THE
VIENNESE

SPLENDOR, TWILIGHT, AND EXILE

THE
VIENNESE

SPLENDOR, TWILIGHT, AND EXILE

PAUL HOFMANN

ANCHOR PRESS

DOUBLEDAY

NEW YORK   LONDON   TORONTO   SYDNEY   AUCKLAND

An Anchor Press Book
Published by Doubleday, a division of
Bantam Doubleday Dell Publishing Group, Inc.
666 Fifth Avenue, New York, New York 10103

Anchor Press, Doubleday, and the portrayal of an anchor
are trademarks of Doubleday, a division of
Bantam Doubleday Dell Publishing Group, Inc.

Library of Congress Cataloging-in-Publication Data

Hofmann, Paul, 1912–
The Viennese : splendor, twilight, and exile /
Paul Hofmann. —1st ed.
p.   cm.
Includes index.
1. Vienna (Austria)—Civilization.   2. Vienna (Austria)—
—Emigration and immigration—History—20th century.
I. Title.
DB851.H64 1988
943.6'13—dc 19   88-22189
                                                                         CIP

ISBN: 0-385-23974-2
Copyright © 1988 by Paul Hofmann

BOOK DESIGN BY MARYSARAH QUINN

PHOTO RESEARCH BY SABRA MOORE

October 1988
First Edition

THE
VIENNESE

SPLENDOR, TWILIGHT, AND EXILE

INTRODUCTION

THE ROOTS OF
AMBIVALENCE

Like most clichés, those of "Viennese charm" and of "merry Vienna" are at once true and false. All too often, Viennese who seem polite, urbane, and amusing turn out, on closer acquaintance, to be also catty gossipers, schemers, lying opportunists, and chronic complainers. The city that inspired Mozart, Beethoven, and Schubert, the capital of *Gemütlichkeit,* of hand-kissing and the waltz, of coffeehouses and wine taverns in the green, of whipped cream and the annual opera ball, has long had one of the highest suicide rates in the world. When Sigmund Freud started investigating hysteria and other neuroses in the late nineteenth century, he found an ominous welter of case histories in the seemingly placid city on the Danube.

A Dutch conductor-composer, Bernard van Beurden, who has worked with schoolchildren in the sylvan mining province of Styria is the author of an observation that may well apply above all to the Viennese: "The Austrian lives in a two-room apartment. One room is bright, friendly, the 'cozy parlor,' well furnished, where he receives his guests. The other room is dark, somber, barred, totally unfathomable."[1] If the visitors in the friendly parlor are not naive, they will nevertheless soon steal glances of the "other room," where the ambivalent Viennese personality also dwells.

1

Consider, for instance, the typical Viennese's impatience with children, especially if they are heard in addition to being seen. Foreigners who bring lively offspring with them are often shocked by the disapproving, even hostile stares and occasional mutterings they encounter in streetcars, eating places, and parks; if, instead, they had a dog with them, everybody would smile and coo. The eyes of many people in Vienna melt when they look at a pet, but harden at the sight of a child, at times even their own. Newcomers find Viennese youngsters strikingly well behaved and quiet; but such good manners may be the result of stern disciplining at home, the source of new neuroses and repression in a city that has always had them in abundance. Child abuse is notoriously much more frequent in Vienna than cruelty toward animals, although only a few dozen cases of battered children ever reach the courts in any given year. Some time ago the city had posters put up showing a little boy and a little girl who were forlornly sitting on the steps of a public stairway. The poignant text: "Be understanding! We are just children!"

Today's Viennese will go out of their way to please tourists. The city's *Gemütlichkeit* industry—its fragrant confectioners' shops, fake Art Nouveau coffeehouses, wainscoted restaurants with courteous waiters, and false-rustic wine taverns in the suburbs—is a big money-maker. Yet, the populace has not lately been known for making foreigners—or people it considers alien—feel at ease in its midst the way it must have done in the days of such beloved or respected immigrants as Prince Eugene of Savoy, Metastasio, Salieri, da Ponte, and Beethoven.

Music students and other young foreigners who spend years in modern Vienna usually complain about how difficult it is to get close to any native. "I practically socialize only with other foreigners," an American music student reported after her first year in the city, "and we usually exchange horror stories about the local xenophobia."

Jews have lived in Vienna since its beginnings and, especially in the nineteenth and early twentieth centuries, have immeasurably contributed to its civilization. A new, racial anti-Semitism, distinct from the much older, religious brand, inflamed a young would-be painter who had been turned down by the Academy of Fine Arts and was leading a down-and-out existence in the Austrian capital—Adolf Hitler. In present-day Vienna, a city almost without Jews, anti-Semitism, though officially condemned, keeps seeping to the surface.

There is no love, either, for the other ethnic groups with which the

German-speaking Austrians have lived together in the same empire for hundreds of years. The Hungarians at least enjoy a measure of respect; they forced the Habsburgs to grant them self-rule in the nineteenth century and have earned new esteem among their more fortunate neighbors, the Viennese, both by their uprising against Soviet domination in 1956 and by the way they have accommodated themselves since Red Army tanks crushed it.

Although many Viennese have Czech, Polish, Croatian, or Slovenian names, Slavs are not popular. Migrant workers from Yugoslavia and Turkey who have found humble jobs in the Austrian capital since the 1950s are euphemistically called "guest workers" but often treated like outcasts. Italians are now highly welcome in Vienna as tourists because many of them are big spenders, but the old prejudice that used to depict Austria's southern neighbors as shifty *Katzelmacher* (roughly, "cat eaters") still lingers.

The Swiss are considered dour, dull and devoid of culture. "Zurich is twice as big as [Vienna's] Central Cemetery, but only half as entertaining," is a proverbial putdown that visitors from the other neutral country in the heart of Europe are likely to hear sooner or later.

The relationship between the Viennese and the Germans is flavored with an ambiguity that was deepened during the period from 1938 to 1945, when Austria was ruled from Berlin. Most Viennese resent the "Prussians" as tactless and arrogant, and deride their ponderous ways, yet at the same time betray that very Viennese syndrome for which a son of the city, the psychoanalyst Alfred Adler, found a name: inferiority complex.

SAY SOFTLY "SERVUS"

For a look into the recesses of the Viennese mind from a different angle, visit what the municipality claims is Europe's only funerary museum. The exhibits in that city-run collection include bizarre catafalques, the certificate of Schubert's death (at the age of thirty-one), and an alarm system whereby persons who find themselves in a coffin after being mistakenly buried as dead may signal to the surface that they are alive.

Or descend into the crypt of the Capuchin Church in the city center with its caskets of 12 emperors, 15 empresses, 135 other members of the

House of Habsburg, and a certain Countess Fuchs who served as governess to Empress Maria Theresa and her daughters. The double sarcophagus of Empress Maria Theresa and her husband, Emperor Franz I (Franz Stephan of Lorraine), by the sculptor Balthasar Moll is almost frivolous in its Rococo playfulness: the imperial couple are shown sitting up in their matrimonial bed with a cherub benignly looking on—an awakening in Schönbrunn Castle one fine spring morning or resurrection at the end of time? In the crypt there are also skulls of rulers carrying the imperial crown, and the tomb of Archduke Rudolf, who ended a suicide at Mayerling, as well as that of his mother, Empress Elisabeth, who was assassinated by an Italian anarchist in Geneva. The Capuchin crypt seems designed to inspire odd and morbid sentiments rather than reverence. The visitor may be most impressed by the stark metal coffin of Maria Theresa's son Josef II, who in his will wrote, "My soul belongs to the Creator; I do not care about my body." Most other people in Vienna, however, are thinking much about death and burials.

Mozart, still waiting for employment at Emperor Josef II's court, wrote to his sick father a famous letter of April 4, 1787, that reflects Viennese fatalism regarding the human condition in moving words: "As death, when we come to consider it closely, is the true goal of our existence, I have formed during the last few years such close relations with this best and truest friend of humankind, that his image is not only no longer terrifying to me, but is indeed very soothing and consoling!" The message, it is true, may not have been much of a consolation for the ailing Leopold Mozart.

Vienna, like Spain and Sicily, has always been fascinated by the macabre. An elaborate funeral is in the local vernacular called *a schöne Leich* ("a beautiful corpse"). Members of the State Opera chorus will pick up a few extra schillings by singing at the graveside—a dirge, an Ave Maria, or, preferably, the evergreen pop tune "Say Softly 'servus' at the Farewell." *(Servus* is Latin for "slave," and the meaning of this Viennese all-purpose greeting between lovers, spouses, relatives, friends, or colleagues is "I am your slave." The Italian *ciao,* from the Venetians' pronunciation of *schiavo,* "slave," has the same origin.)

Is it surprising that in the city of imperial and plebeian suicide and "beautiful" corpses Freud discovered the death wish? At any rate, an impressive number of eminent Viennese have taken their own lives. Among them were the dramatist Ferdinand Raimund; the writers and poets Adalbert Stifter, Ferdinand von Saar, Georg Trakl, Stefan Zweig, and Josef Weinheber; the philosopher Otto Weininger, who rented a room in the house where Beethoven had died seventy-five years earlier to shoot himself in it; the young painter Richard Gerstl, whose motive was an affair with the wife of the composer Arnold Schoenberg; Ludwig Boltzmann, a pioneer of modern physics; the superspy Colonel Alfred Redl; a brother of Gustav Mahler; no fewer than three brothers of the philosopher Ludwig Wittgenstein; the daughter of the writer and dramatist Arthur Schnitzler; and a son of Schnitzler's friend Hugo von Hofmannsthal. When Theodor Herzl died of overwork in 1904, the Viennese were convinced that the founder of modern Zionism had committed suicide. His son Hans later took his own life in France.

Emperor Franz Josef is supposed to have remarked that his only son, Archduke Rudolf, by killing himself with his mistress, had "died like a tailor." Actually, suicides by craftsmen and workers were not then commonplace events, but Vienna was becoming rather used to the news that yet another member of the intelligentsia had died by his own hand, and Rudolf had had intellectual ambitions. As if to negate his son's last decision, the emperor forced reluctant churchmen to give him an imperial funeral.

Today, Vienna's suicide rate hovers around 25 per 100,000 population, about double the United States figure. West Berlin, it is true, now exceeds Vienna in the frequency of suicide, but experts say this is due to the circumstance that even more old people live there than in the Austrian capital. Thousands of elderly Viennese belong to some *Sterbeverein* ("death association"); their monthly dues pay for a decent burial, and surviving members promise to attend the funeral for the deceased.

Burial pomp satisfies the Baroque city's enduring passion for theater. The palaces and churches from the seventeenth and eighteenth centuries, with their extravagant ornamentation and their statues and paintings of gesticulating saints and writhing martyrs, bear witness to the Viennese love of showy facades and of make-believe with a dramatic flourish. Again, the mellow local idiom has a word for it with overtones suggesting a knowing wink: *Schmäh*. The best translation of this dialect term is "blarney, Viennese style."

The schoolboy pretending to have been involved in a traffic accident as an excuse for cutting afternoon classes when he actually had been riding the bumper cars in the Prater amusement park; the computer salesman who praises the advantages of a new system without mentioning to the prospective customer that the software has still to be written; the philandering husband covering up an affair by a phone call to his wife from an alleged high-level conference; the businessman taking a visitor from abroad to a suburban wine restaurant to pull off a deal in an atmosphere of spurious cordiality; and the presidential candidate who writes in his campaign autobiography that he was studying law in Vienna during the last years of World War II whereas he actually served as a Nazi intelligence officer in Yugoslavia and Greece—they all practice the old Viennese art of *Schmäh*.

What is *Schmäh* and what is truth? Which part of their mental two-room abode do the Viennese prefer to inhabit? Were their real feelings revealed when they passionately welcomed Hitler in 1938 or when they tearfully applauded the signing of the 1955 State Treaty, which sanctioned their country's independence, neutrality, and democratic system? Or were both states of mind genuine?

Anyone who observed the frenzy with which hundreds of thousands in Vienna cheered Hitler on April 15, 1938—just forty-eight hours after he had decreed the absorption of his native Austria by the German Reich —will never forget it, although quite a few of the surviving witnesses do not like now to talk about that day. The *Anschluss* ("annexation" or "union") and the increasingly somber five years that had led up to it prompted or forced far more than 100,000 Jewish citizens of Vienna, as well as a few non-Jewish ones, to go abroad. Scientists, physicians, psychologists, writers, artists, musicians, theater people, economists, and outstanding specialists in other fields joined an exodus that has been compared to the flight of the Greek scholars from Constantinople after that imperial city fell to the janissaries of Sultan Mohammed II in 1453. Venice, Florence, and Rome were the main beneficiaries of the skills and learning of the Byzantine emigrés, but in the Nazi period the Viennese refugees went mainly to Switzerland, France, England, Palestine, Latin America, Australia, and—above all—the United States and Canada.

Many Viennese emigrés were signally successful in their new lives. Some became famous on Broadway or in Hollywood; others won professorships at French, British, Australian, or American universities; and still others made their mark on Wall Street, practiced in Manhattan or in Los Angeles as followers of Freud or Adler, preached the message of classic liberalism to a West that seemed to favor economic planners, or managed opera houses. In 1942 one renowned Viennese writer and pacifist, Stefan

Zweig, wrote a nostalgic book about *The World of Yesterday* and then, with his wife, committed suicide in his Brazilian exile.

Intellectually impoverished by the exodus during the Hitler years, Vienna is today a much more prosperous place than it was in 1938; its population, then more than 1.8 million, is now down to 1.5 million and still shrinking. Vienna's politics and, to a large extent, its cultural life have become provincial. The visitor cannot help feeling that Vienna is a museum city, a historical-artistic theme park for tourists who fancy grand opera, hillside wine taverns, *The Merry Widow,* horse ballet, and *Sachertorte.* To be sure, there are stores with Italian designer clothes, fast-food havens and rock clubs too, but new vogues and fads arrive in Vienna usually only when they are already passé in the West. An Old World aura clings to the city, and it enchants many tourists. It is difficult to imagine that Vienna at the beginning of this century was a byword for modernism in the arts and sciences.

Most of the ancient city's civilization and creativity, probably the best part of it, has emigrated. It would be an undue simplification to say that all the "good" Viennese have gone abroad and only the "bad" Viennese, or the dull ones, have stayed behind. Viennese values and talent can be found today in many countries, and so can Viennese character traits. They can be observed even in the children of immigrants from Vienna, although the younger generation may never have learned to speak the original language and idiom of their elders. A good deal of what Vienna used to mean has lived on in the diaspora for some time but will soon be extinct through assimilation and oblivion. Say softly *"servus."*

Viennese personality quirks and typically Viennese gestures endure. Vienna, like other regions and countries—the Middle East, Greece, and Italy, for instance—has a specific body vocabulary that everybody understands. A typical signal of unspoken Viennese language consists in a negligent semicircular counterclockwise movement of the half-open right hand, with the meaning "I don't really care." This body phrase of dismissal, contempt, or renunciation gives away persons who may have long gotten rid of their Danubian accent. Even the children of Viennese will perform this seemingly nonchalant gesture when they do care a lot and want to cover up their frustration.

Wherever the individual fates of the Viennese have taken them, they yearn to make good, to be accepted, to fit in, and their proverbial pliancy often helps them achieve all this. Yet, the ambivalence that almost all immigrants, from wherever they came, feel with respect to their new country and environment is compounded for the former Viennese by their innate tendency to feel at the same time attraction and repulsion, to say yes and no to everything and everybody, their own city not excluded. "Our beloved and hated Vienna," Arnold Schoenberg would say in exile, correctly summing up how many natives of the old capital perceive it. This specific Viennese ambivalence, which depth psychology has identified as an early symptom of neurosis, has roots in the city's landscape, ethnic mix, history, attitude toward religion, and ripe civilization.

THE DANUBE IS RARELY BLUE

The lighthearted mood of Beethoven's Sixth Symphony *(Pastoral)* and the nostalgia and despair of Schubert's *Winterreise* cycle better reflect the diverse emotions inspired by Vienna's natural surroundings than does *The Blue Danube* by Johann Strauss, Jr. To many Viennese, that waltz is the local anthem; it ritually climaxes the New Year's concert of the Vienna Philharmonic Orchestra, which, as relayed by satellite, is seen and heard throughout the world.

The Blue Danube is, however, a pleasant lie—another *Schmäh.* The mighty river that washes the city's northeastern outskirts may look blue on a few clear and sunny days every year, most of the time it is a dull gray. Besides, many residents do not get a glance at the Danube for weeks, or even months, on end. What they are more likely to see as they go about their everyday business is the equally gray Danube Canal, which skirts the oldest part of the city core; this waterway was once one of several arms into which the Danube was split before most of them were channeled into a common broad bed in a vast river regulation project that extended from 1869 to 1877. Lately, the main river has again been bisected near Vienna by a long artificial island that serves recreation and flood control. The Danube, at any rate, is not an essential feature of Vienna's cityscape as it is, majestically, of Budapest's.

The Austrian capital lies at the spot where the river leaves the Alpine foothills behind to roll toward the Hungarian plain. The two elevations closest to the Danube, Kahlenberg (1,585 feet high) and Leopoldsberg (1,388 feet), are the northernmost spurs of the Alps. The twin hills belong to a tender range covered with forests and vineyards whose loveliness has long been praised in music and song as the Vienna Woods. Yet, "the Vienna Woods are a landscape that isn't unproblematic," as Heimito von Doderer wrote. "Everything slightly curving and fragrantly evasive. A certain heaviness, though, is lurking behind it, the heaviness of melancholy, a danger also for very healthy persons, indeed especially for those."[2]

Farsighted conservation laws have saved a good part of the green belt hugging Vienna's western flank; real estate developers have long been barred from it. The eastern sections of the city are flat and seem already steeped in the cheerlessness of the Hungarian lowlands. Metternich, who had his palace in this suburban area, used to remark that from his windows he could see the Balkans and Asia. It is fitting that not far from the Metternich Palace (now the Italian embassy) are the cities of the dead: the Cemetery of St. Marx (an old spelling of St. Mark's), where Mozart's body was lowered into a pauper's grave, and the Central Cemetery, with the tombs of Beethoven, Schubert, Brahms, and many other greats.

On All Souls' Day (November 2), when many thousands of Viennese flock to the cemeteries to visit their dead, and in the following months, when clouds hang low in the sky and the streets are buried under dirty snow, the city and its environs may become singularly depressing, evoking the mood of the *Winterreise*. One hardly expects to see again the smiling lilac time of Vienna's spring.

The western and southern outskirts have always been the most desirable neighborhoods. There the Vienna Woods still offer hillsides, vineyards, parks, and bucolic promenades. Beethoven found that sweet-sad scenery congenial; he used to take long walks in the hills near Heiligenstadt, a northern suburb of Vienna, and spent summers in the hot-springs spa of Baden (the Aquae of the ancient Romans) at the southern approaches to the Vienna Woods. The name of one nearby place, known everywhere, evokes a morbidly romantic event: Mayerling. In a hunting lodge there in 1889, Archduke Rudolf, the crown prince of Austria-Hungary, shot dead his seventeen-year-old mistress, Baroness Marie Vetsera, and then turned the gun on himself—one of the sensations of the Victorian era. (He had spent the night before with a commoner girl friend, Mitzi Caspar.)

A few years later, in a spa-type hillside hotel at another edge of the Vienna Woods, the Belle Vue, "the secret of dreams was revealed to Dr. Sigmund Freud," as a commemorative plaque reads. Freud and his wife spent a few summer weeks at the Belle Vue in 1895, and five years later he wrote to his friend Wilhelm Fliess in Berlin half in jest, "Do you think that at some future time there will be an inscription on that house, 'Here, on July 24, 1895, the secret of dreams was revealed to Dr. Sigmund Freud'? The prospects as of now are dim." The Belle Vue Hotel no longer exists, but the words that Freud would have liked to see on its outer walls were engraved on a tablet unveiled on the spot after World War II. One is tempted to speculate that the emotive landscape helped bring out the Freudian discovery. Freud did not really care for the Vienna Woods (he preferred the Tyrol); but Gustav Mahler did and, while a student at the conservatory, roamed the hillsides. Arthur Schnitzler, the writer whom Freud admired, also went for strolls there. And Franz Kafka found what may have been his only few days of happiness in the Vienna Woods.

The place on the Danube where the green hills give way to the plains has attracted travelers and settlers for thousands of years. Some prehistoric tools and weapons found in the Vienna area tell little about its early inhabitants; we know much less of them, for instance, than of the salt-mining people of the Hallstein civilization in Upper Austria in the early Iron Age (circa 750 B.C.).

What is today Vienna was twenty-five hundred years ago almost certainly a river-crossing settlement on the Amber Road from the Baltic Sea to the Adriatic through which traders from Mediterranean civilizations—Greeks, Etruscans, and Romans—used to pass. They exchanged bronze weapons and pottery from the advanced south for amber and whale tusks from the north. In the third century B.C., Celtic tribes invaded much of what would later be known as Austria. A Celtic root is believed to be hidden in Vindobona, the name that the Romans gave to the spot where the Amber Road traversed the ramified river. They established a small frontier fortress there when Rome's empire had been extended as far north as the Danube under Augustus and Tiberius.

Excavated remains of a military camp with traces of fortifications and billets and with Latin inscriptions can be seen today; visitors descend to them from the Hoher Markt, a square in what was the heart of Vindobona, north of St. Stephen's Cathedral. For nearly four centuries several thousand Roman soldiers were garrisoned there, including the crack Thirteenth Legion and later the Fourteenth. A stone with the seal of the Sixth Cohort of the Fourteenth Legion was much later used, together with other Roman building materials, for the construction of St. Stephen's.

A strategic center much bigger than Vindobona, Carnuntum, was founded on the Danube twenty-eight miles downstream. It had a large civilian population, as the ruins of two amphitheaters and of lavish baths show. The ancient city of Carnuntum is today as dead as Pompeii, whereas Vindobona has survived through the ages.

Vindobona must have attracted Roman and native camp followers, tradespeople, and a motley collection of civilians who came to live alongside older settler families. Relations with the barbarians who roamed the forests and countryside beyond the Danube may at times have been cagily peaceful, but every now and then the near-savages staged surprise incursions or even took on the Roman legions in outright frontier wars.

Emperor Marcus Aurelius, who ruled A.D. 161–180, presumably set up his military headquarters in Vindobona when he steadfastly directed eight successive winter campaigns from the frozen banks of the Danube against the Marcomanni and Quadi, the allied Germanic tribes that were threatening the Roman territory. During military operations Marcus Aurelius found time to write his *Meditations,* conversations with himself in Greek, mirroring his Stoic philosophy and ethics. Probably weakened by hardships, he is known to have died rather suddenly, and the Viennese believe it happened in their city. A street sloping from what was the Roman camp to the Danube Canal is named after one of the many emperors the city claims as its own: Marc-Aurel-Strasse.

Eventually the barbarians overran the Danube frontier of the Roman Empire, and by the end of the fourth century the legionnaires had withdrawn from Vindobona. About four hundred years of confused migrations and raids by Teutons, Huns, Slavs, Avars, and Magyars ensued. A South Germanic tribe, the Bajuvarians, pushed down the Danube and recolonized the territories along the river as far as Vindobona, where some of the old Celtic-Roman populace had probably survived all the invasions.

In 799, Charlemagne established parts of what is today Austria as one of the frontier marches, or defense regions, of his immense empire. The former Vindobona, by then called Wenia, again became a border fortress. In 976 the Holy Roman Emperor Otto II presented Margrave Leopold of Babenberg with the southeastern frontier areas in a move aimed at curbing the power of the Bavarian dukes. Vienna thus owed its resurgence to a power play, not for the last time in its history.

The Babenbergs, a remarkable family, ruled the Ostmark (Eastern March) for 270 years. Margrave St. Leopold III the Holy (1095–1136) built himself a stronghold overlooking Vienna on a hill that was later named after him (Leopoldsberg). Margrave Heinrich II (1141–77), who because of his favorite oath was nicknamed Jasomirgott ("So help me God"), took up residence in Vienna. Under him, in 1156, Austria became a hereditary duchy within the Holy Roman Empire.

Following the extinction of the Babenberg dynasty in 1246, various powers in the region tried to grab their dukedom. Rudolf of Habsburg, an obscure Swiss nobleman who surprisingly had just been elected King of Germany, as Rudolf I, won out. He defeated King Ottokar II Přemysl of Bohemia in battle (1276), took Austria away from him, and six years later proclaimed Vienna and the land around it a Habsburg family possession.

Until 1918, Vienna was to remain—with brief interruptions only—the heart of Habsburg power. The long line of Habsburg emperors began with Albert II in 1438. They were titular heads of the Holy Roman Empire. The title "Emperor of Austria" would be introduced only in 1806. Through conquest and, quite often, through dynastic marriages a vast, multilingual realm grew around Vienna. The city nevertheless continued in a sense to be a border post: always close to the eastern frontier of the German-speaking population bloc in central Europe. Bohemian, Hungarian, Polish, Croatian, Slovenian, and Italian subjects of the Habsburg rulers, not to mention another half a dozen minor ethnic groups, were for hundreds of years frequent visitors to the imperial capital, and quite a few moved to it permanently. Vienna has thus since the High Middle Ages been a cosmopolitan place. Furthermore, the Turkish sieges and wars exposed it, as will be shown later, to Near Eastern civilization.

The many racial and cultural strands that converged and became intertwined in Vienna for centuries are today still discernible in many ways. Open the city's telephone directory at any page, and you will be struck by the prevalence of non-Germanic names—all those Hruskas, Jakoncigs, Novotnys, Prohaskas, Swobodas, Tomasellis, and Zarskis. Before World War I at least one fifth of Vienna's population consisted of Bohemians, Moravians, and Slovaks. All cooks, maids, tailors, building superintendents, musicians, cabinetmakers, and subalterns in government departments seemed to be Czechs.

The Viennese dialect is a cache of terms from Czech and other Slavic languages, Hungarian, Italian, and Yiddish, not to mention many medieval Teutonic words that have long since dropped from what is now standard German. Few Viennese who mention their favorite *Beisl,* or neighborhood tavern, are aware that they are using a derivative from the Hebrew *bayith* ("house"). Scores of Yiddish words, such as *meshuggah, ganef, shiksah,* and *tsores,* are entrenched Viennese idiom. Yiddish syntax, too, has long encroached on the way the Viennese arrange their spoken phrases; in present-day Vienna one still hears people use sentences that in word order and intonation are the equivalent of a New Yorker's "Do I have news for you!" Karl Kraus, who was a master of both the German language and the Viennese dialect and was himself Jewish, made fun of a successful contemporary writer, asserting that the talking animals in Felix Salten's forest stories *(Bambi* and others) were speaking the Jewish way *(jüdeln).*

Thick Viennese dialect is all but incomprehensible to many other German-speakers. Even when the Viennese try to talk in what they think is *Hochdeutsch* (High, or standard, German), their accent and vocabulary betray their origin at once. The gap between the Viennese version of standard German and that which is spoken in, say, Hannover is as wide as that between American and British English.

A refined form of the Viennese idiom was in use for centuries at the Habsburg court *(Schönbrunnerdeutsch,* the German spoken in Schönbrunn Castle) and was imitated in the palaces of the Vienna nobility and in army officers' mess halls throughout the empire. The Viennese upper middle class, including assimilated Jewish families, adopted that slightly nasal speech, about halfway between the High German of books and formal oration and the broad dialect of the Viennese populace. In Emanuel Schikaneder's libretto for Mozart's *Zauberflöte,* High German is reserved for the solemn passages, and Viennese dialect for Papageno's clowning and for the scene where Papagena is disguised as a horrible crone.

The Viennese dialect theater at the time of the *Zauberflöte* already had a long tradition behind it. It was to reach its golden age with Ferdinand Raimund (1790–1836) and the immensely popular actor and playwright Johann Nepomuk Nestroy (1801–62). Dialect words and phrases recur in modern Viennese literature from Schnitzler to von Doderer. The use of the local idiom by today's Viennese newspapers presents difficulties to German-speaking readers in Germany and Switzerland and to foreigners who have learned the standard tongue.

Whenever Viennese speak foreign languages, their accent betrays their origin. Like Germans, they have trouble with the English *th* and will substitute *v* for *w*. They also tend toward a flat pronunciation of vowels and diphthongs, and will say *choint* for *joint* and *Chorch* for *George*. On the other hand, when Czechs, Hungarians, and Yugoslavs speak German, they frequently use Viennese dialectal expressions, for the simple reason that for hundreds of years the German language was filtered to their countries through the imperial capital.

WINE MYSTIQUE

Like the dialect, the cuisine of Vienna is the result of many influences from various directions. Take the schnitzel, considered the epitome of Danubian cooking. Actually, the Viennese way of breading and frying veal cutlets was copied from the Milanese when Lombardy was under Habsburg rule in the eighteenth and nineteenth centuries. The *scaloppina alla milanese* had been imported by the Spaniards, who were in control of the northern Italian city before the Austrians were, and the Spaniards had probably learned to fry meat in bread crumbs from the Byzantines at the eastern end of the Mediterranean. The strudel—thin dough rolled and filled with apples or other fruits, curds, poppyseeds, or chopped cabbage—was probably brought from Hungary, as surely was goulash. Bohemia contributed dumplings and other farinaceous dishes to the Viennese tables; from Germany and Poland came a passion for sausages. Wieners are a Viennese staple but are always called frankfurters. Other popular sausage types are named after the cities of Cracow, Debrecen, and Paris. The sweet tooth of the Viennese, satisfied by their many kinds of torte and other rich desserts and by their indulgence in whipped cream, seems to be a very old characteristic of the city, one probably enhanced by its many contacts with the Turks.

The craving of the Viennese for sugar and starches and their high intake of fats explain why so many of them appear overweight. Their diet is in all likelihood also a major reason for the high incidence of circulatory disorders, which account for 54 percent of all deaths in the city. A 1983 health survey (published in 1987) shows also that the average Viennese reports, or at least feels, sick eighteen days every year, double the number of sick days counted by the average inhabitant of Vorarlberg,

Austria's westernmost province, which shares ethnic and other characteristics with neighboring Switzerland.

In the 1920s a lean female silhouette, then the vogue in the United States, became for a time fashionable in Vienna. Later, in the hungry years during and after World War II, all Viennese looked slim. When food was again plentiful, only relatively few Viennese heeded the advice of their doctors and became diet-conscious. Today many people look as chubby as their ancestors in Baroque and Biedermeier portraits do. Viennese emigrés usually take their fondness for fattening foods with them.

As a wine-growing and wine-drinking city, Vienna has acquired living habits distinct from those of nearby Bavaria and Bohemia, the classic beer-drinking regions, and rather closer to those of the Mediterranean world and Hungary. The Viennese, it is true, have always made beer too, but the product never became as famous as Munich or Pilsen brews. Hard liquor has long been drunk in the Austrian capital, preferably Balkan plum brandy *(šljivovica)* and Hungarian apricot brandy. Wine, however, has since the oldest times held a special place in the social life, folkways, and economy of the Viennese. It is a cherished legacy from the ancient Romans.

A quiet street in the Heiligenstadt section near the vineyards is called Probusgasse, a tribute to Probus, the third-century Roman emperor who is reputed to have introduced the vine to Vienna. (The street is noteworthy also for another reason: the low-slung house at No. 6 is one of many places where Beethoven was a tenant, and it was there that he wrote his "Heiligenstadt Testament" during the summer of 1802—"O ye men who think or say that I am malevolent, stubborn or misanthropic, how greatly do you wrong me. . . .") Marcus Aurelius Probus, a successful general in Gaul, on the Rhine, on the Danube, and in Egypt, was a rigid disciplinarian. To keep his legionnaires from the temptations of idleness between campaigns, he employed them in digging and planting vineyards in Gaul and in Pannonia, the province that comprised parts of what is now eastern Austria and Hungary. His severity was hated by his troops, and in 282 he was killed in a mutiny, but not before he had issued a general permission to the Pannonian provincials to plant vines.

The Roman emperor's experiment of trying to acclimatize a Mediterranean plant north of the Alps was a success. Vines throve on the sandstone hills and in the loamy plains around Vienna, despite severe winters, as they did in the Hungarian lowlands. The natives quickly became hooked on the fermented grape juice and eagerly continued making wine themselves after the legions had left.

In the Viennese dialect, vintners are called *Weinhauer* ("vine hoers"), a reminder of the continual, backbreaking work that vineyards demand, especially in northern lands. Wine growing is a risky business on the Danube: Will there be enough sunny days in the ripening season? Won't a late summer hailstorm destroy the result of a year's labors in half an hour? The vintners around Vienna have nevertheless stubbornly tended their precious plants since Roman times. Soon wine-growing villages sprang up north, west, and south of the city and survived wars and enemy raids.

Throughout the Middle Ages many Viennese made their living through the wine trade and the wine-exporting business. When the vineyards were devastated by the plague of the grape phylloxera in the late nineteenth and early twentieth centuries, they were replanted with improved American vines. There are today still seven hundred families growing wine grapes on eighteen hundred acres within the city limits and many more in the broad vineyard belt of the metropolitan area.

The wine that is drunk in and near Vienna is not Bordeaux, Moselle, or Chianti; it is, frankly, of ordinary, if not mediocre, quality. Wine manipulation is not unknown. The vintages, mostly whites, are best consumed when they are young. Many Viennese fancy even the half-fermented, turbid, and moderately alcoholic juice that wine makers serve as *Sturm* ("storm") just a few weeks after the grape harvest.

Local vintners have since time immemorial poured their product for paying customers right on the spot. The "people's emperor," Josef II, a legendary personage to the Viennese, legalized the old practice by an edict in 1784; the privilege granted by the sovereign has become a law of the Republic. A tuft of pine or fir branches at the end of a pole jutting out of some rustic house in Grinzing, Sievering, or one of the other ancient wine villages on Vienna's outskirts signals that the new wine may be sampled there. What is served is known as *der Heurige;* the term is a derivation from the Austrian word for "the current year," *heuer,* which standard German spurns, and it means "this year's [wine]." *Der Heurige* denotes also the place where the young vintage is sold and drunk.

At present there are a few hundred *Heurige* in and near Vienna. Under Josef II's edict and the Republic's legislation, vintners are forbidden to buy grapes or wine from outside sources and are only allowed to sell their own product for a maximum of three hundred days a year. Many places in the wine villages, however, now have broader licenses, enabling them to purchase wine from faraway producers or from middlemen, to provide full restaurant service, and to keep open all year around. These establishments with their sham-rural decor glare with neon signs, and tourist coaches are parked outside. At times, some high official or the government chief himself entertains important guests from abroad in just such a "typical Viennese" setting—an exercise in *Schmäh.*

The genuine Viennese—retirees with their wives, parties of lower-middle-class people and young couples—stay away from these *Nobel-Heurige (Nobel* means "noble" in the local dialect). At the end of an outing in the Vienna Woods, they will look for the pine or fir tuft on some modest house on the far outskirts of the capital but within walking distance of the last stop of a bus or streetcar line. They will sit down at coarse wooden tables in a bare, whitewashed room or in a garden with flickering candles in storm lanterns. The owner or a relative serves the new wine in stout quarter-liter glasses. Patrons eat cold chicken or sausage they have brought with them, picnic style, or buy dark bread and cheese spiced with onion and paprika laid out on a sideboard. A duo of elderly men, violin and accordion, may wander in and play schmaltzy tunes, and a few guests at the tables will hum the well-known lyrics. One of the classics is a Viennese dialect version of the Horatian *carpe diem:*

There will be wine again
And we won't be around any more;
Therefore let's savor life
While we can enjoy it.

There will be pretty girls
And we won't live any more;
Therefore let's get on to them
Just in time.

The prevailing mood at an authentic *Heurige* is not boisterous but maudlin. "Say Softly 'Servus' at the Farewell" is also a perennial favorite. The atmosphere is probably not much different from that of the suburban taverns where Schubert spent so much of his short life with his friends and where many of his lieder were born.

Schubert, incidentally, may be taken as an extraordinary example of the Viennese who appears bent on merriment and pleasures but thinks compulsively of work to do and business to get on with. Leading what seemed a dissolute existence, Schubert in a dozen years composed six hundred lieder in addition to his symphonies, masses, operas, quartets, and other great music. He was a genius, to be sure, but also a closet worker. Most of his happy-go-lucky friends eventually settled down to lead very respectable, and even successful, bourgeois existences.

Many Viennese of later generations—at home or in distant countries, geniuses or not—have felt obliged to be regarded as debonair while secretly intent above all on getting ahead in their profession. The carefree reveler at the next table at your *Heurige* will probably be up early the next morning and on the job, hangover or not. More than half of the city's population, according to a recent poll, gets up around 6 A.M. every working day.

The devil-may-care figure of Dear Augustin is not really typical of the modern Viennese. A bagpipe player who used to entertain the patrons of the downtown taverns, Marx (Mark?) Augustin imperturbably kept singing his ribald songs to his music between sips of wine when the black death struck Vienna in 1679. Drunk as usual, he stumbled one night into an open mass grave and slept off the fumes of the wine amid heaps of corpses. Next morning he laughingly climbed out of the pit to continue his rakish life, and it was only twenty-five years later, at the age of sixty-two, that, according to a parish record, he died "while drinking wine." An old folk song celebrates his nonchalance: "Ach du lieber Augustin / Alles ist hin!" ("Oh you Dear Augustin / Everything is lost!")

A symbol of recklessness, Dear Augustin is the embodiment of an image of themselves that many Viennese would like to project, although they may in reality be worriers, hypochondriacs, and inveterate grumblers. Neither will there usually be anyone roaring drunk in Vienna's restaurants or at the suburban *Heurige*. Like other societies that have a long experience with wine growing and wine drinking, the Viennese as a rule know how to handle alcohol. Most of them, at home and abroad, are social drinkers with the accent on "social." There are alcoholics (and drunk drivers) also in present-day Vienna and among Viennese expatriates, but compulsive tippling to excess has never been a widespread and characteristic Viennese disease, and the "lost weekend" is not a specific Viennese symptom. The city's relationship with alcohol is typified by the "wine biter," the patron of a tavern, usually in company, who rolls the straw-colored or amber liquid in his mouth before swallowing it while getting into an increasingly mellow mood.

OUT-OF-TOWN SAINTS

The Romans brought to Vindobona not only the wine but also the new religion that was using wine in its central mystery, the mass. (Many legionnaires on the Roman Empire's Danube frontier, however, worshipped Mithra.) One of the quaintest wine suburbs of Vienna, Sievering, may be named after a fifth-century Christian missionary, St. Severinus, who was a lay monk and lay abbot.

We know much about Severinus, who lived in the Vienna area for nearly thirty years, from a vita that a disciple, the presbyter Eugippius, composed in Naples in 511, twenty-nine years after the saint's death. Along with legends, the Latin text gives a vivid picture of the convulsed period when the Roman administration along the Danube had broken down but a few Roman soldiers and many Roman civilians were still living in the region, harassed by barbarian tribes that continually crossed the river to plunder or to trek on to rich Italy.

Severinus was probably a Roman; at any rate, he spoke fluent Latin. He came up the Danube from the Near East and settled near Vindobona in a Roman town, Favianis, whose exact location is controversial. He preached austerity; organized aid for the many victims of famines, diseases, and barbarian rapine; and negotiated with the chieftains of Germanic tribes. One of them was Odoacer, the son of a minister of Attila the Hun. Having made up his mind to seek adventure and riches in Italy, Odoacer called on Severinus to solicit his blessing. The lowness of the door to the cell where the holy man lived forced the strapping barbarian to stoop. Severinus, in the words of Eugippius, told Odoacer, "Proceed to Italy; you will soon cast away this coarse garment of skins; and your wealth will be adequate to the liberality of your mind." The saint's prophecy came true: Odoacer soon deposed the last Roman Emperor of the West, Romulus Augustulus, and proclaimed himself King of Italy.

Severinus died near Vienna in 482. Six years later his body was removed to Umbria and eventually to Naples. An empty grave that, according to scholars, once held the remains of a Christian Roman of some distinction was dug up in 1952 under the parish church of Heiligenstadt, the former wine village that is now part of Vienna's Nineteenth District, Döbling. Archeologists speculate it may have been Severinus's burial site. The holy man is the patron saint of Vienna's vintners and also of the city's textile business (because he collected clothes to distribute to the poor). Naples presented Vienna with presumed relics of Severinus in 1745; a reliquary said to contain some of his bones was taken from Frattamaggiore, near Naples, to Austria in 1935.

Long after the death of St. Severinus, a new thrust of Christianization came from Bavaria. The oldest existing church in Vienna, St. Ruprecht's, is probably named after St. Rupertus, the eighth-century founder of monasteries in what would become Salzburg, near the Austrian-Bavarian border. St. Ruprecht's is a small structure on a low hill above the Danube Canal that has often been rebuilt; its Romanesque remains are believed to rest on foundations that date from around 740.

St. Stephen's Cathedral, the most important Gothic edifice in Austria, marks the geometrical center of the inner city and is a symbol of the capital. It was originally a small Romanesque church southeast of the walls of early medieval Vienna, consecrated in 1147. The structure, destroyed by a fire in 1258, was rebuilt and enlarged over the next few centuries while Vienna continued to be ruled ecclesiastically by the bishop in Passau, the Bavarian frontier city upstream on the Danube. Only in 1469 did Vienna obtain its first bishop; it became an archbishopric in 1722. The mounting power of the Habsburgs led to a practice whereby the archbishops of Vienna were considered princes of the empire and were usually given a cardinal's red hat by the pope. To the Vatican, Vienna is still what it calls a "cardinalitial see," one whose incumbent is almost automatically included in the Sacred College of Cardinals.

Although churchmen proclaimed Vienna a "bastion of Christianity" during the Turkish onslaughts, it has never been much of an ecclesiastical bulwark. Neither has it given a great many saints, towering prelates, or ascetic reformers to the Roman Catholic Church. When a fiery Italian Franciscan, St. John of Capistrano, preached in Vienna in 1451 to call for a crusade against the Turks, he caused such an impression that the pulpit outside the choir of St. Stephen's from which he spoke in Latin was marked with a commemorative tablet. The crusade, however, never got underway, and two years later the Turks conquered Constantinople.

An earthy Augustinian monk from Swabia, Abraham a Sancta Clara (his secular name was Johann Ulrich Megerle), became popular in the late seventeenth century because the Viennese loved to hear him scourge them in his sermons for their lack of religious zeal and their love of the coffeehouse and more wicked pleasures. He wrote also moralistic poetry and a tract, *Remember, Vienna!,* confronting the citizenry with the theme of death, then particularly topical because of the plague. Through his writings the fire-and-brimstone monk secured for himself a niche in the history of literature, but he did not change the Viennese.

Emperor Karl VI, in the midst of another terrifying assault by the black death in 1713, vowed to build a magnificent Baroque church. In 1737 the structure was dedicated to St. Charles Borromeo, the sixteenth-century archbishop of Milan, apostle of plague victims, and champion of the Counter-Reformation, rather than to a homegrown holy man or woman.

The truth is that Vienna, despite its many churches, has always had a reputation for laxity in matters of faith and morals and that even its churchgoers have often been religious cynics and mockers. It is said that at the height of the Protestant Reformation in Germany, no more than four priests in Vienna continued to preach the doctrines of Rome, and contemptuous noblemen rode their horses through St. Stephen's. In many of the city's churches, Protestants had the "pagan images" on the altars covered with cloth; they then presented bills for their expenses to the municipal council.

The Habsburg emperors supported Rome's Counter-Reformation, ruthlessly suppressing Protestantism in Vienna and throughout their domains. The Jesuits and other religious orders had new churches erected in the triumphalistic Baroque style, the architectural celebration of the papacy's presumed victory over the heretics. The drama of the Roman liturgy, reinforced by stirring music and famous preachers, was employed in a broad offensive to lure the tepid Viennese back into the Roman fold.

Yet, when an emperor who was imbued with the ideas of the Enlightenment, Josef II, toward the end of the eighteenth century curbed the privileges of the clergy and closed many monasteries, the Viennese did not seem to mind. Pope Pius VI journeyed to Vienna in 1782 in an attempt to talk Josef II into revoking his anticlerical measures. The city gave the pontiff a warm reception, and the Viennese packed the Church of the Nine Choirs of Angels, then entrusted to the Jesuits, when he celebrated Easter mass: the papal visit was a good show, after all. Pius VI, however, had to return to the Vatican empty-handed.

A zealous member of the Redemptorist Order, Klemens Maria Hofbauer (1751–1820) fought Enlightenment and "Josephinism" as a pastor in Vienna. He was canonized in 1909 and proclaimed patron saint of the Austrian capital. But even Vienna's official advocate in Heaven was not a native: St. Klemens Maria was born in Moravia and worked as a baker's apprentice in Znojmo before studying for the priesthood.

Before and after Josef II, Habsburg rulers generally collaborated with the Church of Rome to mutual benefit. The traditional alliance between throne and altar in effect curtailed church influence in Vienna; the clergy had always to share power with the imperial court.

Until 1918, Vienna's schoolchildren, and their elders, too, sang to Haydn's solemn, though simple, "Emperor's Hymn" the following text:

> *Gott erhalte, Gott beschütze*
> *Unsern Kaiser, unser Land.*
> *Mächtig durch des Glaubens Stütze . . .*

> *God preserve, God protect*
> *Our emperor, our country.*
> *Powerful through Faith's support . . .*

The hymn suggested that the church was to prop up the Habsburg monarchy as it had done for centuries. The Haydn melody, it should be noted, was later appropriated by Pan-German nationalists to accompany the chauvinistic poem "Deutschland, Deutschland über Alles" (Germany, Germany Above Everything), by August Heinrich Hoffmann von Fallersleben (1798–1874), which in 1922 became Germany's national anthem. (The Germans play and sing their purloined anthem at a brisker tempo than Haydn had intended his music to be performed.) Republican Austria, finding itself robbed of a musical theme that had stirred the emotions of its people for a hundred years, looked for a substitute after World War II. The government was swamped by pleas from the populace to keep the Haydn tune, and a committee of the Vienna Academy of Music recommended that a suitable new text be devised for the beloved old melody.

The authorities, however, would not listen. Instead, they organized a competition for a new anthem. Some eighteen hundred proposals poured in, and in 1946 the government selected a musical sequence from Mozart. It is an appendix to the *Kleine Freimaurer Kantate* (Little Freemasons' Cantata), K. 623, one of the composer's last works, conducted by him at the inauguration of a new branch of a masonic lodge on November 18, 1791, a little more than two weeks before his death. (Some scholars doubt the authenticity of the appendix.) The text of the new anthem is by Paula von Preradović, a Croatian-descended poet: "Land der Berge, Land des Stromes" ("Country of the Mountains, Country of the Big River").

To return to Roman Catholic religious practice in the Austrian capital, music has always played an important part in it. Many Viennese used to go to church mainly because of the singing and the orchestral accompaniment at mass, and quite a few still do. Critics inside and outside the church have often dismissed the Viennese way of worship as "Baroque Catholicism," meaning that the Roman pageantry and the musical offerings were detracting from genuine religious devotion. Federal Chancellor Kurt von Schuschnigg recalled a Roman Catholic academic meeting at which priests from western and northern Germany declared themselves scandalized at hearing a mass by the austere Anton Bruckner during a church service; such music belonged to the concert hall, they said. "Small wonder that we worriedly thought of our Haydn, Mozart or Schubert without whom the Catholic Heaven is unthinkable in Austria."[3]

For a long time the Baroque splendor of Vienna's religious life achieved its dazzling culmination in the Corpus Christi procession every spring. The old Emperor Franz Josef, in a white tunic and with a green-feathered hat, rode in the cortege in a splendid carriage drawn by eight white stallions. Handpicked officers from the Hungarian household troops in scarlet uniforms with panther skins over their shoulders flanked the monarch. There were also soldiers with horsetails flowing from their glittering helmets, military bands, and dragoons on horseback. The emperor was preceded by the cardinal-prince-archbishop, who carried the consecrated Host in a golden monstrance under a gold-embroidered canopy, which the Viennese call "the Heaven." The city fathers and other civil dignitaries, the Knights of the Golden Fleece in special coaches, clergy of every description, friars and nuns, student fraternities with caps and ribbons in many colors and with drawn rapiers, and many professional associations took part in the procession, which started at St. Stephen's, proceeded to the Church of St. Michael opposite the imperial castle, and returned to the cathedral. The emperor would get out of his carriage and walk the last section of the circuit. Crown and altar. Thousands of Viennese filled the grandstands and lined the streets, knelt when the Host was being carried past them, and cheered the emperor and sometimes the mayor.

The church pomp of Corpus Christi continued in the "Red Vienna" of the years after World War I. Conservative politicians and groups, members of Christian labor unions, and volunteers from the Republic's small army in uniform walked in the procession. But the Social Democratic Party, which had conquered city hall, was openly anticlerical, and many left-wing Viennese abandoned the church. Later the Nazi Party, too, encouraged its followers to give up church membership and declare themselves nonconfessional "believers in God."

The Roman Catholic Church in Vienna experienced its deepest humiliation in March 1938. The archbishop, Theodor Cardinal Innitzer, who was a native of the German-speaking part of Bohemia (the Sudetenland), felt that the right thing to do after Hitler's triumphant entry into the city was to pay homage. The Führer was staying at the Imperial Hotel on the Ringstrasse, and the cardinal drove up to call on him. Applause and catcalls rose from the Nazi crowd in front of the hotel. The prince of the church turned around and stretched out his right arm in the Nazi salute. (The author, then reporting for a Swiss newspaper, witnessed the shameful scene.) Clerical expediency does not always pay. Nearly seven months later, on October 8, 1938, young Nazi goons raided the archiepiscopal palace, broke twelve hundred window panes, smashed furniture, baited the cardinal's aides, and threw one of them out of a window, causing him serious injury.

Cardinal Innitzer's successor as Archbishop of Vienna, Franz Cardinal König, was one of the power brokers in the Vatican conclave of October 1978. In that unofficial but highly effective capacity, he helped elect Pope John Paul II, the first non-Italian pontiff in more than four centuries.

In 1983 the Polish pope went to Vienna to mark the three hundredth anniversary of the city's relief from the besieging Turks by the combined forces of Poland and the Holy Roman Empire. The Viennese cheered John Paul II as they had cheered Pius VI when he visited the city 201 years earlier. The Polish pontiff—whose father had once served in the

Austro-Hungarian army—addressed the crowds in Vienna in good German tinged with a familiar accent. Hundreds of thousands attended the mass that John Paul II offered in the vast Heldenplatz outside the former imperial castle. Yet, oldtimers who had been present in the same square in 1938 when Hitler harangued the Viennese said that the multitude had then been even bigger and seemed more enthusiastic.

CITY OF COURTIERS

Through the centuries, the commanding presence of a dynastic ruler in the vast empire's "capital and residence city" (Vienna's official appellation until 1918) not only influenced the attitude of its inhabitants toward religion but also contributed to shaping their behavior in many other respects. For more than 750 years, the Viennese have, with only brief interruptions, had a court—margravial, ducal, royal, and then imperial—in their midst. Such a long symbiosis breeds collective traits. It must also be kept in mind that between wars, enemy raids, outbreaks of pestilence, famines, and a few—remarkably few—internal upheavals, the Babenbergs and, after them, the Habsburgs assured Vienna long periods of stability and of relative economic well-being.

The Habsburgs reigned from the Hofburg, a castle one third of a mile from St. Stephen's Cathedral. The original structure dates back to the thirteenth century, but in the course of six hundred years, it was repeatedly enlarged with new wings and annexes, so that it became a city within the city. From the beginning of the eighteenth century, Schönbrunn Palace, the Habsburgs' answer to the splendor of their French Bourbon rivals at Versailles, served as the imperial summer residence, two and a half miles from the Hofburg. The two building complexes, with their thousands of halls and rooms and hundreds of corridors and kitchens (but remarkably few bathrooms), required a large staff—which, of course, functioned as innumerable conduits of hot court gossip. Whenever Empress Maria Theresa's consort, Franz I, slipped out of the palace through some back stairway to find relaxation in a tryst, all Vienna soon knew of it, except perhaps the empress. Maria Theresa herself had sixteen children by her vigorous co-ruler; one of them was Marie Antoinette, the French queen who ended under the guillotine, and another was Emperor Josef II, the employer of Mozart and terror of the Vatican.

The emperors and their kin surrounded themselves with noble families, created new aristocracy, and elaborately kept court in the Hofburg or in the Schönbrunn Palace. Wealthy nobles built palaces all over Vienna and, between court attendance and chores in government or the army, amused themselves with hunts, banquets, masquerades, dances, and musical and theatrical performances.

The Viennese populace, which lived so long in close contact with the imperial family and the aristocracy, serving and observing them, inevitably and imperceptibly took on something of the court manner and no one more so than the bourgeoisie that emerged at the end of the eighteenth century. Enduring Viennese characteristics can thus be explained: ceremoniousness, a love of gossip, a propensity for intrigue, adeptness at maneuvering for preferment, and the dogged pursuit of patronage.

To this day, the Viennese are generally convinced that in order to get on in life, one needs the support of someone in power. Many Viennese expatriates share this deep-rooted conviction, although they may have long lived in societies that cherish the myth of the self-made man. The Viennese term for individual sponsorship is *Protektion*. The strategies of such protection, of how to grant or obtain it, have for centuries dominated the city's political, professional, artistic, and social life. One way of securing patronage is anticipatory obedience, or guessing a bigwig's unspoken or future wishes—whence a certain servility in quite a few Viennese. The feudal system of *Protektion* has survived the Habsburg monarchy, was dominant in Austria's First Republic (1918–38), and has become almost institutionalized in the Second Republic (1945 to the present).

Another remnant of the imperial monarchy is a passion for titles. Viennese who were born long after the fall of the House of Habsburg still attain in bureaucratic service the title Court Counselor *(Hofrat)* or are rewarded with it for some civic or professional achievement. Even a nun may become a *Hofrat* in present-day republican Vienna, in recognition of her work in education or charities, for example. A government official who is promoted to certain posts in the bureaucratic hierarchy is officially called Real Court Counselor.

The court counselors and similar worthies have offices in Baroque palaces that once housed archdukes and high aristocrats. Vienna today appears overadministered because there are so many sumptuous buildings to fill. Out of nineteen resounding bureaucratic titles listed in the 1910 issue of the Civil Service Directory, fifteen are still officially in use. A *Regierungsrat* is not, as the outsider might assume, a consultant to the cabinet chief or some minister (the translation, "Government Counselor," would suggest this) but an official of medium rank who lacks an academic degree; an *Oberregierungsrat* is not much more. Many Viennese titles come in two levels: regular and, with an *Ober-* ("upper") prefixed, superior. A ministerial chauffeur will, after a few years' service without a major accident, be promoted to *Fahrmeister* ("Driving Master").

There are also scores of other baroque honorifics to which the Viennese attach inordinate importance, as they have done for centuries. Almost every day the Official Gazette announces that the Federal President has bestowed the title Professor on a painter who has reached his sixtieth birthday or of Commercial Counselor on some business owner who has never been in bankruptcy court and has shelled out money for worthy causes. Wives share all the honors. The titles Mrs. Lieutenant Colonel and Mrs. Veterinary Counsel do not mean that the ladies so addressed command an army battalion or deliver foals but only that their husbands do or did. Viennese take their titles to the grave, as innumerable headstones in the local cemeteries prove.

On social occasions, addressing persons by their titles alone will not do. In any coffeehouse and at any party in Vienna you may hear such flourishes as "My devotion, Mrs. Superior Medical Counselor," or "My admiration, Mr. Chief Engineer."

The city's Byzantine title mania is compounded by a deep respect for academically recognized learning. Vienna University was founded in 1365 and reorganized under Maria Theresa; its faculty, its graduates, and even its students have always enjoyed considerable prestige. Anyone who has a diploma from law school or from the philosophy or scientific departments is a *Herr Doktor* or a *Frau Doktor,* like every physician, and will be so addressed by everybody. When Leon Trotsky, after his escape from Siberia at the beginning of the century, arrived in Vienna and got in touch with leading Social Democrats, he was shocked to hear them addressed as Comrade Herr Doktor by members of their own party's rank and file. If Trotsky were to return today, he would still have the same experience.

Even peers stick to their titles: a law graduate will address another law graduate as Herr Doktor unless they are close friends. The wife of a Herr Doktor is automatically a Frau Doktor, even if she has dropped out of junior high school. Nonacademic husbands of diploma holders, however, are not yet deemed worthy of being addressed as Herr Doktor, although many will be called so anyway.

A Herr or Frau Doktor who earns a second doctorate, maybe a Ph.D. in addition to a law degree, will have calling cards printed, reading "Dr. Dr." or "DDr." before his or her name, and will henceforth sign that way. The double doctor will, however, have to be content with being addressed as Herr Doktor or Frau Doktor as before. The Viennese love of titles and ceremonious phrases exceeds that of the Germans. In Bonn or Hamburg, two men of the same academic standing simply address each other as Herr. Not so in Vienna. On the other hand, educated Viennese share with educated Germans the pedantic urge to parade their erudition: they are fond of Latin quotations, are often given to recalling presumed historical analogies that have little to do with the matter at hand, and are eager to correct other people's mistakes.

Early in the eighteenth century, Emperor Karl VI, the father of Maria Theresa, introduced the complicated Spanish etiquette at the court of Vienna. Rank and ceremony had to be rigidly observed. As late as 1914, after Archduke Franz Ferdinand and his wife had been assassinated in Sarajevo, her coffin was placed a step below his catafalque when they were lying in state because she had not been of royal blood and their marriage had been morganatic. And in the very last years of the Habsburg monarchy, as Emperor Franz Josef was dangerously ill and the court physician rushed to his bedside, the aged sovereign, who could hardly talk, whispered a horrified "The dress!" The doctor returned to his quarters to get into his morning coat, in which he was supposed to approach his august patient.

Such court punctilio rubbed off on the aristocracy from the beginning and later also on the higher reaches of the middle-class society of Vienna. Hand-kissing and courtseying, remnants of feudal obeisance, are today still being taught to Viennese children by parents who are convinced that such rituals are part of good breeding. Even grown-ups greet their mothers with the words "Küss' die Hand, Mama" ("[I] kiss your hand, Mama," eliding the first-person pronoun). It is considered good manners for a man, on taking leave of a business associate or some other acquaintance, to give him on the way a "kiss on your gracious lady's hand." Such polite phrases are empty formulas that one pays out like small change.

All that hand-kissing and pretended reverence for women point to the notorious flirtatiousness of the Viennese male. For him, no stormy passions or compulsive pursuit of conquest after conquest; neither Romeo nor Don Juan is his model. The Viennese man, instead, usually fancies what Schnitzler called a *Liebelei*—a bittersweet dalliance, lighthearted and at the same time sentimental, with plenty of white lies, or *Schmäh,* and no commitment on either side. Viennese writers appear to assume that there were, and are, uncounted men and women in their city indulging in such playful amours. It was again Schnitzler who coined a name for the archetypal Viennese woman engaged in an affair with some well-to-do and presumably married man—*das süsse-Mädel* ("the sweet girl"). Schnitzler himself would for many years record his erotic exploits in his diaries, painstakingly noting how often he proved his amatory prowess during each encounter.

The Lenten preachers of Vienna have for centuries thundered against adultery, philandering, whore-mongering, and other forms of moral laxity. Much of such licentiousness occurred, as elsewhere, among the upper classes: the word *courtesan* derives from *court,* and not without reason. Prostitutes who had an aristocratic or otherwise wealthy clientele have apparently been thriving in Vienna since the late Middle Ages, as they did in Paris, London, Rome, Naples, and Venice, which had no court but did have an affluent nobility. In modern Viennese literature, prostitutes are portrayed often and usually in a sympathetic light.

Empress Maria Theresa, who was most of the time pregnant and was outraged by what she felt was rampant immorality in Vienna, set up a Chastity Commission in 1747, just as the Venetian adventurer Casanova was surreptitiously tasting the forbidden pleasures of the imperial capital. Maria Theresa had given her commission broad powers to curb sexual license and to carry out house searches, but its activities lasted no more than half a year. Soon Vienna's courtesans were again as little restrained as they had been before. Maria Theresa's son, co-ruler, and successor, Josef II, would don simple dress and go slumming. Popular myth later transformed such imperial escapades into high-minded forays to take the pulse of the common people in the manner of Harun al-Rashid.

Mozart wrote to his father that he was going to marry Constanze Weber because he loathed "wrestling with whores," but he remained overfond of merry female company to the end of his short life. Schubert often consorted with servant girls and prostitutes, and probably caught syphilis, which may have lowered his resistance to his last illness. Johannes Brahms, a bachelor from North Germany who had been playing the piano in a Hamburg bordello and lived in Vienna for more than three decades until his death, soon got into the spirit of the place and, like many other eminent residents, became a regular customer of its broad sex-for-pay market.

SING AND SAY

Vienna's court life was to be of universal cultural importance in two areas: music and the performing arts. The Babenberg dukes began a tradition when they entertained minnesingers, the medieval musicians and poets who, like the troubadours of southern France, drifted from castle to castle to amuse the nobility. Walther von der Vogelweide (1170?–?1230), a Tyrolean who became one of the outstanding lyric poets of the High Middle Ages, wrote that he had learned to "sing and say" at the Babenberg court in Vienna.

The Habsburgs and the aristocratic families clustering around their court favored musicians, poets, and actors even during wars. In the Baroque period, four successive Habsburg emperors were not only patrons of music but musicians themselves. Artistically the most prolific among them was Leopold I (1657–1705): he wrote musical plays in which relatives and members of his court sang, acted, and danced; composed sacred music and many songs; and arranged ballets and musical pageants.

Imperial and aristocratic patronage brought Gluck and Beethoven to Vienna in the eighteenth century. Haydn, born in a village near Vienna, served for twenty-nine years as musical director of the Esterházy princes; and Mozart, after a long search for a well-paying position, at last succeeded Gluck as imperial chamber musician and court composer under Josef II. (More about this stellar age of music in Vienna will be said later.)

The imperial court and the nobility transmitted their love of music to the populace. In the early nineteenth century, good amateur chamber quartets could be heard in many middle-class homes. Otto Nicolai, the German composer *(The Merry Wives of Windsor)* and conductor, founded the Vienna Philharmonic Orchestra in 1841, mainly with musicians of the Hofoper, or Court Opera. The Strauss family—Johann, father and son; Josef; and Eduard—electrified the city with their waltzes, and Wagnerians and anti-Wagnerians clashed at the opera. Vienna was music-mad.

Musical education had by then reached a remarkable level in the Austrian capital. Even families of modest means had their children learn to play some instrument, and school orchestras tackled Beethoven and Schubert. Music is still important in the life of Vienna. In fact, if the city, apart from its museums, continues playing an internationally valid cultural role, it will be as a world capital of music, thanks to the Vienna Philharmonic, the Staatsoper (State Opera), its concerts, and its teachers. The Philharmonic is renowned for its "Vienna sound," a mellowness sets it off from the clipped precision of some other of the world's leading orchestras. The orchestra pit of the Staatsoper is staffed by musicians from the Philharmonic.

Viennese have taken their love of music and their need for it with them into exile. When during World War II the British authorities reclassified as "enemy aliens" hundreds of residents and refugees from Vienna and deported them to Australia, that continent found itself blessed with a sprinkling of new chamber music groups.

Vienna's musical fervor has for hundreds of years been accompanied by its fascination with opera and the theater. The stage had held Vienna spellbound since the morality plays of the fifteenth and sixteenth centuries. For the Jesuits, gripping theatrical shows with a religious message were tactical weapons in their Counter-Reformation battles and brought forth as by-products popular drama and farce. Stage action in any form deeply satisfied the Viennese craving for make-believe, dream life, facade, intrigue, and *Schmäh*.

Maria Theresa had her own theater in Schönbrunn Castle in 1747; it is still in use today as the permanent stage of the Reinhardt Theatrical Seminar. The Hofburg, at the center of the capital, had its own imperial theater, too, in 1751. When the beloved little house facing the Church of St. Michael was at last torn down to make room for a new castle wing and portal, the performances shifted to the new, sumptuous Burgtheater on the Ringstrasse in 1888. (The Viennese called its architecture "Neronian.")

Generations of young Viennese have been initiated into the classics of dramatic literature, as well as some modern works, in the Burgtheater, with its cheap standing-room sections. The Jewish philosopher Martin Buber, who was born in Vienna, fondly remembered in old age how, during his student days, he used to race up the stairs of the Burgtheater as soon as its doors were opened, to assure himself a good place in the top gallery. The Burgtheater is still one of the leading German-language stages. The tenured members of its ensemble are known as "Burg actors" and are sometimes given the title Court Counselor, just as outstanding figures of the British theater are honored with a baronetcy.

The Court Opera moved into its vast, noble building at another spot on the Ringstrasse in 1869 and opened it with Mozart's *Don Giovanni* (then dubbed *Don Juan).* The specifications had called for a special standing-room space for army officers in uniform in the auditorium, and it was duly provided. As Edward Crankshaw said, "In what other army in the world have officers, in or out of uniform, been prepared to listen to an opera?"[4] One of the new opera house's architects, Edward van der Null, shattered by criticism of the building, committed suicide. Now known as the State Opera, the structure, which was severely damaged during World War II and reopened in 1955, is to many Viennese the most important place in their city.

There were already several private stages in Vienna and its suburbs when Maria Theresa inaugurated her Schönbrunn theater. One of them was Schikaneder's little Freihaus Theater, where Mozart's *Magic Flute,* with a libretto by Schikaneder, had its first performance in 1791. Schikaneder complained, "My *Zauberflöte* was so nice, but that fellow Mozart spoiled it all with his music."

At the apogee of popular comedy, around the middle of the nineteenth century, the playwright Nestroy could with some justification be called the Viennese Aristophanes. Like Giuseppe Gioacchino Belli, the Roman vernacular satirist who was his contemporary, Nestroy would have become far better known outside his homeland if he had written in the standard form of his mother tongue rather than in dialect. Karl Kraus—who will often be cited in this book as a merciless critic of Vienna's intelligentsia—was a great admirer of Nestroy, the consummate manipulator of language. Himself stagestruck, Kraus read from Nestroy farces in his highly successful lectures.

When he was still a student, Kraus acted in a suburban production of Schiller's *Die Räuber* (The Robbers). He was playing opposite another young theater enthusiast, Max Goldmann, who would later, as Max Reinhardt, become an internationally acclaimed stage director. Reinhardt helped get the Salzburg summer festivals started in 1920, and in the 1930s was one of several leading figures whom Vienna's theatrical culture would give to American drama, opera, and film. Rudolf Bing, Fritz Lang, Otto Preminger, Erich von Stroheim, and Billy Wilder were among them.

Musicians and theater people in Vienna have always had to reckon with the daunting power of the bureaucrats who helped parcel out patronage, administered the court theaters, and exercised censorship. Maria Theresa and her son Josef II had shaped the Austrian civil service into a formidable instrument that, along with the army, held the multilingual empire together for another century and a half.

THE FILES, THE FILES!

Emperor Franz Josef was, during the sixty-eight years of his reign, the supreme bureaucrat. He got up from his iron field bed at dawn every day and spent long hours at his desk, reluctant to delegate authority and insisting on examining all the files—up to four hundred dossiers a day. "He may have been just a pedant, not a tyrant, only cold and not cruel," wrote Karl Kraus in a diatribe against the old emperor soon after Franz Josef's death in 1916.[5] Today, pictures of the aged monarch with his porcelain-blue eyes and his muttonchops are on postcards and book jackets all over Vienna. They are signs of a cult of Franz Josef, the father figure under whom things were supposedly better and people happier than they are now. The overwhelming majority of the Viennese nevertheless supports the republican form of government, as all polls and elections show; there is no organized monarchist party.

The records *(die Akten)* that crowded Franz Josef's days were always the fetish of the Viennese bureaucracy, much more important than the individuals they recorded. The civil service of the Austrian Republic has inherited this attitude. The writer Elias Canetti remembers that when a rioting mob had set the Palace of Justice in Vienna on fire in 1927, he observed a man in a nearby street throwing up his arms and wailing, "The files are burning, all the files!" The desperate bystander—perhaps a civil servant or a lawyer—seemed not to care that wild shooting between the police and the rioters was going on and that scores of people were being killed.

The awesome government machinery followed immutable procedures. It was slow but honest. Corruption was extremely rare, as was blatant incompetence. "In the lands of Austria it is not possible to keep an important post without having the kind of talent that the slow and complicated, but very reasonable, administration of that old monarchy requires," wrote Stendhal in 1838.[6] That old monarchy had turned him down when the French government wanted to send Stendhal to Trieste, then an Austrian seaport, as a consul.

Modern Italian writers have acknowledged that Trieste, Milan, and other cities that were once ruled from Vienna were well run and that later administrative experiences were less satisfactory. Austria-Hungary, according to Robert Musil, was governed "in an enlightened manner that was little felt, and which prudently cut off all sharp edges, by the best bureaucracy in Europe, which could be blamed for one shortcoming only: it resented as brashness and presumption any genius and enterprising imagination in private persons who were not authorized to possess them by high birth or official mission."[7]

Not everyone among the emperor's subjects, though, had such a bland perception of Austria-Hungary's administrative apparatus. Its ponderous procedures surely inspired the theme of Kafka's *The Trial, The Castle,* and some of his short stories: the defenseless individual confronted by a cruel, incomprehensible power in a frightening labyrinth. The author, it is true, found even the simplest transaction at the post office an ordeal, as his lover, Milena, wrote when their affair was over.

Another Prague-born writer, Jaroslav Hašek, showed instead in *The Good Soldier Svejk* (1921) how a sly dealer in stolen dogs who has been redrafted into his regiment after being medically discharged on account of "chronic feeblemindedness" manages to fool the bureaucracy and survive World War I. Svejkism, or passive resistance disguised as mental dimness, has since been practiced in Central Europe under Nazi and Communist domination. In Austria-Hungary it could work because Emperor Franz Josef's system of government was "absolutism mitigated by *Schlamperei,*" as Viktor Adler, one of the founders of the Austrian Social Democratic movement, observed. *Schlamperei,* which means messiness, inefficiency, and lack of exactitude, is what the North Germans and the Swiss always reproach the Viennese for. But in Vienna, *Schlamperei* may have amiable overtones of humane laxity.

The favorite technique of the Austro-Hungarian art of government was *fortwursteln,* a Viennese dialect term that may be rendered as "muddling through" or "soldiering on." Literally, the word seems to suggest subsistence on small sausages for long periods, but it may also derive from Hans Wurst, the male clown of Punch-and-Judy shows and popular farce. For generations, carrying on through expediency, avoiding showdowns and radical solutions, was the guiding principle for Austrian officials.

Fortwursteln has always been a Viennese way of coping with problems outside the affairs of state. Thus, a disgruntled employee will forever complain about his boss and try to obtain favors from customers, but he will rarely think of walking out to start his own business. A wife may close her eyes to the infidelities of her husband and, rather than ask for a divorce, console herself with discreet affairs of her own. Shunning clear-cut decisions and persisting in ambiguity are typical Viennese strategies.

As the core of an intricate administrative mechanism, Vienna has for hundreds of years housed legions of officials and pensioners, many from Bohemia, Croatia, Poland, and other non-Germanic parts of its empire. To maneuver their sons into some state job was the chief aim of innumerable Viennese families, and all their connections were used to get the necessary *Protektion.* The security and prestige of employment in some government department by far outweighed the relatively low pay and slow advancement.

Proverbial virtues of the Viennese bureaucrats were urbanity, frugality, moderation, and punctuality—no *Schlamperei* in reporting for work on time! Franz Josef had been an admired model: his iron bed was legendary, as was the meticulousness with which he invariably appeared at the exact moment scheduled for an official function, not a second early, not a second late. His stock response to every opening of an art show, agricultural fair, or new building was to say, "It was very nice, I was very pleased." On the last day of his life, on November 20, 1916, the eighty-six-year-old emperor went to bed earlier than usual, telling his attendant to wake him at 3:30 A.M. because "there is so much to be done." He died in his sleep.

The values and limitations of officialdom and its sense of hierarchy, rank, title, and authority have pervaded Viennese life for centuries. Everything that is not expressly permitted is forbidden, residents joke even today. If for some reason crime were allowed in Austria, Musil wrote, it would be committed by officially authorized criminals only. Warnings on doors in Vienna read "Entry Prohibited!" where a simple "No Entry" would do. *Verboten* ("prohibited") is a recurring word in the city, often reinforced by *streng* ("severely") and an exclamation point! Signs on many buildings caution that panhandling and door-to-door sales calls are forbidden; so are stepping on the grass in some public parks and many other things. What the city gains in orderliness it loses through the grimness of the many *Verboten!* signs.

No matter how long Viennese may have lived abroad, they will instinctively assume a respectful attitude toward the authorities of their host countries, pay their taxes to the last cent, and refrain from publicly criticizing official measures. Viennese emigrés, and even their children, are often perceived as paragons of punctuality, rather than *Schlamperei,* and may show annoyance toward people who do not keep commitments or are habitually late. Quite a few diaspora Viennese are also sticklers for accuracy in professional life and private conversation, just as many bureaucrats back home were.

A position in the government administration, the army, the judiciary, or the higher-education system has for at least two centuries carried far more cachet in Vienna than mere moneymaking. Even one who had a lucrative practice of medicine or law—let alone a great income from industry or trade—was long regarded as not quite on the level of a ministerial section chief or a court counselor. What is more, a senior civil servant could, at the end of a staid forty-year career, hope to be elevated to the petty nobility by the emperor, and put the coveted *von* in front of his name, a privilege he might bequeathe to his children.

JEWISH VIENNA

Vienna's Jews, long barred from public service, gravitated in the nineteenth century toward industry, commerce, and the free professions, in which they were joined by successful Jewish immigrants from the outlying lands of the empire. The fathers of Sigmund Freud, Arthur Schnitzler, and Karl Kraus were among the many Jews who moved to the capital and did well there; the sometime distiller and taverner Bernhard Mahler, too poor to emigrate from Jihlava, Moravia, with his large family, did manage to send his gifted son Gustav to study music in Vienna.

Jewish traders are believed to have been doing business in the Vindobona of the Romans. Some ancient myths even have it that the first Jews settled in the Danubian town eighty years after Joshua, the successor to Moses, had crossed the Jordan River, and even that Vindobona had actually been founded by Jews. According to Josef Fraenkel, "All these legends probably originated from the need to make quite clear how deep the roots of the Jews in Vienna are, and how strongly they are attached to that city."[8]

The oldest documents referring to Jews in Vienna date from the twelfth century; the existence of a Jewish cemetery near the site of the present State Opera was recorded in 1244. The first Viennese Jew identified by name was one Shlom, a jeweler who melted down the silver ingots received as ransom for King Richard the Lion-Hearted. The English monarch took part in the Third Crusade and, in the eyes of another high-ranking participant, Duke Leopold V the Virtuous of Austria, insulted the red-white-red Austrian flag by hauling it down from the bastions of the captured city of Acre. In 1192, on his way back from the Holy Land in disguise, King Richard is said to have been recognized in the Erdberg suburb of Vienna, arrested on orders from Leopold, and held prisoner in the castle in Dürnstein on the Danube. According to a romantic legend, Richard's favorite, the French minstrel Blondel de Nesle, located the king and procured his release against payment of a huge ransom in 1194. Pope Celestine III excommunicated Duke Leopold for his inhospitable treatment of a fellow crusader, but the silver plate or coins supplied by Shlom may have been a consolation.

Vienna's Jewish community seems to have flourished for some time in the late Middle Ages. A Jewish school, rabbi's house, and hospital on a little square in the center near the Judenplatz that is still officially known as the Schulhof, the name of a former building, were mentioned in chronicles in 1294. This old Jewish establishment seems to have survived until 1421, when 92 men and 120 women of wealthy Jewish families were publicly burned at the stake after a pogrom, and poor Jews were herded onto Danube boats for deportation to Hungary.

In the centuries following this grisly outbreak of anti-Semitism, periods of persecution alternated with spells of reluctant and relative tolerance. Various emperors permitted the Jews to live in ghettos in the oldest part of the city and beyond what is now the Danube Canal. In 1670 a popular bishop, Count Leopold Kolonitz, brought about another expulsion of the "enemies of Jesus."

All the time a few Jewish financiers, known as "court Jews," were raising funds for the emperors and advising them on money affairs. One of them was Samson Wertheimer, whom Emperor Leopold I in 1684 called from Worms on the Rhine to Vienna to help him replenish his treasury. Vienna had just barely survived a long Turkish siege, and the emperor needed money to reconstruct the battered city and to pay the forces who were pursuing the retreating Turks into Hungary. Wertheimer seems to have obtained new loans or income for Leopold I. A scholar as well as a financial expert, he not only served for several years as court Jew of the Habsburgs but was also named chief rabbi of their Jewish subjects in Hungary and Bohemia. Because of his influence in high places, Wertheimer came to be called the "Jewish emperor." He settled in Eisenstadt, a rural town near the border between Austria and Hungary, and built himself a stately mansion with a private synagogue in the ghetto there. The restored Wertheimer House in Eisenstadt became in 1982 the site of the Austrian Jewish Museum.

A turning point for Jews in the Austrian capital came in 1781, when Emperor Josef II, in the spirit of the Enlightenment, issued his Edict of Tolerance *(Toleranzpatent)*. Jews were admitted to public schools and institutions of higher learning, the civil service, and other professions. Outward signs of discrimination, such as yellow badges, were prohibited. However, there was no provision that would have enabled Austrian Jews to organize themselves in religious communities; this would only come in the middle of the nineteenth century. The thrust of Josef II's reforms was toward assimilation. Jewish families had to take on German-sounding names—whence Vienna's many Rosenthals, Schönfelds, and the like—and their sons were to serve in the Imperial Army like all other young Austrians.

There was some pressure on Jews to get baptized. Josef II's mother, Maria Theresa, had already relied on the advice of Baron Josef von Sonnenfels, a leading jurist and political scientist who was the son of a baptized Jew from Moravia. Sonnenfels persuaded his empress to abolish torture in ordinary criminal procedure, helped liberalize Vienna's business life, and was a patron of the arts and the theater, credited with founding the stage at the imperial castle.

Many Viennese Jews rose quickly in commerce and finance. Their money permitted the building of a large synagogue, from 1824 to 1826, on a central site (2–4 Seitenstettengasse) where a Jewish house of worship is believed to have existed in the Middle Ages. In compliance with a building code that denied street frontage to any religious building that was not Roman Catholic, the structure had to be hidden behind a nondescript dwelling-house facade. Members of the Jewish community must to this day walk across a small entrance hall to reach a courtyard and the domed synagogue that is tucked away in it.

Two years before the start of the synagogue construction in the old Vienna ghetto, Emperor Franz II of Austria had conferred baronies on the five sons of a Frankfurt banker, Mayer Amschel Rothschild, in recognition of financial services rendered by the family. Only one of the five settled in Vienna; of the others, one lived in Frankfurt, one in London, one in Paris, and one in Naples. Baron Salomon von Rothschild was the first Jew to be awarded full Viennese citizenship, but not before he had granted the municipality a low-interest loan of 340,000 florins for inner-city rehabilitation.

The Jewish Viennese attained complete legal equality with the majority of the population after the middle-class revolution of 1848. During the uprisings in that turbulent year, Jews manned barricades and fought side by side with Gentiles against Metternich and absolutism. Leading Jews were elected to the Parliament that was the result of the 1848 upheavals. A Jewish community of Vienna was formally established in 1852.

In the second half of the nineteenth century numerous Jews excelled in Vienna's intellectual and artistic life—as writers, musicians, scientists, physicians, scholars, theater people, and patrons of all kinds of talent. "It was the pride, the ambition specifically of the Jewish middle class," Stefan Zweig was to write when it was all over, "that they could participate here in a leading position in maintaining the fame of Viennese culture in its old splendor. Immeasurable is the part that the Jewish middle class has thus taken in Viennese culture. They were the real audience. They filled the theaters and concerts, they bought the books, the pictures. They visited the exhibitions and, with their more agile perception less burdened by tradition, became everywhere the champions and sponsors of everything that was new."[9]

The Jewish contribution to Viennese civilization at the turn of the century, one of the most creative eras in the history of that—indeed, of any—city, can hardly be overrated. Many Viennese Jews sincerely loved the capital, as their writers made plain and as their enthusiastic involvement in urban beautification projects and other municipal affairs showed. Nowhere, except in fifteenth-century Spain, had there been a more fruitful collaboration between Jews and a Christian majority of the population than in Vienna, Zweig wrote.

A Hungarian-born Jew who had become a widely read Viennese

journalist, Theodor Herzl, strove for assimilation into the German-speaking Gentile society of the city before the shocks of anti-Semitism that he experienced at home and in Paris prompted him to write his epochal pamphlet *Der Judenstaat* (The Jewish State) in 1896. Other Viennese Jews scoffed at Herzl, none more acerbically than the young Karl Kraus in the pamphlet *Eine Krone für Zion* (A Crown for Zion, 1898). An avowed assimilationist, Kraus formally abandoned the Jewish community, embraced the Roman Catholic faith, and was baptized in the Church of St. Charles Borromeo in 1911, with Adolf Loos, the innovative architect, as his godfather; but after World War I, Kraus left the church.

When the novelist Jakob Wassermann, a native of Fürth, near Nürnberg, first arrived in Vienna around the turn of the century, he found that "almost all persons with whom I got spiritually or cordially in touch were Jews. Furthermore, this was always underlined by others, and they themselves underlined it." In his autobiography, Wassermann recalled that at home, in Bavaria, he had hardly met any Jews, whereas in Vienna "the entire public life was dominated by Jews. The banks, the press, theater, literature, social events, everything was in the hands of the Jews. . . . The court, the petty bourgeoisie and the Jews gave their imprint to the city. That the Jews, as the most mobile group kept everybody else in movement, is not particularly astonishing; I was nevertheless surprised by the multitude of Jewish doctors, lawyers, club members, snobs, dandies, proletarians, actors, journalists and poets."[10] Himself Jewish, Wassermann married a high-strung Viennese, became a friend of Viennese literati, and wrote one bestseller after another.

The resurgence of Viennese anti-Semitism toward the end of the nineteenth century started among the church-influenced lower middle class of artisans, small shopkeepers, petty bureaucrats and other state employees, and among chauvinistic, Pan-German academics, schoolteachers, and students, many of whom were from the lower middle class. Vienna's industrial workers and proletariat were for a long time unaffected by the anti-Semitic tide; Viktor Adler and many of the other leaders of the increasingly powerful Social Democratic Party were in fact Jewish. Emperor Franz Josef and the high aristocracy were known to despise the anti-Semites.

As for the attitude of many Viennese Jews, listen to Hans J. Thalberg, an Austrian diplomat who was descended from the Jewish upper middle class: "It wouldn't have occurred to anyone in either branch of our family to take Zionism seriously. One gladly left that to the eastern Jews on which one looked down with disdain."[11] Poor neighborhoods of Vienna were then filling up with Jewish refugees from the pogroms and hardships in Russia.

Thousands of Jewish Viennese served valiantly in the Austro-Hungarian army from 1914 to 1918, and many died for their country. In 1922 a most unusual novel, *Die Stadt ohne Juden* (The City Without Jews), found many readers in Vienna. Its author was Hugo Bettauer, who had earlier written some successful, though shallow, books and for some time published a sexual-emancipation magazine, *Er und Sie* (He and She). A native of Baden, near Vienna, Bettauer had been a schoolmate of Karl Kraus and, as a young man, had emigrated to the United States and become an American citizen. He later worked as a journalist in Berlin before returning home. One of his novels, *Die freudlose Gasse* (The Street Without Joy, 1923), was used for a film by G. W. Pabst, who gave a part in it to a young Swedish actress, Greta Garbo.

Bettauer's *Die Stadt ohne Juden* was a stroke of genius. In this "novel of the day after tomorrow," which was also filmed, a conservative government chief introduces a bill in Parliament ordering the expulsion of all Jews from Austria on the grounds that they dominate the press, the theaters, and the banks; fill the coffeehouses, restaurants, and night spots; and generally lead lives of luxury. The Christian Democratic floor leader, a priest, hails the government chief as a modern apostle worthy to be proclaimed a saint. The Pan-German deputies Wondratschek and Jiratschek—two Czech names—praise the proposed legislation as a decisive step toward racial purity. Only the Social Democrats vote against the bill, and are thrown out of the Parliament chamber by the majority.

As soon as all Jews have left Vienna, life in the city changes radically. Gentiles take over the businesses, homes, and automobiles of the Jews, and it becomes "no longer necessary to line up to conquer a seat at the opera house; life [becomes] quieter, more solid, simpler." But soon economic stagnation sets in, unemployment spreads, and Christian artists, scholars, and physicians begin to emigrate because Vienna can no longer afford them. The people who stay behind go around in Alpine dress, the women in dirndls and the men in short pants and loden suits with green Styrian hats. Coffeehouses are deserted, and the Viennese greet each other with "Heil!" Eventually life becomes so drab that the city realizes it needs the Jews and calls them back.

Rightists in Austria and Germany, including Hitler's racist ideologue Alfred Rosenberg, denounced Bettauer as a Jewish propagandist. In Vienna the writer got into trouble when he started a campaign for repeal of the penal code's provision that declared abortion punishable. Church-supported newspapers and groups joined the Nazis in an outcry against the feminist crusader. In March 1925 a dental technician who was a member of the Nazi storm troops, Otto Rothstock, walked into Bettauer's office and killed him with five revolver shots. "He had it coming," was the burden of many press reports about the crime. At the assassin's trial, the victim seemed to be the real accused. Rothstock's defense counsel was Walter Riehl, a lawyer who had founded the Austrian branch of the Hitler party; the murderer told the court he had acted to protect young people from being corrupted by Bettauer. The defendant received a lenient sentence and was later released from prison by the Nazis. Bettauer's book was in some respects prophetic, yet he could not imagine the horrors that Vienna would see in only a few years. At least sixty thousand Viennese died in the Holocaust. Today, the Austrian capital is almost a city without Jews, but anti-Semitism has endured.

COFFEEHOUSE AS REFUGE

Many Viennese who went abroad because of Hitler were to find that they missed few things of their former life as badly as their *Stammcafé,* their regular coffeehouse. They often felt uncomfortable with that distinctly non-Germanic institution for socializing, the cocktail party, and would seek out places that, however faintly, reminded them of the coffeehouse atmosphere back home, such as Sardi's Restaurant in New York or Fink's Restaurant in Jerusalem. In Vienna the coffeehouse was more a manner of urban living than a type of catering establishment. It used to provide the highlight of the day, of every day, for generations of Viennese before 1938. (How the city picked up the passion for coffee and the coffeehouse habit will be told in the following chapter.)

Coffeehouse civilization peaked in fin-de-siècle Vienna and in the first three decades of our century. Sigmund Freud favored the Café Landtmann near the university; Gustav Mahler was a regular at the Café Imperial; Alfred Adler, founder of the anti-Freudian individual psychology, frequented the Café Central. Another habitué there was a Russian,

Lev Davydovich Bronstein, also known as Leon Trotsky. When Count Leopold von Berchtold, the Austro-Hungarian foreign minister from 1912 to 1915, was told that a Communist revolution might break out in czarist Russia, he exclaimed with an incredulous guffaw, "And who, if you please, will make that revolution? Mr. Bronstein who is playing chess at the Central all the time?" Josef, the Central's headwaiter, is reported to have shown no astonishment when the news came in 1917 that the Russian Revolution had broken out and that Trotsky was one of its leaders: "I always knew that Herr Doktor Bronstein would go far in life, but I shouldn't have thought that he might leave without paying for the four moccas he owes me."

Lenin, too, is believed to have been seen at the Café Central occasionally. Franz Lehár, whose operettas helped keep the myth of merry Vienna alive in the years between the two world wars, was long a revered figure at the Café Sperl. At about the same time, Elias Canetti, who was to receive the Nobel Prize in literature much later, spent many afternoons with other literati in the Café Museum.

The Landtmann, the Imperial, the Sperl, and the Museum have remained in business, and the Central has been reopened as a tourist attraction, but their former vibrancy has long since gone. There are still a couple of hundred other coffeehouses in Vienna today, but most of them now offer snacks and simple meals, which few cafés did before the 1930s. Quite a few Viennese, especially older ones, keep dropping in at their *Stammcafé* to drink a "little brown one" or a "mélange" (cappuccino) and read the newspapers and magazines that the management provides free. The dailies are still kept in holders of bamboo or hardwood, and the periodicals in brown covers that tend to get greasy as they, with their contents, are passed on by first-rate cafés to more-modest establishments, the crossword puzzles already filled in. Some coffeehouses still keep an encyclopedia—though maybe no longer the most recent edition—on a shelf for the convenience of patrons who need help in solving puzzles or deciding disputes.

The glass of water that comes with the coffee will still be replaced from time to time as a silent message to the patron: You are welcome to stay as long as you like, without any reorder. Waiters are still mostly men, and the headwaiter will probably be dressed in black and acknowledge a tip with what would sound like obsequiousness if it were not uttered so mechanically: "Thank you very much, many thanks, Herr Doktor, see

43

you again, *Herr Doktor!"* or "Kiss your hand, thank you so very much, gracious lady!"

The regulars know the headwaiter at their *Stammcafé* by his first name only, but always address him as "Herr Ferdinand" or "Herr Richard." Vienna coffeehouse lore postulates that the accomplished headwaiter will betray no surprise on seeing a former patron who has not shown up for five years and that he will not ask any questions, but will say, "Good morning, my respect, Herr Professor. The usual? A mélange, rather dark, in a teacup?" The headwaiter will at once bring the onetime habitué the Swiss newspaper that he had always perused. Café managements and patrons have often encouraged waiters to develop quirks and become originals. They may have tics, mutter to themselves, or betray other eccentricities, but their mechanic politeness should never degenerate into excessive familiarity with guests.

In Vienna's coffeehouses students still meet today to cram for exams, and middle-aged women, to gossip or play bridge while spooning the thick layer of whipped cream off their cappuccino. Chess players ponder their next move, surrounded by silent kibitzers. Architects sketch apartment interiors and salesmen work out their commissions on the marble tops of coffeehouse tables. Couples who crave anonymity seek out some café where they have never been before, as do spies and their contacts.

Then there is still the stock character of the coffeehouse loner who appears at the same time every day, speaks to no one but the headwaiter, and hogs the newspapers, stacking them on the empty seat next to him. When he is through with the papers, he prowls the place and pounces on any daily or magazine that he sees lying around; once in a while he may break his habitual taciturnity and say, "Excuse me, is *Die Presse* free?," and take it even before the person so addressed has had time to nod. While seeming absorbed in his reading, the coffeehouse loner often observes everything that is going on around him, and after months and years of watching the other regulars and overhearing snatches of what they say, he will have a fairly good idea of their role in society, without ever having talked to any of them—except maybe to ask for a newspaper.

A joke that made the rounds of Vienna around the middle of the 1930s had a Dr. Altschul or Commercial Counselor Kornfeld tell his wife how he wanted Hitler to end: "He should go around our coffeehouse, down at heel, and look for newspapers to read, and you should say, 'Isn't he that fellow Hitler, that nebbish?' And he should come to our table and ask, 'Excuse me, is *Die Presse* free?' And I would say, 'Not for you, Herr Hitler, not for you!' "

Around the time when Vienna café patrons wished Hitler such an inglorious but mild fate, they may have noticed a bespectacled, dark-haired man looking for newspapers to read. He was Karl Kraus, the critic, satirist, poet, magazine publisher, lecturer, and moralist who would move on to a new coffeehouse whenever too many people tried to talk to him in the one he had lately been frequenting. Then in his sixties, Kraus worked all night at his home in the Lothringerstrasse—between Vienna's two leading concert halls—and slept until the early afternoon, when he would make his coffeehouse visit. He had first startled intellectual Vienna in 1896 by pouring scorn on coffeehouse writers in a pamphlet, *The Demolished Literature*. What had really been demolished was the Café Griensteidl, which had stood on the Michaelerplatz opposite the imperial castle and had long served as a meeting place of the intelligentsia.

Another compulsive coffeehouse habitué was Robert Musil, the author of *The Man Without Qualities*. He always chose a table with great circumspection, wanting to be sure that nobody could be behind him. At the Café Central or Café Museum he would often stand around for quite some time until one of the tables close to the wall became vacant.

Much of the writing in Vienna between the 1880s and 1938 was done in coffeehouses. One essayist, Peter Altenberg (his real name was Richard Engländer), actually lived in the Café Central. He used his room number 51 at the Graben Hotel in the narrow Dorotheergasse for sleeping or, as he used to say, "camping." The prostitutes who were habitually in and out of the hotel would pamper him, put bottles of šljivovica under his bed, and send him picture postcards in summer when they took their trade to some resort. He pinned these greetings on the room's walls alongside pictures of his child loves. (Altenberg shared with the architect Adolf Loos and the painter Egon Schiele a fascination with adolescent girls.) At the Café Central, Altenberg, one of the few contemporary Viennese writers whom Kraus respected, spent most of his waking hours until late at night. He talked with other patrons, read the newspapers, received his mail, wrote his impressionist sketches, ate his meals, and also took a hand in, as he put it, "educating" the junior waiters. Almost always wearing sandals, he was the eccentric-in-residence.

If the coffeehouse was the habitat of the Viennese literati, it served also as setting for the fiction and drama they produced or was mentioned in them. In Schnitzler's *Reigen* (La Ronde), ten dialogues before and after the sexual act, the son of a bourgeois family takes his parents' housemaid to bed and informs her right afterward, "I now go to the coffeehouse." In another vignette of the same cycle, an aristocratic officer, awakening in the squalor of a prostitute's room, remembers through the fog of his hangover that the night before he had been in a "whores' café."

In Karl Kraus's leviathan of a drama, *Die letzten Tage der Menschheit* (The Last Days of Mankind, 1922), the second scene takes place in the Café Pucher, where the Prime Minister and the Minister of Domestic Affairs on the day after Archduke Franz Ferdinand's assassination in Sarajevo profess their utter boredom.

When Franz Ferdinand von Trotta, the antihero of Joseph Roth's 1938 novel *The Capuchin Crypt*, returns to Vienna after years in a Russian prisoner-of-war camp at Christmas 1918, it takes only a few days before he goes back to his former *Stammcafé*. Many of his old friends are there, most of them still in military uniform. They have all lost something in the lost war—the aristocrats their titles and privileges, others the money they had invested in war bonds. They drink ersatz coffee, read newspapers, talk from table to table, and banter as they had done before the war. "I felt good; I was home again," von Trotta muses.

In Heimito von Doderer's 1956 novel *Die Dämonen* (The Demons), set in the Vienna of 1926–27, one or the other coffeehouse is mentioned in almost every chapter. In the grim period immediately after World War II, coffeehouses were quick to function again, somehow, amid the ruins caused by Allied bombers and the final Soviet assault. In Graham Greene's *The Third Man* and the Carol Reed film classic based on it, racketeers use a coffeehouse near the State Opera, the still-existing Café Mozart, as a meeting place.

Looking back on the "world of yesterday," Stefan Zweig described the Viennese coffeehouse as a "democratic club." It did favor informal contact and discussions, but at the same time, it permitted the kind of solitude in company that Kraus and Musil craved. At least by sight, most of the few thousand persons that made up Vienna's intelligentsia before 1938 knew one another, thanks to the coffeehouses. Playwrights spoke to philosophers of the neopositivist Vienna Circle, high government officials rubbed elbows with bohemians, Freudians nodded at operetta stars, and Alma Mahler, née Schindler, the widow of Gustav Mahler, divorced wife of the architect Walter Gropius and mistress of, successively, the painter Oskar Kokoschka and the writer Franz Werfel, knew everybody.

Thus, rather than being a subculture, the coffeehouse was an essential part of the Viennese manner of living. It made the drab housing to which hundreds of thousands of Viennese were condemned a little more bearable. Behind the palatial buildings of the Ringstrasse that had gone up in the second half of the nineteenth century, a broad belt of working-class neighborhoods with tenements known as "rental barracks" or "bed-bug castles" encircled the city. In them, a typical apartment opened from the staircase right into the kitchen, and from there one might reach a bedroom and perhaps a smaller room, the *Kabinett*. A toilet on the landing was shared by several families, as was the nearby water faucet and sink, the *Bassena,* which in dialect comedy and in real life played a big role as a social center and scene of occasional quarrels between tenants.

In a single generation the number of Vienna's inhabitants had almost doubled, and the poor districts were monstrously overcrowded. Many lower-middle-class and workers' families sublet extra beds to single persons, who were consequently called *Bettgeher* ("bedgoers") and were entitled to space for their few belongings in some dresser or cabinet, but never to a room of their own or to any privacy. Between 1900 and 1910, one out of every twenty residents in the city was a *Bettgeher.* They were living in a world far from the febrile cultural brilliance of fin-de-siècle Vienna. The escapist literati and artists of the epoch and aestheticists like Hugo von Hofmannsthal preferred to ignore the mean reality of *Bettgeher* and workers' flats without indoor toilets and running water and with seven or more people sleeping in one room.

The traditional refuge from the rental barracks was the tavern, but lower-middle-class Viennese who had had a chance of attending high school would later in life be drawn to the café. There, amid the relative opulence of marble-topped tables, plush banquettes, bright lights, and plate-glass windows, they could meet wealthier friends without embarrassment. Even quite recently, many Viennese were ashamed of their inadequate or outright shabby lodgings. "It is almost impossible to penetrate the secret of a Viennese apartment," Ingeborg Bachmann, among Austria's most important writers after World War II, remarked. "Even a person's best friends cannot do it."[12]

Newcomers to Vienna who had to put up with sordid housing found a haven in the city's cafés too. Joseph Roth has described how the refugees from Eastern Europe got their first Viennese acculturation in the noisy little coffeehouses in the Leopoldstadt, the then predominantly Jewish section between the Danube Canal and the Danube River: "The Jews like to go to the coffeehouse to read newspapers, play tarok and chess, and make business deals. . . . They come 18 times to the place in the course of a morning. Business requires this."[13]

The relatively low cost of the basic order in a café, a cup of "black" or "brown," enabled almost anyone to patronize the place and to partake of all its amenities, at least from time to time. Coffeehouses, however, could not have functioned the way they did for so many years unless some of their habitués were spending more. Pastry was always a big money-maker, and so were brandies and other alcoholic drinks. (Most cafés had liquor licenses). The staff was badly paid and relied mainly on tips, whence the waiters' oily courtesy. Management had nevertheless to cope with daunting overheads, especially rent and the cost of the many newspapers and magazines patrons expected to find there. At the height of the Café Central's reputation, guests could choose there from two hundred Austrian and foreign publications, listed in a special catalog.

During the 1920s several well-known cafés had to close because they could no longer afford the rising rentals; bank branches, then burgeoning, took over their premises. Other cafés managed to survive by starting to serve warm meals in addition to beverages and snacks like eggs, sandwiches, and frankfurters. In the 1930s such "café-restaurants" proliferated. Today many of the coffeehouses in Vienna have lunch and dinner service, and during meal times they reserve their best tables for patrons ordering more than a mere cup of coffee.

In the 1950s a new threat to the classic Vienna coffeehouse was the increasing number of espresso bars, small places with an Italian-made espresso machine behind a stand-up counter and just a few tables. There were no newspapers on wooden holders and no black-suited headwaiter. Patrons were supposed to move on quickly. The Viennese, however, unlike most Italians, want to linger over their coffee, so many espresso bars gradually transformed themselves into small cafés with upholstered seats, a few free newspapers, and a clientele of regulars who would stay a little.

Amid an affluence that Vienna's populace has never known before, housing conditions have generally improved since World War II, and television keeps former café habitués at home during evening hours.

Motorization empties the city on weekends, when many of the surviving coffeehouses now stay closed. Young people flock to fast-food emporiums, the new pizza parlors, and rock-music haunts rather than to the cafés, which they find too sedate. Such generational shifts in tastes, combined with economic pressures—rising labor costs and rents above all—do not bode well for this old institution. In its golden age, more than thirty glittering coffeehouses could be found along the Ringstrasse alone. Banks, auto dealerships, and airline offices have long since supplanted most of them. The few embattled Ringstrasse cafés that have remained and a few other old-time establishments in various neighborhoods, some of them kept alive only by tax abatements and other official favors, seem memorials to the world of yesterday.

Distinguished by politeness and intellectualism, Vienna's former coffeehouse civilization seems a remote ancestor of what the glossy magazines now call "café society" or the "beautiful people," who are as much at home in the trendy places of Manhattan as they are in those of Acapulco, St. Moritz, and Monte Carlo. Uncounted Viennese who could speak knowledgeably about art, music, literature, business, and a dozen other subjects and, possibly, were chess mavens, too, felt really comfortable only in their *Stammcafé* with its faded draperies, its newspapers on bamboo holders, and Herr Oskar, the headwaiter, with his black suit and slightly unctuous manner.

GEMÜTLICHKEIT AND ITS FALLACIES

Like the playing fields of Eton, which reputedly won the Battle of Waterloo, or the frontier experience, which is supposed to have nurtured a spirit of self-reliance in Americans, the Vienna coffeehouse has generated a specific personality type—genial, gossipy, and *gemütlich.* But it must be pointed out that the most creative Viennese of the last hundred years —Freud and Mahler, Kraus and Musil, Klimt and Kokoschka, Schoenberg and Loos—lacked any *Gemütlichkeit,* although they all at least occasionally showed up in the city's coffeehouses.

Any discussion of character traits that persons of the same background are supposed to share should note that the Viennese are frequently accused of not possessing any character at all. Austrians from the Alpine regions of the country are often particularly harsh in dismissing the inhabitants of their capital as brash, vulgar, cynical, spoiled, and overbearing opportunists. It sounds like the bad-mouthing of New Yorkers by other Americans or of Parisians by provincial Frenchmen. Germans and German-speaking Swiss are usually amused to hear the idiom of Vienna on the stage, in films, and on television, but in general, they distrust the Viennese, whom they regard as unprincipled, slack, unreliable, and inefficient, their *Schlamperei* masked by suavity.

Musil, the coffeehouse regular, has described the deep ambivalence and ambiguity felt by the Viennese himself in *The Man Without Qualities:* "When he is angry, something laughs in him. When he is sad, he is preparing something. When he is moved by something, he rejects it. Every bad action will in some respect appear good to him. Only a possible connection will always decide for him how he regards something. Nothing is firm for him. Everything is transmutable. . . . Thus every one of his answers is a partial answer, every one of his sentiments only a view."[14]

Musil's great unfinished novel weaves the eminently Viennese themes of neurosis, alienation, incest, insanity, and suicide into a tapestry of a declining civilization. Ambivalence overshadows everything: like the double-headed Imperial Eagle, the true Viennese manages to gaze in opposite directions at the same time.

NOTES TO INTRODUCTION

1. Quoted by Erwin Ringel in *Die oesterreichische Seele,* Vienna-Cologne-Graz, 1986, p. 25.
2. *Die Dämonen,* Munich, 1956, p. 32.
3. *Dreimal Oesterreich,* Vienna, 1937, p. 200.
4. *The Fall of the House of Habsburg,* The Viking Press, 1963, p. 331.
5. *Die letzten Tage der Menschheit,* Frankfurt, 1936, p. 501.
6. *La Chartreuse de Parme,* Paris, 1983, p. 42.
7. *Der Mann ohne Eigenschaften,* Reibeck bei Hamburg, 1978, p. 33.
8. *Sündenbock Jude,* in *Versunkene Welt,* Vienna, 1984, p. 159.
9. *The World of Yesterday,* Frankfurt, 1970, p. 28.
10. *Mein Weg als Deutscher und Jude,* as quoted in *Versunkene Welt,* Vienna, 1984, pp. 55–59.
11. *Von der Kunst Oesterreicher zu sein,* Vienna, 1984, p. 33.

12. *Der Fall Franza,* Munich-Zurich, 1982, p. 364–65.
13. *Juden auf Wanderschaft,* 1927, as quoted in *Versunkene Welt,* Vienna, 1984, pp. 155–6.
14. *Der Mann ohne Eigenschaften,* P. 65.

1

THE GOLDEN APPLE

Among the earliest historical dates that are still being hammered into the heads of Vienna's elementary school children are A.D. 1529 and 1683, the years when the Turks laid siege to the city. There are few Viennese anywhere who do not remember 1529 and 1683 all their lives, even though they may have forgotten much else of what they had to learn when they were young. To this day, traces of the times when the Turkish guns and the Janissaries' tents ringed the imperial capital abound in Vienna: Turkish cannonballs are displayed on inner-city house walls; there is a Türkenstrasse (Turks' Street) close to where Freud lived and where centuries earlier fierce battles were fought; a Türkenschanze (Turkish Bulwark) is one of the choicest residential neighborhoods; and the steeple of the Minorite Church near Austria's government headquarters has remained as it was since Turkish artillery truncated it in 1529.

The Hungarians occupied Vienna in 1480–85, the French under Napoleon in 1805 and 1809, the Nazis in 1938, and the Red Army in 1945. Yet, the Turks, who twice beleaguered but never took the city, play a much more important role in its collective memories than the other invaders. The reason may be that the sieges of 1529 and 1683 were parts of a confrontation between East and West, Islam and Christianity, that lasted for centuries, from the Crusades to the Enlightenment. The drums, cymbals, and piccolos of the Janissaries that once so frightened the Viennese can still be heard in the *alla turca* episodes in eighteenth-century music, like the "Turkish" movement of Mozart's Violin Concerto no. 5, K. 219, of 1775.

Geography designated Vienna as the West's "breastplate" against the Turks. The Ottoman Empire, as heir to Islam's dynamism, advanced in all directions for hundreds of years—in the Mediterranean Sea by the nearly annual expeditions of its fleet, in the Middle East, toward Asia, and toward Europe. The Danube and the Hungarian plains tempted the sultans to mount military campaigns in a northwesterly direction. Budapest was for a century and a half in Turkish hands, administered by a vizier. If Vienna had fallen, Bohemia and Bavaria would have been the next Turkish objectives.

Between Turkish wars, sieges, and naval battles, and the establishment of a military frontier in the Balkans by the Habsburgs, there were many behind-the-scenes deals. The emperors in Vienna paid yearly tributes to Constantinople as the price for nonaggression during long periods, without making any fuss about it. The French kings, the wealthy Republic of Venice and other Italian states, and even the papacy at times would negotiate with the sultan and reach secret or open agreements with him. Espionage was flourishing on all sides. The French historian Fernand Braudel has found plenty of evidence in the archives that in Vienna "they were always well-informed on Turkish moves" and occasionally tipped off the Venetians when an armada was again about to sail out of Constantinople.[1]

Even in times of official peace between the emperor and the sultan, bands of Moslem raiders on fast horses might sweep out of Hungary during the warm months and plunder the villages around Vienna right under the noses of His Imperial Majesty and his garrison within the capital's fortifications. Every now and then traders who were journeying up and down the Danube brought back rumors from Constantinople that the sultan had grandiose plans for a thrust into the Christian heart of the continent and that military preparations for such an enterprise were already afoot. Vienna was not a very *gemütlich* place then.

Two years after the terrible sack of Rome in 1527, when the Spanish and German soldiery of Charles V had for weeks run wild in the papal city, Vienna was threatened by a similar fate, though from a different direction. The menace came from Sultan Suleiman I, "the Magnificent," who had achieved a brilliant string of conquests: he had taken Belgrade in 1521 and crushed the Hungarians in the Battle of Mohács in 1526, while his fleet had been victorious in the Mediterranean. Vienna sensed, correctly, that it was next on Suleiman's agenda. The city clamored for help, and an imperial army of ten thousand men arrived in August 1529 and took up quarters in Vienna—none too early.

UNFORGOTTEN SIEGES

Turkish reconnaissance patrols on horseback were sighted in September, and toward the end of that month the bulk of the sultan's awesome forces rolled toward Vienna, escorted on the Danube by crafts carrying shock troops and by supply boats. Chroniclers wrote later that Suleiman had moved 120,000 men up to Vienna, but many of the troops, as always with armies in that period, must in fact have been auxiliaries and camp followers.

The defenders of the Austrian capital were commanded by Count Niklas Salm. At age seventy, he was one of the top generals of the Habsburg Empire, on which, then, "the sun never set." Almost at the last moment, as the Turks were approaching, he took the stern decision to have all of Vienna's suburbs burned down to deprive the enemy of cover by creating a scorched-earth belt around the city. Within the city walls he had seventeen thousand men at his disposal, including a Viennese citizens' militia. For nineteen days Salm managed to repel all assaults; fighting was particularly savage around the northwest bastions, near the present Türkenstrasse.

Since winter was not so far away, the military situation became perilous for the besiegers because they were being decimated by dysentery, and their long supply lines through the Balkans could not be relied on indefinitely. On October 15 the Turks tried to force a decision with an all-out attack near a tower in the area of the present State Opera. Count Salm, who took part in the battle, was wounded, but the enemy was again thrown back. After that ultimate defeat, the Turks withdrew eastward, but not before strangling a number of their Christian prisoners. In a sortie, the defense forces killed any Turkish stragglers they could lay their hands on and brought back four camels but apparently no prisoners.

As the Turkish Danube fleet was sailing downstream, the Viennese managed to sink a few of the boats. Count Salm died of his injuries seven months later.

During the next 145 years there were periodic Turkish scares, but apart from the usual raids, no major Ottoman force appeared again near Vienna. The city saw the ruthless suppression of Lutheranism by the Habsburgs and was frightened whenever the confusing marches and countermarches of the Thirty Years' War (1618–48) brought the ragged armies of the belligerents too close for comfort.

In 1679 the black death made another one of its sinister visits to Vienna. Dear Augustin survived, but almost one sixth of the population perished in a matter of weeks. Emperor Leopold I, the music lover who through most of his long reign was embroiled in wars with the Turks and the French, vowed he would erect a monument as a sign of gratitude to the Deity if the epidemic subsided. He made good on his pledge, as is shown by the Trinity Column (popularly known as the Plague Column) in the central Graben, now an elegant shopping street. A peak of Austrian Baroque art, the soaring marble landmark is covered with panels of complicated symbolism by various sculptors.

Four years after Leopold made his vow, the Turks were back before Vienna, but this time their threat was much more fearsome than in 1529. The Ottoman Empire of Sultan Mohammed IV stretched then from the Crimea to Morocco and from the Persian Gulf to Hungary. With central Europe still exhausted from the Thirty Years' War, a military push toward Vienna, and maybe even beyond, seemed promising to the Turks. At the sultan's order, his grand vizier, Kara Mustafa, assembled a formidable army in Hungary for such an enterprise—a motley host of 150,000 men that included Tartar troops and that had the elite corps of the Janissaries as its cutting edge. A French renegade and former Capuchin friar who had assumed the name Ahmed Bey commanded an artillery force with three hundred guns.

In Vienna there had for years been forebodings of the coming ordeal. In 1680, Emperor Leopold I named Count Ernst Rüdiger von Starhemberg military commander of the city. Then forty-four years old, the serious, dignified count was one of the emperor's highest military officers, but habitually affected a simple soldier's uniform. He at once went about strengthening Vienna's fortifications, but the municipal administration under Mayor Andreas Liebenberg was not too efficient in preparing for the dreaded emergency, so that Starhemberg would eventually be burdened also with civilian problems.

When at last the long-feared Turkish hordes were surging toward the capital in July 1683, the emperor, with his family and court, hurriedly sailed up the Danube to Linz, and the commander of the imperial field troops in the Vienna area, Duke Charles of Lorraine, withdrew his cavalry to the north bank of the Danube. Starhemberg, left with six thousand regulars, ordered his soldiers to go from house to house to press every able-bodied civilian man into defense service. Refugees from the suburbs were crowding into the city. Soon Vienna was confronted by a huge semicircle of Turkish guns, siege machines, and twenty-five thousand Turkish tents. Communications with the outside world across the Danube were haphazard, and during long periods the city was completely isolated because Turks roamed the left bank of the river. Dysentery and other diseases spread quickly among the populace, still shaky from the plague of 1679; the mayor, too, fell ill and was eventually killed by a Turkish cannonball.

Count Starhemberg had been ordered to hold out until the emperor succeeded in drumming up a relief army. Conditions in the beleaguered city soon became nightmarish. The Turkish guns caused many casualties and extended damage; enemy sappers tunneled below the ramparts and, with their mines, blew up fortifications, creating large breaches through which the Janissaries poured in. Although the attackers were always repulsed, it seemed only a question of time before Vienna would fall. Visitors who climb the steeple of St. Stephen's Cathedral today are shown a little bench from which Starhemberg is supposed to have peered out anxiously toward the northwest for some sign that the promised succor was approaching. For nearly two months he looked in vain, and the Turks were smugly confident that they would eventually get hold of the "golden apple," as they called the bright metal ornament that topped the tower of St. Stephen's and glittered in the summer sun. Just the place to hoist the green banner of the Prophet!

A Christian force did at last assemble upstream. It was composed of a Polish army and imperial troops. The Poles were led by King John III Sobieski, a military leader of towering stature and proven skill; he had brought ten thousand foot soldiers, fourteen thousand cavalry, and twenty-eight guns with him. Duke Charles of Lorraine commanded the Imperials, comprising the Austrians and contingents contributed by Bavaria, Saxony, and some small German principalities—in all, eight thousand infantry, thirteen thousand cavalry, and seventy guns. From the hard-pressed city, Starhemberg sent out a secret agent who, dressed up as a Turk, managed to cross the lines and the tent rows of the besiegers to convey to Duke Charles an urgent message: "My lord, time is running out!"

After the Turks conquered some outworks near the imperial castle, Starhemberg signaled the city's desperate situation by firing flares during the night into the sky. They were seen by the rescuers, who by that time were already in position on the hills in the city's northwest (September 3). Before the decisive battle, King John and Duke Charles attended mass in the hermitage of the Camaldolensian monks on top of the Kahlenberg, then called the Pigs' Mountain. The legate of Pope Innocent XI, the Capuchin friar Marco d'Aviano, celebrated at the rite and gave a fiery sermon. (Polish-born Pope John Paul II visited the little hilltop church three hundred years later.)

The Christian troops pounced on the Turks while Starhemberg's soldiers, though nearly exhausted, stormed out of the bastions. Caught between two fronts, Kara Mustafa and his men fled confusedly toward the east, leaving most of their three hundred guns and their tents behind. King John was the first to enter Kara Mustafa's tent while his Poles vied with the Imperials in lustily plundering the riches that the enemy had abandoned.

The chronicles assert that the Turks took with them six thousand men, eleven thousand women, fourteen thousand girls, and fifty thousand children from the ravaged countryside around Vienna. The separate listing of the girls from the villages means that they were nubile and would in all likeliness join the Turkish harems. Some boys among the children might be pressed into the Janissaries' Corps. The prisoners, most of whom destined to increase the vast slave population of the Ottoman Empire, had been captured by raiding parties that were sent as far as the Alps in the south and the Bavarian border in the west, and many had been taken to the Ottoman Empire before the final battle. The defenders of Vienna themselves had suffered two thousand casualties. An illustrious victim of the unsuccessful Turkish enterprise was Kara Mustafa. The grand vizier was still on his way home when the sultan's executioners arrived with the ominous silken cord and strangled him on December 25, just as the Christmas service was being sung in St. Stephen's, below the golden apple.

The Viennese were not in the mood for much celebrating, though, as their city was recovering only slowly from sixty days of an increasingly harrowing siege. The leaders of the relief troops had, inevitably, started bickering soon after their joint victory, and Emperor Leopold was miffed that King John had made a grand entry into his liberated capital without waiting for him to share in the triumph. Count Starhemberg received high honors from his sovereign, but he would always look melancholy; he died eighteen years later, after having lost both of his sons in the Turkish wars.

The captured Turkish cannon were melted down and founded into a huge bell, weighing forty-six thousand pounds, that was hung in the steeple of St. Stephen's. Beloved as Vienna's *Pummerin* ("boomer"), it was struck with hammers instead of being rung the way smaller bells are, because its boom (whence its nickname) and vibration might have caused the tower to collapse. The *Pummerin* crashed to the ground and burst when St. Stephen's was burning during the battle for Vienna in April 1945. The fragments were later collected and refounded, together with material donated from all over Austria, into a new bell, nine feet high and thirty-three feet around.

Although Vienna was safe from the Janissaries after 1683 and was to remain so, the struggle between the Habsburg and Ottoman empires would go on for more than a century. The failure of the Turks to capture Vienna when they seemed to have their best chance of success is nevertheless considered the turning point in the fortunes of the Ottoman Empire, and its decline is generally dated from 1683. One is tempted to speculate what might have happened if Kara Mustafa had tied the banner of the Prophet to the golden apple of St. Stephen's. Using Vienna as their new advanced base, Ottoman forces might have pushed up the Danube or into the rich Bohemian lands. True, the sultan's domains were already overextended when his forces were ringing Vienna, yet decades might have passed before the Habsburg emperors and allied Christian powers would have been able to recapture the city and roll back the Turks. Vienna, at any rate, would have grievously suffered.

As it was, the Turkish setback below the walls of Vienna opened the road toward the reconquest of Budapest by the Habsburgs. Belgrade, farther down the Danube, would be stormed by Austrian forces in 1688, 1717, and 1789, but would have to wait until 1867 to see the last Turkish soldiers march out. In Constantinople, the Janissaries emerged as the dominant force soon after Kara Mustafa's disgrace. Whenever they were not tied up in the still far-flung provinces of the Ottoman Empire, the elite troops rioted in the capital to exact back pay they claimed was due to them; the Janissaries would pick sultans and push them off the throne the way the Praetorian Guard of ancient Rome had made and unmade emperors.

TURQUERIES ON THE DANUBE

The Turkish sieges of 1529 and 1683, when disaster seemed impending, may have contributed to a certain fatalistic streak in the Viennese personality. Even today the foreigner will be surprised or annoyed to hear Viennese say all the time, "Da kann ma halt nix machen," a dialect formula that means roughly "Whatever you may say or try, nothing really can be done about it." The desperate straits of 1683, in any case, linger vividly in the city's collective memory.

Between campaigns, sieges, and cavalry raids, however, the Ottoman and Habsburg empires exchanged tradesmen and diplomatic agents, ransomed prisoners, and infiltrated spies into each other's territories. Such osmosis over three centuries has—more than did periodic military clashes —introduced quite a few Near Eastern elements into Vienna's everyday life.

Steam rooms became popular in the city on the Danube as "Turkish baths" and were only recently supplanted by saunas. The show windows of old-style candy shops in the suburbs today still display "Turkish honey," the local name for Turkish delight. In one period in the eighteenth century, Vienna favored fashions *à la turque,* and they spread westward to Paris. Viennese painters and popular comedy indulged in *turqueries,* such as harem scenes on the Bosporus with languid beauties, fat eunuchs, and lustful pashas. In 1782 the Imperial Court Theater presented a novelty by Kapellmeister Mozart entitled *The Abduction from the Seraglio.* The pasha of the German-language singspiel was, remarkably, a humane character, a Moslem gentleman, and the Janissaries sang in chorus.

Armenian traders—Christian subjects of a Moslem empire that was religiously rather tolerant—brought Persian rugs up the Danube and found many buyers. Some of the merchants settled in Vienna near the river bank, establishing a small Armenian colony, which still exists.

Nothing, however, of all the things that the Viennese learned or borrowed from the Turks had such an impact on their way of life as the coffeehouse. It was to become the epitome of Viennese civilization, the fulcrum of social, intellectual, and political life.

Public places where coffee was served were opened in the city soon after the siege of 1683. Coffeehouses existed at that time already in Venice, Marseilles, London, Hamburg, and maybe in other seaports trading with the Levant. It is quite possible that the first coffee beans really reached Vienna by way of Venice through normal commerce, but the Viennese have always wanted to believe a more romantic story.

According to the venerable tale, still told in Austrian schoolbooks, the introduction of coffee and the coffeehouse is due to a clever and courageous Pole, Georg Franz Kolschitzky. Tradition depicts him as an adventurer who traveled in the Ottoman Empire as far as Armenia, picked up the Turkish language, and made a living in Constantinople as a dragoman (interpreter). Finding himself in Vienna just as the troops of Kara Mustafa were closing in, Kolschitzky supposedly offered his services as a secret operative to the city's defenders. The astute Pole, dressed in Eastern garb and accompanied by a similarly disguised servant, was said to have wandered across the broad belt of Turkish tents and artillery emplacements more than once to gather military intelligence and take messages to and from the Christian relief forces that were gathering northwest of the beleaguered city.

As legend has it, Kolschitzky was asked after Vienna's liberation to name his reward for his exploits during the siege. He reportedly said with a show of modesty that he wanted nothing but the "camel fodder" —bags filled with greenish beans—that the fleeing Turks had left behind, together with their tents, guns, armor and other material, and which nobody wanted. There were about five hundred pounds of those beans. Kolschitzky was familiar with them from his travels in the East; he knew how to roast and grind them and how to boil the powder into a stimulating brew. (To this day, the Viennese dialect calls a coffeehouse owner a *Kaffeesieder,* or "coffee boiler.")

Kolschitzky is said to have applied for a license to sell the newfangled beverage to the public and to have been authorized by imperial decree to do so. According to a variant of the story, the city even gave him a house, known as the Court at the Sign of the Blue Bottle, in what is today the narrow Domgasse, east of St. Stephen's Cathedral. Thus, the "Blue Bottle" is believed to have become Vienna's first coffeehouse.

About a hundred years later Mozart would take an apartment nearly opposite it and compose there *Le Nozze di Figaro*. In Vienna *kahve,* as the Turks called it, met initially with only moderate success, the story goes, but when the resourceful Pole started adding sugar and milk to it, business picked up. The mixture, which Italians, with an allusion to a Capuchin friar's brown cowl call cappuccino, became the rage of Vienna.

It is a good yarn, but modern scholarship has cast doubt on it. A Kolschitzky probably existed, and he may have done services for the city under siege. Poland had once been a mighty power, reaching from the Baltic to the Black Sea, and it is plausible that a Pole would have traveled in the Ottoman Empire. The real problem with the story is that coffee was known in Vienna before 1683, at least as an exotic drink fancied by some connoisseurs. One Johannes Diodato, described as an Armenian, is now believed to have actually opened the first commercial coffee operation in Vienna. Diodato is not an Armenian name; it is Italian, meaning "Given to [or by] God," and it is how foundlings were often called. Maybe Diodato came from Venice, where a large Armenian community lived and where coffeehouses were already flourishing.

Whatever Diodato did in Vienna, Kolschitzky's fame is deeply rooted in the city. He is even credited with the invention of the croissant, the crescent-shaped roll that is the classic accompaniment for cappuccino. Actually, croissants, the gustatory caricature of the Turkish banner's crescent, were munched in Vienna, as elsewhere in Christian Europe, long before 1683—but no matter.

It may be for the sake of the croissant that the confectionary workers of the Polish capital in 1983 had a commemorative plaque put up on the building at the site where the "Blue Bottle" is supposed to have been located. The brass plaque, in Polish and German, at 8 Domgasse, reads in translation, "Franciszek Jerzy Kolschitzky, 1640–1694, court courier and scout during the siege of Vienna, 1683, lived and died in this house. Offered to their fellow countryman by the Warsaw confectioners."

Vienna took pains in its tricentenary celebrations in 1983 not to grate on Turkish and Moslem sensibilities. For one thing, thousands of Turks were by then living as "guest workers" in newly prosperous Vienna, employed in humble jobs and often relegated to substandard housing. Even more important to the organizers of the 1983 commemorations was the Austrian government's policy of seeking good relations with modern Turkey and with Moslem countries in general.

For the 1983 anniversary, Vienna dressed up again *à la turque*. The horsetail insignia of the Janissaries were flowing from lampposts, and the crescent symbol was displayed on various spots where fighting had taken place three hundred years earlier. The Renaissance-revival facade of the nineteenth-century Künstlerhaus, one of Vienna's major halls for art shows, was masked with the giant shape of a Turkish gala tent. Inside, hundreds of exhibits gave a vivid idea not only of the siege and the final battle of 1683 but also of the way the Viennese were living at the time, with samples of period furniture, musical instruments, books, pictures, and Judaica. Nor were Kolschitzky and the coffeehouse forgotten.

TRIUMPHANT BAROQUE

The siege of 1683 and the Turkish wars are linked in Viennese memories with a foreigner, a great military leader, whom they eventually considered one of their own—Prince Eugene of Savoy. Of unassuming appearance, if not outright ugly, he became the terror of the Turks and commander in chief of all Austrian armies; the Viennese called him the "secret emperor." He signed his name in three languages, Italian, German, and French: Eugenio von Savoie. He amassed immense wealth, had castles and palaces built for himself in and around the imperial capital, collected books and works of art, and outlived his own fame, an enigmatic lifelong bachelor who may have been a homosexual.

Prince Eugene's father, a French prince of the blood royal, Eugène Maurice de Savoie-Carignan, Count of Soissons, was a general who died early. His widow was Olympe (or Olimpia) Mancini, a niece of Cardinal Mazarin, who was the Italian-born chief aide to kings Louis XIII and Louis XIV of France and whose astuteness was matched by his greed. Beautiful and scheming, Olympe was implicated in an affair of scandalous poisonings in the 1670s and fled to the Netherlands, abandoning her children. Prince Eugene was brought up by relatives, had a sketchy education, and was pressed to enter the priesthood. Louis XIV haughtily denied his repeated pleas for being allowed to follow in his father's footsteps and take up a military career.

Not yet twenty years old, Prince Eugene left France to offer his services as a soldier to the Austrian emperor. The year was 1683, and any volunteer was welcome. The young Frenchman, who had brought his own horse with him, took part in the battle to liberate Vienna. Duke Charles of Lorraine noted his valor and asked the prince to follow him in the campaign that culminated in the reconquest of Budapest. After distinguishing himself in other military enterprises in the Balkans and the west, Prince Eugene received the supreme command of the Imperials in the east, at the recommendation of Starhemberg, in 1697. He defeated the Turks at Senta in that year and took Belgrade from them in 1717. The song of "Prince Eugene, the Noble Knight" who captured the city and fortress of Belgrade became one of the traditional hymns of the Habsburg armies; the soldiers of the neutral Austrian Republic still parade to its martial strains today.

The French-Italian prince led imperial troops also in western Europe and shared the glory of victory over the allied French and Bavarian forces at Blenheim in 1704 with the Duke of Marlborough. In later years, Prince Eugene served as a diplomatic negotiator for the successive emperors Josef I and Karl VI, and administered two wealthy territories that they had gained in the War of the Spanish Succession, Lombardy and the Low Countries. Back in Vienna, Prince Eugene developed a highly personal network of agents and informants all over Europe, and reported only to Karl VI ("my master") personally. Thousands of letters by Prince Eugene in the archives are proof of his industriousness and his very Viennese propensity for underhanded dealings. His voluminous correspondence, however, reveals almost nothing of his elusive personality.

Foremost among the monuments that Prince Eugene created is his summer residence, the Belvedere Castle, on a slope overlooking Vienna from the southeast. The architect Johann Lukas von Hildebrandt, who had already designed fine buildings in the city center, erected the garden palace for Prince Eugene between 1700 and 1723, by which time the outskirts of the imperial capital had no longer to fear Turkish raiders. The Belvedere, a celebrated example of Baroque splendor, consists of two large structures, at the lower and upper ends of a terraced garden. Prince Eugene lived in the Lower Belvedere during the summer months and used the Upper Belvedere for formal receptions. After his death, his niece inherited almost everything; she sold off the art treasures with which the prince had filled both buildings. The Belvedere today houses three museums of Austrian art, with collections that range from the Middle Ages to the twentieth century. Prince Eugene's fifteen thousand books in precious morocco bindings were bequeathed by him to the Court Library, now the Austrian National Library, in the former imperial castle.

Prince Eugene's winter palace, in the heart of the old city, was built by the famous architect Johann Bernhard Fischer von Erlach between 1694 and 1698; Hildebrandt added a western wing in 1723–25. The sumptuous structure in the narrow Himmelpfortgasse now houses Austria's Ministry of Finance; the magnificent staircase and the grandiose halls, with their gilded and painted ceilings, do not convey a sense of the fiscal frugality that a small republic with limited resources requires.

On April 21, 1736, Prince Eugene died in his winter palace, and people flocked to it to see his body lie in state. The funeral cortege to St. Stephen's Cathedral nearby took two hours, with the bells of all of Vienna's churches tolling all the time. All officers and soldiers of the imperial garrison were escorting the coffin, carrying their weapons upside down in sign of mourning; their drums and standards were covered with black crepe. It was one of those grand obsequies that the Viennese so thoroughly enjoy. The former generalissimo of the Habsburg armies was laid to rest in a chapel of the cathedral, at the left side of the main entrance.

With the Turks pushed far back into the Balkans, thanks mainly to Prince Eugene, construction work now went on vigorously all over the suburbs of Vienna, which had for so long been periodically harassed by enemy incursions. The largest of the building projects was the imperial summer residence at Schönbrunn. Leopold I, whom Prince Eugene called "my father," had started it in 1694 on the site of a hunting lodge that had been destroyed during the siege nine years earlier. Schönbrunn ("Beautiful Fountain"), two and a half miles southwest of Vienna's center, was to be the Habsburgs' Versailles; every dynasty in Europe then felt the urge to imitate the architectural pomposity of Louis XIV's court. Fischer von Erlach was originally entrusted with the design of the new palace, but it took half a century to complete it. The main palace, a central section and two straight wings, is 656 feet long. It is flanked by service buildings and stables, and its south side looks out on a 500-acre formal park with straight promenades, clipped hedges and trees, symmetrical ponds and fountains, calculated vistas, and a colonnaded pavilion on a hill, the Gloriette.

Schönbrunn, the Belvedere, the Church of St. Charles Borromeo (erected after the cessation of the plague of 1713), and other large buildings that went up in the decades after the siege of 1683 are architectural expressions of the political and religious triumphalism of the era. Baroque art, with its exuberance and theatrical character, was to shape the face—or at least the facade—of Vienna for centuries to come. With Islam no longer an imminent threat, and Lutheranism rooted out in the Austrian lands, Habsburg power, supported by the Church of Rome, was at its zenith.

Karl VI, who ruled from 1711 to 1740, had been educated by Spaniards and trained for the Spanish throne; when he became instead emperor in Vienna, he took the rigid Spanish court ceremonial back with him to the Austrian capital, introducing a degree of artificialness and formality into the city's aristocratic society that it had not until then known. A good deal of the enduring ceremoniousness of the Viennese goes back to that time.

The supple white Lipizzaner stallions of the emperor's Spanish Riding School, which dates from the reign of Maximilian II, had to perform the courbettes and other refined figures of classical horsemanship. Karl VI loved the horse ballet, and in 1735 inaugurated a Winter Riding School, a new annex to the Hofburg, with a gala performance presenting fifty-four foals from the imperial studs. The intelligent, ambitious, and discreetly pampered animals are descendants of the Andalusian horses that were much in demand in ancient Rome; from circa A.D. 1580 they were crossbred in Lipizza, a small town near Trieste, with imports from Italy and Araby. Today, before the riders of the Lipizzaners take them through their pirouettes for the benefit of tourists, they still doff their bicornes under a portrait of Emperor Karl VI in the Winter Riding School. In Vienna, the Baroque era lives on in many such gestures.

The members of Karl VI's Spanish entourage were not the only foreigners in Vienna during his long reign. Craftsmen, artists, scholars, fortune seekers, and adventurers from the Austrian Habsburgs' new provinces, the Netherlands and the Milan region, flocked to the imperial capital. There were newcomers also from Hungary, France, the various Italian states, and other countries.

In 1729, Karl VI called an Italian writer, Pietro Antonio Metastasio, né Trapassi, to Vienna as his new court poet (*poeta cesareo* in Italian). Metastasio, a native of Rome, would live in the Austrian capital for more than half a century until his death in 1782 without ever learning to speak German; he did not have to, because everybody at court, and many other people, too, were fairly fluent in Italian, owing to the craze for Italian opera. In Vienna, Metastasio wrote more than two dozen libretti, some of them set to music by twenty or more composers; Gluck and Mozart, too, used his texts. Famous all over Europe at a time when Italian opera was triumphant from Naples to London and St. Petersburg, Metastasio by his harmonious, gentle poetry refined the Italian language and created the Rococo stereotype of the cagey protagonist, the lyrical "Metastasian hero."

In Metastasio's time a great deal of Italian was heard in the coffee-houses of Vienna, mingled with French, Hungarian, Czech, Polish, and the various German dialects. A cosmopolitan society was developing. Patrons of the coffeehouse of a Herr Kramer near St. Stephen's Cathedral could read all the local gazettes and a few foreign ones free of charge. Kramer's idea of a "newspaper café" was an enormous success and was soon imitated. Vienna's coffeehouses were the places where newcomers could make their first contacts, meet the local habitués, and strike up useful acquaintances. Contemporary prints show that travelers arriving by road or Danube boat found suburban coffeehouses greeting them; there were also tables and chairs for sitting outside in fair weather—the first Viennese café terraces.

Canaletto, the Venetian master, painted a famous *View from the Belvedere* and did other work in Vienna. Italian architects helped build Baroque churches and palaces in the city, and Karl VI commissioned one of them, Donato Felice d'Allio, to design a replica of the Escorial for the town of Klosterneuburg, five miles upstream of Vienna. The project, inspired by the palace of the kings of Spain near Madrid, would never be completed, but what can be seen today—a Baroque church and abbey with a dome bearing a ducal hat and an imperial crown of copper—are evidence of Habsburg pride and ambitions in the early eighteenth century.

"THERE MUST BE SPECTACLES"

Karl VI had no male heir, and most of his—and Prince Eugene's—diplomatic actions were aimed at having the European powers recognize his daughter, Archduchess Maria Theresa, as his rightful successor. In 1713 the emperor issued a Habsburg family statute proclaiming the indivisibility of all lands ruled by the dynasty and reserving succession to the throne for a female heir if the male line were to become extinct. This Habsburg house law, known as the Pragmatic Sanction, did not apply to the imperial dignity, which remained elective and had long been little more than a high-sounding title. Voltaire wrote in 1756 that "the agglomeration that is called, and which still calls itself, the Holy Roman Empire is neither holy nor Roman nor an empire." Most of its elected emperors, but not all, were Habsburgs. The Habsburg heads of the Holy Roman Empire had many other titles besides, stemming from their own kingdoms and other domains that were forming their hereditary power base. They would assume the title "Emperor of Austria" only in 1806 following the collapse of the Holy Roman Empire. After protracted bargaining most of the powers formally accepted the Pragmatic Sanction, though not without wresting political or territorial concessions from Karl VI in return. Prince Eugene warned before his death that "100,000 men and a full treasury are the best guarantees for the Pragmatic Sanction." Karl VI left behind neither. After he died in 1740, several European monarchs promptly challenged Maria Theresa's right to the Austrian hereditary lands.

When the Viennese today think of Maria Theresa, they are likely to visualize her the way she is represented by the showy monument that was erected in 1887 between the then new Museums of Art History and of Natural History on the Ringstrasse opposite the Hofburg: the matriarch loftily enthroned, holding her scepter and the Pragmatic Sanction in her hands, surrounded by allegories of Wisdom, Strength, Justice, and Mercy, by equestrian statues of her field marshals, by life-size figures of her chief aides, and by group reliefs of such outstanding contemporaries as Gluck, Haydn, and the young Mozart—a marble-and-brass apotheosis suggesting majesty, benevolence, and serenity. Yet, most of Maria Theresa's forty-year reign was filled with conflict and war.

Another likeness of the empress, as a full-bosomed dowager, is seen on large silver coins that were introduced during her lifetime and are still a welcome monetary vehicle in such faraway places as Ethiopia and the two Yemens. After Mussolini conquered Ethiopia in 1935, he obtained from the Vienna mint the dies for striking Maria Theresa thalers; the hard-pressed Austrian government of that time thought it could not deny the request by its chief supporter, Il Duce. Since 1946 the Maria Theresa thalers have again been struck in Vienna.

The last Habsburg monarch in an unbroken line from the thirteenth-century Rudolf I has long been recognized as one of history's great woman rulers. Maria Theresa was a leading figure in European affairs just when two other remarkable women were wielding power in two large nations—Catherine the Great in Russia and Madame Pompadour as the mistress of King Louis XV in France. Maria Theresa's main antagonist on the Continent was Prussia's King Friedrich II, "the Great," who succeeded his father—by whom he had been despised and at one point sentenced to death as a deserter—in the same year as she succeeded hers. What a cast for a Baroque power play!

At age nineteen, Archduchess Maria Theresa became the wife of Franz Stephan, Duke of Lorraine, who was soon to take over the Grand Duchy of Tuscany, whereas Lorraine, in a complicated barter deal, was destined to become French. Maria Theresa's wedding to Franz Stephan looked like a typical dynastic marriage, one of the many through which the Habsburgs had over the centuries won plenty of new territories. The archduchess was nevertheless in love with her "Franzl" and would dote on him until his death. At the end of a letter she wrote to him in stilted French (probably dictated by a governess) when they were engaged, she had impulsively scrawled an endearment in Viennese dialect: *Mäusl* ("little mouse"). The yellowed document in the archives does not indicate whether she or he was the little mouse.

French was then spoken, together with Italian, at the court and in the aristocratic and intellectual society of Vienna. The presence of noblemen from Duke Franz Stephan's Lorraine was a reason, as was an upper-class mania for imitating Versailles. French words seeped into the everyday language of Vienna. To this day, the Viennese say *malheur* for a mishap and *rendezvous* for a date (as long as it is romantic; a business appointment is now designated by a frigid legal expression, *Termin*). A score or so of similar Gallicisms is still embedded in the Viennese patois. Maria Theresa often wrote in French to her children; that language also dominated the correspondence conducted by Austrian diplomacy, as it did that of the other powers then and later.

The husband of Maria Theresa was hanging around the Vienna court most of the time. In 1737 the last male Medici, the debauched Grand Duke Giovan Gastone, died, and Franz Stephan became his successor, to the disgust of the Florentines, who did not like to be ruled as an appendage to Austria. Maria Theresa's Franzl spent only a few weeks in Tuscany and later governed it as an absentee grand duke through agents from Lorraine who conducted themselves in Florence like haughty viceroys.

When Maria Theresa succeeded her father in 1740, she did so as Archduchess of Austria and later became Queen of Hungary and Queen of Bohemia; but she never held the title of empress in her own right. An ambitious neighbor, Duke Karl Albrecht of Bavaria, who was married to another Habsburg archduchess, did not recognize the Pragmatic Sanction and managed to have himself chosen as the new emperor, styled Karl VII. Friedrich of Prussia, his supporter, swooped down on a rich Habsburg possession, Silesia, dispensing with the formality of a declaration of war.

In Vienna, Maria Theresa had just given her consent to the proposal by a theatrical entrepreneur, Franz Selliers, to adapt a ballroom in the northeast corner of the Hofburg as a stage. "There must be spectacles," she is supposed to have said as she signed her decree, a remark that sums up Baroque attitudes.

At the arrival of the news that the Prussians had invaded the Habsburg territory of Silesia, Maria Theresa's ministers "slumped back in their chairs, pale as corpses, while only one heart remained stout: the queen's,"[2] according to a secret report to London from the English envoy in Vienna. Maria Theresa was then twenty-three years old and lacked international experience. To her, the Prussian king would never be "the Great," but always "the monster" and "the robber of Silesia."

A jumble of military campaigns, shifting alliances, and diplomatic deals—grouped by historians as the War of the Austrian Succession (1740–48) and the Seven Years' War (1756–63)—kept the Continent in turmoil for more than two decades. Parallel to the struggle between Maria Theresa and Friedrich, between Austria and Prussia, for predominance in central Europe was the worldwide rivalry between France and England, in which of course their respective allies were entangled. Colonial interests in North America and India became involved. In the end, Prussia emerged as a new great European power and England as the globe's foremost owner of overseas territories.

The Austro-Prussian wars, which were to have a second edition a little more than a century later, left the Viennese with an enduring inferiority complex regarding Prussia and Berlin, as noted earlier. Some Viennese have at different times voiced admiration and sympathy for Berlin, and quite a few moved there during the two world wars because the German capital offered better opportunities than their own city, but most Viennese will always think of Berlin as a latecomer and a pushy upstart. When the Austrian Patriotic Front was set up in Vienna in 1933 in a desperate attempt to stem the Nazi flood, it recalled in a manifesto Friedrich's "rape of Silesia" nearly two centuries earlier and declared, "Austria was a great German country when the Prussians didn't yet speak a word of German and sacrificed horses' blood to their pagan gods! When Walther von der Vogelweide sang in Vienna, Potsdam was a little Slavic hamlet!"

The young Maria Theresa scored an early political success when she courted the Hungarian nobles at a gathering in the city east of Vienna that is called Pozsony in Hungarian, Bratislava in Slovak, and Pressburg in German. The Magyar aristocracy gallantly declared its support of Karl VI's daughter, and she was solemnly crowned Queen of Hungary in 1741 amid jubilation.

MRS. EMPEROR

Emperor Karl VII, the Bavarian, died in 1745, and the Prince Electors of Germany (except Brandenburg and the Palatinate) voted for Maria Theresa's husband as his successor. Franz Stephan, now Emperor Franz I, was duly crowned in Frankfurt, and Maria Theresa went along for the fun of it, but she herself never received the imperial crown. She is supposed to have remarked that another coronation ceremony would cost too much money. As it was, the ruler who during her lifetime and ever afterward would generally be called Empress Maria Theresa had, strictly speaking, no right to that title. True to the customs of her native city she was "Frau Emperor," the wife of the emperor, whose dignity she was supposed to share the way the wife of a professor is automatically "Frau Professor."

During his years as emperor, Franzl was as lazy and fond of good living as he had been before, and so he gladly left the affairs of state to Maria Theresa and, in their occasional quarrels, yielded quickly. He did, however, take a skilled hand in Austrian and Habsburg finances, and not only became one of the richest men of his time but also helped balance the state budget, despite the continual wars. Maria Theresa bore him five sons and eleven daughters, to whom he was an affectionate father. He spent much time with his growing family—when he was not sneaking out of the Hofburg through the Confectioners' Stairway for his stealthy amours with one or the other of his wife's ladies-in-waiting.

With her many pregnancies, Maria Theresa soon looked matronly and became very stout. Contemporaries say, and portraits show, that Maria Theresa did not give much thought to dressing up; she would put on what her ladies-in-waiting had laid out for her and looked frumpy in the English-style hoopskirts she fancied. She was taller than most of the Viennese women of her time and had what those who saw her described as a majestic bearing. Her bright blue eyes were vivid and usually gentle, but she could also look stern. Most of the time, her expression was merry, and she had a way of encouraging persons who were timid in her presence to speak their mind. One can understand why the six-year-old Mozart was captivated by the imperial charm, climbed onto Maria Theresa's ample lap, and kissed her.

Actually, the benignant sovereign must have regarded the Mozart family, whom she received with their wunderkind in audience in Schönbrunn in 1762, as a kind of traveling group of circus performers, like sword swallowers or jugglers. When one of her sons, the Archduke Ferdinand, asked her from Milan a few years later whether he should give the young musician Mozart a job, she wrote back that the Mozarts were "useless people . . . running around the world like beggars."

Maria Theresa was a devout supporter of the Church of Rome. She did suppress the Jesuit Order and seize its properties in her domains, but only after Pope Clement XIV had dissolved the Society of Jesus in 1773. (Most of Europe's rulers did the same, except Friedrich the Great and Catherine the Great, with the result that the Jesuits were able to hibernate in Prussia and Russia until their order was officially reestablished in 1814.) Maria Theresa's son and successor, Emperor Josef II, was to look at the church with a much colder eye.

The short, unpopular experiment of Maria Theresa's Chastity Commission has already been mentioned. The empress, who was so obviously enjoying her matrimonial bliss and was either unaware of her husband's womanizing or chose to ignore it, remained a zealous guardian of public morals all her life. Her priggishness extended also to statuary. One day her gaze fell on a new fountain in the square in front of the Capuchin friary in whose vaults her father and other Habsburgs had been laid to rest. The fountain, commissioned by the city of Vienna, was the work of the renowned sculptor Georg Raphael Donner; he had surrounded an allegorical Providence with four lead figures of buxom maidens, symbolizing tributaries of the Danube, the Austrian rivers Traun, Enns, Ybbs, and March. (Why Donner had omitted the Danube itself is not clear; maybe Providence was to mean also the big river.) The straitlaced empress was scandalized by the shimmering nudity of the statues and ordered them to be removed to the armory to be melted down and used for gunmetal. A sculptor named Johann Martin Fischer saved the leaden maidens and in 1801 obtained their return to the fountain in Neuer Markt. (What can be seen in that square today is a set of copies; the originals, threatened by corrosion, were dismantled in 1873 and are now in the Baroque Museum in the Lower Belvedere.)

Maria Theresa's prudery and her continual wars did not endear her at first to the Viennese. As years went by, however, respect for her grew, and at the end the people in the capital genuinely loved their empress. The success of her forty-year reign was due largely to her fortunate choice of her chief aides, one of whom, Baron von Sonnenfels, we have already encountered. Her imperial chancellor, Count Wenzel von Kaunitz, was a resourceful diplomat who shared his sovereign's distrust of the Prussians and was cynical enough to obtain for Austria a slice of Poland when it was partitioned in 1772. Field Marshal Count Leopold von Daun, a native of Vienna, defeated Friedrich II in a battle at Kolín in Bohemia, reorganized the Austrian army, and founded the Theresian Military Academy at Wiener Neustadt, south of the capital, which is today training the officers of the Austrian Republic's small armed forces. Count Friedrich Wilhelm von Haugwitz reformed and unified the administration of the Habsburg territories.

In 1745 the empress called to Vienna a distinguished physician from Leiden in the Netherlands, asking him to reorganize her capital's medical services. Dr. Gerhard van Swieten became not only Maria Theresa's personal physician but also her trusted adviser in many other fields. He founded orphanages and schools for midwives, created a veterinary college, and revamped Vienna University, inviting outstanding scientists from abroad to join its faculty. Van Swieten also found time for the Court Library and opened its reading room to anyone who wanted to consult its books. The Dutch-born doctor's son, Gottfried van Swieten, became director of the library; a learned pedant and a musical dilettante, he was to play a part in the careers of Haydn, Mozart, and Beethoven.

In 1765, Maria Theresa's Franzl died of a stroke in Innsbruck, at the age of 57. Their oldest son, Josef, became co-ruler of Austria with his mother and soon succeeded his father as emperor. After Maria Theresa's death in 1780 he was the sole sovereign during the ten years he had still to live, the first monarch of the Habsburg-Lorraine line.

BENEVOLENT AUTOCRAT

Viennese folklore has long canonized Josef II as the "People's Emperor." Even good-natured parody on suburban stages could still, a century and a half after his death, bring out emotional applause and a few tears: A stranger steps up to the young lovers who through five acts have suffered unspeakable adversities, and presents them with a purse full of florins that will at last permit them to get married; while the young fellow remains open-mouthed, his girl timidly takes the money and asks, "Noble stranger, who are you?" The benefactor replies mysteriously, "My name you shall never know—for I am the Emperor Josef." As he opens his plain overcoat under which the imperial sash becomes visible, the young couple fall to their knees, and the orchestra strikes up the imperial hymn. (Never mind that Haydn composed the hymn seven years after Josef II's death.) The author remembers having seen such a spoof in his young years.

Josef II, who admired Friedrich II and, like the Prussian king, had been won over to the ideas of the Enlightenment, did make many populist gestures. In 1766 he opened the Prater, the vast imperial hunting reserve on the right bank of the Danube, to all Viennese as a "place for amusement and recreation." Nine years later he threw open also another imperial park closer to the city, the Augarten. A plaque at its entrance reads that the gardens were dedicated to the pleasure "of all the people, by their Esteemer." The restless emperor is said to have proved his particular esteem for young females among his subjects by striking up casual acquaintances when he roamed the Augarten in disguise.

In more substantial reforms, the People's Emperor freed peasants from serfdom and, with keen foresight, prohibited aristocrats from buying up their land. As has been noted earlier, he issued the Edict of Tolerance, according freedom of worship and civil equality to Protestants and members of other Christian denominations; and he improved the condition of Jews. When he was asked whether Vienna's church bells could be rung to welcome Pope Pius VI on his visit to the capital, the emperor replied, "Why not? Every army has its own artillery." The pontiff's solemn entry proved fatal to at least one resident: Metastasio, watching the papal cortege from his open window near the Hofburg, caught a cold and died soon afterward.

Josef II did much for public education and health; the sprawling General Hospital that he founded in 1784 was still the center of Vienna's medical establishment two hundred years later. The emperor's lapidary dedication over a doorway reads, "To Humankind."

A benevolent autocrat, Josef II was also reckless and high-handed. He continually disagreed with his mother and, after her death, undid much of the goodwill toward the dynasty that she had patiently built up. He was a ruthless centralizer, wanting the complicated empire to run like a clockwork. He increased taxes and imposed German as the official state language on Czechs, Magyars, and the other peoples under his rule. He was "a man of utmost coolness and utmost disunion."[3]

Late in his reign Josef II realized he had legions of critics at home. He said to Chancellor Kaunitz, whom he had inherited from his mother, that he hoped posterity would judge him more favorably than his contemporaries did. In his last will he claimed, "I have lived as a servant of the state, and have guarded it." When he died in 1790, a feeling of relief was almost general in Vienna; in Hungary, the Cardinal-Archbishop of Esztergom sang a Te Deum, and the citizens of Pest lighted rows of torches as a sign of joy. The new emperor, Leopold II, who until then had been Grand Duke of Tuscany, had not yet reached Vienna when he promised he would restore the status quo in the Habsburg lands, and he actually rescinded many of the reforms that had been enacted by his brother. Yet, myth soon took over, and the People's Emperor became posthumously a Viennese folk hero. Along with his legend, "Josephinism"—a cult of bureaucratic integrity, coolness toward the Roman Catholic Church, and populist attitudes—was to linger in the city for a long time.

Historically, Maria Theresa and Josef II marked a process of unification of the Habsburg territories, which until then had been a conglomerate of countries and peoples that had little in common. Vienna's effort to bring about a measure of cohesion in the empire through new laws and administrative practices occurred during that pregnant era when America became independent and the French Revolution was about to erupt.

WORLD CAPITAL OF MUSIC

It was during the reigns of Maria Theresa and Josef II, too, that Vienna's musical civilization approached its peak—a process that to the world means immeasurably more than do the fortunes of the House of Habsburg. The patrons of the great composers were at the beginning the imperial court and the high nobility, who at times attempted to outdo the court in splendor; with Schubert the bourgeois middle class of Vienna took over music.

Maria Theresa did not suspect she was making cultural history when she hired a new court kapellmeister, Christoph Willibald Gluck, in 1754. He would in the next few years do away with the rigid conventions of Italian opera seria—its pathos, its lack of dramatic action, its endless coloratura sung by castrati—and clear the road for Vienna's classical masters. The merit of having brought Gluck to the Habsburg court belongs to one of those versatile Italians who were adding sparkle to Rococo Vienna, Count Jacopo Durazzo. He had arrived as envoy of the Republic of Genoa, married a Viennese countess, and become a well-known society figure; Maria Theresa had eventually appointed him manager of the court theaters. (Much later, in 1771, Durazzo would serve as Austrian ambassador to the Republic of Venice and would be of help when the young Mozart wanted to organize a concert there.)

Gluck, whose court salary was fixed at two thousand florins annually on Durazzo's recommendation, was born in 1714 in the Upper Palatinate, a region west of the Bohemian Forest that was later to join Bavaria. Prince Lobkowitz, a member of the high Bohemian aristocracy, was the local overlord at the time, and it was only natural that the gifted young Gluck would go to Prague to study and make a living. He became a professional musician and entered the service of the Lobkowitz family, the former employers of his father. Soon moving in the circles of music-loving nobility, Gluck turned up in Vienna, met with Metastasio and other well-connected Italians, and wrote operas in the Italian and French styles then fashionable.

With his knack for getting on with aristocrats, Gluck had no difficulty in finding wealthy patrons. A Count Melzi took him to Milan, where Gluck became a pupil and friend of the famous musician Giovanni Battista Sammartini; he accompanied Prince Lobkowitz to London, visited Hamburg, and held down a job as kapellmeister of the rich Prince of Sachsen-Hildburghausen in Vienna. In 1750, Gluck married an heiress, Marianne Perg, the daughter of a wealthy Vienna merchant and banker, and settled down in the imperial capital for good. All the time, he kept composing operas in the taste of the time, drawing his subjects from classical mythology or ancient history, and paying due regard to the talents and requirements of some prima donna or renowned castrato who was to sing a main part.

It was as kapellmeister at Maria Theresa's court that Gluck wrote his masterpiece, *Orfeo ed Euridice.* The libretto was by Raniero da Calzabigi, an Italian from Livorno who in Vienna had joined an anti-Metastasio faction; he collaborated with Gluck on achieving a perfect balance between words and music. The premiere at the court theater made an enormous impression because the intent of freeing opera seria from tedious formalism was clear to the sophisticated audience. "Madness, tumult, noise," Metastasio muttered, sensing that Gluck had challenged a tradition that he, Metastasio, embodied.

On October 6, 1762, the day after *Orfeo ed Euridice* was first performed, Leopold Mozart and his two children, Wolfgang and Nannerl, arrived in Vienna by boat from Linz. The customs official frowned on the travel piano they were carrying with them (it was no bigger than a small table), but little Wolfgang softened the man by playing a minuet on the spot, and there were no duties to pay. A week later Wolfgang was performing for Empress Maria Theresa in Schönbrunn Palace and announced he would marry Archduchess Marie Antoinette, the sovereign's lively daughter who was there too.

After Marie Antoinette became the wife of the future King of France eight years later, she summoned Gluck to Paris. In 1779 he produced there his much-admired *Iphigénie en Tauride.* Eventually Gluck returned to Vienna and lived in his comfortable house in the southern suburb of Wieden for the rest of his days, a wealthy and respected personage. After he suffered a stroke, he mostly stayed at home, but he did attend a concert by Mozart in 1783, and the following Sunday had the Mozarts and the young composer's sister-in-law with her husband as guests for luncheon. Gluck and Mozart seem to have got on well enough, although Mozart's father had always warned Wolfgang to keep away from Gluck, whom he considered a master of intrigue.

Actually the well-to-do Gluck, who in 1778 received the title of court composer, seems to have been a jovial man who instinctively knew what he could do and say, and what he could not, in the Vienna of Maria Theresa and Josef II. One of his protégés was Antonio Salieri, a native of Legnago, near Verona. Salieri became director of the Italian opera in Vienna in 1774; he wrote thirty-nine operas and singspiels, in addition to oratorios and other music, entered a close, though ambiguous, relationship with Mozart, and directed the court choir until 1824. The durable Salieri also gave music lessons to the young Beethoven, Schubert, and Liszt, and honored Haydn in the old master's last public appearance.

Gluck's death in 1787 was a typically Viennese episode. He was having friends from Paris as guests for lunch. While his wife was out of the room for a moment, the ailing composer, defying his doctor's strict orders, emptied a glass of liqueur. Afterward he took his customary coach trip around town, but came home in a coma. His demise caused a vacancy in the court's musical establishment, and Josef II at last hired Mozart as his new court composer. The stingy ruler, whose wars were straining the treasury, paid Mozart only eight hundred florins a year, much less than Gluck had been receiving.

It is characteristic of much of Vienna's intellectual and social history that most of the outstanding figures knew one another personally, were friends, rivals, or adversaries, became involved in intricate cabals, and kept go-betweens busy. One reason for this cultural inbreeding, which will again be encountered early in the twentieth century, is the relatively small number of people who really counted—a few thousand at most, if not only a few hundred. The easy contacts in salons and coffeehouses, and the resulting gossip, also may explain why everybody seems to have met everybody at one time or another.

Thus, the young Franz Joseph Haydn was still living in a drafty garret above Metastasio's pleasant apartment near the Hofburg when a friend of the court poet's, Niccolo Porpora, introduced him to Gluck. It is to Gluck's credit that he took interest in the young musician and soon had some of the early quartets by Haydn performed in his house. Haydn, then eighteen years old, had been giving music lessons—at two florins an hour—to Metastasio's niece (some people said she was really his daughter) when he met Porpora, a composer and voice coach from Naples. Haydn, who became something of an assistant to Porpora, later said he had learned a lot from him, despite the Neapolitan's bad temper.

Haydn's early years had been grim by our standards. One of twenty children (by two marriages) of a wainwright in the village of Rohrau, close to the border of Hungary, he was found to have musical talent and therefore sent to school in the nearby city of Hainburg on the Danube. "I received there more spankings than food," he would remember later, adding that he nevertheless was grateful to his teacher for instructing him in the rudiments of his art.

A court kapellmeister, Georg Reutter, discovered the little Haydn during a family visit to Hainburg and took him to Vienna as material for the long-established Boys' Choir. Until age sixteen Haydn lived with five other young singers in a cramped attic of the choir house near St. Stephen's Cathedral. When his voice broke, he was dismissed and, knowing he could not count on any support from his struggling father, he made a try at starting a career as an artist in Vienna. His first move was to rent the cheap garret at 1220 Michaeler Platz, which was also Metastasio's address.

Besides giving music lessons, the young Haydn picked up a few florins by playing the organ in churches and private chapels. He composed quartets and piano sonatas, and a comic opera, *Der krumme Teufel* (The Stooped Devil), which was a joke on a limping Italian theater manager commissioned by a mischievous actor; it brought the nineteen-year-old Haydn the princely sum of twenty-four ducats.

When he was about twenty, Haydn was one day surprised and happy to see his name on sheet music in the show window of a bookshop: pupils of his had sold sonatas that he had written as learning aids for them to a publisher without bothering to tell him. Haydn was soon able to raise his fee for an hour's instruction to five florins. In 1759 he landed a job with Count Karl Joseph Franz Morzin, a court chamberlain who kept a private orchestra. As the nobleman's music director, Haydn got two hundred florins a year, in addition to free lodging and board. The Morzin family spent winters in Vienna and summers on their estate at Lukavice, near Plzeň (Pilsen), in Bohemia.

At twenty-eight Haydn thought he had a solid enough position to get married—but the prospective bride, the daughter of a wigmaker and a student of his, preferred to enter a convent. Determined to found a family anyway, Haydn married a sister of hers, Maria Anna Aloysia Apollonia Keller. (Mozart, too, would marry the sister of the woman who had jilted him.) Haydn's fallback choice turned out a disaster. His wife was a nag, a religious zealot, and a bad housekeeper, and she did not have any children. They separated after a few unhappy years; many years later Haydn wrote to one of his Viennese woman friends from London that his estranged wife, with whom he had stayed in touch by letter, was a "devilish beast."

THE BIRTH OF THE SYMPHONY

By 1761, Count Morzin was broke and had to disband his orchestra. Haydn, who had become well-known among Vienna music lovers, quickly found a new employer, and an immensely rich one at that— Prince Paul Anton Esterházy, a Hungarian magnate who made occasional appearances at the imperial court in Vienna but most of the time held court himself in splendor at his castle in Eisenstadt (now the capital of the Burgenland, Austria's easternmost region). Prince Paul Anton died in 1762 and was succeeded by his brother Nikolaus, also a musical connoisseur. A few years later Prince Nikolaus built himself a little Versailles or Schönbrunn, the château of Eszterháza, complete with a theater, twenty miles southeast of Eisenstadt, on the far side of what is now Austria's borderline with Hungary.

Haydn, soon the chief conductor of the twenty-four member Esterházy orchestra, shuttled for twenty-eight years between Eisenstadt and Eszterháza, with only a few occasional trips to Vienna. When he was performing before the prince and his guests, he wore the blue-and-gold Esterházy livery like the members of the orchestra and was duly powdered and bewigged. He was responsible for the discipline of the musicians, had been told not to fraternize with them, and was, in the words of his contract, "to instruct the songstresses so that they won't forget in the country what they have learned in Vienna with much effort and expense." Above all, Haydn was expected to furnish always new music for the princely ears, was forbidden to have copies of his scores made, and was permitted to accept commissions from outside patrons only if authorized by his employer.

During those nearly three decades in Eisenstadt and Eszterháza, Haydn produced an impressive number of symphonies and string quartets, as well as a few operas and other music. In the isolation of the princely court he developed his own idiom and created the pattern of the classic symphony—a sonata for orchestra with tension and contrast—that would remain the standard for composers from Mozart to Mahler. Through various channels, many of Haydn's works did reach Vienna and, from there, other countries. He himself did not realize for a long time how famous he had become all over Europe. Haydn must have had an inkling of his spreading prestige, though, when he received a request from the cathedral chapter in Cádiz, Spain, in 1785, to write music for a Holy Week rite. With the consent of his prince, Haydn complied, and the result was *The Seven Last Words of Our Savior on the Cross,* an extraordinary test of his skills, consisting of seven contemplative adagios for orchestra.

During his last season in Eszterháza, in 1790, Haydn wrote to a woman confidante in Vienna, Marianne von Genzinger, the wife of a noted gynecologist, that "the Viennese [had] done many good things" to him. What were those episodes of Viennese benevolence? Surely not the hunger and cold of Haydn's teenage years nor the tirades of his Viennese wife. In the autumn of 1790, Prince Nikolaus Esterházy died, and Haydn was free, with a pension from the new chief of the noble family, Prince Anton, who had decided to disband the orchestra. The retiree moved to Vienna and saw much of Mozart there. It is one of the fetching traits of Haydn that he had from the beginning recognized the genius of the younger composer without showing any envy. Mozart, on the other hand, respected only Haydn among all contemporary musicians. The two influenced each other, and Mozart dedicated six string quartets to Haydn. Haydn and Mozart occasionally made music together, and on at least one evening were joined by von Dittersdorf and Vanhal in playing string quartets—one of the great, fleeting moments of cultural history.

When Haydn told Mozart in merry company late in 1790 that he was about to accept an offer from an English impresario to go to London, he was warned by his colleague and friend, "You are no longer young enough" for such an arduous journey. Mozart, who addressed Haydn familiarly in the second person singular *(du),* had stayed in the English metropolis as a child prodigy, and all his later life fantasized about going back there. Haydn, fifty-eight years old at the time, was undaunted, although he spoke no English and had never been abroad. Several months later he wrote to Marianne von Genzinger from England, "How sweet a certain liberty tastes!" He was lionized in London, was entertained by royalty, and received an honorary doctorate from Oxford University. He also wrote his series of "London" symphonies, which show the impact of Mozart. Haydn would not see Mozart again.

In 1794–95, Haydn made a second visit to London; during his two sojourns there he earned twenty-four thousand florins. Even considering that his travels cost him six thousand florins, he was a wealthy man, able to buy a snug house in Vienna's western suburb of Gumpendorf. He nevertheless reentered active service with the Esterházys when a new chief of the family, Prince Nikolaus II, revived the orchestra. Haydn's duties under his fourth Esterházy prince were greatly reduced. As honorary chief kapellmeister, he was obliged to reside in Eisenstadt only during the summer months and for the remainder of the year was free to live in his own house in Vienna.

The young Beethoven was for a short time Haydn's student but soon went his own way. Haydn wrote soaring church music and two great oratorios, *The Creation* and *The Seasons,* both with texts supplied by Gottfried van Swieten. The son of Empress Maria Theresa's personal physician was described as ponderous and opinionated by contemporaries. The younger van Swieten did, however, wield much influence in Vienna's musical life and cultural politics at a crucial juncture, favored the revival of works by Bach and Handel that seemed to have slipped into oblivion, and helped bring music-making out of the palaces of the aristocracy into the theaters and public halls. Haydn grumbled about van Swieten's wooden verses, but earned much additional fame and money with the two compositions. There was money also for the poor of Vienna when the oratorios were performed at fund-raising concerts and the composer was awarded honorary citizenship of the imperial capital.

Haydn had not yet moved into his own house when, in 1797, he wrote the simple melody that sounded like a folk tune and was to become Austria's national anthem until 1918 and again 1934–38. The words—"God preserve Franz the Emperor . . ." changed to "God preserve, God protect our emperor, our country . . ." for Franz's successors —were supplied by a poet with a Slavic name, Lorenz Leopold Haschka. Haydn had during his stay in England been impressed by the solemnity of "God Save the King" and wanted to create a similar hymn for his own homeland. It was first played in public when the emperor entered his box at the Court Theater on the eve of his twenty-ninth birthday, February 22, 1797. Haydn himself loved the tune, used it in a string quartet (Op. 76, no. 3), and had it played at his home a few days before his death as Napoleon's guns were pounding Vienna.

During his last years Haydn, because of failing health, stayed mostly in his house. He passed the long winter evenings playing cards with his faithful copyist and valet, Johann Elssler, whose father he had brought with him, also as a servant, from Eisenstadt. (The younger Elssler had a beautiful daughter, Fanny, who was to become a dazzling prima ballerina who toured Europe and America, took rich lovers, and lived as a millionairess until old age.) Haydn liked also to gossip with his Gumpendorf neighbors, ordinary people who spoke to him in broad dialect. The famous composer was by then "Papa Haydn" to everybody. Mozart had been the first to address him in this affectionate way when Haydn was still in his fifties, and the slightly patronizing appellation had stuck, although later generations would recognize his innovating genius.

On the eve of Haydn's seventy-sixth birthday in 1808, Vienna offered him a concert that has remained in the city's annals as one of its great historic tableaux: The scene was the main hall of the old university; the Italian version of *The Creation* was on the program; Salieri conducted; and Beethoven was in the audience. Everybody got up when Haydn was carried in on a portable chair and even the proud Beethoven bowed. Haydn was seated in the front row, next to the Princess Esterházy and other aristocratic or prominent personages. Musicians and members of the audience crowded around the frail master to kiss his hand, and Haydn had tears in his eyes. He could not stay to the end of the concert, his apotheosis.

Haydn died the following year when Vienna was for the second time occupied by the French. Napoleon had an honor guard posted at Haydn's house, where the composer was lying in state. Mozart's Requiem was performed at a funeral service in the Schottenkirche two weeks after Haydn's death, and several French generals attended. At an auction of Haydn memorabilia, Prince Liechtenstein paid fourteen hundred florins —seven times the yearly salary that Count Morzin had once paid his kapellmeister—for a parrot that the composer had brought from London and that spoke a few words taught to it by Haydn.

MOZART MYSTERIES

Mozart was twenty-three years younger than Haydn and died seventeen years before him; during Mozart's ten years in Vienna the two were, as we have seen, very close. This book is not meant to add to the immense Mozart literature, but it must point to a puzzle: Why did one of the greatest geniuses ever born spend the decade of his early, and all too short, maturity in a city that he did not particularly like?

Mozart notoriously hated Salzburg, his birthplace, since his teenage years and made no bones about it in his letters. He loved Prague, where *Le Nozze di Figaro* had made him popular, where his *Don Giovanni* had what today would be called its world premiere, and where he had good friends. He spoke all his life with nostalgia about London. He had lived there for fifteen months when he was a wunderkind, eight and nine years old, although his father pretended he was even younger.

Mozart was twenty-five when his and his father's Salzburg employer, Prince-Archbishop Hieronymus Colloredo, a Josephinist and Voltairean, ordered the young musician to accompany him to Vienna. Mozart wrote home that "it seemed as if fortune was awaiting me here. . . . I feel I *have* to remain here." But fortune was to prove elusive.

Before the prince-archbishop's chief of the kitchen staff, Count Karl Arco, administered the famous kick into Mozart's backside to signify that his employment, as the young musician had desired, had come to an end, he gave the rebellious fellow a piece of sensible advice: Do not allow yourself to be excessively dazzled by Vienna, for "here the fame of a man lasts very briefly—at the beginning one hears plenty of praise and also earns a lot, that's true—but how long? After a few months the Viennese want something new again." Count Arco, who as the prince-archbishop's *Oberküchenmeister* had to deal with such lowly people on the payroll as cooks and musicians, might have made the same observation about any other metropolis.

The very fact that Vienna at the time was one of the world's important capitals, fickle though its public might be, must have appealed to Mozart after the stifling years in Salzburg when he was no longer the traveling boy wonder. Surely, the environs of the Austrian capital did not attract the young musician; the even lovelier countryside around Salzburg had not either. Unlike Haydn and Beethoven, Mozart did not need inspiration from nature, for he was a city person and got his musical ideas out of himself. He was, above all, a man of the theater, and Vienna had plenty of that.

During his ten years in Vienna, Mozart had a dozen different addresses. Financial difficulties may have been one reason why he and his wife, Constanze, moved so often, but not always. Their frequent apartment changes reflected also great restlessness. From the beginning, Mozart had hoped to obtain a well-paying job at the imperial court or in the musical establishment of some princely house, but there never seemed to be any vacancy. After Gluck's death in 1787, a court post did at last become available, and Josef II named Mozart *Kammer-Compositeur*. For the small salary of eight hundred florins a year, Mozart did not have much work to do.

He was not in financial straits all the time. The apartment where he wrote *Le Nozze di Figaro* (now a museum) was comfortable by the standards of the era, and Constanze had a servant girl. At one time Mozart even owned a horse and rode out every day because the doctor had advised him to get some sort of regular exercise. The Mozarts often entertained friends, held musical parties at home, and went to the theater.

Whatever ominous legends have been spun around the figure of Salieri, Josef II's favorite kapellmeister, the Italian was always courteous to Mozart and would be one of the very few mourners at his bleak funeral. Lorenzo da Ponte worked for Salieri before writing his masterly librettos for *Le Nozze di Figaro, Don Giovanni* and *Così fan tutte.* He was one of the fascinating cosmopolitan personages then to be encountered in Vienna. The son of a Jewish leather merchant on the Venetian mainland, he was fourteen years old when he was baptized and took on the name of the local bishop; his father had converted to Roman Catholicism before remarrying and had his three sons by his first wife become Catholics too. In due course, Lorenzo even received holy orders and taught in various seminaries, which did not prevent him from having mistresses on the side and probably getting one of them with child. He seems to have left the Venice region in a hurry, and turned up in Dresden before arriving in Vienna with an introduction to the well-established Salieri.

It did not take long for da Ponte to get himself a title in Vienna: Poet of the Imperial Theater. Posterity must be grateful that he met Mozart. Although he would much later tend to magnify his part in the creation of three of the greatest operas that have ever reached the stage, there is no doubt that he did stimulate their composer. It is tempting to follow the remainder of da Ponte's career after his job in Vienna was eliminated because of budget cuts following Josef II's death. The Italian librettist moved to Trieste and fell in love with a young Englishwoman there; they got married, lived in London for thirteen years, and eventually emigrated to the United States. Da Ponte made a living as a language teacher in

New York, and for some time belonged to the Columbia College faculty. He died at age ninety-eight, in 1838. He did not get the name right that ensured his immortality: in New York he spelt it "Motzart."

When Mozart composed the last of his da Ponte operas, *Così fan tutte,* in 1789 he was already in deep financial trouble. One would not guess his anxiety—expressed in many begging letters—from the musical score, with its arias ranging from the airy to the passionate. It was in that year that Mozart, in a note to his brother Freemason and friend Michael Puchberg, wrote in justification of yet another request for a quick loan that "my fate is unfortunately, *but only in Vienna,* so adverse that I cannot earn anything." Why stay on then, rather than escape the presumed Vienna jinx and move to some other city, such as Prague or London, where fate might be more merciful to Mozart? Some scholars have suggested that the composer was kept in Vienna by his debts, maybe incurred at the gambling tables. Da Ponte simply would have skipped town.

The relative success of *Die Zauberflöte* came too late; Mozart died nine weeks after its first performance at Schikaneder's suburban theater. The mystery of Mozart's last months and of his fatal disease will probably never be cleared up.[4] The composer's wife was again at the spa of Baden, taking the waters, and he, alone in Vienna, was seeing odd people instead of the old friends who had lately withdrawn from him.

When Mozart died on December 5, 1791, he left two hundred florins in cash, shoddy furniture, and books with an estimated value of twenty-three florins and forty-one kreuzers. His debts amounted to three thousand florins, which would be paid back rather easily by Constanze in the following years with the proceeds from the sale of the manuscripts her husband had left behind.

BEETHOVEN AND THE BIRDS

One reason why the young Beethoven came to Vienna has to do with the intricate machinery of that bizarre old conglomeration that was known as the Holy Roman Empire of the German Nation. Bonn, his birthplace, was the residence of the archbishops of Cologne, who were also quasi-sovereign lords of their territory and had the right to cast their vote whenever a new emperor had to be chosen. As one of the Prince Electors

—there were nine of them in Beethoven's time—the Archbishop of Cologne was an influential personage. The spiritual-secular position was then filled by Archduke Maximilian Franz, the youngest (and favorite) brother of Emperor Josef II. Beethoven's father had been a singer in the choir of the Prince Elector–Archbishop in Bonn and had later been promoted to assistant kapellmeister. In 1787 the archbishop, who was also a Habsburg archduke, was persuaded to send the talented young pianist Beethoven to Vienna for further music study under Mozart.

The lad played before the composer in Vienna, and Mozart is supposed to have remarked to those present, "Keep an eye on this one; he will tell you something one day." The Viennese phrase meant that the student would become a master. It is doubtful whether Mozart ever gave Beethoven any actual lesson, because the young Rhinelander soon hurried home, having been informed that his mother was sick. Beethoven's mother, a former maid, died soon afterward, and he found himself burdened with having to take care of his two younger brothers while their father was drinking himself to death.

In 1792, Haydn passed through Bonn on his return from his first visit to England, auditioned the promising pianist, and declared himself ready to take him on as pupil should the Prince Elector–Archbishop send him again to Vienna. When the time for Beethoven's departure had at last arrived, one of his Bonn patrons, Count Ferdinand Ernst Gabriel von Waldstein, wrote a farewell note into his album (young people then kept such books to have words of wisdom written on the blank pages): "Receive Mozart's spirit at the hands of Haydn!" Mozart had died the year before.

Beethoven arrived in Vienna for the second time with some money from the Prince Elector, and with a sheaf of introductions to the music-loving nobility. Despite his gaucheries and frequent rudeness, the newcomer was well received in the imperial city's aristocratic palaces. Gottfried van Swieten, the chief of the court library, presented the pock-marked, badly dressed pianist to many of his high-ranking friends. Beethoven studied with Haydn until the old composer started out on his second journey to England; Salieri and other pillars of the Viennese music establishment also gave lessons and advice to the Rhinelander. Beethoven made his public debut as a pianist in a concert at the Court Theater in March 1795, and it was a great success.

Among the early admirers of Beethoven were Prince Karl Lichnowsky and his wife, Maria Christiane. The couple would for many years favor him and patiently put up with many oddities. Beethoven soon counted friends and pupils also in other princely families—the Schwarzenbergs, the Liechtensteins, and the Odescalchis. His favorite disciple, Karl Czerny, was to write much later that Beethoven's "preference for Vienna" arose from the forbearance with which everybody accepted his outlandish ways and his fits of temper; "he was always admired and esteemed as an exceptional being."

Beethoven's biographers have enumerated the women in his life and speculated that the pianist wife of an Austrian officer, Dorothea von Ertmann, may have been the "Immortal Beloved" to whom he wrote three passionate letters when she was undergoing the cure in the Bohemian spa of Karlsbad in 1812. One of his pupils, Ferdinand Ries, wrote that Beethoven was always in love with one or another of the society ladies who studied with him or were friends of his but that he did not talk about his sentimental attachments.

Modern Beethoven research has found some indications that the composer may have contracted syphilis in his late twenties or early thirties, which would not have been surprising in the Vienna of that epoch (or of later ones as well). As early as 1796, Beethoven wrote in a letter from Prague to his brother Nikolaus Johann he hoped the brother would increasingly like Vienna, "only, beware of the entire guild of bad women." The passage sounds as if Beethoven had had terrible experiences with them.

As Beethoven became more and more isolated and crotchety, he often vented his unfavorable opinions of the Viennese in general in the presence of foreign visitors. "All the Viennese, from the emperor to the bootblack, are worthless," he told Xavier Schnyder, a Swiss, in 1811. Other callers from abroad heard the composer grumble that any commitment in Vienna had to be put down in writing because otherwise it would not be honored. Beethoven also complained that the Viennese nobility was vain and arrogant and was showing bad taste, observations that might as readily have applied to aristocrats elsewhere.

What kept Beethoven in Vienna until his death? In addition to the general tolerance of his unconventional behavior and of his lack of the social graces, which Czerny and other sources have mentioned, Beethoven's love of the city's surroundings was surely a weighty reason. He liked to stroll for hours on the hills, in the valleys, and through the dense

Vienna Woods on lonely and often impenetrable paths, in any weather. "On such occasions he was most disposed to be creative," Ries reported.

Beethoven himself would point out the exact spot where he had composed the second movement of the *Pastoral* Symphony: the Wiesental (Meadow Valley) between the wine-growing suburbs of Heiligenstadt and Grinzing. "The yellowhammers and quails, the nightingales and cuckoos all around me were playing their parts." By the time Beethoven thus reminisced in the company of his friend Anton Schindler, he could no longer hear the birds.

The composer's hearing had started deteriorating in his late twenties. He was not yet thirty-two years old when he wrote in his "Heiligenstadt Testament" that six years earlier a "desperate condition"—deafness—had befallen him, that the doctors had been of no help, and that "only art" had prevented him from taking his own life. (The "Heiligenstadt Testament," discovered among his papers after his death, is a sealed letter addressed to Beethoven's brothers, but throughout its text the name of Nikolaus Johann, with whom he had fallen out, is replaced by blank spaces.) Beethoven's depression at the time of this self-revelation may have been deepened by his rejection by a young and pretty Italian pupil, Countess Giulietta Guicciardi; she married a composer of trashy ballet music. Fifty years later she would recall, "Beethoven was very ugly, but noble, sensitive and educated."

The composer's deafness worsened during the next years, but Beethoven often insisted on conducting the orchestras that were playing his compositions, even though he could not hear the instruments. He would wildly gesticulate and often was a few measures behind or ahead of the players who did not look at him but at their concertmaster while irreverent snickers were heard from the audience.

When Napoleon's forces bombarded Vienna in 1809, Beethoven could still hear the artillery, and had a cushion tied around his head in the basement of his brother's city apartment, where they had taken refuge. Napoleon was at that time sitting at an outdoor table of the Casa Piccola coffeehouse in the western suburbs, which in quieter times had been favored by Vienna's Italians, and watched the effects of the guns.

FAMOUS ECCENTRIC

By 1809, Beethoven no longer admired Napoleon. Every Beethoven biography re-creates this scene: In May 1804 the composer was preparing to send a neat copy of a new symphony, his Third, to the First Consul of the French Republic; the work is dedicated to Napoleon Bonaparte, and the signature reads "Luigi van Beethoven." Prince Lichnowsky is there when Ries brings the news that Napoleon has just proclaimed himself emperor, and Beethoven snatches the score, tears off the dedication page, and curses the new "tyrant." The symphony would henceforth be known as the *Eroica.*

Napoleon had occupied Vienna for the first time when Beethoven's only opera, *Fidelio,* had its premiere in the Theater an der Wien in November 1805. Many French officers and soldiers were in the audience, but few Viennese, for most civilians did not dare to go out to the new suburban theater at night during enemy occupation. *Fidelio* was a mild flop, and its composer reworked it later.

In 1808, Beethoven was reconciled enough with Napoleonic dominance in Europe to move toward acceptance of an offer from the French emperor's brother, King Jérôme of Westphalia, to become his court composer in Kassel. The promised salary: six hundred gold ducats a year. Beethoven's friends and admirers in Vienna were stunned, none more so than Archduke Rudolf, a brother of the Austrian emperor and a sometime composer who was later to become Archbishop of Olomouc in Moravia. The archduke got together a group of sponsors who undertook to raise a fund that would enable Beethoven to stay in Vienna. The easygoing Rudolf, a Beethoven pupil, committed himself to fifteen hundred florins a year, Prince Franz Joseph Max Lobkowitz (in whose palace the *Eroica* was first performed) to seven hundred florins, and Prince Ferdinand Kinsky to eighteen hundred florins. As might have been predicted, Beethoven was to have trouble collecting the promised four thousand florins annuity because his patrons died or lost part of their wealth, and he would eventually have to sue. At any rate, the composer did not move to Westphalia, which was as well because King Jérôme did not last all that long.

From 1813 on, each of Beethoven's concerts in Vienna was considered an important event. His music was one of the artistic attractions during the giddy days of the Congress of Vienna in 1814–15, and the secret police were not too busy to omit reporting that there were pro-Beethoven and anti-Beethoven factions among the concertgoers. At a gala for the monarchs and statesmen who were assembled in the Austrian capital, Beethoven conducted his *Wellington's Victory* while his former teacher, Salieri, was taking care of an apparatus that simulated gun salvoes; the future composer of grand opera who called himself Giacomo Meyerbeer worked the thunder machine; and a disciple of Mozart, Johann Nepomuk Hummel, beat the drums. The *Wellington* extravaganza was preceded by Beethoven's Seventh Symphony.

"That's just the way he is," Archduke Rudolf used to say laughingly whenever somebody complained about the composer's uncouth ways. Beethoven had become a famous Vienna original. Nobody cared anymore how negligently he dressed or how absentminded he was. People greeted him reverently in the streets, and coffeehouse habitués were proud when the celebrity, maybe with a two-day stubble on his chin, strode in to read the newspapers. Beethoven's shiftless nephew, Karl, it is true, was ashamed of being seen with him; the composer was using Karl as a famulus, sparing neither affection nor reproaches. Eventually Karl took to drinking and, exasperated by his uncle's nagging, tried to kill himself, holding two pistols to his head and pulling the triggers. He bungled his suicide, as he did many other things in his life, and apologized to his uncle with the abject phrases that can be read in the deaf composer's "Conversation Book" of that period. The entry shows that Karl called his uncle "Father."

For several years before his death, Beethoven always carried writing books and a coarse carpenter's pencil with him to be able to communicate with other people. Since he never went out without notepaper either, his pockets were bulging. His seedy appearance was completed by the high hat in the style of the time, which had long since lost its original shape and had taken on an undefinable color. The Viennese, notoriously meddlesome and gossipy, nevertheless knew he was a genius and left him alone. Vienna has always loved for its personages of great repute to behave in bizarre ways, especially if they belonged to the world of the arts.

Beethoven cannot, however, have been very popular with his landlords, of whom he had at least three dozen during his thirty-six years or so as a resident of the imperial city. He continually moved from the center to the suburbs and back again, a quarrelsome, often noisy, and always messy tenant. There are many descriptions by visitors who were appalled by the untidy and squalid quarters in which they found the famous composer, often with an unemptied chamber pot under his bed.

When the Ninth Symphony—which had been commissioned by the Royal Philharmonic Society in London—was completed, Beethoven dedicated it to the King of Prussia and planned to have it first performed in Berlin. There was consternation in Vienna. A group of friends and devotees, including Prince Lichnowsky, appealed in a public petition to the composer to allow the work to be first heard in Vienna, and it was. During the premiere at the Kärntnertor Theater in 1824, Beethoven conducted erratically, as had become usual, but the concertmaster Jean Louis Duport brought the great symphony to a good end.

During his last years, while Beethoven was exploring the depths of his own mind and the outer reaches of pure music in his last quartets, Vienna was being dazzled by the novelty of Rossini's melodies. Beethoven felt the Viennese did not care for "real music" any more, and he said so; and in this mood, he drank more than usual. Even so, after he died in his Spartan apartment in the Schwarzspanier-Strasse during a snow flurry with lightning and thunder on March 26, 1827, Vienna did go into profound mourning.

Unlike Mozart's hasty burial, the funeral rites for Beethoven were a lavish Viennese pageant, *a schöne Leich*. Twenty thousand people— more than a tenth of the city's population—turned out, and the cortege from the house where the composer had died to the Church of the Most Holy Trinity, half a mile distant, took an hour and a half. Eight singers of the Court Opera carried the coffin, Hummel and other famous musicians were the pallbearers, and Austria's foremost poet and dramatist, Franz Grillparzer, together with Schubert, Czerny, and other prominent admirers of the dead composer were holding torches. The city's engravers were able to sell prints showing the funeral procession a few days later. After the requiem, two hundred carriages followed the coffin from the church to the suburban Währing Cemetery, where an actor, Heinrich Anschütz, delivered a eulogy composed by Grillparzer: "An artist he was, but also a man, a man in every, in the highest, sense."

THE TORCHBEARER

Franz Schubert, who had carried a torch at Beethoven's funeral, would die eighteen months later and be buried next to the older man in the Währing Cemetery. He never moved in the society of princes and counts. His brief, thoroughly unconventional, and astonishingly productive life marks the transition from aristocratic to middle-class culture in Vienna. The princes and counts were losing their interest in serious music and intellectual life, and untitled people were flocking to the more than one hundred public concerts that were held in the capital every year and were listening to chamber music in the homes of the bourgeoisie almost every night.

Of all the great figures of the Vienna classical era in music, Schubert was the most Viennese. Gluck, Haydn, Beethoven, and occasionally even Mozart liked to live in the city's village suburbs, but Schubert was born and raised in one, Lichtental on Vienna's northwestern outskirts. Outwardly easygoing, he also was a compulsive worker, as has been mentioned earlier. Much of what he created is lost because, unlike Mozart, he never drew up a list of his compositions and he allowed visitors to carry off any of the manuscripts that were scattered around his disorderly living quarters—usually a room in some friend's home.

The *Unfinished* Symphony was not known until 1865 when the Viennese conductor Johann von Herbeck discovered it in the drawer of a friend of Schubert's, Anselm Hüttenbrenner, in Graz. Other compositions were retrieved from relatives, friends, and admirers of Schubert; the composer himself left behind nothing but "a few old musical scores estimated at 10 florins," according to the official death record. Schubert never liked to write letters or notes; he preferred conversation with his friends, who were almost always around, but he had no real disciples who might have collected and conserved his manuscripts.

At times Schubert did keep a journal, and what he entered in it is additional evidence that the composer, portrayed by cloying films as a carefree bohemian who was timid with women and preferred to play the piano while his friends were dancing with pretty girls, had moods of deep melancholia. "Nobody understands another one's pain, nobody understands another one's joy," he wrote in 1824. "One always believes one is going toward each other, and one only goes side by side. Oh, it is torment to him who understands this!" Sadness hides behind the lyricism and seeming gaiety in much of Schubert's music, suggesting a character makeup that is found fairly often in Vienna; it may lead to alienation and angst, sometimes to suicide.

Vienna appears to have been singularly tolerant of the short, pudgy-faced musician whose genius was suspected by very few people during his lifetime. Most of his contemporaries regarded Schubert as a nice enough drifter and sponger who would gladly move in with some friend for a few months or longer if there was an extra bed, a table for writing, and an old piano. He liked to take potluck and did not mind sharing clothes with his hosts either.

After three years of grudging service as an assistant to his schoolmaster father, Schubert never held down any regular job during the remaining eleven years of his life. He did give music lessons to the two daughters of a Count Esterházy in a castle near the present border between Hungary and Czechoslovakia—Schubert's only brush with nobility—for a few months in 1818, but nostalgia for Vienna and the free life in it soon drove him back to it. Almost everybody in his circle of friends who attended the "Schubertiads," musical gatherings devoted largely to his music in various middle-class homes, eventually became a civil servant, landed lucrative painting commissions or had some other reputable career, and started a family—but not Schubert.

In 1826, pressed by his intimates, Schubert applied to the emperor for a job as a deputy kapellmeister at court. There seemed to be an opening because the musician who had filled that rather lowly post had been promoted when Salieri (who had been insane at the end) had at last died. Emperor Franz, however, wanted to save money, and neither Schubert nor any one of the eight other candidates was hired.

Compositions by Schubert were sometimes performed publicly, at the Kärntnertor Theater and in other concert halls, but Vienna's critics were condescending or unresponsive. His only public concert in a city where music was then publicly played almost every night was held shortly before his death. It was a success and netted him eight hundred florins, a highly welcome sum that enabled him to pay all his debts and buy a spinet. He was nevertheless soon broke again and had to be taken in by his brother Eduard when he fell sick.

Schubert's ailments, from his twenty-sixth year on, were in all likeliness consequences of a badly treated venereal disease, probably syphilis.

At one time he had a nasty skin rash, his hair was shorn (possibly in a hospital), and for a period he wore an ill-fitting wig. He was known to indulge in brief affairs with maidservants and may also have frequented prostitutes, who then, as always, abounded in Vienna. He probably fell really in love only once, with a neighborhood girl, Therese Grob, who had a sweet soprano voice and was sixteen years old when she sang at the first performance of a Schubert mass in the Lichtental parish church in 1814. He was 17. By that time Schubert had already left the live-in convent school of the Piarist Fathers, where he had received a good education, at the emperor's expense, as a member of the Vienna Boys' Choir. (Salieri had been present at his entrance exam.) The Piarists' school, attended also by many students from well-to-do families, long remained a second home for the alumnus Schubert, who would go back there on weekends to see friends and make music.

Therese (whom Schubert himself described later as not very pretty, but kind) eventually made a sensible marriage, becoming a baker's wife. Schubert would for the rest of his life speak very little about love. There were some young women at the Schubertiads, but they appear to have been interested in him only as a musician. During a later short return visit to the Esterházys, Schubert seems to have been smitten by one of his former pupils, Countess Karoline, who was then seventeen years old, but he must have realized how hopeless such a passion was, and is supposed to have found solace, as he did during his earlier stay, in the servants' wing of the castle. Scholars assume that it was there that he contracted the disease that would shorten his life.

Schubert had since his Boys' Choir days revered Beethoven; it is likely that he knew him by sight from casual encounters in taverns and coffee-houses and that Beethoven recognized his young admirer. Schubert, however, was always too shy to approach his idol. He was probably among a group of musicians who called on Beethoven during his last illness. Beethoven's disciple Anton Schindler reported that the master had seen some of Schubert's lieder and piano pieces and had commented that "in that Schubert there truly dwells a divine spark." Legend has it that the evening of Beethoven's funeral Schubert repaired with friends to the Mehlgrube restaurant and drank a toast on "the first one who will follow" the dead master. True or not, he may have felt then that time was running out for him.

When he sang the lieder of his just-completed *Winterreise* cycle to friends, they were perplexed by the somber, enigmatic music; Schubert told them he liked the twenty-four songs better than any other ones of his, "and one day you will too." He made a trip to Hungary and visited Haydn's tomb in Eisenstadt, fell ill again on his return, read *The Last of the Mohicans* and other books by James Fenimore Cooper in bed, received the last sacraments of the church, and died of what the doctor described as "nerve fever," probably typhoid.

GLITTER AND TORPOR UNDER METTERNICH

The year of Schubert's death, 1828, marks the end of the great era of Viennese music that had started with Gluck. The Turkish wars and even Napoleon, who had died on St. Helena in 1821, were just memories. Vienna had become stagnant and would remain so for another twenty years, until "mad" 1848.

The Congress of Vienna in 1814 and 1815 had been the last event that had brought genuine and protracted excitement to the imperial city. About two hundred states, lordships, cities, and other corporate entities sent delegations to Vienna, where, after the collapse of the Napoleonic system, a new European order was to be mapped. There was never a plenary meeting; a steering committee on which the leading powers were represented did all the work, amid incessant lobbying and intrigues. Prince Klemens Wenzel Nepomuk Lothar von Metternich, the brilliant and cynical Rhinelander who had been Emperor Franz's foreign minister and state chancellor since 1809, presided at the committee meetings, earning the sobriquet as "the Coachman of Europe." Then forty-one years old, he was also a relentless womanizer.

Upon Napoleon's declaration of the end of the Holy Roman Empire in 1806, the Holy Roman Emperor Franz II had become Emperor Franz I of Austria. As such, he successfully played his role as the genial host of the glittering congress, talking in homely Viennese dialect even on formal occasions. Czar Alexander I of Russia struck poses as the liberator of Europe, and King Friedrich Wilhelm III of Prussia, although older than the czar, deferred to him in public so demonstratively that the Viennese found he was behaving like Alexander's valet. Viscount Castlereagh, the British foreign secretary, advocated leniency toward France, and Talleyrand, the deft and corrupt French representative, triumphantly won acceptance as the fifth of the "Big Five." Visitors to the Office of the Federal Chancellor in the Ballhaus Platz are today still shown the hall with enough doors to allow the main delegates to enter simultaneously for committee meetings—none would yield precedence.

Congress logistics and entertainment for the delegations cost the Austrian treasury eighty thousand florins a day, a hundred times what Mozart's yearly salary as court composer had been. Concerts, receptions, and balls crowded everybody's agenda. The bon mot that "the Congress doesn't get on; it dances" has become proverbial. It was coined by the seventy-eight-year-old Prince Karl Joseph von Ligne, a retired Austrian field marshal who inhabited a pink house near one of the city's ramparts and was known as the "Pink Prince," a bon vivant and witty holdover from the Rococo age. Still a redoubtable ladies' man despite his age, he is supposed to have caught a cold during a late-hour tryst and died before the congress had finished dancing.

Vienna was crawling with foreign spies and homegrown police informers. One of the innumerable secret reports that were filed noted that the Russian Princess Katharina Pavlovna Bagration, called "the Naked Angel" by her admirers, was running a high-class house of assignation and that a Prince Starhemberg had broken into a locked room in her elegant apartment and found his young daughter in the buff with a Russian nobleman.

With all its dances and dalliances, the Congress of Vienna did eventually produce political results. It enacted territorial changes in Europe, reinstated dynasties that the French Revolution and Napoleon had dispossessed, and led to the Quadruple Alliance. This coalition—comprising Austria, Prussia, Russia, and initially Britain—pledged to maintain the status quo in Europe; Metternich skillfully pulled the levers of the alliance mechanism. For Vienna, the era of Metternich meant about two decades of political and cultural immobility, of reaction, and of censorship. The police informers who had had to shadow all the foreigners in the city during the congress now concentrated on their fellow Viennese. Even a recognized literary figure like Grillparzer had reason to be afraid of the snoopers.

The Viennese's answer to the stifling climate of police-state absolutism after the age of Napoleon was withdrawal to private life and enjoyment of its consolations. The Schubertiads were by no means exceptional social affairs during those years. All over the city and in the suburbs middle-class people gathered often to make music in private homes, read poetry to one another, and organize outings to some attractive spot in the environs. The mood to be cultivated by the paternalistic authorities was *Gemütlichkeit*. Until a few years earlier the word had meant "soulfulness"; its new Viennese significance, "coziness" or "snugness," developed only at the beginning of the nineteenth century.

Those years of personal noninvolvement in public affairs, of the cultivation of friendships and other private values, and of modest but *gemütlich* hedonism has come to be called the Biedermeier epoch. The term is derived from the name of a philistine, law-abiding, and timorous character satirized in verses by the Swabian poet Ludwig Eichrodt in the 1850s. "Gottlieb Biedermaier," as Eichrodt called his caricature of the model citizen in the domains of the Quadruple Alliance, translates into something like "God-loving Goody-goody." (The spelling *Biedermeier* came to be accepted later.)

Vienna was the center of Biedermeier culture: one could enjoy a serene life as a middle-class citizen in the imperial capital if one kept one's nose out of politics, did not profess liberal ideas, and did not harbor excessive pretentions, but sought personal fulfillment instead in one's family, love, friendship, and the arts. The Biedermeier style in furniture and interior design was characterized by sober lines, modest proportions, and soft colors. A residue of Biedermeier feeling lingered among Viennese craftsmen, small-business owners, petty bureaucrats, and other members of the lower bourgeoisie for a long time; even today, Biedermeier moods seem sometimes to float through simple *Heurige* wine taverns.

The atmosphere of the Metternich years was one of intense snugness, especially in Vienna's coffeehouses. The strong aroma of the coffee, the cigar and pipe smoke, the rustle of the newspapers, the clicking of billiard balls, the sound of chessmen being moved, the shuffling of cards, and the reverent voices of the waiters were a soothing mix, the very essence of *gemütlich* Vienna. Some cafés were more elegant than others, and one, the Silberne, even had door handles of silver, but the important things were the ambience, the clientele, and the newspapers. The woman cashier was seated behind her desk like a queen on her throne, jotting down the orders reported to her by the staff, and coquettishly or haughtily acknowledging the compliments of flirtatious patrons.

The Biedermeier coffeehouses were notoriously saturated with police spies, but nevertheless served also as places where habitués who knew and trusted each other could prudently exchange their political opinions.

Delightful gossip was to be picked up too: "Have you heard the latest, it seems the Duke of Reichstadt is getting his first love lessons from that ballerina, Fanny Elssler?" The Duke of Reichstadt was Napoleon's son by his Habsburg-born empress, Marie Louise. He was to die in Vienna of tuberculosis in 1832, a mere twenty-one years old. Elssler, already launched on her way to becoming one of the richest women in the city, may actually have consoled the unfortunate "Eaglet," although he was a virtual prisoner in the Schönbrunn palace.

Beethoven and Schubert were still alive when a new, mocking voice was heard from the Vienna stage, and during the years to come it would help to shatter the Biedermeier idyll with merciless skepticism: Johann Nepomuk Nestroy. A dropout from the law school of Vienna University, he started his theatrical career in 1822 as a basso in the daunting role of Sarastro in Mozart's *Zauberflöte;* through the more than eighty dramatic works he was to write, he became the harbinger of a new Viennese era of realism and psychological insights.

Even after he was famous, Nestroy was in everyday life ill at ease with other people. On the stage he seemed transformed: fluent, cutting, and aggressive. Tall and angular, he eventually found his ideal straight man in the actor Wenzel Scholz, who was short, stout, and jovial. The hilarious pair guaranteed full houses at the Carl Theater—named after the impresario Karl Carl—in the Leopoldstadt suburb night after night. After a brief, unhappy marriage Nestroy lived for thirty years with the singer Marie Weiler, who bore him two children.

The plays that Nestroy wrote for himself and his troupe sharply portrayed the Viennese society of his day: the greedy speculators, scheming widows, smug shopkeepers, sly servants, pompous officials, languid bourgeois girls and their romantic suitors, the sales clerk who wants to get some fun while the boss is out of town, and, in *The Evil Spirit Lumpazivagabundus,* the outcasts and vagrants. "Lumpazivagabundus," a name formed with the German words for "rascal" *(Lump)* and "vagabond," is an example of how Nestroy played with language. In his farces and his parodies of high-flown serious drama, he contrasted the ponderousness of rhetorical High German with the earthiness and force of the Viennese dialect. Exploring the possibilities of verbal manipulation, Nestroy created many neologisms that are hard to translate—for instance, as an invective hurled at an unpleasant woman, *Krokodiless,* a nonexistent word that everybody understood to mean "she-crocodile."

In *Freiheit in Krähwinkel,* a satire on the misuse of freedom in the fictional backwater of Crows' Corner that he wrote during Vienna's brief liberal spring of 1848, Nestroy had one of his characters say, "Censorship is the younger of two shameful sisters; the name of the older one is Inquisition." During most of his acting and writing career, Nestroy had trouble with the disgraceful sister. But he managed nevertheless to puncture the facade of Biedermeier placidity.

NOTES TO CHAPTER I

1. Braudel, *The Mediterranean and the Mediterranean World in the Age of Philipp II*, New York, 1973, II, p. 1,014.
2. Walter Kleindel, *Oesterreich*, Vienna-Heidelberg, 1978. Entry for year 1741.
3. Hermann Broch, *Hofmannsthal and His Time*, University of Chicago Press, 1984, p. 68 trans. Michael P. Steinberg.
4. Wolfgang Hildesheimer, *Mozart*, Frankfurt, 1977, p. 294.

2

REVOLUTION, SPLENDOR,

DECADENCE

Long inertia ended when the feverish year 1848 saw the traditionally docile Viennese in the unwonted role of rebels. The spectacle was so extraordinary that no less a radical than Karl Marx came to watch it and, possibly, play a part too. He had just won control of the *Neue Rheinische Zeitung* of Cologne and, as its editor in chief, traveled to the Austrian capital in August 1848, ostensibly to report on the events. At one point he changed from journalist into agitator and delivered a harangue at a rally of Viennese workers. Marx soon decided, however, that what was going on was not the class struggle that he and Friedrich Engels had advocated in their *Communist Manifesto* (published in February 1848), but a bourgeois insurrection, and so he left Vienna. Another young firebrand whom the turmoil drew to the imperial city for some time was Richard Wagner.

What had happened in the Austrian capital was that middle-class people, inflamed by popular movements against monarchic absolutism in France and in various German states and, above all, by an anti-Habsburg uprising in Hungary, were defying Metternich's police state. Unorganized laborers soon joined in the revolt. The disorders came on the heels of Vienna's traditional carnival frenzy. The public dances had been crowded, Franz Liszt had enchanted capacity audiences at his concerts, and Meyerbeer had attended the opening of his new opera *Vielka*.

In stark contrast to the glitter at the capital's center, workers and other poor people were miserably vegetating in overcrowded dwellings or even in the gutters of some of the suburbs—early outcasts of the industrial age, which somewhat belatedly had begun also in the Habsburg domains.

On March 13, 1848, a group of students, university teachers, professional men, booksellers, and coffeehouse intellectuals demonstrated against Metternich—not against the emperor—in the heart of the city. Later that day the rioters clashed with army detachments that had been called out, while on the capital's outskirts unemployed workers stormed factories and smashed machinery. By the evening, fifty people had been killed.

The Viennese malcontents demanded freedom of the press and other political and civil rights. Emperor Ferdinand I, who in 1835 had succeeded his father Franz, was feebleminded and suffered from bouts of insanity. The members of the imperial family and court dignitaries who unofficially were ruling in his name quickly decided that to appease the rebellious capital Metternich had to be jettisoned. The longtime coachman of Europe, by then frail and stone deaf, hid in a laundry cart to get safely out of the city and found a refuge in London. He was to return to a becalmed Vienna in 1851, and would still exercise some influence behind the scenes until his death at the age of eighty-six in 1859.

The seven months following the March troubles were dizzying. Citizens set up a National Guard, and students, an Academic Legion, arming themselves with weapons taken from the imperial armory. There were new riots and barricades. A Hungarian-born Jewish physician who was serving in Vienna's General Hospital, Dr. Adolf Fischhof, emerged as an articulate spokesman for the Vienna liberals. The emperor and his court fled first to Innsbruck in the loyal Tyrol, then returned to Vienna, and fled again, this time to Olomouc in Moravia. A legislative assembly in the capital discussed constitutional reforms. For a few heady months the newspapers and theaters were not bothered by government censorship, and Nestroy let himself go in extempore remarks from the stage.

In autumn 1848 the Imperial Army command ordered a part of the Vienna garrison to move to Hungary to help quell the nationalist revolution there. Viennese insurgents tore up the tracks of the new railroad from the capital to the east of the monarchy. A mob lynched the war minister, Count Theodor Baillet von Latour, in front of his offices in the city center and strung up his body on a lamppost. There was fighting around St. Stephen's Cathedral. Eventually military forces loyal to the Habsburg dynasty, including fifty thousand tough (and anti-Hungarian) Croats, closed in on seething Vienna. Many prudent residents left the capital, while the rural population in the surrounding countryside remained apathetic.

When Vienna failed to surrender at once, the commander in chief of all imperial troops outside Italy, Prince Felix von Schwarzenberg, ordered his artillery to fire into the capital. At the end of October 1848 the city's resistance was broken, two thousand people had been killed, and the courts-martial and executions began. The events had at any rate proved that the Viennese were not all that easygoing; seventy years later their city would become known throughout Europe as Red Vienna.

The court camarilla in Olomouc decided that the mentally subnormal, though usually amiable, emperor had to go, to save the dynasty, and Ferdinand I gladly abdicated. (He was to live in retirement in Prague's gloomy Hradčany Castle until 1875.) His eighteen-year-old nephew, Franz Josef, became the new ruler of the Habsburg monarchy. He styled himself Franz Josef I, as if he expected a series of emperors of the same name to succeed him. During his long—overlong—reign Vienna would become a modern metropolis with a sparkling intellectual and artistic life, but also a city of decadence and despondency.

Five years after the turmoil of 1848, Franz Josef, supported by the army and the high aristocracy, reintroduced absolutism. But the system no longer worked. Another fifteen years later, after a few lost wars and new secession threats by the Hungarians, Austria-Hungary—as the Habsburg dominions were officially called after 1867—had ample civil rights legislation, a free press "within legal restraints," parliaments in both Vienna and Budapest, and a liberal government.

THE ECLECTIC BOULEVARD

For Vienna, the crucial event of that period was an imperial edict of 1857 whereby the fortifications surrounding the core of the city were to be razed, and the army-controlled belt of unobstructed land between the bastions and the suburbs, called the *Glacis,* was to be made available for public and private development on either side of a projected circular boulevard.

The walls and ramparts around Vienna went back to the Middle Ages, and had been reinforced in the sixteenth and seventeenth centuries because of the Turkish threat. Later they had become the favorite promenades of the Viennese. The imperial army held exercises and parades on the Glacis and had long insisted that the half-mile-wide space between the fortifications and the suburbs must be kept open like a shooting range. Vienna had thus remained squeezed into a military corset at a time when other European cities were already free to spread far beyond their old walls. The imperial army had acquiesced in the plans for Vienna's expansion because it envisaged the proposed boulevard, the Ringstrasse, as a thoroughfare over which troops could be moved rapidly. The events of 1848 had taught the generals that the enemy might not be outside the capital but inside. Baron Georges Eugène Haussmann conceived his grands boulevards in Paris in the same vein.

The Ringstrasse was to be 2.5 miles long and was to enclose the inner city like a horseshoe, its two ends joined by a stretch of the Danube Canal embankment (Franz Josef Quay). The landscaped boulevard, embracing the historic core on three sides, was to be 185 feet wide and lined with representative public structures and stately residential buildings. By 1860 the first Ringstrasse constructions were completed. On May 1, 1865, Emperor Franz Josef officially inaugurated the boulevard, but another two decades would pass before it could be considered finished.

The military saw to it that army barracks were placed at strategic points near the new Ringstrasse. A huge red-brick building, the Rossau Barracks, went up near the northwest end of the horseshoe boulevard between 1865 and 1869. The Viennese tell one another to this day that when the first soldiers moved in, they could not find any toilets: the architects had forgotten to allot space for such facilities and had to be sent back to their drawing boards to make the necessary adjustments.

In 1890, by which time the Glacis had been built up and a few remaining open spaces had been transformed into public parks, forty-three suburban communities were administratively incorporated into the city of Vienna, causing its official population to jump from 525,000 to 1,365,000. The people living on the outskirts had in culture, dialect, customs, and economic interests been Viennese all along, even though they might cling to their particular parochial identities.

Even today many Viennese will make a point of describing themselves as natives or longtime residents of a certain neighborhood, thereby emitting subtle cultural and social signals that only another Viennese can read. It makes a difference if someone is from Neustift am Wald, where vintners' traditions linger, or Ottakring, with its proletarian self-respect; the name Erdberg conveys the notion of lower-middle-class roots, whereas Hietzing suggests elegance. There are scores of districts where old village characteristics survive.

The architects of Vienna's "city expansion"—the bureaucratic term—in the second half of the nineteenth century filled the monumental belt between the core area and the suburbs with buildings in what has come to be known as the Ringstrasse style. A polite description of it is eclectic historicism; it may also be defined as a hodgepodge of borrowed architectural idioms from the periods between 500 B.C. and A.D. 1700. The new home for the parliament of the "Kingdoms and Countries" of Austria-Hungary's western half was built in the classical Greek manner —for after all, wasn't Athens the cradle of democracy? The City Hall nearby became a Gothic extravaganza, an allusion in stone to the free communes of the Middle Ages (Vienna never was one). Many offices in that mock-medieval structure are so dark that the lights burn in them throughout the working day, but its builders cared more for historical symbolism than for functional design.

A new university building, larger even than City Hall, rose north of it in the Italian Renaissance style. Further north is a large neo-Gothic church, the Votive Church, or Church of the Divine Savior, commemorating Emperor Franz Josef's escape from an assassination attempt in 1853. (The would-be murderer, a young Hungarian, was executed.) The new Burgtheater, opposite City Hall, imitated the style of the early Baroque; as has been mentioned earlier, the Viennese found the theater, with its lavish foyer and sumptuous staircases in wings on either side, Neronian. The twin Museums of Art History and Natural History, opposite the last remaining city gate, the Burgtor, were designed in the Italian Renaissance style.

The French Renaissance inspired the builders of the new Court Opera. Even before it was finished in 1869, almost no Viennese seemed to like it. One critic wrote that the building resembled an "elephant lying down to digest its dinner." The structure seemed indeed to be squatting because the city's development had raised the street level by three feet. Scoffers spoke of a "sunken box," and even the emperor found that the building was a trifle low. The jeers so depressed one of the opera house's two architects, Eduard van der Null, that in 1868 he hanged himself, leaving his widow destitute; friends started a fund-raising drive to help her. The other architect, August von Siccardsburg, died two months later —of heartbreak, the Viennese said. It took quite a few years before the citizenry recognized the opera house as one of the most convincing achievements of Ringstrasse architecture. It became a beloved landmark and was painstakingly rebuilt in every outward detail after it had been gravely damaged during World War II.

Alongside the public buildings, the parks, and the statues of the Ringstrasse and in the new city blocks bordering the showy boulevard, private developers erected large residential structures. They became at once the favorite addresses of the new bourgeoisie. It was an assertion of newly acquired status when the father of Arthur Schnitzler, the laryngologist Johann Schnitzler, moved from the Praterstrasse to No. 1 Burgring; Dr. Schnitzler was by then teaching at Vienna University and was treating actors and singers of the court theaters and other prominent patients. The father of another future writer, Stefan Zweig, had around the same time made enough money in the textile business to be able to afford an apartment at No. 14 Schottenring; when the family became even richer they moved into a larger place near City Hall.

The "apartment palaces" along the Ringstrasse, with their imposing facades and marble staircases, echoed the stylistic medley of the new boulevard's public buildings. A young critic and essayist, Alfred Polgar (né Polak), cast a sober eye on the Ringstrasse in 1897 and wrote in an 1897 essay in the *Wiener Allgemeine Zeitung* that the main characteristic of its architecture was its lack of character: "The new style is clumsy and flashy, it is full of pretension, that is, ordinary and vulgar."

The Ringstrasse architecture was copied in cities throughout Austria-Hungary, and Musil noted ironically that the buildings of that period "didn't content themselves with being Gothic, Renaissance or Baroque, but made use of the possibility of having all that simultaneously." The word *Kitsch* had not yet been invented when the City Hall and the Burgtheater were built in Vienna, but much of the Ringstrasse style prefigured it. And yet, even now, with the patina of more than a century, Vienna's circular boulevard does not seem devoid of a certain grandeur.

Nineteenth-century visitors pose in the terraced gardens between the upper and lower structures of Belvedere Castle. The baroque palace was erected between 1714 and 1723 for Prince Eugene of Savoy, hero of the 1683 Turkish siege of Vienna. *(The Bettmann Archive, Inc.)*

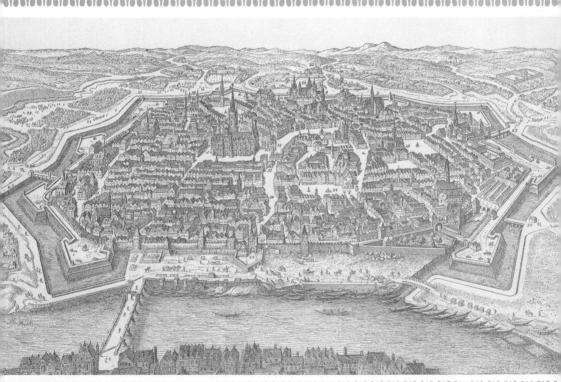

Eighteenth-century print of the fortified city of Vienna. The walls and ramparts were razed through an imperial edict of 1857, allowing the city to expand into the surrounding countryside. *(The Bettmann Archive, Inc.)*

Three persons symbolizing Austria, Russia, and Prussia dance in precarious balance while others perform to different political tunes, in a contemporary French commentary on the 1814–15 Congress of Vienna. *(Giraudon/Art Resource)*

Franz Schubert's compositions were mostly performed at musical gatherings in various middle-class homes. Here, a Schubertiade of 1826. *(Bildarchiv d. Österreichisches Nationalbibliothek, Courtesy of the Austrian Institute)*

The child prodigy Mozart and his sister playing before Empress Maria Theresa. Vienna was the world capital of music during the reigns of Maria Theresa and Josef II. *(The Bettmann Archive, Inc.)*

Beethoven playing for Mozart, who warns distinguished guests to keep quiet. "Keep an eye on this one. He will tell you something one day," Mozart is supposed to have remarked about the young composer. *(The Bettmann Archive, Inc.)*

Mozart's friends gather at his deathbed, singing the Requiem Mass, in a fanciful painting after H. N. O'Neil. No one recorded Mozart's actual death scene; he died leaving his wife three thousand florins in debt. *(The Bettmann Archive, Inc.)*

The coffeehouse—the fulcrum of Viennese social, intellectual, and political life—is an unlikely legacy of the Turkish siege of 1683. *(Photo by Fritz Kramer, Courtesy of the Austrian Press and Information Service)*

Scene in a public park in Vienna in the 1930s. Unlike its German-speaking neighbors, Vienna is a wine-growing and wine-drinking city. *(The Bettmann Archive, Inc.)*

Photograph of composer Arnold Schoenberg in 1910. Listeners fought on the floor and in the gallery of the Musikverein during a 1906 concert of his *Kammersymphonie. (Bildarchiv d. Österreichisches Nationalbibliothek, Courtesy of the Austrian Institute)*

Alma Schindler, daughter of painter Emil Schindler, stepdaughter of painter Carl Moll, was married three times: to Gustav Mahler, Walter Gropius, and Franz Werfel. Mahler described her love affair with the painter Kokoschka as "one sole, vehement love struggle." *(Bildarchiv d. Österreichisches Nationalbibliothek, Courtesy of the Austrian Institute)*

Photograph of Gustav Mahler in 1892. The great composer also directed the Court Opera for a decade, a brilliant period in Vienna's musical history. *(Gustav Mahler Archive, Courtesy of the Austrian Institute)*

Alban Berg, member of the Schoenberg circle of composers. *(Bildarchiv d. Österreichisches Nationalbibliothek, Courtesy of the Austrian Institute)*

The funeral procession of Emperor Franz Josef in 1916. His body was placed in the crypt of the Capuchin Church in the city center, among the caskets of 11 emperors, 15 empresses, 135 other members of the House of Hapsburg, and one Countess Fuchs. *(Courtesy of the Austrian Institute)*

The Viennese are fascinated by the macabre. Vienna is the only city in Europe with a funerary museum. ABOVE: The death mask of the composer Ludwig van Beethoven. *(Courtesy of the Austrian Institute)* RIGHT: The death mask of Viennese composer and Court Opera director Gustav Mahler. *(Courtesy of the Austrian Institute)*

TOP LEFT: The Viennese love an elaborate funeral, *a schöne Leich* (a beautiful corpse) in the local vernacular. More than a tenth of the city's population attended Beethoven's funeral. His tomb is in the Central Cemetery of Vienna. *(Courtesy of the Austrian Institute)* TOP RIGHT: Franz Schubert, torchbearer at Beethoven's funeral, is buried next to him. His tomb was designed by architect Theophil Hansen and sculptor Karl Kundmann. *(Courtesy of the Austrian Institute)* BOTTOM LEFT: The city of Vienna accorded Gustav Mahler a "tomb of honor," designed by Josef Hoffmann, at the suburban Grinzing cemetery. *(Courtesy of the Austrian Institute)* BOTTOM RIGHT: The tomb of composer Hugo Wolf. Wolf died in a Vienna lunatic asylum. *(Courtesy of the Austrian Institute)*

Gustav Klimt, the painter who led the artists' rebellion in 1897 that formed the Secession. *(Bildarchiv d. Österreichisches Nationalbibliothek, Courtesy of the Austrian Institute)*

Joseph Hoffmann, one of Otto Wagner's best pupils at the Vienna Academy, was a founding member of the Secession. *(UPI/Bettmann Newsphotos)*

Architect Otto Wagner joined the Vienna Secession in 1899. His buildings combined functionalism with art nouveau elements. *(Courtesy of the Austrian Institute)*

Adolf Loos, architect, friend of satirist Karl Kraus and composer Arnold Schoenberg, shocked Vienna with his unadorned "house without windows," the Loos House of 1909–1912. *(Courtesy of the Austrian Institute)*

SELF-CELEBRATION AND SECESSION

While the Ringstrasse was still being developed, the imperial capital, in a spirit of self-celebration, staged a World Exhibition in 1873. It was born under an evil star. On May 9, 1873, a week after its inauguration, the Vienna stock exchange crashed. The wave of bankruptcies and suicides that followed and the ensuing economic recession, which lasted for years, did not prevent the Danish architect of the Parliament, Theophilus von Hansen, from doggedly completing his new *Börse* ("stock exchange") on the Schottenring in Renaissance style. The World Exhibition was still on when a cholera epidemic broke out in Vienna, taking three thousand lives.

By 1879 the imperial capital was nevertheless in the mood for self-glorification and escapism again. The occasion was the twenty-fifth wedding anniversary of Emperor Franz Josef and his Bavarian-born wife, the beautiful and high-strung Empress Elisabeth. A celebrated "painter-prince" of Ringstrasse Vienna, Hans Makart, organized a lavish historical parade along the circular boulevard, with costumes designed by him. When the pageant could at last be held after two postponements due to the fickle April weather, Makart, decked out in a black suit in seventeenth-century fashion, was riding on a white horse at the head of 14,000 marchers dressed up as Renaissance and Baroque artists, craftsmen, and noted personages from the city's past. At least 350,000 people—50,000 on grandstands—were watching and cheering. The enthusiastic newspapers spoke later even of a million spectators.

Makart, a friend of Richard Wagner, was the foremost representative of neo-Baroque painting, and for many years a darling of Vienna's upper crust. In a studio that in size and opulence might have been worthy of a Rubens (his avowed idol) or a Titian, he toiled in the mornings on huge historical or fleshly allegorical canvases with gorgeous colors; in his afternoons he played host to aristocrats, wealthy admirers, visiting foreigners, and less fortunate artist colleagues. Society beauties—his mistresses?— were rumored to have been models for his nudes. In 1881, Makart married a member of the Court Opera ballet, Berta Linda, and died three years later, apparently of an inadequately treated syphilis.

The Court Opera was in those years under Wagner's spell. The new building had been opened in 1869 with Mozart's *Don Giovanni* in the presence of Emperor Franz Josef and the King of Hannover, but not of the unpredictable Empress Elisabeth. In 1875, Giuseppe Verdi triumphantly conducted his *Requiem* and *Aida* in the opera house. It was Wagner, however, who generated most of the operatic excitement. The composer, who had long since shed his political radicalism, lived in 1863–64 in a sumptuous villa with ankle-deep rugs and heavy draperies near the Schönbrunn Palace, and worked there on *Die Meistersinger.* In 1875 he was back in Vienna to produce his *Tannhäuser* at the Court Opera, with, among other stunts, live dogs on the stage. For the cavalcade in *Die Walküre,* the imperial-and-royal cavalry had to provide horses and riders (disguised in flowing blond wigs to portray Valkyries), and their backstage trotting path was padded with mattresses. And all the time Eduard Hanslick, the learned critic of the *Neue Freie Presse,* whom *Die Meistersinger* had caricatured as the pedantic Beckmesser, kept savagely panning Wagner's music.

While the anti-Wagnerians at the Court Opera were fighting their losing battle, Johann Strauss, Jr., the "Waltz King," went from success to adulation in the popular theaters and ballrooms of the city. It had been his father who, together with Josef Lanner, had popularized the waltz, the three-quarter-time dance that toward the end of the eighteenth century had developed from the cheerful *Ländler* of the farm folk in the Danubian countryside. Schubert and Weber had dabbled in the new waltz mode, but the worldwide rage for the new electrifying dance was caused above all by Johann Strauss, Sr. (1804–49) and his sometime associate and later rival Lanner (1801–43). The elder Strauss composed also a military tune in honor of Field Marshal Count Joseph Wenzel Radetzky, Austria's foremost army leader in the nineteenth century; it became, as "Radetzky March," a classic of martial music.

The younger Johann Strauss (1825–99) started as a bandleader, against the will of his father, and soon employed several orchestras playing at the same time in different restaurants and ballrooms while their nominal conductor was rushing from place to place to put in a token appearance and wield the baton for a few minutes. As a composer, he was even more talented and productive than his father, and he won the admiration of both Richard Wagner and Johannes Brahms, the two hostile champions of heavyweight music. When he was forty-five, Strauss started composing scores for operettas and turned out a classic with *Die Fledermaus* (1874). In 1877 the first of a still continuing series of opera balls was held, with Emperor Franz Josef attending, and Strauss appeared at midnight to conduct the orchestra in some of his waltzes. His sensationally successful *The Gypsy Baron* (1885) marked the peak of what has later been called the golden era of Viennese operetta; a silver era with Franz Lehár and Emmerich Kálmán would follow.

An immensely popular actor, Alexander Girardi, played the Gypsy Baron, and Strauss, in the orchestra pit, would shake his jet-black mop of hair after yet another salvo of applause, and would call up to the stage, "Thank you, Xandl!" using the Viennese pet name for Alexander. The composer-conductor was notorious for dyeing his hair; he received so many letters begging him for a lock from his artist's head that he would soon have been bald, had he satisfied all his fans; his secretary mailed out snippets from the coat of his black poodle. "Xandl," on the other hand, impressed the Viennese by his favorite headgear, the straw boater, which today is still called locally the "Girardi hat." Girardi, whose father had been an Italian immigrant from the Dolomite Mountains, started out in Vienna as an apprentice in his father's trade, locksmithing, and later as an actor enchanted his audiences with his mastery of every subtle shade of the Viennese dialect.

Privately, the younger Strauss, who married three times, was not a particularly sunny person; he seemed a driven man, given to dark moods. His waltzes, polkas, and operettas nevertheless helped, like nothing else, to convince the world, and quite a few people in the Austrian capital itself, that Vienna was a place full of merriment and frivolity. The gaiety of Strauss and of such other composers of the era as Karl Millöcker and Franz von Suppé pleased a smug bourgeoisie that did not seem to care about lost wars, the mounting discontent of many ethnic groups in the empire, and the misery of hundreds of thousands of proletarians on Vienna's own outskirts.

The tunes in three-quarter time that were pouring out of the Austrian capital wafted around the globe, and people everywhere danced to them as a generation a century later would dance to the rock beat. The waltz has remained the jolly signature of Vienna. It welcomes the passengers of Austrian Airlines the moment they board their aircraft. Vienna radio stations play waltzes all the time. Music by the Strausses, Millöcker, von Suppé, and their contemporaries is heard at the New Year's concert of the Vienna Philharmonic, an annual media event with a worldwide audience of hundreds of millions. The waltz and *Die Fledermaus*—this is how many Viennese, and surely the local tourist industry, want their city to be perceived in the world at large. Maybe even some natives are convinced that is the way Vienna really is.

One Viennese, Hermann Broch, pointed out in an essay he wrote in America much later that the Strauss operettas lack the satire that Nestroy had cultivated, the sober acerbity that distinguishes also the operettas of Jacques Offenbach and of Gilbert and Sullivan. What was offered instead by the Strauss genre, Broch said, was "pure idiocy." Broch's essay also coined the fortunate phrase "joyful apocalypse" to characterize the Vienna of the 1880s.[1] One might add that the lilting merriness and mawkish sentimentalism of the Viennese waltz and the operettas of the "golden" and "silver" eras stem from the same gift for self-deception as the Ringstrasse architecture and the Makart parade of 1879—*Schmäh* fooling its own purveyors.

The Ringstrasse builders, Makart, and virtually all other recognized architects, sculptors, and painters of the epoch belonged to the Association of Visual Artists of Vienna, a group founded in 1861. One of its number, August Weber, designed a spacious exhibition hall in the Italian Renaissance style, the Künstlerhaus (Artists' House), which went up on a choice plot off the Ringstrasse, near the Court Opera, in 1868. The Künstlerhaus association organized shows, dominated Vienna's art market, and provided its members with useful contacts for obtaining lucrative commissions. The Viennese practice of *Protektion* was thriving in and around the Künstlerhaus, and the coffeehouses in the neighborhood buzzed with gossip about artists, models, critics, patrons, dealers, and collectors. The ruling faction in the Künstlerhaus and in the nearby Academy of Fine Arts—another Italian-Renaissance palace—was conservative; Makart was long their king.

Some Künstlerhaus affiliates were nevertheless interested in the new artistic currents in western Europe—Pre-Raphaelitism, Impressionism, Symbolism, and Art Nouveau—and advocated modernism and experimentation in Vienna. The critics of the prevailing conservatism at the Künstlerhaus and in the Art Academy faculty found encouragement by a literary coffeehouse group that in the 1890s became known as *Jung Wien* ("Young Vienna"), a coterie of writers and intellectuals who frequented the Café Griensteidl in the Michaeler Platz, near the imperial castle.

After a chain of coffeehouse cabals the revolt against Künstlerhaus historicism and naturalism and against Ringstrasse pomposity came into the open in April 1897 through a walkout of nineteen prominent members of the Association of Visual Artists. The secessionists were led by Gustav Klimt, a painter who had decorated important Ringstrasse buildings, and was backed by an already well-known architect, Otto Wagner. The Young Vienna clan lent literary and journalistic support. The rebel group founded a new Association of Visual Artists of Austria/Secession, with Klimt as its first president. Plenty of funds were offered by local patrons, including the industrialist Karl Wittgenstein, whose son Ludwig would become one of the twentieth century's great thinkers.

The new movement had soon its own exhibition building, known as the Secession. It was defiantly erected near the palace of the Art Academy by a disciple of Wagner, Josef Maria Olbrich. The windowless structure in Assyrian-Egyptian style, which got sunshine through skylights, was topped by a globe of gilded iron leaves that were supposed to represent laurel, and was promptly dubbed the "golden head of cabbage" by mockers. Inside there were movable partitions that could be adjusted according to the requirements of specific shows. A bronze group showing Mark Antony in a chariot drawn by lions, by the Secessionist sculptor Arthur Strasser, was placed outside at a corner of the unconventional building. An inscription over the entrance read, "To the Age Its Art—To Art Its Freedom."

JUGENDSTIL

The Secessionist group itself split later, and new modern-art factions organized their own separate exhibitions. The Viennese offshoot of the Art Nouveau movement in Europe took its name, Jugendstil ("youth style"), from a Munich magazine, *Jugend.* Its leading representatives were Klimt, Otto Wagner, and, a little later, the architects Josef Hoffmann and Adolf Loos and the painters Oskar Kokoschka and Egon Schiele. By 1908, Vienna's turn-of-the-century art revolution appeared to have triumphed when the imperial-royal postal administration commissioned a series of mail stamps commemorating the sixtieth anniversary of Emperor Franz Josef's accession to the throne to a Secessionist graphic designer, Koloman ("Kolo") Moser. Austria-Hungary's money bills also were soon in Jugendstil patterns. (The empire had introduced a new currency on January 1, 1900, issuing two crowns for each old florin.)

Otto Wagner wanted to do for twentieth-century Vienna what Baron

Haussmann had done for nineteenth-century Paris. Freeing himself from Ringstrasse pretentiousness, Wagner developed into a city planner on the grand scale, elaborating an architectural vocabulary that increasingly did away with decoration and stressed efficiency and functionalism. Wagner, the son of a Vienna notary, studied under van der Nüll and Siccardsburg, the Court Opera builders, at the Art Academy, and started putting up apartment houses and villas in the manner of historical-revival eclecticism.

A turning point in Wagner's career came in 1893 when he won a contest for a municipal development and transportation project. As chief architect of a new transit system, including the elevated and subway sections of a new belt railroad, he became absorbed in technical problems down to the shapes of nuts and bolts. Designing the bridges, tunnels, and stations of the new transportation network, he refined a utilitarian idiom that he sought to make aesthetically pleasing with Art Nouveau elements. One of Wagner's subway stations that is no longer in use, in the Karlsplatz near the Künstlerhaus, has been designated a historical landmark by the city; it is now a memorial like the Art Nouveau artifacts of the Métro in Paris.

As professor of architecture at the Art Academy from 1894 on, and in his writings, Wagner insisted that builders keep the purpose of the structures they had to erect foremost in mind. He himself presented an impressive achievement of the "new architecture" in his Postal Savings Office (1906), a building near the eastern prong of the Ringstrasse. It has a vast, functional cashiers' hall on the ground floor and outer walls covered with marble slabs fastened by aluminum bolts. Several Wagner apartment houses of his later period show a growing tendency to use Jugendstil ornaments sparingly and to stress practical sobriety.

Wagner's Church of the Hospital for Mental Diseases (1905–7) on the Steinhof, a slope on Vienna's western outskirts, is a textbook example of early use of modern style elements in a Roman Catholic sanctuary. A dome of gilded copper surmounts the edifice, visible from afar. The church itself has the form of a cross, its walls masked with white marble. Wagner also designed the Byzantine-inspired main altar and other fittings. The stained-glass windows are by Kolo Moser, the mail-stamp Secessionist. The church in the sprawling mental institution is a solemn cathedral for the insane, an emblematic landmark in a city where Freud and others were just then plumbing the human psyche. Musil would a few years later choose the Steinhof complex as setting for the haunting lunatic-asylum episodes of his *Man Without Qualities.*

Kolo Moser and Josef Hoffmann founded in 1903 a cooperative enterprise for design in the Secession spirit, which they called Wiener Werkstätte (Viennese Workshop). The Guild of Handicrafts in London's Essex House was the model for the undertaking, and an Anglophile industrialist, Fritz Wärndorfer, provided financial backing. The artists of the Wiener Werkstätte designed furniture, tableware, ceramics, metal and glass objects, book bindings, textiles, leatherware, jewelry, and occasionally clothes. The cooperative's craftsmen were, at least in the beginning, busy in bright workshops, maintaining close contact with the designers and customers. At one time, the Wiener Werkstätte even decorated an avant-garde cabaret, Fledermaus, on the Kärntnerstrasse in the city center, and furnished the costumes for its shows.

Early Wiener Werkstätte artifacts were characterized by a geometrical style, with straight lines and squares as a standard ornament. Elegance in simplicity was the trademark; black-white patterns often prevailed; inlaid work and mosaics found many applications. The Wiener Werkstätte also adopted the plainness of the neoclassical Biedermeier style in furniture that had been revived by the Vienna bentwood manufacturers Thonet Brothers and J. & J. Kohn. Influences from Expressionism, Cubism, and other advanced art currents, as well as fantastic shapes, lavish materials, and extravagant color combinations, came later. The Wiener Werkstätte was to survive World War I, was to open sales outlets in New York and Berlin in the 1920s, and would be forced by the Depression to go out of business in 1932. Products of the Viennese cooperative are today displayed in many museums. A veritable monument of the Wiener Werkstätte is represented by the lavish Art Nouveau villa that Hoffmann built and furnished for the Belgian financier Adolphe Stoclet in Brussels, the Palais Stoclet (1905–11).

MODERNIST SHOCKERS

The most uncompromising of Vienna's early twentieth-century architects was Adolf Loos, a friend of the satirist Karl Kraus and of the austere composer Arnold Schoenberg. The Viennese remember Loos above all—and maybe solely—as the builder of the "house without eyebrows" opposite the Michaeler Platz entrance to the imperial castle. Erected between 1909 and 1912 for the tailoring firm Goldman & Salatsch, the building caused a sensation that we have difficulty nowadays to understand. The "Loos House," with its plain walls and windows without any decoration, stares at the neo-Baroque facade of the Michaelertrakt of the Hofburg and its heroic statuary, put up only twenty years earlier, as if in defiance. Many critics at the time condemned the juxtaposition as a deliberate insult to Vienna's traditions and even to the emperor. Loos himself used to joke that he had accepted the commission as a means of settling his tailor bills. A fastidious dresser, he was in fact a customer of Goldman & Salatsch, and he was also notoriously incapable of managing money. When his wife at last opened a bank account for him after World War I, Loos never figured out how to use it properly.

The son of a sculptor who owned a stonecutting business in Brno, Moravia, Loos had visited the United States when he was twenty-three years old, and had done odd jobs for some time in Chicago, Philadelphia, and New York. Back in Austria, he apprenticed himself to a bricklayer and would for the rest of his life remain proud that he had thoroughly learned that trade. He later studied under Otto Wagner at the Vienna Art Academy, but would always bristle at being described as an architect. "I have more internal affinity with valets and beekeepers than with architects," he wrote back when the Association of Architects invited him to join.

Loos hated useless ornamentation; one of his essays was characteristically entitled "Ornament and Crime" (1908). He did not build much, wrote a little, and made a living mainly as an interior designer. He converted from the Jewish faith to Roman Catholicism and acted as Kraus's godfather when his friend followed his example. No all-out pacifist like Kraus, Loos volunteered for military service as an officer during World War I; afterward he played for some time a role in the housing program of Red Vienna, as will be shown later.

Vienna's fin-de-siècle moods—languor, eroticism, decadence, elitism, deepening anxiety, and search for new art forms—are epitomized by the later paintings of Gustav Klimt, the first Secession president. The son of a Viennese engraver and goldsmith, he had graduated from the Art Academy and shown a versatile talent in the Makart mode just in time to get commissions for helping to decorate some of the most sumptuous Ringstrasse buildings. With his brother Ernst, he contributed ceiling paintings and other frescoes to the grand staircases of the Burgtheater and the Museum of Art History. By age thirty, Klimt was considered a remarkable success. After the death of his brother in 1892, however, he dropped out of sight for some years. Klimt never talked much about himself and gave very few interviews; little is known about what he did before he led the Künstlerhaus rebellion in 1897 that resulted in the Secession. He seems to have read a lot during those years of withdrawal and to have immersed himself in the new art trends that were advancing in western Europe.

The first Secession show of Klimt works in 1898 caused astonishment, even scandal, among traditionalists. Controversy centered on the painting *Pallas Athena,* which represented the goddess of wisdom and patroness of the arts as an enigmatic "demon of the Secession," holding in her right hand a globe with a realistic nude female figure, Naked Truth. There was even more outrage when Klimt delivered three paintings—*Philosophy, Jurisprudence,* and *Medicine*—for the ceremonial hall of the new university building, commissioned in 1895 by the government's education department. Artistic and political conservatives joined forces in denouncing the panels as unacceptable: they combined dreamlike allegory with what was resented as crude naturalism in picturing female nudes. In *Medicine,* above all, a naked woman seeming to float in the air with a full view of her pubic hair and the equally nude figure of a pregnant woman were found by the critics to be aggressively obscene. More than eighty members of the university's faculty petitioned the government to reject the Klimt paintings. The writer Hermann Bahr and other intellectuals of the Young Vienna group came out in support of Klimt.

The embattled painter was ensconced in his studio in the garden-courtyard of an old residential building in the Josefstadt district near City Hall. At work he usually wore a dark blue cassock, cut like a long nightshirt, with his brindled pet cat often on his shoulder. His bald pate behind a tuft in front and his nimbus of hair on the sides gave him a faunlike appearance. A bachelor, Klimt was notorious for having affairs with many of the models who went in and out of his studio. He was rumored to have fathered at least a dozen children, most of them boys named Gustav, by various women he had painted.

At one point in the quarrel over the university paintings, Klimt withdrew them, but the government bureaucracy insisted he hand them over, although they had little chance of ever being mounted in the academic hall. Klimt threatened to use his revolver to defend the panels if policemen were sent to get them. At last he returned his fee (with borrowed money) to the government, to buy back the paintings. They were unfortunately destroyed toward the end of World War II in a fire in the castle where they had been stored. Some preparatory studies by the master still exist.

Later, Klimt developed a style of sensual aestheticism with mythical and exotic quotations, and the establishment made peace with him. When his painting *The Kiss* (1908) was first exhibited, the Austrian State Gallery purchased it at once, and the erotic icon became one of Klimt's most popular works. With its gold-textured background, it belongs to his "golden period," betraying the impression that the Byzantine mosaics of Ravenna had made on him when he visited the ancient city on the Adriatic Sea in 1903; reminiscences of his father's precious-metal workshop may also have reemerged.

During his golden period, Klimt painted the portraits of several Viennese society ladies, including the celebrated one of Adele Bloch-Bauer (1907), a dark orchid wrapped in ornamental gold on golden background. In his sultry *Salome* (1909), knowledgeable people thought they recognized a well-known beauty whom Klimt was believed to have already portrayed in his *Pallas Athena* eleven years earlier, Alma Schindler Mahler. She was the daughter of Emil J. Schindler, a landscape painter who suffered no lack of wealthy patrons but, because of his free-spending ways, was always oppressed by debts. After his death he got his own monument in the Stadtpark.

Alma first met Klimt when she was eighteen, and the painter, who was seventeen years her senior, was said to have fallen in love with her. Shapely Alma, a dilettante wanting to become an artist or a composer, was then just starting her gallery of famous men: she was having an affair with Alexander von Zemlinsky, her gnomish composition teacher (the mentor also of Arnold Schoenberg); she would marry Court Opera director Gustav Mahler, Walter Gropius, and Franz Werfel; and she would become the mistress of Oskar Kokoschka before adding more trophies to her amorous collection.

Kokoschka was twenty-one years old when he burst on the Vienna art scene as the wild man of a modern-art show in 1908. The Klimt group, which had split from the Secession in 1905, had organized the exhibition, called "Kunstschau," and Josef Hoffmann had built for it a cluster of temporary showrooms on a large grassy plot near the Künstlerhaus. Kokoschka's book illustrations, drawings, and paintings outraged visitors by their erotic expressionism, and the room where they were on display became quickly known as the "horror chamber." One critic wrote that according to Klimt that young man, Kokoschka, was talented, but "one wouldn't believe this at first and might think a savage had painted the stuff." The exhibition had a second edition as "Internationale Kunstschau" in 1909, when works by van Gogh, Matisse, and Munch were shown together with productions by local artists, again including Kokoschka.

The provocative young painter was the son of a Bohemian goldsmith. He was born in a small town on the Danube fifty miles west of Vienna, when his mother, who had grown up in the forests of Styria, was spending a rest period there. Kokoschka was brought up, in increasingly modest circumstances, on the capital's outskirts. He attended Vienna's arts and crafts school, and was already then able, like other students, to do work for the Wiener Werkstätte, the cooperative founded by Kolo Moser and Josef Hoffmann. Among other things, Kokoschka contributed designs for decorative picture postcards and for the Fledermaus cabaret. His early two-dimensional fairy-tale illustration style soon turned into a raw expressionism.

A play written by Kokoschka, *Mörder, Hoffnung der Frauen* (Murderer, Hope of Women), caused a scandal at the 1909 Kunstschau when it was performed on an open-air stage on the exhibition grounds. (It was later made into a short opera by Hindemith.) The brief drama's theme of lust and cruelty was illustrated by the author with ink drawings that have later been said to anticipate the Picasso of *Guernica*. The performance led to such a tumult that police were called to restore order.

To shock the philistines, Kokoschka had shaved his head. Among the few who took him seriously was Loos, and the two became lifelong friends. Through Loos, the young scandal-courting painter met Karl Kraus; the standoffish writer even permitted Kokoschka to portray him. By then, Kokoschka had developed a thoroughly personal manner, characterized by pointillism and bold brush strokes in garish colors; since his student days, he had signed all his works "OK." Restless in Vienna, he moved to Berlin and contributed there to the avant-garde magazine *Sturm,* received commissions for portraits, and for the first time made a little money.

At the 1909 Kunstschau, a nineteen-year-old artist had a small room to himself, his first exposure to the Viennese public. His name—Egon Schiele. He was to become one of the most powerful designers and painters of the early twentieth century. Schiele met Kokoschka a few times but was snubbed by him. The critics ignored the newcomer, whose portraits seemed to stamp him as just another follower of Klimt. According to one story, Schiele had indeed got encouragement from the former Secession leader. Still a student, Schiele is supposed to have one day called on Klimt with samples of his works. "Do I have talent?" he asked. "Much too much," the older man replied.

Schiele was born in Tulln, a Danubian town less than twenty miles northwest of Vienna. His father, the town's stationmaster, was pensioned off early, apparently owing to his increasingly odd behavior, and he died eventually of progressive paralysis, then a frequent consequence of poorly treated syphilis. Egon therefore grew up in the care of his mother and an uncle who was acting as his legal guardian. Against the uncle's will, he entered the Vienna Art Academy, passing its admission test at the age of sixteen. From the beginning, he seems to have been obsessed by the female body; he drew portraits of both his sisters, one four years older than he and the other four years his junior, in the nude with painstaking attention to anatomical details.

An accomplished draftsman at an early age, Schiele never used or needed an eraser. At the Art Academy he was nevertheless considered a mediocre student and obtained just passing grades. Like many of his classmates, he started frequenting the coffeehouses near their school and came to know major artists and critics at least by sight. At eighteen he had his first show—landscapes mostly—in the abbey of Klosterneuburg (Emperor Karl VI's ersatz Escorial), just outside Vienna. The exhibition for local talent—the Schieles were then living nearby—was sponsored by a prelate, Friedrich Gustav Piffl, who would later become Archbishop of Vienna and a cardinal. One collector with sure instincts became interested in Schiele even then and started buying works by him.

Soon after the 1909 Kunstschau, Schiele attracted also the attention of such leading modernists as Josef Hoffmann and Otto Wagner and of the art critic of the Social Democratic Party newspaper *Arbeiter-Zeitung,* Arthur Roessler. They got him commissions for portraits, and the young artist seems to have produced enough erotic drawings to make a living. At the International Hunting Exhibition in Vienna in 1910, he was represented by a female nude with her arms spread out. At the inauguration, Emperor Franz Josef glanced at the picture, turned away, and muttered, "This is quite awful."

During the following years Schiele took up with a former Klimt model, Wally Neuzil, and lived with her in various places. She appears to have helped him get pubescent girls to pose for him, which meant courting trouble. The couple were virtually run out of the hometown of Schiele's mother, Krumlov in Bohemia. In Neulengbach, a large village in the hills twenty miles west of Vienna, the artist was arrested in 1912 on charges of sex offenses involving a girl under fourteen. He spent twenty-four days in detention and eventually got a sentence of three days' imprisonment for having shown pornographic material to a minor, whereas a charge of sexual molestation was dropped after the girl in court retracted earlier testimony. During his weeks in prison Schiele turned out a series of watercolors showing his chair, his bed, his water jug, and an orange that he described as "the only light" in his cell. The pictures are now treasured by the famous Albertina gallery in Vienna.

Schiele had by then found his own angular and seemingly tortured style of probing intensity. His figures, alone or entwined, often without any paraphernalia on the canvas, seem defenseless, exposed to his merciless scrutiny. His many self-portraits attest to his angst-ridden preoccupation with himself. He also wrote poetry in free verse in which the many color adjectives, not surprisingly, indicate the predominance of visual elements in his perception.

In 1915, Schiele married one of two pretty sisters who were living across the street from his attic studio in the Hietzinger Hauptstrasse; he had paid much attention to both of them in a curious window-and-mail courtship. His wife, Edith Harms, three years his junior, had to put up with much. The convent-educated young woman often posed in the nude for her husband and soon acquiesced also in his employing professional and occasional models again. One of the latter told a friend that she did not really like to sit for Schiele because "he is interested in one thing only." The painter's wife was adamant, however, in barring his longtime mistress, Wally Neuzil, from his studio; Wally died in 1917 of scarlet fever in a Dalmatian military hospital where she was serving as a nurse.

In March 1918, Schiele was able to exhibit nineteen works in a Secession show, achieving a resounding success. He was acknowledged as Vienna's leading painter, Klimt having died a month earlier. But Schiele himself would have only half a year to live.

CAFÉ MEGALOMANIA

Modernism in the visual arts was, as has been mentioned, from the beginning supported by several literati belonging to the clique known as Young Vienna. They acted as intellectual brokers between the avant-garde painters, designers, and architects, on the one hand, and, on the other, their public—wealthy patrons, collectors, and eventually museum officials and other members of the state bureaucracy.

Particular influence was wielded by Hermann Bahr, a protean coffee-house sage with a long beard, who over the next few decades would play many different literary roles. When he returned to Austria from a sojourn in Paris in the late 1880s, he told the art critic Bertha Zuckerkandl, the Viennese were not just sleeping but snoring, and "I am going to wake them up." He was soon the ranking *maître à penser* at the Café Grien-steidl, where the progressive intelligentsia of the Austrian capital had its headquarters until the place was torn down and its patrons migrated to the Café Central and other coffeehouses.

To outsiders and critics, the Griensteidl was the "Café Grössenwahn" (Café Megalomania). None of its detractors was more biting than Karl Kraus, who had himself been a hawk-eyed regular of the place for some time. The satirist was to carry on a lifelong campaign against Bahr, whom he often called "the gentleman from Linz." The virtual leader of Young Vienna who ever since his stay in Paris affected big-city ways, had indeed been born in Linz, in 1865. The name of the Danubian city rhymes with the German word *Provinz* ("province"), and to a Viennese it conveyed a sense of semirural parochialism and stuffiness. (While Bahr was pontificating in Vienna coffeehouses, the young Adolf Hitler flunked out of high school in Linz. He would nevertheless love the city all his life and promise to make it a cultural center of his Third Reich.)

Bahr wrote ten novels, forty plays, and innumerable essays, reviews, and fluffy feuilletons. Greedy for novelty, he was always looking out for new intellectual and artistic trends, which earned him the nickname "the Man of the Day After Tomorrow." A Pan-Germanic nationalist during his student days in Vienna, he was for a few years entranced by French symbolism and the *décadents,* and championed Oscar Wilde, Ibsen, and Strindberg in literature, the Secession and Jugendstil in the visual arts, and Mahler and Schoenberg in music. In 1909 he married the Court

Opera soprano Anna von Mildenburg, who had once been a protégée of Cosima Wagner, the composer's wife, and in Hamburg had between 1895 and 1897 been a very good friend—probably more than that—of a promising young conductor, Gustav Mahler. After his marriage, Bahr who had affected free-thinking ways, began leaning again toward Roman Catholicism and in 1914 became a ranting war propagandist. And Kraus kept goading him all the time, charging Bahr with turgid writing, bad taste, and the changeability of a chameleon.

The "gentleman from Linz" was already a celebrity when a young Jewish doctor joined the Young Vienna group—Arthur Schnitzler. He was a son of the Ringstrasse laryngologist who had come from a small Hungarian town and worked his way up to a Vienna University professorship and chief of its medical school. The two sons of Professor Johann Schnitzler became physicians, too, but Arthur, the older one, soon drifted into literature, turned into a coffeehouse and theater habitué, and indulged in gambling bouts. Elegant and handsome with his dark goatee, he was also a redoubtable skirt-chaser.

Not yet thirty, he began writing a series of seven one-act plays with the narcissistic, lazy, and sometimes melancholic philanderer Anatol as the protagonist. The "sweet girl" from the suburbs and other women on the stage were brilliantly characterized. During those years Schnitzler lived very much like the decadent hero of his plays, letting his mother and her servants take care of his physical comfort and conducting his many affairs, with their epilogues in hotels or rented rooms. In 1894, when he was thirty-two, the Burgtheater accepted one of his plays, *Liebelei* (Flirtation; usually called *Light o' Love* or *Game of Love)* and at its premiere a year later an archduke was in the imperial box.

Liebelei is still performed by German-language theaters from time to time. It and the *Anatol* cycle of short plays have become emblematic of the hedonism, frivolity, and underlying angst of an affluent sector of Viennese society at the turn of the century and of the mentality of the people of more modest circumstances, like the "sweet girl" and her relatives, who came in touch with it.

The portrayal on the stage of what was then called "free love" outraged conservatives; yet, Schnitzler was looking for more trouble. During only six days in 1900 he wrote a novella, *Leutnant Gustl,* that, with the then new technique of the interior monologue, described the agonies of an army officer who is insulted by a baker. Nobody else has witnessed the scene, but the lieutenant, unable to challenge the chunky baker to a duel because of the difference in social class, convinces himself that he cannot in good conscience wear his uniform anymore and that suicide is the only way out. When he learns that the baker has died in an accident, he feels relief: I'm off the hook. The story, with its exposure of the archaic mentality of the officers' caste, caused displeasure in military circles. The proarmy newspaper *Reichswehr* attacked Schnitzler, and when he failed to conform with the officers' code of honor by challenging the author of the criticism to a duel, the army deprived him of his rank as a reserve lieutenant in the medical corps.

In 1903, Schnitzler married his mistress of four years, Olga Gussmann, by whom he already had a son. In 1908, a long novel on which he had been working for several years, *Der Weg ins Freie* (The Road Toward Freedom), came out, providing a panorama of Vienna's society at the beginning of the twentieth century. It portrayed various types of Jewish Viennese, but largely ignored orthodox and proletarian Jews, whom Schnitzler hardly knew. The book is relevant because some of the century's outstanding Jewish thinkers, including Martin Buber, Theodor Herzl, and Sigmund Freud, were then living in Vienna while anti-Semitism was surging.

By the time he was fifty, in 1912, Schnitzler was the most frequently performed playwright in the German-speaking countries, and several of his works had been translated and were being produced in faraway places. He had bought a villa in the posh "Cottage District" on Vienna's northwestern outskirts from the renowned court actress Hedwig Bleibtreu and was leading an intense social life. His friends were above all fellow literati, but "friendship" did not necessarily mean personal closeness: one saw others at the coffeehouse or tried out unpublished works on them in private readings. "Friends?" one of the writers of the Schnitzler set, Richard Beer-Hofmann, said. "We just don't get on each other's nerves."

MEN OF PRECIOUS LETTERS

One Viennese man of letters was for some years quite intimate with Schnitzler and would stay on affectionate terms with him to the end of his life, the poet Hugo von Hofmannsthal. He is today known above all as a librettist for Richard Strauss. Hofmannsthal, born in 1874, was almost twelve years younger than Schnitzler, but the two hit it off marvelously right from the beginning and made long bicycle trips to Switzerland and Italy together just as the first automobiles were appearing on Europe's highways.

The young Hofmannsthal had written a few verses as an introduction to a collection of Schnitzler's *Anatol* playlets that the author had had printed at his own expense. Those verses have since then been quoted over and over as an epitaph of fin-de-siècle Vienna:

Also spielen wir Theater
Spielen unsre eignen Stücke
Frühgereift und zart und traurig
Die Komödie unsrer Seele.

Thus we are playing theater
Playing our own pieces
Premature and delicate and sad
The comedy of our soul.

As in lyric poetry in general, the word *music,* with its evasive overtones, gets lost in translation if the exact sense is to be given, or the meaning escapes the translator if an attempt is made to render the mood and melody.

The early maturity evoked by Hofmannsthal in his verses for *Anatol* was above all his own, though comparable to that of Keats. His first poems and essays were signed "Loris" the first name of the Russian general Melikow who had died a few years earlier; Hofmannsthal needed a pseudonym because he was then a sixteen-year-old high school student and, as such, was not supposed to be published. Hermann Bahr has often recalled how he met "Loris" for the first time. The leader of Young Vienna had been struck by an elegantly perceptive criticism of one of his writings that had appeared under that pseudonym. Bahr expected the author to be a Frenchman, or at least a Viennese who had long lived in Paris, between forty and fifty years old. He was stunned when a boy "with a girl's eyes" was introduced to him as Loris at the Café Griensteidl. At about the same time, Schnitzler recorded his first encounter with Hofmannsthal in his diary: "Knowledge, clarity, and, it seems, genuine artistry; it is unheard-of at that age." For the first time in his life, he had had the feeling of having met a genius, Schnitzler told Stefan Zweig.

Still a student at the Academic Gymnasium, an elite high school, Hofmannsthal was, at age seventeen, an acknowledged poet, besieged for contributions by newspapers and magazines. The school ostensibly kept ignoring the success of Loris, but unofficially basked in it, and many others among its students started writing verses, too, though with less-convincing results. A young German poet who had come from Stéphane Mallarmé's circle in Paris, Stefan George, sent Hofmannsthal a bunch of red roses into his classroom by one of Vienna's public messengers, to the huge amusement of the other boys. While Hofmannsthal's classmates were grappling with Latin and Greek verbs, the young paragon produced polished translations from Sophocles; he also spoke French, Italian, and English.

Hofmannsthal had never attended elementary school. The only child of a bank official, he had been carefully prepared for the Academic Gymnasium by private tutors and had learned a lot of other things beside. He had a Jewish great-grandfather, Isaak Löw Hofmann, who had moved from Prague to Vienna in 1788, had promoted the silk trade in the eastern lands of the Habsburg monarchy, had headed the capital's Jewish community for some time, and had eventually been raised to hereditary nobility by Emperor Ferdinand I. Hofmannsthal's grandfather, also in the silk business, had converted to Roman Catholicism before marrying a Milanese countess. The poet was dark, brown-eyed, delicate, and Italianate, and all his life, he affected a slightly nasal upper-class Viennese dialect that contrasted with the formal perfection of his verses and prose in standard German.

He wrote various lyrical plays, gradually turning away from his early aestheticism. At age twenty-seven he married the daughter of a bank director, Gertrud ("Gerty") Schlesinger, and went to live in Rodaun, a village near the southern outskirts of Vienna. The house that the Hofmannsthals inhabited for many years went back to the time of Empress Maria Theresa and was said to have been built by a Prince Trautsohn for his mistress. Thomas Mann, Rainer Maria Rilke, Richard Strauss, and many other noted personages would at one time or another be guests at the Rodaun villa and admire its frescoes, stuccoed ceilings, Rococo-style ceramic stoves, and terraced garden with many fruit trees.

In 1906, Richard Strauss asked Hofmannsthal whether he could use the poet's free adaptation of Sophocles' *Elektra.* Hofmannsthal consented, and a long collaboration developed. Years later, however, Hofmannsthal wrote in a letter that he would feel more comfortable if he were working with a composer "less famous but closer to my heart, better attuned to my thinking."[2]

A high point in the cooperation between the Viennese writer and the Bavarian composer was *Der Rosenkavalier* (1911). Hofmannsthal's "comedy for music" pretends to depict the era of Empress Maria Theresa when one of her armies stood in the Netherlands and an imperial field marshal was able to take time off to hunt the bear and the lynx in the Balkans while dalliance and adultery enlivened the palaces of the capital. A woman singer plays the role of a young nobleman, Octavian Maria Ehrenreich Bonaventura Fernand Hyazinth, Count Rofrano, who lards his refined Viennese dialect with French and Italian phrases. When *Der Rosenkavalier,* after its world premiere in Dresden, was first performed at the Court Opera, the Viennese critics savaged it, contending, among other things, that its waltzes were anachronistic, that the dance was still unknown under Maria Theresa. The public nevertheless loved the glorification of a Baroque Vienna that may have never existed quite the way Hofmannsthal represented it, in an idiom that he had invented and that had probably never been spoken in reality. *Der Rosenkavalier* has become one of the most popular operas of the Vienna repertoire. Hofmannsthal, it is true, is supposed to have sighed much later, "How nice it would be if Lehár had composed the music for *Rosenkavalier* instead of Strauss."[3]

Hofmannsthal was an ardent patriot all his life. In 1912 he publicly broke with Gabriele D'Annunzio, whom he had once admired, after the Italian poet and nationalist had attacked Emperor Franz Josef and Austria-Hungary.

A despairing patriot in his own way, another Viennese writer, Robert Musil, resolved around that time to portray the fatuity and repressed strains of early twentieth-century Vienna in a large novel, *The Man Without Qualities;* critics would compare it later to the masterpieces of Joyce and Proust. Musil had already attracted attention, even stirred a minor literary scandal, in 1906 with a slim volume, *Die Verwirrungen des Zöglings Törless* (published in English as *Young Törless).* The novella is, on its face, a study of adolescent homosexuality and sadism in a military junior college of the Habsburg empire, but at a deep level loom disquieting questions about authoritarianism and the limits of rational thinking. The respected *Berliner Zeitung* devoted six columns to an admiring review by Alfred Kerr, then the "literary pope" of the German capital. Austrian military circles, instead, were miffed by *Törless*.

Musil's first book was in part autobiographical. The author had been twelve years old when his mother had persuaded his father, a professor at the Polytechnic College in Brünn (now Brno), to bundle the boy off to a military institution in Hungary. Two years later he was transferred to another such military school—which he was to describe as "hellish"—in Moravia. The pretty, vivacious mother had her reasons to want the teenager out of the way: a male "house friend," in all likelihood her lover, was living with her and her husband in the same apartment, and she seems to have also had other affairs. The "house friend"—since the Biedermeier period, a recurrent figure in bourgeois Viennese family life and a stock character in popular comedy—has always meant semipublic, or even institutionalized, adultery; observers of the Viennese scene will be able to spot house-friend situations around any *Heurige* table in the suburbs even today.

Musil would always nurse a grudge—not so much against his mother as against his father. The professor does not seem to have deserved such hard feelings; whenever his wife ordered a birching of the boy, the elder Musil usually first soaked the twigs in water so that they would not hurt very much, and he provided financial support until his son was thirty. Musil, who held degrees in engineering and philosophy, also got his first job through his father, but served in the post—a librarian at the Vienna Polytechnic—only for three years, always complaining about the "intolerable, murderous" office routine the way many Viennese intellectuals in the bureaucracy have always done. He married a divorced woman from Berlin almost seven years his senior (a mother substitute?), took several leaves of absence, and eventually resigned from his library job.

Like virtually all Viennese literati, Musil read *Die Fackel* (The Torch) regularly. Like most of his fellow writers, Musil also detested the magazine's acerbic publisher, editor in chief, and (after 1909) sole contributor, Karl Kraus. Musil had probably met "Fackel Kraus" at one of the coffeehouses both frequented, but neither felt the urge to deepen the acquaintance.

A large part of the Vienna intelligentsia had chosen to ostracize Kraus after he dared in his 1896 pamphlet *The Demolished Literature* to ridicule the pretensions of the Young Vienna coterie. A few friends of Arthur Schnitzler's, including the writer Felix Salten, the author of

Bambi, had ambushed the young Kraus and administered a beating to him. In 1899, Kraus, the son of a well-to-do paper manufacturer, started *Die Fackel,* and sold thirty thousand copies of the magazine's first number. The German poet Richard Dehmel, the playwrights August Strindberg and Frank Wedekind, the café essayist Peter Altenberg, and others were contributors during the publication's first few years—until, that is, Kraus decided to write *Die Fackel* all by himself, as if it were an intellectual diary. Until his death in 1936, Kraus produced 922 issues, some of them bunched together in fat volumes. A complete set of the magazine, bound in its original red paper covers, is today a collector's dream.

One recurrent theme of Kraus's writings is criticism of Vienna: "My hatred of this city is not love gone astray; rather, I have discovered a completely new way of finding it intolerable." Kraus was one of the many intellectuals who were always railing at Vienna yet would never leave it. His main preoccupation was with language, "the mother, not the maid, of thought."

Kraus forever exposed the venality, bombast, and sham in contemporary writing, especially in Vienna's chatty newspapers. He denounced cultural corruption through merchandising, and banned advertisements from his magazine. One regrets that the great satirist died before the coming of television. Kraus's many enemies charged him with monumental vanity—which he obliquely admitted—as well as with enviousness, monomaniacal worry about words, and Jewish self-hatred; indeed, quite a few of his polemics sounded anti-Semitic.

This nemesis of sloppy writers was born in Jičin, northeastern Bohemia, in 1874. The family moved soon to Vienna, where the young Kraus attended school and dabbled in the theater. While an older brother was taking care of the family enterprise, including a paper factory east of Vienna, Kraus was soon self-supporting. A lifelong bachelor, Kraus was close to few people in Vienna, among them Adolf Loos and Oskar Kokoschka. Kraus liked Altenberg, as noted, and professed admiration for Otto Weininger, that tragic figure who shot himself in 1903, at age twenty-three, in the house on the Schwarzspanier Strasse where Beethoven had died.

Weininger, the son of a goldsmith, had suddenly become famous in the year of his suicide through an enlarged version of his doctoral dissertation, *Sex and Character: A Fundamental Inquiry.* From the thesis that every personality contains male and female elements in varying proportion, Weininger derived antifeminist and anti-Semitic conclusions. He has long since become one of the chief figures in the literature on Jewish self-disparagement. Weininger knew Sigmund Freud and had probably learned of his ideas about the bisexuality in every human being even before meeting him.

FREUD IN THE HOUSE OF ATONEMENT

"No other thinker of the 20th century, Austrian or otherwise, has so impregnated contemporary consciousness, permeating every facet of economic, social and intellectual life" as Freud.[4] At the beginning of the century, the founder of psychoanalysis was known only to a small circle. His *Traumdeutung* (Interpretation of Dreams) was brought out by the textbook publisher Franz Deuticke in Vienna at the end of 1899 (with the portentous date "1900"), but only 123 copies were sold in the first six weeks. It took another seven years before the entire first printing, all of six hundred copies, had found buyers. Like Mozart and many lesser figures in the arts and sciences who are today identified with Vienna, Freud did not care for the city and often voiced disgust with it. Yet, he stayed on through all his creative years and did not want to leave, as will be seen, even when the Nazis were marching in the streets and raided his home.

Freud's father, Jakob, was born in Galicia in the far northeast of the Habsburg empire, and his mother, Amalia ("Malka") Nathanson, in Odessa, on the Black Sea. The father came from an orthodox Jewish family and was in the wool trade. The Freuds moved to Freiberg (now Příbor) in Moravia, where Sigismund was born on May 6, 1856. As a student, Sigismund would shorten his first name to Sigmund, but for his doting mother he would remain her "golden Sigi." The Freuds went to live in Vienna when the boy was three years old. After doing very well in high school, the young Freud studied medicine at the University of Vienna and graduated, somewhat belatedly because of research work, at age twenty-five. Four years later he became an instructor in neuropathology in the university's medical department. A grant enabled him to do post-graduate work in Paris under Jean Martin Charcot, a specialist in nervous diseases, in 1885; the year afterward Freud married Martha Bernays of Hamburg.

The young couple lived first in the House of Atonement, a fake

Gothic edifice that Emperor Franz Josef had had built by the architect of City Hall, Friedrich von Schmidt, on the site of a theater that had burned down in 1881. Anton Bruckner, who was then living opposite the theater, had witnessed the catastrophic fire, which caused 386 deaths. When the Freuds' first child, Mathilde, was born in 1887, an aide-de-camp of the emperor brought flowers and a letter with Franz Josef's congratulations on the first appearance of new life in a place where so many persons had perished.

In 1891 the young doctor and his family moved to a second-floor apartment at the lower end of a sloping street five blocks to the north of the Ringstrasse and the House of Atonement. It would remain Freud's residence for forty-six years, an address that for Freudians everywhere took on a hallowed ring: Berggasse 19, Vienna IX. The neighborhood is within walking distance of the main building of the university on the Ringstrasse and major medical institutions. Later Freud rented three more rooms, looking out on a small garden, on the ground floor of the Berggasse building, to use as a waiting room, consulting room, and study. In 1908 he gave up the ground-floor premises and, from then on, would see his patients in the professional area of his vast second-floor apartment —a separate entrance, a hall, a waiting room, an office, and a library.

Freud was named extraordinary (associate) professor in the university's medical department in 1902, and on October 13 of that year, he appeared before Emperor Franz Josef in a formal audience to thank him, as was the custom, for the appointment. He would never attain a full professorship. (When the government of the Austrian Republic in 1920 conferred on Freud the honorary title of ordinary, or full, professor he had already ceased giving academic lectures.) Anti-Semitism has been blamed for this lack of official recognition of Freud's scientific achievements, but this explanation must be qualified. "The number of eminent professors of medicine, of heads of clinics, and famous specialists, of Jewish extraction was strikingly high" in Vienna at the beginning of the twentieth century, Ilse Barea has pointed out. "The fact makes nonsense of the notion that Freud, for the mere reason of his being a Jew, did not stand a good chance of an academic career."[5] What caused the persistent diffidence of the Vienna medical establishment, which included many Jewish scientists, was mainly the circumstance that Freud developed his psychoanalytical school and movement completely outside the university structure and that it seemed to take on a cultist character.

In 1902, Freud started his famous Wednesday Society, informal gatherings of psychologists who shared his ideas. The Vienna Psychoanalytical Society grew out of the Wednesday meetings in 1908 and two years later became the International Psychoanalytical Association. Rivalries, dissent, and apostasies bedeviled the movement almost from the beginning. Alfred Adler, a Vienna physician who had attended the early Wednesday meetings, went his own way and founded the school of individual psychology. Carl Gustav Jung, the son of a Swiss Protestant minister and the first president of the International Psychoanalytical Association, broke with Freud in 1913.

Abroad, psychologists denied the universal validity of Freud's discoveries and theories, contending that Vienna was a very special environment. An American scientist, Allen Starr, in an address to the Neurological Section of the New York Academy of Medicine denounced Freud as "a typical Viennese libertine." Members of the International Psychoanalytical Association suggested that the organization's headquarters be moved from Vienna to Zurich. Freud, in a letter to a Hungarian follower, Sandor Ferenczi, ridiculed what he described as the notion that "Viennese sensuality is not found anywhere else." He added, "Between the lines you can read further that we Viennese are not only swine but also Jews!"[6]

In Vienna itself, detractors of Freud abounded; their deepest motives may have been not anti-Semitism but a desire to repress the phenomena and syndromes that he had bared. Of the many aphorisms that Karl Kraus crafted, probably the most famous is his assertion that "psychoanalysis is the mental disease whose therapy it believes itself to be."

Freud was very Viennese in some of his traits and un-Viennese in others. He liked to play tarok—an old card game popular throughout Austria-Hungary—with three friends in the few hours of relaxation he allowed himself. Whenever he did not have to skip his constitutional, he would walk the entire length of the Ringstrasse at a rapid pace, as quite a few spry natives of the city did, and still do. He was jealous of his privacy, and even secretive, the way many of his fellow residents were. At the same time, he was a bit of a gossip who did not find it easy to keep someone else's secrets, which is particularly surprising in a physician. According to Ernest Jones, "he had indeed the reputation of being distinctly indiscreet."[7]

He spent many of his summer vacations in the Alps, especially in the South Tyrol and, like other visiting Viennese, would dress up in a Tyrolean costume with a chamois brush on his green hat. Freud's hobby was hunting for mushrooms (a psychoanalytical clue?); the scarcity of mushrooms in the Vienna Woods seems to have been a reason for his dislike of the green hills near the city, although his children loved them. He was an accomplished writer who set forth his thoughts in a German distinguished by great power and inventiveness, and he often declared his preference for what he called the suppleness of the Viennese idiom.

In the original, Freud's writings are those of a highly erudite, polished, and articulate Viennese essayist of his time; even the best translation loses some of the flavor. Bruno Bettelheim, the Viennese psychoanalyst who survived the Dachau and Buchenwald concentration camps and immigrated to the United States, has pointed out that Freud's eloquent style has in English turned into a jargon peppered with "ego," "id," and "cathexis," and that where Freud wrote about "the soul's activities," the English-speaking Freudians discuss "mental processes."[8]

It was quite un-Viennese that Freud rarely went to the theater and that he had little use for music. He nevertheless met the dominant musical figure of his early years, Gustav Mahler, in 1910, less than a year before the conductor-composer was to die. Mahler, back from the United States, had asked to see the founder of psychoanalysis, and after some telegrams were exchanged, a meeting with Freud, then on a long vacation tour, could be arranged in Leiden, the Netherlands. Mahler unburdened himself for a few hours, and Freud, who normally would see patients for many sessions over years, exceptionally gave the musician an instant diagnosis: "You are looking for your mother in every woman." This, at least, is how Mahler's widow reported what she had been told about the Leiden meeting; Freud himself wrote much later about Mahler's *Mutterbindung* ("mother-bond") in a letter to a disciple.

MAHLER'S VIENNA

Mahler's mother was a small woman who, because of a congenital defect, limped; she patiently endured her husband's insensitiveness and bore him twelve children (half of them died in infancy or early childhood). Mahler's father, Bernhard, sold liquor and later owned a small distillery. The future composer was born in the village of Kališt in Moravia, but the family soon moved to the nearby town of Jihlava (Iglau), about halfway between Vienna and Prague, then a German-speaking enclave in a Czech-language area. Young Mahler showed his talent early, and a well-situated family friend persuaded his father to send the fifteen-year-old boy to the Music Conservatory in Vienna. Mahler would later speak of the imperial city as his *Heimat,* the place where he really felt at home.

Until his twenty-third year, Mahler lived in Vienna, except during vacation visits to Jihlava and, later, during his first professional assignments in provincial cities. The music student received financial support from his father, but it was never enough, and he gave piano lessons to earn a few extra florins. Mahler may have had more addresses in Vienna than Beethoven or Schubert did, usually sharing his lodgings with some fellow student. One of those who, off and on, roomed with Mahler was a budding musician from a town in the south of the monarchy, now Slovenj Gradec in Yugoslavia, by the name of Hugo Wolf. A protest against a plodding teacher led to Wolf's expulsion from the conservatory, but he remained Mahler's friend.

Wolf was the embodiment of the adulation that surrounded Richard Wagner then. Once, when the German composer in his extravagance had rented no fewer than seven rooms at the Imperial Hotel, young Wolf would wait for hours outside in the ice cold to catch a glimpse of his idol and maybe open the door of Wagner's carriage; then Wolf would outrun the horses to the nearby Court Opera and again open the carriage door for the master. Eventually Wolf became, in capricious spurts of creativity, one of the greatest of lieder composers, but he would remain disappointed in the hope that his friend Mahler, by then Court Opera director, might produce his opera *Der Corregidor.* Wolf died in a Vienna lunatic asylum, aged forty-three; later the Court Opera did get around to performing his only opera.

Another one of Mahler's friends in Vienna, Anton Bruckner, was thirty-five years his senior and a professor at the Music Conservatory. The two shared admiration for Wagner and distaste for the romanticism of Johannes Brahms. At the time the Jewish student Mahler and the devoutly Roman Catholic Professor Bruckner were periodically meeting in some tavern for a snack and a stein of beer, musical Vienna was split into feuding Wagnerian and Brahmsian camps. Bruckner, the son of a schoolteacher in Upper Austria, had for fourteen years served as an organist at the cathedral in Linz; he had come to the imperial capital at age forty-four. Bruckner was forever revising his mammoth symphonies, with their huge blocks of sound. After Bruckner's death in 1896, Mahler would often conduct his works, but considerable time was to elapse before they became a part of the international concert repertoire.

Mahler was not yet twenty-one years old when he signed a contract as kapellmeister at the civic theater in Laibach (today Ljubljana in Yugoslavia), not far from the hometown of his friend Hugo Wolf. During the following years he held conducting jobs in theaters and opera houses in Olomouc, Kassel, Prague, Leipzig, Budapest, and Hamburg. As a far-sighted strategist, he built a coalition of supporters who would eventually maneuver him into the position he really wanted—the directorship of the Vienna Court Opera.

One influential Hungarian political figure whom he had impressed during his stint at the Budapest opera house, Count Albert Apponyi, proved a great help in getting Mahler the Vienna appointment. In a formal application for the Court Opera post in 1896, Mahler wrote in a postscript that "in view of the present situation in Vienna I don't deem it superfluous to mention that I have, in accordance with an old project, converted to Catholicism a considerable time ago."[9] Alma Mahler was later to write that her husband "was a Christian believer" who would not pass a church without entering it. Others have suggested that for Mahler the Vienna opera house was "well worth a mass," as another famous convert, King Henry IV of France, is supposed to have said about Paris. (Mahler, incidentally, never composed a mass.) He already had three symphonies, many lieder, and other music to his credit when he was named deputy director of the Court Opera in 1897; a few months later he was the director of the institution. He was thirty-seven years old and would remain in charge of the opera house for ten years, a brilliant period in Vienna's musical history.

Mahler's younger brother Otto, for whose education in Vienna he had been paying, had shot himself in 1895. The twenty-two-year-old suicide had left a note: "I no longer like to live, I am returning my admission ticket." Gustav Mahler at the time seemed to have no doubt that the price he had to pay for *his* ticket was not too high.

A famous dictum by Mahler as Court Opera director was that "tradition is *Schlamperei.*" From the beginning he strove to impose stern discipline on singers, musicians, and audiences. The names of conductors—even when they were Mahler himself, Hans Richter, Franz Schalk, or Bruno Walter—were not mentioned in posters and programs. In the interest of ensemble performances, he fought the star system that earlier directors had favored, and requested solo singers to sign pledges that they would not pay the claque. Rent-an-applause was a venerable institution, and its leaders had routinely been given a number of free gallery tickets by earlier opera directors; Mahler stopped that practice. The claque nevertheless survived in barely masked clandestinity. (Between the two world wars there were two rival claques in the State Opera. After the Nazi takeover, the leader of the "gallery claque," Josef Schostal, emigrated to New York and continued his old line at the Metropolitan Opera; the chief of the more aggressive "pit claque," Otto Stieglitz, remained in Vienna and was killed by the Nazis.)

Mahler, during his many exhausting rehearsals, insisted on faithful execution of a composer's directions. He would often leap from his pulpit to some empty chair in the bass violins' section and from there up to the stage to make a point to a singer. According to one (unverified) story, it seems he chased a delinquent tenor all the way backstage, and when the frightened singer locked himself into a toilet, the director pummeled at the door, shouting, "And a *coward* you are, too!" (Up to this day there are backstage toilets in the State Opera, marked "For Soloists Only.")

The easygoing ways of Vienna's operagoers irritated Mahler. Habitués had long regarded the house as their salon, greeting one another and chatting from box to box during the overture, unconcerned about people arriving late. Mahler ordered lights out and all doors closed before the first notes were heard; latecomers had to await the end of the first act in the corridors outside. Whenever Mahler, before raising his baton, heard a whisper or a cough from the audience, he turned around, and through his sparkling eyeglasses glowered at the section where the offense had been committed. Opera personnel and operagoers soon denounced the short, dark, sharp-faced director as a pedant and a dictator.

To Mahler, the Court Opera was not a glorified Viennese coffeehouse with music but an artistic shrine. To deepen the reverent atmosphere, he ordered the orchestra pit to be lowered so that the lights for the musicians would not be visible to the audience. He called one of the Secession artists, Alfred Roller, as stage designer to the opera house, and their cooperation resulted in a series of memorable productions, beginning with a *Tristan* in 1903 that won wide acclaim. Roller introduced new lighting effects and explored the technical possibilities that electricity had opened; admirers spoke of a "music of light." The Court Opera under the Mahler-Roller team became an exciting place where full houses were the rule.

In 1901, Mahler met Alma Schindler in the apartment of Emil Zuckerkandl, a renowned anatomist and sometime dean of the Vienna medical school. Dr. Zuckerkandl's wife, Bertha, was a journalist and art critic; her father, Moritz Szeps, was a liberal newspaper publisher who had been an intimate of the late Archduke Rudolf. Bertha had many friends in the intelligentsia, including Hermann Bahr, as has been mentioned, and she delighted in their gossip and frequent flirtations in her salon. Alma, then twenty years old, impressed the opera director by her artistic interests no less than by her full-bosomed beauty; she, on the other hand, was fascinated by famous men. Three months later they were married in the Church of St. Charles Borromeo. On the day after, Mahler's sister Justine became the wife of Arnold Rosé, the Rumanian-born concertmaster of the Vienna Philharmonic, who during performances was sitting at Mahler's elbow. Justine, seven years Mahler's junior, had for years been taking care of his household; the two were close, but Justine had told her brother of her romance with Rosé only at the last moment. Not surprisingly, Alma and Justine resented each other.

Alma asserted later that Mahler had asked her before their wedding to give up composing. She had studied musical theory with private teachers and had had a few lieder with texts by Heine, Rilke, and other poets published. Mahler must have thought that one composer in the family was enough; Alma, at any rate, would not resume her interrupted musical career as a widow. As for Mahler's own composing, his intense work at the Court Opera and concert tours abroad, which tended to become increasingly frequent, hardly left him time for it during the music season. He described himself as a "vacation composer."

He conceived most of his works during holidays near Salzburg, in Carinthia, and eventually at Toblach in the South Tyrol, and often would attend to the instrumentation during the winter months. His experiments in polyphony, vast assemblages of sound, and his introduction of unconventional instruments—cowbells and a hammer in his Sixth Symphony, for instance—exhilarated some concertgoers and infuriated others. After Mahler's "friendly" Fourth Symphony was first performed in Vienna in 1902, a group of young enthusiasts raided the composer's dressing room, and one of them, Alban Berg, was happy to get hold of his baton, taking it home as a relic.

As Mahler was becoming much in demand abroad as conductor of his own and other music, his concert tours provided new fuel for the conspiracies against him that had long been smoldering in Vienna coffee-houses, newspaper offices, and salons. Disgruntled singers, music critics who opposed Mahler's modernism, and rivals who coveted his job had from the beginning been intriguing to get him out of the opera house. Anti-Semitism was doubtless an element in the whisper campaign, but its impact at the time must not be exaggerated. Mahler did, after all, head the Court Opera for the respectable span of a decade; opera directors before and after him who were not Jewish did not last nearly that long. Ganging up on the opera chief is a popular Viennese pastime, the way bearbaiting was a few centuries earlier. (Characteristically, the Viennese dialect word that once applied to animal-baiting, *Hetz,* now means "fun" in general.) Even Viennese who have never been inside the opera house will gleefully talk about the forthcoming downfall of its incumbent director.

In 1907, after yet another cabal that also involved Roller, the opera's production chief, Mahler had enough of the baiting and resigned. It was a harrowing year for him. His older daughter, Maria Anna, had died of scarlet fever, and doctors had diagnosed that Mahler himself was suffering from a serious heart condition. He had a favorable offer from the Metropolitan Opera in New York in his pocket and said he wanted to make some money to be free to compose at will.

A group of friends and admirers publicly appealed to him to stay on in Vienna. Among them were the writers Altenberg, Bahr, Hofmannsthal, Schnitzler, and Stefan Zweig, as well as Freud and other scientists, leading actors and singers, and many artists who belonged, or had belonged, to the Secession. Mahler, however, would not be swayed, appeared in the opera pit for the last time to conduct *Fidelio,* and left. He was surprised to find two hundred people at the West Railroad Terminal on December 9, 1907, to see him off. When the Paris express had pulled out, the painter Klimt turned to the others, and said, "Vorbei"—"It's over."

Mahler spent three seasons in the United States, conducting at New York's Metropolitan Opera and leading the reorganized New York Philharmonic Orchestra. On concert tours, he saw a great deal of the country; when he visited Niagara Falls, the composer remarked, "At last, a fortissimo."

Before his last voyage to New York, in the autumn of 1910, Mahler conducted in Munich the premiere of his giant Eighth Symphony. Soloists from the Court Opera and 250 members of the chorus traveled from Vienna to the Bavarian capital to take part in the "Symphony of a Thousand" (actually, 171 instrumentalists and 858 singers). In the United States that winter, Mahler took the New York Philharmonic as far as Seattle, but was forced by illness to break off his concert engagements. He sailed back to Europe in April 1911 to seek treatment in Paris; his daughter Anna Justine said later that when he realized there was no cure for him, he wanted to die in Vienna. He was transferred to the Austrian capital, and the end came on May 18, 1911. Before dying, Mahler moved his hands as if conducting an orchestra, smiled, and twice whispered, "Mozartl," or "Little Mozart."

The City of Vienna accorded the former opera director a "tomb of honor" at the suburban Grinzing cemetery, and thousands attended the funeral. The wreath from the Vienna Philharmonic was so big that two men could hardly carry it. "Yes," said Alexander Girardi, the popular actor who was among the mourners, "that's what the Viennese are great in: staging funerals." A Mahler bust by Auguste Rodin was placed in the lobby of the opera house, and a nearby street was named Mahler-Strasse. When the Nazis were the masters of Vienna, they removed the bust and renamed the street Meistersinger-Strasse. Today the Rodin bust is back, and the street signs read again Mahler-Strasse.

Mahler's widow, Alma, was then thirty-two years old and soon provided Vienna with new gossip. In the house of her stepfather, the Secession painter Carl Moll, she met Kokoschka, who had just returned from a long sojourn in Berlin. A flaming liaison developed. Alma was to write in her memoirs that her three-year affair with the strapping "OK" was "one sole, vehement love struggle. . . . Never before had I experienced such strain, such hell, such paradise." The painter's jealousy "bordered on the absurd," if Alma is to be believed. Kokoschka wrote in his autobiography, "She could not forget that she had been married to a world-famous conductor and composer whereas I was ill-famed—and that only in Vienna, at the most—and penniless." The pair traveled together to Naples and the Dolomite Mountains, and lived off and on in a farmhouse that Alma and her late husband had bought in the Alpine foothills south of Vienna. When all was over, Kokoschka painted a portrait of Alma and himself in a storm-tossed sea *(The Tempest)* in his black-daubed two-room studio on the Stubenring, where she had been a frequent visitor.

After World War I, when Kokoschka was a professor at the Art

Academy in Dresden, he had a life-size doll made, anatomically accurate and with flowing blond hair, and painted it to resemble Alma. He dressed it in underwear and toilettes that he asserted he had ordered from Paris. He called it "The Quiet Woman" and took it with him to the theater. After a boisterous celebration with friends, the doll, spattered with red wine, was lying in Kokoschka's garden, and a mailman reported to the police he had seen a blood-stained corpse. Thus, "OK" managed to shock Dresden.

Not the paragon of discretion, Kokoschka would write decades later that Alma had been pregnant by him in Vienna and had had an abortion. Mahler's widow married the German architect Walter Gropius at the beginning of World War I, and in 1916 had a daughter, Manon, by him. "It is the most remarkable marriage one can imagine," she wrote at the time. "So unmarried . . . , so free and yet so committed."

As for her first husband, the composer Arnold Schoenberg called him a "saint" and a "martyr" in a commemorative speech in 1912. (Mahler is supposed to have once said as a child that he wanted to become a martyr.) Schoenberg, in his characteristic sardonic way said he found it quite right that Mahler during his lifetime should have been misunderstood and insulted. "Somehow a great artist must be punished in life for the admiration he will later enjoy." Vienna has often excelled in punishing its artists.

KNIFING AT THE CONCERT

Schoenberg himself received an ample share of attacks and insults in Vienna. His father had come to the empire's capital from a Slovak town near Bratislava at age fourteen, had started as a messenger boy, had risen in a merchant firm, had married a girl from Prague, and had eventually opened a shoe business in the predominantly Jewish Leopoldstadt district. Arnold was barely sixteen years old when his father died; the youth abandoned science high school and went to work in a bank. After a few months in his first job, he knew he wanted to be a musician—he had composed a waltz at twelve—rather than a banker. He walked out and soon was picking up some money as director of a workers' choir whose singers addressed him as "comrade."

The fledgling musician took to dropping in at the Café Griensteidl before that bivouac of the intelligentsia was dismantled, and there met Alexander von Zemlinsky, one of the music teachers of Mahler's future wife. From Zemlinsky, the young Schoenberg received his first systematic instruction in musical theory (he never attended conservatory), and in 1901 he married Zemlinsky's sister Mathilde. Three years earlier he had asked a Protestant pastor to baptize him, apparently in the interest of his career. Schoenberg was introduced to Mahler by the opera director's brother-in-law Arnold Rosé, and stayed in touch with the Mahler camp.

Backed by Zemlinsky and Rosé, Schoenberg had some of his compositions played in concerts and soon had students of his own. He showed an early knack for attracting loyal followers; two Viennese middle-class music enthusiasts, Alban Berg and Anton von Webern, became his chief disciples, twin pillars of what came to be known as the Schoenberg circle. They seemed to aim at shocking musical Vienna.

At a performance of works by Schoenberg and Berg in the Bösendorfer Hall in 1907, the majority of the audience started laughing and booing. Mahler, who was present, sitting next to a burly railroad official and modern-music enthusiast named Josef Polnauer, turned around to a heckler who was whistling on a house key, and told him, "Don't whistle when I applaud!" The baiter, recognizing Mahler, sneered, "I whistle at your symphonies too!" Polnauer hit the whistler, who thereupon pulled a knife and slashed Polnauer's face. The railroad official was for the rest of his life proud of his scar, a proof of his commitment to modern music.[10]

Schoenberg's private life did not lack drama either. His wife Mathilde fell in love with the gifted young painter Richard Gerstl, who had his studio in the Liechtenstein-Strasse building where the Schoenbergs were then living, and ran off with him. After a while, Berg, Webern, and Mathilde's brother talked her into returning to her husband; Gerstl, who had been artistically influenced by van Gogh and Munch and had painted portraits of the Schoenbergs and of Zemlinsky, committed suicide at the age of twenty-five.

At the time Schoenberg's wife was having her affair with Gerstl, the composer himself took up drawing and painting. His about ninety known visual works include many self-portraits and a portrait of Mahler; in later years, he tended toward caricature and grotesqueries. Schoenberg was also a handyman who built his own desks and bookshelves, and would do so in exile in the United States too. When he organized a show of his paintings in 1910, mainly to raise badly needed cash, the ailing

Mahler anonymously bought some of the works on display to help his friend without embarrassing him. By that time Mahler used to say he did not understand Schoenberg's music anymore. On earlier occasions, too, Mahler had come to the rescue whenever the Schoenbergs were unable to pay their rent. Schoenberg expressed his gratitude later by dedicating his *Theory of Harmony* (1911) to the memory of Mahler.

In the last years before World War I, Schoenberg was developing a musical language based on a twelve-tone system in a personal style mixing a cerebral concentration that today seems to have anticipated the computer age, with spurts of fantasy. He had the support of Bahr and Loos, and found Kraus interested. He conducted a harmony class at Vienna's Music Academy (the former Conservatory), but was becoming restless. The last straw was a physical assault by a deranged fellow tenant in the house near Schönbrunn Castle where he was then living with his wife and their son. Schoenberg moved to Berlin, found himself almost famous there, and accepted a teaching job at the Conservatory.

The Vienna Music Academy offered Schoenberg a professorship in 1912, but he declined. He did revisit his native city the year afterward to conduct a concert in the fabled great hall of the Musikverein; his own Chamber Symphony no. 1 (1906) and works by Berg, Mahler, Webern, and Zemlinsky were on the program. The evening turned into the worst musical scandal in Vienna's modern history. Listeners fought on the floor and in the gallery. Modernists and antimodernists were seen climbing over rows of seats to slap adversaries; some men challenged each other to duels. Schoenberg, his face pale, interrupted the concert and shouted toward the seething audience that he would call in the police to have the protesters ousted. Police did eventually clear the hall, and the concert was never finished. Schoenberg and Webern—who had earlier joined the master in Berlin—returned in disgust to Germany.

Alban Berg stayed behind in Vienna as the ranking member of the Schoenberg circle. The son of a Vienna export merchant, he had been a devotee of modern music since his early teens, had attended Hugo Wolf's funeral, and, together with Webern, was at the railroad terminal to see off Mahler in 1907. Berg knew Freud, was introduced to Kraus by Altenberg, and became a lifelong friend of Loos—another example of how closely members of the Vienna intelligentsia were interrelated.

SOMBER PARALLEL CITY

There were hundreds of thousands of Viennese to whom atonal music, the Court Opera, Expressionist paintings, literary coffeehouses, and psychoanalysis meant nothing: they had other worries. The worker families in the outlying districts, the little people in the tenements, and the servant girls—most of them from Moravian or Slovak villages—in the homes of the bourgeoisie seemed to inhabit another Vienna, a parallel city that stood in dismal contrast to the imperial capital's surface gloss.

Housing for the proletarians and the lower middle class was, as has been pointed out earlier, shockingly poor; tuberculosis, then often called "the Viennese disease," was rampant. Landlords unmercifully evicted families that missed a sole rent payment, so that at the beginning of every month carts with the poor belongings of newly homeless families were crisscrossing the suburbs. Working hours in factories and sweatshops were long, pay was generally low, and child labor was tolerated and widespread.

The Young Vienna of the coffeehouses, authors like Bahr, Schnitzler, and Hofmannsthal, so sensitive to the angst of the well-to-do, so alert to intellectual novelties from France, Belgium, and Britain, seemed blind to the appalling social reality all around them. The musicians did not seem to hear the sighs and groans from the city's poorer quarters; the anguish in Mahler's symphonies may have anticipated the imminent doom of Austria-Hungary, but it surely was not caused by Vienna's "bedbug castles." Freud's case histories originated in the upper middle classes. The painters, through their professional models, did have direct contact with what Victorians called the lower orders, but before Kokoschka and Schiele, they hardly seemed to respond to poor people's miseries.

The turn-of-the-century intellectuals and artists knew, at least by sight, the man who would become the beloved champion of Vienna's underprivileged—Viktor Adler. He and other Socialists, too, had their regular tables, first at the Café Griensteidl and then at the Café Central. Adler was born in Prague in 1852 into a German-speaking Jewish family that eventually moved to Vienna. As a medical student in the Austrian capital, Adler was a Pan-German nationalist; in 1878 his father and he became Protestants. Later, with many poor people among his first patients, the young physician immersed himself in social problems and took trips abroad to study the situation of workers in other countries. He met Social Democratic leaders in Germany and, in England, Friedrich Engels, the friend and collaborator of Karl Marx. Back in Vienna, Dr. Adler joined the young Austrian Socialist movement and unified its factions. Undeterred by arrests for alleged anarchism, he organized a congress in the town of Hainfeld in the Vienna Woods in 1888 that resulted in the birth of the Austrian Social Democratic Party.

Adler's new party impressed Vienna with an orderly show of strength in its first May Day celebration in 1890. The government had ordered the army to stand by, and many timorous Viennese stayed indoors that day for fear of disorders, but no incidents occurred. Seventeen years later the Social Democratic Party had won universal suffrage in the western half of Austria-Hungary and had become the strongest group in the Austrian Parliament. The workers' movement was torn between a doctrinaire Marxist faction that advocated revolution and a moderate faction that strove for social reforms; Adler always managed to avoid an open split in his party. With characteristic skepticism regarding Marxist theory, he told Trotsky he preferred political predictions based on the Book of Revelation rather than on dialectical materialism. Year after year, the Viennese Social Democrats flexed their muscles in their May Day parades in the Prater.

Red Vienna would, however, come only a generation later. For the time being, the imperial capital was politically dominated by a church-inspired lower-middle-class force, the Christian Social Party, and its able but demagogic leader, Karl Lueger. The son of a janitor at Vienna's Polytechnic College, he had earned a law degree and early entered politics, doing grass-roots work for the Liberal Party, which had run Vienna for three decades. Sensing the discontent of the artisans and shopkeepers who felt threatened by new economic realities, Lueger started inveighing against capitalists and "the Jews." He drifted toward the moderate Left and in the late 1880s helped found a new political movement.

Lueger's Christian Social Party proclaimed itself the advocate of the little people who resented corruption in City Hall, the power of industrialists and the banks, and Jewish influence in business and cultural life. The lower Roman Catholic clergy, the parish priests and the curates, backed the new movement, but the higher clergy had reservations. In 1895 a group of Austrian churchmen led by the Cardinal-Archbishop of Prague, Count Franz Schönborn, at the Vatican denounced Lueger and his party as dangerous because of their radicalism and anti-Semitism. Lueger obtained the support of the Apostolic Nuncio in Vienna, Archbishop Antonio Agliardi, and succeeded in justifying himself in the eyes of the Roman Curia, pointing out that the Christian Social Party was adhering to the social doctrines of the church, and that its attitude toward the Jews had nothing to do with racial anti-Semitism. Pope Leo XIII upheld Lueger and sent the Vienna populist his apostolic blessing.

By then the good-looking, tall, and elegant Lueger, with his decorative beard, was already highly popular as *der schöne Karl* ("Handsome Karl"). He had promised his mother he would never marry, so as to be able to take care of his two sisters, and indeed remained a bachelor all his life. His Christian Socials became the strongest party in Vienna. The city council elected Lueger mayor, but the emperor refused to confirm him in the post. When Sigmund Freud learned of Franz Josef's veto, he lit a cigar to celebrate the decision. The city council insisted in another vote, and the emperor again rejected Lueger's election. After the city parliament had voted in favor of Lueger a third time, Franz Josef in a one-hour audience prevailed on the Christian Social leader to step aside "for the time being" and to content himself with the post of deputy mayor. Lueger was elected mayor in a fourth council vote in April 1897, and this time the emperor confirmed him.

Lueger was reelected mayor three times and stayed in office until his death in 1910. He opportunistically used anti-Semitic rhetoric to retain the support of the artisans, who felt threatened by industrial manufacturing, and of the shopkeepers, who feared competition by department stores and mass-marketing—economic modernism blamed on "the Jews." Yet, Lueger had also Jewish friends, and one of his confidantes, Deputy Mayor Josef Portzer, was half-Jewish. When Arnold Schoenberg was once again in financial trouble and applied for a city grant, Lueger's signature brought the Jewish-born composer 1,000 crowns. Lueger's dictum that *"I decide who is a Jew"* has become famous. The young Hitler, who lived in Vienna during Lueger's last years, was mightily impressed by his anti-Semitic tirades and later, in *Mein Kampf,* would praise him as "the most formidable German mayor of all time."

As the uncrowned "King of Vienna," Lueger in fact modernized the city. He broadened the public sector of services by municipalizing the gas works and electric power plants and had a modern slaughterhouse built. He developed Vienna's transportation network, instituted labor exchanges, and dotted the city with more than a hundred new schools. He improved Vienna's water supply by the construction of a 150-mile aqueduct from the Alps in its south, and promoted afforestation in the Vienna Woods to save the capital's green belt.

After Lueger died of diabetes in 1910, he received the grandest funeral the city had seen—and enjoyed—in a generation. Emperor Franz Josef and a cluster of archdukes attended the requiem in St. Stephen's Cathedral. A large statue of Lueger, overlooking the eastern part of the Ringstrasse, was unveiled under a Social Democratic city administration in 1926.

Much more virulent than Lueger's populist brand of anti-Semitism was that of a onetime ally and later adversary, Georg von Schönerer. His father, Mathias Schönerer, was a railroad builder who had acquired great wealth and was raised to the nobility by the emperor. Georg von Schönerer, born in Vienna in 1842, developed the family estates near the Bohemian border—Hitler's family had come from the same area of Lower Austria—as a political basis. He was elected to Parliament and started a crusade against the interests of the Rothschild family in the railroad linking Vienna with Bohemia. Lueger, in the Vienna city council, went along with the anti-Rothschild campaign for some time. Soon Schönerer stressed racial anti-Semitism, advocated the inclusion of Austria's German-speaking areas into the German Empire that Bismarck had created, and turned against both the Roman Catholic Church and the House of Habsburg. In the Reichstag, the lower house of the Austrian Parliament, Schönerer kept ranting against Jewish capitalists but also against the poor Jews from the east of the monarchy who were peddling merchandise from house to house in Vienna and, above all, against the Jews on the Viennese newspapers.

Schönerer's hostility to the liberal press caused his sudden political end in a bizarre way. The *Neues Wiener Tagblatt,* a daily founded by the father of the journalist and critic Bertha Zuckerkandl, published an extra with the news of the death of Emperor Wilhelm I of Germany in 1888 a few hours before it actually occurred. An enraged Schönerer with a few followers of his German National Party, raided the newspaper's editorial offices and shouted, "You Jews can't even wait for the death of our illustrious emperor!" A telephone operator named Cäcilie Jaczko tried to talk the invaders into leaving, but Schönerer yelled, "Back! We won't spare Jewesses either!" At that moment, printers from downstairs rushed into the editorial offices and threw the intruders out.

Tried for assault, Schönerer was sentenced to a short prison term and had his political rights suspended for five years. The loss of his seat in Parliament and of the *von* before his name were consequences of the verdict. Schönerer, admired by Hitler, lived until 1921, but never reemerged from political limbo. His German National Party nevertheless remained entrenched at Vienna's university and other institutes of higher learning, among the judiciary, in the civil service, and in the ranks of professional people. Latter-day followers of Schönerer were eventually to pave the way for the Nazi conquest of Vienna.

HERZL AND HITLER

Anti-Jewish agitation among university students was a traumatic experience for the young Theodor Herzl. He was born and brought up in Budapest, but his family moved to Vienna in 1878. As a law student, Herzl joined the Pan-Germanic dueling fraternity Albia and revered Bismarck and Richard Wagner. One of his fraternity brothers was Hermann Bahr, the future standard-bearer of Young Vienna; for the time being, the young Bahr was an anti-Semite. Herzl offered to resign when he realized that other fraternity members were sharing Bahr's views, and felt insulted when his name was instead struck off Albia's rolls, which was tantamount to expulsion.

Already as a student, and after graduation, Herzl contributed feuilletons to various Vienna newspapers and was soon widely read. His good looks, his elegance to the point of dandyism, and his winning ways made him a man-about-town who could dream of a diplomatic career or of elevation to the nobility. He was then a convinced assimilationist. In 1891 the *Neue Freie Presse*, Vienna's leading liberal newspaper, appointed Herzl as its correspondent in Paris, an assignment that carried prestige because of the daily's elite readership throughout Austria-Hungary and abroad. How Herzl went to Paris as a Francophile, was shaken by French anti-Semitism during the Dreyfus affair, and became the founder and first leader of modern Zionism has been told often and in many languages.

Herzl would not have anything to do with the Society for Defense Against Anti-Semitism, which Austrian and German liberals had created. (In Vienna, Johann Strauss, Jr., was among the members of these "anti-

145

antis.") "Polite and moderate responses" to the haters of Jews were use-less, Herzl declared. After returning from Paris to Vienna, he held a position as feuilleton editor of the *Neue Freie Presse* from 1896 to 1904, at the same time organizing the Zionist movement and its first congresses.

He was exhausted from overwork in 1904 when he was taken to Edlach in the foothills of the Alps south of Vienna for a rest cure at nearly two thousand feet altitude. His wife, Julie, was with him, and topped fifteen years of a tempestuous marriage with what eyewitnesses described as an outbreak of hysteria. Among Herzl's visitors in Edlach was Bahr. Doctors blamed "cardiac sclerosis" for Herzl's death on July 3, 1904, but the morbid story in Vienna was that he had killed himself. Herzl's burial at the cemetery of suburban Döbling brought more than ten thousand Jews from all over Europe to Vienna. His remains were flown to Israel in 1949 and rest now on Mount Herzl, the highest eleva-tion of modern Jerusalem.

Less than two years after the leader of the Zionist movement died, a seventeen-year-old high school dropout from Upper Austria, Adolf Hitler, made his first visit to Vienna, a provincial admiring the marvels of the imperial capital during a few weeks. He was back in 1907, and would spend six drab and purposeless years in the city before emigrating to Germany. He had probably been an anti-Semite already when he first arrived in the Austrian capital, imbued as he was with the Pan-Germanic nationalism then prevalent in the middle class of Linz, the Danubian city where he had grown up. Hitler's sojourn in Vienna was nevertheless to be of utmost importance for his intellectual formation because it rein-forced the ideas and resentments of his earlier years.

At the beginning of his stay in Vienna, Hitler was shattered when the Academy of Fine Arts twice rejected his applications for admittance. He lacked a high school graduation certificate, and the tests he submitted were judged unsatisfactory. His hopes of an artistic career squelched, the provincial without family and friends drifted into the squalor of cheap rented rooms and men's hostels. He was not, at least not in the begin-ning, outright poor; he had inherited some money from his parents and, as the orphan of a government worker (Hitler's father had been a minor official in the customs service), received a small state pension for a few years. Later he earned some crowns by selling, in person or through associates, the watercolors that he painted in the dayroom of the hostel that housed him during his last three years in Vienna.

The Männerheim (Men's Home) built in 1905, offered Spartan living quarters to 544 men; it charged very little for occupancy of one of its iron beds, served cheap meals, had a resident physician, and boasted central heating, washrooms, and a library. The house rules were stern. Fellow guests at the institution later recalled Hitler as a loner in worn-out, dirty clothes who on occasion ranted about the Jews or the Socialists. During his six years in Vienna, Hitler lived in at least sixteen different places, including a refuge for homeless men at which nobody was allowed to stay longer than five nights in a row, a shelter that Jewish philanthropists had helped finance. He may also have slept on some park bench in the Prater during hot summer nights.[11]

Hitler himself would later dwell on the deep impression that the architecture of the Ringstrasse and Wagner's music at the Court Opera had made on him. He claimed to have attended about every performance of *Tristan und Isolde;* if so, what had enthralled him was the famous 1903 production by Gustav Mahler and Alfred Roller. Hitler seems to have been unaware of the Secession artists, the Young Vienna writers, the music of Mahler and Schoenberg, and all the intellectual ferment in the Austrian capital during those years. He saw, instead, Jews and Marxists everywhere: "Vienna was and remained for me the hardest, but also the most thorough school in my life," the high school dropout would later write in *Mein Kampf,* explaining that his stock of basic ideas was formed in that city "at so early a time under the pressure of fate and through my own learning."

Hitler's early memoirs contain visions of swarthy Jews taking advantage of blond Teutonic maidens and pulling the strings of prostitution and white slavery in Vienna: "An icy shudder ran down my spine when seeing for the first time the Jew as a cold, shameless and calculating manager of that shocking vice." That was the language of sexual envy and sexual anxiety that Hitler had picked up from *Ostara,* a nutty magazine that he had been reading regularly in Vienna. At the men's hostel he had a stack of *Ostara* issues and once even called in person on the magazine's crackpot publisher, who called himself Jörg Lanz von Liebenfels, to ask for back numbers. Lanz recalled later that he let the destitute-looking young man have the requested issues free of charge and gave him two crowns too.

The son of a Vienna teacher, Adolf Josef Lanz—the real name of Hitler's guru—had been a Cistercian novice before he broke with the

Roman Catholic Church and founded his own "Aryan" religion, the Order of the New Temple.[12]

In his magazine and in many other writings, Lanz preached the superiority of the blond nordic race over bastardized subhumans like Jews. *Ostara,* which took its name from a Germanic goddess of spring, also had readers abroad, including Britain's Lord Kitchener and Sweden's August Strindberg.

Hitler was already living in Vienna, but had not yet met the "Grand Master," Lanz, when the latter's Knights Templars gave themselves a new symbol, the Indian (Aryan) swastika. At a ruined castle at Werfenstein in Upper Austria, which the apostate monk had picked as the seat of his order, the raving racists hoisted their first swastika flag at Christmas 1907. A little more than three decades later it would flutter over Nazi-occupied Europe. By then, Lanz would be silenced, for in 1938 the Gestapo would forbid him to publish. The maniacal mentor, however, was to survive the disciple: Lanz died in obscurity in Vienna in 1954.

The commonplace judgment about the Vienna of the last few years before World War I is that it was decadent. Edward Crankshaw, among others, rejects this "received idea." Who was decadent? Certainly some of the old ruling families who still enjoyed undue prominence but had been left far behind culturally and were carrying little weight. The stirring proletariat was proving its dynamism. And was not the cliché of Vienna's degeneracy belied by the "business men who were turning the Empire into a modified capitalist society with confidence and verve" and by the middle classes "who, besides making their contribution to administration and industry, were bursting out in all directions in the sciences, in medicine, in the arts?"[13]

NOTES TO CHAPTER II

1. *Hofmannsthal and His Time,* in Collected Works, Zurich, 1955, p. 83.
2. Werner Volke, ed., *Hugo von Hofmannsthal in Selbstzeugnissen und Bild-dokumenten,* Hamburg, 1967, p. 97.
3. Alma Mahler-Werfel, *Mein Leben,* Frankfurt, 1960, p. 354.
4. William M. Johnston, *The Austrian Mind,* Berkeley-Los Angeles-London, 1973, p. 399.
5. Ilse Barea, *Vienna,* New York, 1966, p. 302.
6. Ernest Jones, *The Life and Work of Sigmund Freud,* New York, 1968, II, p. 116.

7. Ernest Jones, l.c., II, p. 412.
8. *Freud and Man's Soul,* New York, 1985, passim.
9. Quoted in Kurt Blaukopf, *Gustav Mahler,* Vienna-Munich-Zurich, 1969, p. 152.
10. Joan Allen Smith, *Schoenberg and His Circle,* New York-London, 1986, p. 70.
11. William A. Jenks, *Vienna and the Young Hitler,* New York, 1960, p. 36.
12. Wilfried Haim, *Der Mann der Hitler die Ideen gab,* Munich, 1958, passim.
13. *The Fall of the House of Habsburg,* London, 1974, p. 320.

3

REDUCTION SHOCK
AND RED VIENNA

On June 12, 1908, people from all over Austria-Hungary paraded on the Ringstrasse to celebrate the sixtieth anniversary of Emperor Franz Josef's accession to the throne. It was not as grandiose an affair as Makart's pageant in 1879 had been, but it nevertheless took two colorful hours. Nineteen groups in historical costumes and delegations from the fifteen peoples that cohabited in the Habsburg Empire filed between cheering crowds. The young Hitler probably witnessed the parade, too, but it is unlikely that he cheered, for he hated the Habsburgs.

The concord that for one day seemed to reign among the representatives of the empire's fifteen ethnic and linguistic communities was spurious, a Viennese *Schmäh*. In Parliament, the deputies of the various nationalities had for years been fighting viciously; they hurled inkwells at one another, often came to blows, and chanted their national songs or blew children's trumpets to prevent adversary orators from being heard. The emperor suspended the legislature for long periods, and his imperial-royal government ruled by decree, backed by a bureaucracy that commanded almost universal respect and trust.

Many Viennese in the years before World War I sensed that the

Habsburg Empire, despite a measure of prosperity, was being kept from falling to pieces only by the old sovereign. "Only one person in those motley multitudes was really Austrian, the Emperor Franz Joseph whose flesh magically united them all."[1] It was generally realized that after his death great changes would take place. For the time being, the tactics of the Vienna administration was *fortwursteln,* muddling through.

The emperor, the supreme bureaucrat, examined official dossiers every day and made his decisions on their basis. He did grant audiences and listen to reports by his ministers and other aides, even inaugurated exhibitions or new public buildings from time to time, but only what was in black and white, what was in the files, seemed really to exist for him. He read documents all day, but hardly anything else. It was said that for many years he had never taken a book in his hands except the volume of army regulations. The army and the civil service, closely supervised by Franz Josef, kept functioning at the deliberate pace that had become a century-old tradition; the emperor's more than fifty million subjects (only one fifth of whom spoke German as their mother tongue) had the justified feeling to live in a well-ordered commonwealth.

In his personal life, Franz Josef was austere. He lunched every day on boiled beef that had to be so tender that he could eat it with his fork alone, garnished with potatoes and vegetables; one glass of champagne was all he allowed himself with it. The emperor who appeared more an institution than a living being—Hermann Broch would later describe him as the "abstract monarch"—had nevertheless a human side: his friendship with the court actress Katherine Schratt. She provided affection and Viennese warmth for the aged, lonely sovereign, whose brother Maximilian had been executed by Mexican nationalists; whose only son, Rudolf, had killed himself; and whose wife, Elisabeth, had been assassinated.

Katherine Schratt was the daughter of a baker in Baden, the spa south of Vienna. As a young actress, she had a liaison with a colleague, Alexander Girardi, and later she had married a Hungarian baron. Divorced, she was hired by the Burgtheater in 1888 and, according to usage, had within two weeks to appear in audience before the emperor. A friendship developed, favored by Empress Elisabeth. After Archduke Rudolf's suicide, the court actress consoled his imperial parents.

Franz Josef's confidante moved into a villa close to Schönbrunn Palace that the emperor could reach through a side door in the wall surrounding the imperial residence's park. Franz Josef saw her almost daily for many years, and, as a true Viennese, enjoyed the actress's tidbits of theatrical and society gossip. Mrs. Schratt never played a political role, but sometimes used her influence with the emperor to have her way at the Burgtheater.

When the government censor forbade performance of Schnitzler's play *Professor Bernhardi,* Mrs. Schratt asked Franz Josef to lift the ban so that the drama could be performed at the court theater. The emperor is supposed to have said that if only the bureaucrats were against the Schnitzler play he might be able to do something for it, but if "the clericals," too, were opposing it, the ban would have to remain in force. Roman Catholic groups did object to a scene in which a priest and a Jewish doctor are antagonists, and *Professor Bernhardi* did not then reach the Burgtheater. In other interventions on behalf of playwrights and actors, Mrs. Schratt was more successful.

Schratt quarreled with a Burgtheater director, Paul Schlenter, in 1900, however, and retired; after that, Franz Josef never again set foot in the imperial-royal theater, although he kept subsidizing it out of his personal funds. Mrs. Schratt apparently reproached the emperor bitterly for his failure to come to her defense in her row with the theater management. In a letter to the angry actress, Franz Josef expressed the hope that the "black storm clouds will roll away and that the old, happy friendship will be restored." But it was not. The emperor's daughter, Archduchess Maria Valerie, was nasty toward Mrs. Schratt, and Empress Elisabeth, who had always protected her husband's friend from court intrigues, was dead. Franz Josef told his daughter on his seventieth birthday that he would call on Mrs. Schratt for the last time, and there was a formal farewell. For once, the old emperor, always so self-possessed, appeared moved. He saw Mrs. Schratt a few more times in brief, melancholic encounters, and they kept writing each other, but the old confidential relationship was over. At the Burgtheater, younger actresses were in the limelight.

For the Viennese, the Burgtheater was in those years more than just a stage on which actors were interpreting roles, as Stefan Zweig would write later: it was a mirror of the world. Both the court theater and opera were galvanizing young people: "We somehow represented the last generation imbued with that fanaticism for the arts that today can hardly be evoked, a fanaticism that has always distinguished this old city of the theater and of comedians."[2] Such enthusiasm is today generated only by sports events and rock concerts.

In the first few years of the twentieth century, the conviction of Viennese intellectuals that their city had a special mission in the realms of the arts and learning could console them for feeling that they were living in a stagnant empire that, in economic and military importance, compared poorly with the superpowers of the time, Britain, France, and Germany. Musil has, with nostalgic irony, described the mood in dying *"Kakania,"* his mocking name for a monarchy that was both *kaiserlich und königlich* (or *k. und k.,* "imperial and royal") and *kaiserlich-königlich* (or *k.-k.,* "imperial-royal"), according to subtle legal distinctions: roughly, "imperial and royal" were officials, institutions and matters that were common to both halves of the dual monarchy; "imperial-royal" was a term focusing exclusively on the western half of the empire, while *königlich ungarisch* ("royal Hungarian") was used for the eastern half. In Musil's words, "Of course, automobiles were rolling also on these highways [of Austria-Hungary]; but not too many automobiles! The conquest of the air was being pioneered here too; but not too intensively. Some vessel sailed for South America or East Asia every now and then; but not too often. One had no ambition for world economy or world power. . . . One spent enormous sums for the army; but, then, just as much money as to make sure one remained the second weakest among the great powers. The capital too was somewhat smaller than the other biggest cities in the world, yet considerably larger than mere big cities were."[3]

The instinctive trust of the Viennese in the authorities was badly shaken in 1913 by a scandal in that holy of holies, the general staff of the Imperial-and-Royal Army. It centered on the chief of counterespionage, the forty-eight-year-old Colonel Alfred Redl. Russian agents had been shadowing him and discovered that he was having a homosexual affair with a young cavalry lieutenant in Stockerau, a town northwest of Vienna. Blackmailed by the czar's secret service, the colonel supplied it with the names of Austrian spies inside Russia and the plans of Austrian fortresses in the frontier province of Galicia. As a double agent, Redl received messages from his control officers in St. Petersburg by general-delivery mail in Vienna under the code *Opernball* ("Opera Ball"), not a highly ingenious method of clandestine communication.

Colonel Redl was observed as he was collecting payment for his betrayal. Four military officers called on him in his lodgings, Room 1 at the Hotel Klomser in the central Herrengasse, and confronted him with the evidence. The traitor made a full confession, and the officers' commission withdrew, apparently after putting a loaded revolver on his desk. It seems the four officers had to wait for hours outside the hotel in the chilly spring night before they heard the expected shot from inside. At the morgue, the body of the suicide was stripped of its general-staff insignia and clad in the uniform of a simple soldier. But the attempt at hushing up the scandal failed. A young newspaper reporter from Prague, Egon Erwin Kisch, brought it into the open, causing an international sensation.

END OF AN ERA

The Redl affair, through its repercussions in the military hierarchy, widened the chasm between Emperor Franz Josef and his nephew, Archduke Franz Ferdinand, the heir presumptive to the throne. As inspector general of Austria-Hungary's armed forces, Franz Ferdinand had set up a kind of shadow government in his residence, Belvedere Palace. With his aides and advisers he was mapping reforms that he intended to enact when he would at last rule the empire. He was known to favor greater autonomy for the Slavic peoples in the Habsburg Empire, mainly to counterbalance the influence of the Hungarians, whom he detested (a sentiment fully reciprocated in Budapest). The old emperor resented the activities of his nephew and the "Belvedere Party," and the meetings between Franz Josef and his heir presumptive were always tense, sometimes even stormy.

The archduke, who went to mass daily and was cultivating clerical connections, felt deeply offended by the way his wife was being treated by the imperial court. Franz Ferdinand had in 1900 married a Bohemian countess, Sophie Chotek, and since she was not of royal blood, she had been obliged to renounce all dynastic claims and prerogatives for her and their children. The archduke's wife was later named Duchess of Hohenberg, but Franz Josef's court kept rubbing it in that she was of inferior rank. Franz Ferdinand hated above all the supreme guardian of the Spanish court etiquette, High Chamberlain Prince Alfred Montenuovo, for always relegating his morganatic wife below the youngest of the archduchesses at formal banquets or processions and for devising other snubs. Montenuovo, who enjoyed the old emperor's complete trust, was a descendant of the one-eyed Count Adam Adalbert von Neipperg, an Austrian general and diplomat who became the lover and eventually the second husband of Marie Louise, the wife of Napoleon and Empress of France. (Montenuovo is the Italian translation of Neipperg or Neuberg.)

Montenuovo even managed to inflict posthumous indignities on Archduke Franz Ferdinand's wife, as has been mentioned. After the couple's assassination in Sarajevo by the Serbian nationalist Gavrilo Princip on June 28, 1914, the high chamberlain of the imperial court, clearly with Franz Josef's consent, made funeral arrangements that at every step emphasized Duchess Sophie's lowly court status. Franz Ferdinand had known that as long as he was not on the throne, the Spanish etiquette would bar his wife from burial in the Capuchin vaults, the Habsburg family tomb; he had ordered in his will that both she and he should be laid to rest at their country estate at Artstetten near the Danube, nearly fifty miles west of Vienna.

After a few weeks of frantic diplomatic activity, World War I broke out. Patriotic fervor swept Vienna for a few months, and the city's intellectuals helped inflame it further with manifestos, newspaper articles, and instant poetry. The Social Democratic Party, which had consistently opposed the emperor's governments, supported the war, and several of its leaders volunteered for military service. Friedrich Austerlitz, editor in chief of the Social Democratic Party newspaper *Arbeiter-Zeitung* wrote chauvinistic editorials. Freud, then fifty-eight years old, greeted Austria-Hungary's declarations of war with "youthful enthusiasm," and Ernest Jones reported that "for the first time in thirty years [Freud] felt himself to be an Austrian."[4] Freud's sons Ernst and Martin were in uniform as officers, and his third son, Oliver, was building barracks and tunnels for the army.

Hermann Bahr, the champion of Young Vienna and coffeehouse chameleon, became overnight an enraged war propagandist. Various other Viennese writers found cushy jobs in the military bureaucracy—Hofmannsthal in the War Welfare Agency, and Felix Salten, Stefan Zweig, and the essayist Alfred Polgar in the War Archives. Each military unit at the front had orders to send regular reports to the Vienna archives; staff members there were expected to cull from the material "three events worthy of glory" every day. The idea was to develop great literary works.

One day at the beginning of 1916 a bemused figure with a drooping mustache, in the uniform of a simple soldier, turned up to report for duty at the War Archives—Rainer Maria Rilke. For some the most illustrious living poet in the German language, he had just been rescued from field service through *Protektion*. Hofmannsthal was later entrusted with editing an "Austrian Library" of many patriotic volumes, which was to find few buyers.

Karl Kraus, who had remained a civilian because of his crippled spine, was pouring scorn on his favorite target, Bahr, and on the War Archives literati. He flayed them, not for shirking front service, but for their contributions to the war frenzy. Kraus himself was a vocal pacifist from the beginning of the hostilities and scathingly exposed the idiocies of war propaganda. His magazine *Die Fackel* appeared with many white spots, indicating passages that military censorship had suppressed.

Zweig had at first routinely done his duty at the War Archives, but in 1916, after a visit to battle-ravaged Galicia, he wrote a pacifist play, *Jeremiah*. It was accepted by a theater in Zurich, and its author obtained a furlough to attend rehearsals. Zweig, who was accompanied by his wife, did not return to Austria; he moved to Geneva and joined a group of pacifists around the self-exiled French writer Romain Rolland, who in 1915 received the Nobel Prize for literature.

Schnitzler, now in his fifties, also proved immune to the patriotic fever. When the *Neue Freie Presse* asked him to contribute something about the war, he answered that what he could write would be unprintable. Musil, the product of military schools, served as an officer on the Italian front, was hospitalized in 1916, and later edited a soldiers' newspaper in Bozen in the South Tyrol, calling in his editorials for unity among the peoples of the Habsburg Empire. He eventually found himself called Captain von Musil because his father had just been raised to hereditary nobility. At the end of the war, Musil was monitoring enemy propaganda at military press headquarters in Vienna. Joseph Roth, the Jewish Habsburg loyalist from eastern Galicia, had volunteered for the army right at the beginning of the war, and served as an officer on the eastern front until he was captured by the Russians.

Schoenberg differed from his supporter, Kraus, in his attitude toward the war; assigned to an officers' school in 1915, he composed a patriotic hymn. After a long leave he was back in uniform in 1917, but did not see any action. His disciples and friends Alban Berg and Anton von Webern also served in the army.

Oskar Kokoschka was a volunteer and suffered head injuries on the Russian front. After he recovered, he was sent to the Italian front and, eventually, to Stockholm in neutral Sweden, where an Austrian doctor who had won the 1914 Nobel Prize in medicine, Robert Bárány, conducted therapeutic experiments on the war-wounded painter. Kokoschka noted in his memoirs much later that during his stay in Stockholm he had an affair with a Swedish woman who would eventually marry a German fighter pilot, Hermann Goering.

Egon Schiele was called up to military service soon after his wedding and, because of his weak constitution, was assigned to the home front. A pacifist like his friend Kraus, he was fortunate enough to get soft jobs in the army throughout the war. His wife was near him most of the time. In one rural place where Schiele was supposed to do paperwork in a prisoners' camp for Russian officers, he was permitted to set up his own studio, where, between lettering camp signs, he painted landscapes.

Another Viennese intellectual, the son of the Social Democratic leader Viktor Adler, decided in October 1916 that he had to do something dramatic to protest against the government's war policy. Friedrich Adler, then thirty-six years old, phoned his mother one morning and said that he would not be home for lunch, took the tramcar to the city center, and entered the dining room of the Hotel Meissl & Schadn, where Count Karl von Stürgkh, the Austrian prime minister, was having lunch with friends. Adler sat down at a table near Stürgkh's, ate through three wartime courses to steady his nerves but drank only mineral water, at last got up, approached the prime minister, and fired four shots from his Browning revolver at the distinguished, gray-haired count.

Adler was arrested on the spot. At his court-martial he explained that by assassinating the prime minister he had wanted to strike at the embodiment of the "absolutist" war government. The court sentenced the younger Adler to death, but suspended the execution. Friedrich Adler was to play a political role after the war.

When Emperor Franz Josef died a month after the political murder, the patriotic enthusiasm and the initial optimism as to the outcome of the war had long waned in Vienna. Operations against Serbia and the Russians had gone badly, requiring assistance by German units—a humiliation for the Habsburg army. The Austro-Hungarian forces had suffered fearful losses, and in 1915, Italy had entered the war on the side of the Allied powers, opening a new front in the south of the multiethnic empire. Vienna was apathetic, if not outright gloomy.

"From the newspaper we learn the death of the old emperor," Schnitzler noted in his journal. "With Olga [Schnitzler's wife] into the inner city out of curiosity. A few black flags; his pictures are being sold on the Graben; a few fashion-store windows are dark. The mood was hardly aggrieved, certainly not shaken, as it would have been—despite his advanced age—in peacetime. There is no event today that is in any way 'affecting.'—No victory, no defeat, no imperial death."5 A couple of weeks later Schnitzler saw a newsreel of Franz Josef's funeral and recorded in his diary, "At the end a few people wanted to applaud!"

The high point of the newsreel in the Urania cinema must have been that oft-described ritualistic scene at the entrance to the Capuchin Church: The coffin had been brought there from the funeral service in St. Stephen's Cathedral, and when High Chamberlain Prince Montenuovo rapped at the church door, the prior of the Capuchins asked, "Who is seeking entry?" Montenuovo replied, "His Majesty, Franz Josef I, by the grace of God, Emperor of Austria, Apostolic King of Hungary, King of Bohemia, Dalmatia, Croatia, Slavonia, Galicia, Lodomeria, and Illyria; King of Jerusalem; Archduke of Austria; Grand Duke of Tuscany and Krakow; Duke of Lorraine, Salzburg, Styria, Carinthia, Carniola, and the Bukovina; Grand Prince of Transylvania; Margrave of Moravia; Count of Habsburg and the Tyrol." The prior said, "We don't know him. Who seeks entry?" The High Chamberlain: "Emperor Franz Josef, Apostolic King of Hungary, King of Bohemia." Prior: "We don't know him. Who seeks entry?" The sixty-two-year-old Prince Montenuovo knelt down, and humbly said, "A poor sinner, Franz Josef, who begs God's mercy." The prior opened the door to the church and its crypt, and commanded, "Enter!"

When Franz Josef was lying in state, his successor, Emperor Karl, broke Spanish etiquette by leading Katherine Schratt to the catafalque. The retired court actress placed two white roses on the breast of her longtime friend, whom she was to survive by twenty-four years.

Karl was the grandnephew of the deceased monarch. He had had little time to prepare himself for the dynastic role that history had in store for him—little more than the two years since the assassination of the heir presumptive, Franz Ferdinand. "Karl the Sudden," the Viennese called the new emperor. They never took the twenty-nine-year-old successor to Franz Josef very seriously. When the slender new emperor with the soft eyes and the little mustache styled himself Karl I, people in the Vienna coffeehouses did not bother to lower their voices speaking of him as "Karl the Last."

At the beginning of a reign that many Viennese felt would be short, Emperor Karl tried to save the monarchy and his throne by taking Austria-Hungary out of the war. The brothers of his empress, Zita of Bourbon-Parma, the Princes Sixtus and Xavier, were officers in the Belgian army, and were chosen as middlemen to make confidential overtures to the Allied powers. The emperor's advisers on the peace initiative included Hans Kelsen, an expert on legal and social questions who would later write the first Constitution of the Austrian Republic and eventually teach at the University of California at Berkeley.

In a meeting at the out-of-the-way Castle of Laxenburg, ten miles south of Vienna, Emperor Karl handed peace proposals, destined for French President Raymond Poincaré, to his brothers-in-law. The secret leaked out in the West, and Kaiser Wilhelm II summoned his junior colleague in Vienna to his military headquarters at Spa in Belgium; there, the Habsburg emperor was bullied into signing a declaration that Austria-Hungary would stick with Germany to the end. For the rest of the war Karl's empire was a mere vassal of Germany.

SALOME AND INFLUENZA

Throughout World War I, Vienna's coffeehouses and most of its theaters —the city's two all-important institutions—kept functioning. In the month when Friedrich Adler assassinated the prime minister in the Hotel Meissl & Schadn, the Court Opera nearby presented a brilliant premiere: Richard Strauss's revised ("Vienna") version of *Ariadne auf Naxos,* with not just one prima donna, but two—Maria Jeritza and Lotte Lehmann. Works by Puccini and other living composers from enemy countries were banned; an Italian who was safely dead became "Josef Verdi" on the official program.

At the beginning of 1918 the Court Opera brought out a novelty that was supposed to please the Czechs, Leoš Janáček's *Jenufa,* but any attempt at kindling pro-Habsburg loyalty in Prague was by then hopeless. During the spring of the last war year, the Court Opera tried to brighten up glum Vienna with a Richard Strauss Week, which was a big success. Shortly before the end of the monarchy, the censors, who since 1905 had kept Strauss's *Salome* from being performed at the imperial-royal opera, at last relented; the work had its premiere in October 1918 with an exciting Maria Jeritza in the title part.

While Strauss's eroticism in music enraptured the operagoers, all Viennese were then fretting about what they would have for dinner and how they could keep warm. They were eating horse sausages, dried fruits and vegetables, ersatz meat made in part with the pulverized bark of birch trees, beet jam, and vile-tasting make-believe "chocolate." Saccharine replaced sugar. Cooking and frying was done with ersatz fat derived from petroleum residues and plants. Bread was mostly of corn-meal and more questionable ingredients. Chicory and ground beets were boiled to yield a beverage that had to do as coffee substitute. Textiles were woven with yarns of nettle fibers and paper. Shoe soles were hydraulically pressed cardboard and sawdust bonded with tar. Some war-time industrialists made fortunes turning out ersatz products.

In 1918 the official daily food rations for every Viennese were 5.8 ounces of bread, 1.2 ounces of flour, 1.6 ounces of meat, 0.175 ounces of fat, 0.9 ounces of sugar, and 2.45 ounces of potatoes. The trouble was that the stores quickly ran out of supplies and often were unable to honor the ration cards. Hungry and shivering people, mostly women, were lining up all night for the scant rations. In the winter of 1918–19, after the end of the war, the fat quota would be reduced to 0.7 ounces per person per week. The Austrian capital had for generations been relying on flour, pork, salami, fat, poultry, eggs, and other food supplies from rural Hungary; shipments of the Hungarian farm surplus to Vienna were throttled during the first war years and eventually ceased completely.

The meager provisions on which Vienna had to subsist were increasingly strained by the thousands of refugees crowding into the city. Most visible—and unpopular—among them were the Chasidim from the shtetls of Galicia who had fled when the Russians overran the Habsburg monarchy's easternmost province at the beginning of the war. The Viennese, including many Jewish residents, did not welcome the newcomers with their black hats and long black coats, their beards and side curls. Most of the estimated twenty-five thousand Chasidim, as well as other Jewish refugees from the east, found nowhere to live but in the old ghetto neighborhood between the Danube River and the Danube Canal, the Leopoldstadt. "Their cousins and coreligionists who are sitting in the newspaper offices in the First District [the city center] are 'already' Viennese and don't want to be related to, let alone be confounded with, the eastern Jews," Joseph Roth, himself a Galician Jew, was to write a little later.[6]

The hunger and cold in Vienna were eventually joined by an even more sinister companion, influenza. The pandemic scourge was to take the lives of an estimated twenty million persons in an exhausted world between 1918 and 1920. In Vienna, it raged for many months.

One of the first to die was the painter Gustav Klimt. Egon Schiele made a sketch of his body and in a eulogy praised him as an "artist of unbelievable perfection." Seven months later, Schiele's wife was down with the disease. His portrait of her, designed just before her death, was his last work: Schiele died two days after his wife. Other victims of the epidemic were Freud's daughter Sophie, the architect Otto Wagner, and the editor-in-chief of the *Neue Freie Presse,* Moritz Benedikt. Viktor Adler, the sixty-six-year-old leader of the Social Democratic Party, succumbed to it just as the Austrian Republic was to be proclaimed. "I don't mind dying," he said. "But I am so curious." His funeral brought more Viennese into the streets than had that of Emperor Franz Josef two years earlier: it was the first mass demonstration of Red Vienna.

In a few weeks in October and November 1918 the old Habsburg Empire fell apart. Vienna underwent a reversal not unlike the downfall of a manorial family that, after living in comfort for generations, faces poverty and must subsist on dry bread and potatoes amid the faded splendor of their now unheated residence while their former retainers and tenants take over the bulk of the estate. The dramatic change in Vienna's fortunes came by no means unexpectedly. Forebodings that the collapse of the monarchy was near had pervaded Vienna for decades. Karl Kraus had warned that Austria was a "laboratory for the end of the world." Yet, when the metropolis found itself radically downgraded, the experience was shattering. Joseph Roth wrote that the great conflict was called a "world" war, "not because the entire world had conducted it but because, owing to it, we all lost a world, our world." What the Viennese were then undergoing was later called a "reduction complex," a syndrome that might lead to a nagging feeling of inferiority.[7]

URBAN HAS-BEEN

Thus, in 1918, Vienna joined the ranks of those once-illustrious cities that have fallen on hard, or drab, times. Like Alexandria, Athens, Istanbul, Lisbon, Naples, Venice, and a few other centers, Vienna became an urban has-been and had to learn to live in reduced circumstances. For the Austrian capital, the fall from greatness came almost overnight. Emperor Karl proposed in the last weeks of World War I that his empire should transform itself into a federation of self-governing peoples. The Czech, Slovak, Hungarian, Polish, Croatian, Slovenian, and Italian leaders in the areas that had until then belonged to the old monarchy ignored the imperial manifesto and went their own political ways. The German-speaking members of the Parliament that had been elected in 1911 proclaimed themselves a provisional national assembly and announced their intention to create a "sovereign state of German-Austria."

Vienna had for hundreds of years been the hub of an empire that, by the beginning of World War I, had come to number fifty-four million inhabitants—the second European power in terms of territory and the third by population. Now the city was the oversize capital of an impoverished republic that, after its peace treaty with the victorious Allies, would take in only about one eighth of the area, and only one ninth of the population, of old Austria-Hungary. More than one third of the shrunken state's people lived in Vienna; the Alpine provincials, who had always been distrustful of their capital, called it a "hydrocephalus." To make matters worse, the once-imperial city, considered much too big for the modest new republic, was located at its eastern periphery, geographically and culturally distant from its mountainous regions.

Early in November 1918, Emperor Karl was persuaded by his advisers to renounce "any part in the affairs of the state." The document that the last Habsburg sovereign signed amid the Rococo chinoiseries of the Blue Room in Schönbrunn Palace was less than a formal abdication, although he pledged he would recognize any decision that "German-Austria will take regarding its future form of government." Vienna reacted to Emperor Karl's withdrawal with indifference. There were rumors, however, that a revolution might break out any moment. The Vienna-born wife of Jakob Wassermann, the German novelist, followed

163

the example of many other frightened householders, burying the silverware in the garden for fear of looters.

On November 12, 1918, a rainy and chilly day, the Provisional National Assembly convened in the Greek-style Parliament building on the Ringstrasse and voted a law that proclaimed in its Article I that "German-Austria is a democratic republic," and in Article II that "German-Austria is a part of the German Republic." Here, then, was "a country that with the first sentence it uttered committed suicide."[8]

The creation of the republic of German-Austria was the result of a power-sharing deal between its three main political forces: the Social Democratic Party, which maintained hegemony in Vienna; the church-backed Christian Social Party, controlling large areas in the provinces; and the much smaller German National Party, backed by professional and other middle-class people in the capital and in provincial cities and towns.

As the birth of the republic was to be officially announced to the Viennese from the steps of the Parliament building, armed Communists rushed forward from the crowd that had gathered in the Ringstrasse. Communists tore the white middle sections out of the red-white-red banners that were about to be run up on two tall flagpoles, and hoisted the remaining red rags instead. The men of the new Communist "Red Guard" attempted to occupy the building of the legislature, but they were thrown out by Social Democratic deputies and, after a shooting, dispersed by the police. Two persons were killed and forty-five injured.

The Red Guard had been founded a few days before the disorders by a group of radicals, including Egon Erwin Kisch, the newspaper reporter who five years earlier had exposed the Redl espionage affair. Another young writer from Prague, Franz Werfel, had joined the Red Guard and, on the day of the republic's proclamation, harangued a crowd from a military monument facing the Stock Exchange on the Ringstrasse. Werfel urged his listeners to storm the nearby bank palaces; the throng applauded him, but left the banks alone. For a few days the police were looking for the agitator, and Werfel wisely stayed away from his room in the distinguished Bristol Hotel. Karl Kraus, once a friend of Werfel's, was quick to ridicule him for posing as a revolutionary so soon after having undertaken propaganda assignments for the Habsburg cause abroad. Werfel had indeed given lectures in Switzerland on behalf of the

Vienna military press headquarters, to which he had been transferred from a lowly army job as a switchboard operator.

Friedrich Adler, the murderer of Prime Minister Stürgkh, derided the abortive Red Guard coup as a "bad operetta." Emperor Karl, in one of the last decisions of his reign, had pardoned the assassin who formally had been awaiting execution, and a large, cheering crowd had been at hand when Adler was released from prison. The small, newly founded Austrian Communist Party offered its chairmanship to him, but Adler refused it and became one of the major figures in the Social Democratic Party, which his father had unified. In the following years the younger Adler would be identified with the left wing of the party that ruled Red Vienna.

The Communists and their Red Guard tried again to seize power in two more putsch attempts in April and June 1919. Béla Kun was then the Communist despot of Hungary—but only for four months—while Bavaria, Austria's western neighbor, was also going through a brief experiment as a "soviet republic." Russian and Hungarian agents were busy in Vienna in 1918 and 1919 to bring about a pro-Moscow regime in Austria, too, but the Social Democratic Party foiled all Communist plots.

In June 1919, in the last of the attempted coups in Vienna, twenty persons were killed. Sigmund Freud and one of his daughters were taking a Sunday stroll when they heard shots fired in the Hörlgasse, close to the university; they ran to the safety of their home in the nearby Berggasse. After that, the Communists never tried revolutionary action in Vienna again, and Austria has to this day remained the sole country in Central Europe without a sizable Communist Party.

During the Communists' unsuccessful "Maundy Thursday putsch" in April 1919 (in which five policemen and a woman were killed), the horse of a mounted police officer was hit during a shooting. The animal fell to the pavement, a mob surrounded it, and a young man drew a bayonet or large knife and finished it off. The dead horse was cut into pieces on the spot within a few minutes. Men and women scuffled to wrest a bloody chunk of horsemeat, and those who did forgot all about revolution and hurried home with the unexpected Easter treat.

Coal and gas were desperately short in the years after the war. Householders burned wood that they had torn off park benches or trees. Instead of the two hundred railroad cars of coal that until 1914 used to arrive in Vienna from the mines in Bohemia and Moravia every day, only twenty, at most, were now delivered by what had become Czechoslovakia. Owing to the scarcity of fuel there were few railroad trains that would bring eatables from the Austrian provinces to the starving capital; electric power was lacking most of the time. Newly independent Hungary did not send any food at all.

Sure enough, the officers of the Allied military commissions who had ensconced themselves in the plush hotels and the war profiteers were still able to eat tasty schnitzels if they paid in pounds sterling or French francs. Eventually, a lawsuit brought by a horse butcher against the deluxe Sacher Hotel, alleging that a bill for two thousand crowns had not been paid, revealed that the chargers of the imperial-and-royal cavalry had ended up in hotel kitchens.

To scare up some food, the Viennese made private forays into the surrounding countryside of Lower Austria in one of the few overcrowded trains that were running, on bicycle, or on foot, with knapsacks on their backs. In such foraging expeditions, money was useless because it had lost all purchasing power during the war. The farmers, themselves hard-up, might be amenable to letting the humble visitor from the capital have a couple of pork chops or a few eggs only if in exchange they were given something of substance, table silver, for instance, or fine prewar linen. There was the story of the piano that everybody claimed to have seen in some farmhouse near the Hungarian border: a hungry Viennese family was supposed to have carted the instrument out there to barter it for sausages and cheese, and the new owners of the piano were proudly displaying it in their "good room," but had put it to use storing potatoes in it.

To make a trip into Lower Austria or more distant provinces in search of something to eat was known as *hamstern* ("to hoard"). For years, it was a way of survival for thousands of Viennese families. Others tried, with varying results, to grow potatoes and green vegetables in courtyards, vacant lots, and suburban land. Horse manure was much in demand as fertilizer for such improvised kitchen gardens; on the outskirts of the capital little boys equipped with pails and brushes were stalking the meager cart horses to sweep up their droppings.

Thousands of Viennese children were taken in for months and even years by foster families in Switzerland, the Netherlands, and the Scandinavian kingdoms; when they came home eventually, the temporary expatriates spoke the language of their host country. Quite a few of the Viennese who had tasted their first chocolate and butter in Amsterdam or

Oslo would return during World War II in the uniform of Hitler's armed forces as invaders and occupiers.

Fritz Kreisler, the Viennese virtuoso who had long been living in the United States but had returned to the old country and been wounded in the war, gave a concert in New York's Carnegie Hall as his contribution to the Milk for Vienna's Children Fund. The Society of Friends and several other groups sent humanitarian missions to Vienna. The author of this book was among the many Viennese children who were generously fed and clothed by American Quakers.

The famine of 1918–20 strained the relations between Vienna and the surrounding countryside. The rural population, long condescended to, and on occasion made fun of, by the city slickers, often drove hard bargains when the skinny, sallow visitors came from Vienna to beg for a few kilos of potatoes or some pork fat. And as international help began arriving in Vienna, the provincials became envious. The alienation of the capital from the hinterlands deepened their political antagonisms and psychologically prepared the constitutional separation between Vienna and Lower Austria that was soon to take place.

In the overpopulated capital, the *Ostjuden* ("eastern Jews") were for years a favorite target of demagogues. Typical was a harangue that the founder of the Christian labor movement in Austria, Leopold Kunschak, delivered during a City Hall rally in 1919 that had been organized expressly to demand the ouster of all refugees from Vienna. Kunschak described the Jewish newcomers as "a band of middlemen, blackmarketeers, and usurers."

The eastern Jews, however, were not the sole newly arrived people who were swelling Vienna's multitudes. Many German-speaking civil servants and military officers from Prague, Bratislava, Budapest, Zagreb, and other centers of the old empire that now belonged to independent states converged on Vienna and expected to be given state jobs in little postwar Austria. Eventually hundreds of thousands of Viennese men who had been at the front or in prisoner-of-war camps came home after four or five years' absence and wanted too to eat and find work. Many of them kept wearing their military uniforms because they had no civilian clothes or wanted to save their one good suit for important occasions. Former officers, however, had removed their insignia and decorations because they would surely be insulted or even roughed up by angry Viennese if they had continued sporting them. Once-elegant streets were now populated by throngs of haggard men in uniforms that became more ragged by the week.

After Emperor Karl's renunciation in November 1918, the first American newsmen had arrived in Vienna, and the children of the last Habsburg ruler, all little archdukes and archduchesses, gratefully accepted chocolate bars and cookies that the correspondent of the Associated Press offered them. The white Lipizzaner stallions from the imperial stables were put in harness to draw coal carts. The imperial family was moved from Schönbrunn to a Baroque castle near Eckartsau, in the plain east of Vienna. Near there 640 years earlier, Rudolf of Habsburg, the founder of the dynasty, had vanquished his rival, King Ottokar of Bohemia, in battle.

Soon the republican government seized all Habsburg property and ordered the former emperor and his family to leave the country. Switzerland offered them asylum, and on March 24, 1919, a British military escort took Karl, ex-Empress Zita, and their children there. Several other Habsburgs who had formally renounced all their dynastic prerogatives were allowed to stay in Austria. After the Communist dictatorship of Béla Kun in Hungary had collapsed and the country had been declared a monarchy with Admiral Miklós Horthy as regent, Karl tried in April and again in October 1921 to reassert his claim to the throne of Budapest. He managed to set foot on Hungarian soil, but the majority of the country's armed forces failed to support him. The National Assembly in Budapest voted a definitive ban on the House of Habsburg. Switzerland refused further hospitality to the troublesome former emperor, and the Allied powers relegated him to the Portuguese island of Madeira. He died there on April 1, 1922, only thirty-five years old.

In Vienna, a small legitimist movement kept for years talking about a Habsburg restoration, but the overwhelming majority in the Austrian capital and in the provinces supported the republican form of government. No serious attempt at bringing the Habsburgs back was ever undertaken. Parliament abolished all aristocratic titles and privileges, but after the first few years of republican fervor, it could not prevent Vienna coffeehouse waiters from greeting certain patrons again as Herr Baron or Herr Graf. The republic, for its part, had no qualms about perpetuating many bureaucratic titles inherited from the monarchy, like *Hofrat*.

During the negotiations about Austria's peace treaty at St.-Germain-en-Laye, near Paris, in 1919, the French wartime premier Georges Clemenceau, "the Tiger," is supposed to have said when the frontiers of the defeated empire's heartlands were discussed that "Austria is what is left." That remainder looked puny enough. The treaty cut off Vienna from the mining and industrial districts of Bohemia and Moravia, from the fertile farming areas of Slovakia, Hungary, Slovenia, and Croatia, and from its maritime supply line by way of Trieste. Would the new entity with its six million inhabitants and its large capital on its far end be able to survive as an independent state? Most politicians, economists, and scholars agreed that the new Austrian Republic would never be viable, and the population believed them.

One of the very few experts who affirmed the vitality of postwar Austria was Josef Alois Schumpeter, then secretary of state for finance; he was later to achieve a distinguished career as an economist in the United States. Schumpeter told the new Austrian Parliament in July 1919 that the small country's economic recovery could be brought about within a few years. When Austria was restored after World War II within its 1919 frontiers, it soon prospered, a belated proof that Schumpeter was right.

In 1918 and 1919, however, the Viennese not only doubted the new state's chances for survival but were not even sure how it should be called. Some proposed German Alpine Land, others Southeast Germany. The name German-Austria *(Deutschoesterreich)* came eventually to be accepted and, for some time, official. For the large majority of the population, there was no doubt that the German-speaking remnant of the Habsburg Empire could have a future solely as a part of a Greater Germany.

That only an *Anschluss* ("union") with Germany would solve little Austria's problems was axiomatic for the Pan-Germanists in Vienna and, especially, in the provinces. They had for generations been clamoring to join the German Reich of the Hohenzollern emperors; they had been naming streets after Bismarck in Austria's provincial towns and had been shouting "Heim ins Reich!" during their nationalistic demonstrations. The Social Democrats, long the strongest force in Vienna, favored union with republican Germany, too, wanting to link up with the powerful Social Democratic Party of Germany. The conservatives in Vienna and in the Austrian countryside, for their part, were frightened by the leftward drift, and many of their leaders reckoned that an *Anschluss* would strengthen the Roman Catholic element in the resulting Greater Germany, thereby enhancing their own importance.

Vienna's delegates at St.-Germain-en-Laye were at once made to realize that the Allied powers, France above all, had not fought a world war to see an aggrandized Germany emerge from it. A formal veto of any *Anschluss* was written into the Austrian peace treaty in September 1919 and reluctantly ratified by the Vienna Parliament. The Austrian government was then based on an uneasy coalition between the Social Democrats and their ideological adversaries, the Christian Social Party. This "Strindberg marriage," as a newspaper called the radical-conservative setup, broke up in 1920. The Social Democrats, entrenched in Vienna's City Hall, would stay outside the Austrian Republic's government until the country's capitulation to Hitler eighteen years later.

Austria had to repeat the pledge that it would not seek union with Germany when Federal Chancellor Monsignor Ignaz Seipel, a dour priest-politician, obtained a $126 million loan for his country from the League of Nations in 1922. That hard-currency injection into the republic's sick economy was vital. Inflation, which had started during the war, was galloping: the Austrian crown fell within three months in 1922 from 10,000 to the U.S. dollar to 74,450, and the cost of living soared during the same period from 1,364 times the nominal 1914 level to 14,153 times.

THE FEVERISH TWENTIES

In 1920 four Austrian crowns could be exchanged for one Czechoslovak crown; two years later a Czechoslovak crown fetched three thousand Austrian crowns. A successful author like Hofmannsthal wrote in a letter to his old friend Schnitzler that inflation had created an "almost untenable situation" for him. Hofmannsthal confessed that his wife was unable to put together a decent dinner to entertain the Schnitzlers. About that time, Hofmannsthal sold a Rodin bronze to raise some money.

One of the strings attached to the League of Nations loan was an obligation to dismiss more than eighty thousand government workers—a catastrophe for Viennese middle-class families. Many of the fired bureaucrats would soon become Nazis. Seipel's rigorous austerity program under League of Nations supervision did, however, stabilize the currency; on January 1, 1925, a new monetary unit, the schilling, worth ten thousand old crowns, was introduced. (In 1923, Weimar Germany had launched a new mark, worth four trillion old marks, the textbook case of hyperinflation.) The price of Seipel's stabilization policy was a sudden rise in the cost of living and sharply increased unemployment. By 1926 a disastrous 18 percent of the Austrian labor force was jobless; the near impossibility of finding any kind of salaried work, especially for many young people, would haunt the first Austrian Republic to its end and swell the Hitlerite camp.

Uncounted Viennese families had lost their life savings, which they had invested in war bonds, and the roaring inflation had wiped out many remaining fortunes. Not all Viennese, though, were poor. A small and arrogant tribe of profiteers, racketeers, and newly rich people had come into the open too. Some of them had during the war procured raw materials, weapons, food, or uniforms for the military authorities and had shrewdly bought inflation-proof assets with their huge profits. Others were playing the roulette of monetary fluctuations with success, at least for some time, speculating on the ups and downs of the French franc or the Czech crown. In the hectic atmosphere of runaway inflation in Vienna, new banks were mushrooming.

The *Schieber* ("profiteers") lived in the top hotels, rode in chauffeured limousines, dined in expensive restaurants, danced the fox-trot and the shimmy in the new nightclubs, and during the cold months wore the fluffy greatcoats or the belted fur coats that were then the uniforms of the hard-currency millionaires. Their wives and mistresses were hung with jewelry when they went to the opera, where they talked from box to box about luxury trips to Venice or Paris. There were rumors of orgies and cocaine sniffing. Camillo Castiglione appeared like a comet: obscure one day, he was by the next president of a rubber company and a bank, and then founded an aircraft corporation and subsidized newspapers and the theaters of Max Reinhardt. When Castiglione acquired the majority interest in Austria's largest iron-and-steel combine, many believed him to be the richest man in Vienna, richer than Rothschild. It was not true. Baron Louis Nathaniel Rothschild owned banks, hotels, and many other solid enterprises, but did not flaunt his old-money wealth.

Castiglione traveled in his own special cedarwood railroad coach, which contained, among other amenities, a marble bathtub. Government members socialized with him, and the stars of the State Opera sang at his parties for fees far exceeding their monthly pay. Another presumed financial wizard of Vienna's giddy postwar years was Sigmund Bosel. Many of the *Schieber* were Jewish, and they often behaved, as the philosopher Karl Popper noted in his autobiography, like typical nouveaux riches, thereby reinforcing the local anti-Semitism. Karl Kraus's journal

Die Fackel and the Social Democratic press ceaselessly assailed the parvenu profiteers. The flimsy bank empires of Castiglione, Bosel, and the other *Schieber* eventually collapsed overnight, and tangles of bankruptcy cases kept the courts busy for years.

The febrile years when fortunes were quickly made and lost saw also the vogue of the shimmy and the other new dances and the local imitations of the American flapper. Innumerable families of the impoverished Viennese middle class were thrown into domestic turmoil by their young women, who had their hair bobbed, starved themselves with crash diets, or openly took up with lovers. Such a consummate expert on the female psyche as Arthur Schnitzler was confounded when his fifteen-year-old daughter Lili one day came home with one of the then-fashionable short hairdos and a story that someone had surreptitiously cut off her tresses. The writer informed the police of the presumed outrage, but they would not believe the girl. Lili confessed later that she had made it all up. (At age eighteen she would kill herself.)

Right after World War I, when Austria's economy was a shambles and government ministers were shivering in their unheated offices, the new Parliament, in an uncontested vote, decided to keep subsidizing the former Court Opera with state money to almost the same extent as the emperor had done out of his private funds. The republican largesse was not felt to be extravagant: Vienna sensed that the shrine of the musical drama, now renamed the State Opera, was an incalculable asset. For once, the deputies from the provinces went along with the interests of the capital city.

STAGE TRIUMPHS AND SCANDALS

After the wartime Strauss Week, imperial officials had offered the directorship of the Court Opera to the Bavarian composer. Strauss accepted and stuck to his commitment after the Vienna court had vanished. He served as codirector with the conductor Franz Schalk, a Bruckner disciple, from 1919 to 1924. One of the first postwar productions was a new Strauss opera, *Die Frau ohne Schatten,* in October 1919. It was a world premiere, but only a moderate success; critics found the symbolism of the Hofmannsthal libretto about "the woman without a shadow" hard to grasp. A year later, Puccini came again to Vienna to attend the State

Opera premiere of his *Trittico*, comprising three one-act works, *Gianni Schicchi, Il Tabarro*, and *Suor Angelica*. This time the operagoers' response was much warmer.

Strauss nevertheless became a Viennese by adoption. He built himself a spacious villa on a choice plot near the Belvedere that had been given to him by the city in exchange for the original score of *Der Rosenkavalier*, and on his sixtieth birthday in 1924 he was made an honorary citizen. Coffeehouse patrons delighted in anecdotes about the henpecked composer being hectored by his wife, Pauline, a former singer. When she bullied him in front of other people, Strauss would whisper in a sheepish aside, "I need that." Someone got hold of a letter by Pauline in which she had treated her husband to such epithets as "donkey," "ox," and "idiot." Ah, but you must read between the lines, Strauss commented; "she does love me."

In 1921 the State Opera staged the world premiere of a work by a local wunderkind, Erich Wolfgang Korngold's *Die tote Stadt*. It was not his theatrical debut; the son of the influential music critic of the *Neue Freie Presse*, Korngold had at age eleven composed a ballet, *The Snowman*, which had been performed by the Court Opera. The scintillating production of *Die tote Stadt* was a triumph above all for the lead soprano, Maria Jeritza, then at the height of her career.

Born in Brno (then Brünn), the Moravian capital, one of the greatest dramatic singers of the century arrived in Vienna as Mitzi Jedlitzka, soon changed her name, and in 1912 was hired by the Court Opera. Her rivalry with another star, Lotte Lehmann, became a Viennese legend; fans of the two divas often fought outside the stage door. Jeritza gave the Viennese a lot to talk about. During one stormy *Walküre*, Maria Olczewska, a singer from Bohemia, spat at Jeritza in a quarrel onstage. The State Opera fired Olczewska, whereas Jeritza went on from triumph to triumph. When Puccini saw her sing "Vissi d'arte" in the second act of his *Tosca* nearly supine instead of standing, he was enthusiastic and declared that this was the way it should be done. From 1921 on, Jeritza commuted every year to New York to appear at the Metropolitan Opera.

Strauss, despite the occasional brilliance of his tenure at the State Opera, inevitably had his critics too; they would say that the favorite composer of the opera director Strauss was Richard Strauss. By then he was holding a dominant position in Vienna's musical life, but he knew when to be broad-minded. As the Gustav Mahler Fund was about to award a prize to Arnold Schoenberg, who badly needed the money,

Strauss wrote to Alma Mahler, the composer's widow, it would be better if Schoenberg "shoveled snow rather than waste notepaper." Schoenberg, however, got the prize anyway with Strauss's consent.

Schoenberg had founded the Association for Private Musical Performances in 1918 as a forum for presenting compositions by himself, his disciples, and such other moderns as Bartok, Busoni, Debussy, Mahler, Ravel, Scriabin, and, yes, Richard Strauss to an elite of experts while professional critics were barred. Rehearsals were endless; after a seven-hour stint, Schoenberg would ask the worn-out musicians, "What's the matter, are you tired?" Supported by private contributions at a time when Vienna had little to eat, Schoenberg's association offered 113 performances during the three years or so of its activity.

By 1920, Schoenberg had perfected his twelve-tone system, and six years later he started working on his opera *Moses und Aron*. Carl E. Schorske has described the work as "a comprehensive rejection of all the formative Austrian tradition—the Catholic culture of grace, its secular adaptation by the bourgeoisie, and eventually the middle class's turning to art as a substitute for religion."[9]

Alban Berg, the outstanding Schoenberg pupil, was unsuccessfully trying to get his opera *Wozzeck* performed at the State Opera at the time Strauss was its codirector. The masterpiece was accepted in Berlin and had its premiere in 1925 under Erich Kleiber, the Viennese conductor who was then general music director of the State Opera in the German capital. Like their master, Schoenberg, neither Berg nor Webern was ever offered any official position in Vienna's musical establishment after World War I. Whenever Berg's name was mentioned at a Vienna coffee-house table, someone would say, "Do you know that he married a daughter of the old emperor?" Helene Berg, née Nahowski, was indeed presumed to be the result of a brief romance between Franz Josef and a pretty basketmaker fifty years the sovereign's junior.

Richard Strauss had already left his State Opera post following the usual intrigues, and Schalk was its sole director, when the jazz opera *Jonny spielt auf* by the Viennese composer Ernst Křenek had its Viennese premiere on the last day of 1927. Musical conservatives were outraged, and early militants of the Nazi movement staged anti-Křenek demonstrations, passing out leaflets in which the "Jewish-Negro perversities" at the opera house were denounced. The title role of the opera in fact demanded blackface. The work was nevertheless a success, and Křenek, who had been close to Schoenberg and for a short time was married to Gustav Mahler's daughter Anna, became popular in his native city.

Thus, the State Opera, amid much gossip, gave a scruffy capital an illusion of glamor and grandeur with its novelties and its world-class stars Jeritza, Lehmann, the tenor Leo Slezak, and a sensational young Polish singer, Jan Kiepura. At the same time, the Vienna operetta, on a more modest intellectual and artistic level, was emitting the last shimmer of its silver age before the newfangled talkies would draw part of its audiences into the moviehouses.

One of the most successful, and despicable, operettas of all times had been cobbled together during World War I: Heinrich Berté's *Dreimäderlhaus* (Lilac Time), with a caricature of Schubert as the lead role and a farrago of plundered Schubert music accompanying banal lyrics. And on any evening during the 1920s the Theater an der Wien, the Bürger Theater, the Johann Strauss Theater, and maybe the Volks-oper would perform the latest efforts by Franz Lehár, Emmerich Kál-mán, Ralph Benatzky, and other masters of the genre. Yet, usually the world premiere of a new "Viennese" operetta no longer took place in Vienna but in Berlin or some other German city.

Denounced as a "soul whore" by its many critics, the operetta of the post–World War I years nevertheless satisfied the need of the Viennese for escapism and catered to the deepening nostalgia for the city's imperial past. Kálmán's *Gräfin Maritza,* for instance, with its Hungarian countess and its adulation of Vienna, packed the Bürger Theater on hundreds of evenings in a row. The "operetta king," Lehár, by then a millionaire, felt no compunction about writing alternative music (in *Friederike)* for a Goethe poem that Schubert had used for a sublime lied or about imitating the Puccini of *Madama Butterfly* and *Turandot* in his *Das Land des Lächelns.* Such a formidable enemy of artistic compromise as Schoenberg nevertheless respected Lehár's technical expertise. The inventor of the twelve-tone system sent some of his compositions to the operetta composer, and in an accompanying letter addressed Lehár as "Dear Master." In 1934 the Hungarian-born Lehár would receive the ultimate Viennese accolade by having his *Giuditta* produced by the State Opera as a world premiere with a then-idolized tenor, Richard Tauber, in the male lead.

Like the State Opera, the Burgtheater had its traditional state subsidy confirmed by the young Austrian Republic, and it even kept its august name, dropping only the "k-k." ("imperial-royal"). It kept providing the local newspapers with an unending flow of anecdotes and rumors about its directors, would-be directors, producers, and actors.

Greater intellectual excitement originated from the old Theater in der Josefstadt (founded in 1788) when Max Reinhardt took over as director in 1923. This prodigy of stagecraft was born in Baden, near Vienna, in 1873 and early left a promising bank job to devote himself entirely to his passion, the theater. In the 1920s he was shuttling between Berlin, Vienna, and Salzburg, where he had in 1920 been one of the founders, together with Richard Strauss and Hofmannsthal, of the summer festival. Reinhardt bought Leopoldskron Castle, near Salzburg, and gave lavish parties there. He found time to teach at an actors' school (the Reinhardt Seminar) at Leopoldskron and in Vienna's Schönbrunn Palace, while at the Theater in der Josefstadt he was alternating brilliant productions of the classics with Hungarian or French boulevard fare or plays by his friend Hofmannsthal.

One of Reinhardt's stars was Alexander Moissi, a Jewish Italian from Trieste who enchanted his many devotees by his slightly exotic German diction. Young Viennese would queue up for hours to see him in a Shakespeare or Ibsen role. In 1920, Moissi was the first actor to interpret in Salzburg the lead part in *Jedermann* (Everyman), the drama that Hofmannsthal had patterned after medieval morality plays and that has since then opened every edition of the Salzburg summer festival.

In 1921 a theatrical scandal rocked Vienna when Schnitzler's *Reigen* (La Ronde) reached the stage for the first time since it had been written twenty-five years earlier. At the small Kammerspiele theater, the curtain fell in the middle of each of the ten scenes, to be raised again after a few minutes during which intercourse was supposed to have taken place on the stage. There were stink bombs and tussles in the theater and soon fistfights in Parliament. Street demonstrations against Schnitzler and the Kammerspiele management quickly turned anti-Semitic, and the police banned further performances. Schnitzler's maid walked out on him because her boyfriend was convinced the playwright's household was a den of immorality. The ban on *Reigen* was later lifted, but Schnitzler would never again authorize any theater anywhere to produce the work.

As in Berlin, the 1920s in Vienna were a golden age for the cabaret. The most successful practitioners were a team of two comic actors, Karl Farkas and Fritz Grünbaum, who wrote much of their material—a lot of it political—themselves. Farkas, who was of Hungarian descent, would later manage to flee from the Nazis to France; Grünbaum, a native of Brno in Moravia and an army officer during World War I, was to die in the Dachau concentration camp.

THE ARCONAUTS

Quite a few of Vienna's once-sumptuous cafés became banks overnight in the economic rubble of World War I, but there were still enough places throughout the city that afforded the Viennese and the new immigrants a refuge amid decor that had become threadbare. Czech, Hungarian, Polish, Yiddish, and the other languages of the defunct Habsburg Empire could then be heard in the crowded coffeehouses of the Austrian capital almost as frequently as the local idiom. Visitors from Prague and Budapest were numerous, and they inevitably showed up in some coffeehouse within hours of their arrival.

A group of literati and other intellectuals from Prague who had moved to Vienna temporarily or for good met regularly in the Café Herrenhof. Karl Kraus called them the "Arconauts" because they had earlier had their headquarters at the Café Arco in the Czech capital. One of them, the essayist Willy Haas, would later reminisce about "the erotic and intellectual promiscuity of a Vienna literary café in the wild years after 1918." Female company was readily available. "Never were the women prettier, more supple, and more charming," the writer Alfred Polgar wrote about those years of hunger, unheated rooms, and ersatz coffee. "From the combined effects of sadness and its overcompensation through frivolity, there resulted a type of woman strangely avid for life, haunted by the fear of missing a minute."[10] After endless conversations around a coffeehouse table, the habitués would walk each other home, the scanty streetcar service having long since ended for the night, and indulge in more talk, and maybe stay at their companion's place until morning.

The Arconauts included the writers Max Brod, Egon Erwin Kisch, and Franz Werfel, as well as a Prague intellectual who was holding down a bank job in Vienna while working for a doctorate in philosophy, Ernst Polak. Usually with him was his wife, Milena Jesenska Polak. Ill at ease in the Austrian capital, unconventional, and speaking German only haltingly, she was considered an eccentric. She was soon to become the recipient of Franz Kafka's *Letters to Milena*.

Milena had already met Kafka briefly in Prague. In Vienna she read some of his short stories in 1920 and translated a few of them from the original German into Czech. The author was just then seeking a cure for his lung ailment in Merano, the resort that, with all of the southern Tyrol below the Brenner Pass, had a short time earlier been ceded by Austria to Italy under the peace treaty.

Milena wrote to Kafka, he replied, and they fell in love by correspondence. Milena, then twenty-four years old, urged the author, who was twelve years her senior, by letter and telegram to visit her in Vienna. He did so eventually, but only for four days because he was anxious to report back to the director of the insurance office in Prague where he was employed. During his short stay in Vienna, Kafka lived at the vermin-infested Riva Hotel, near the South Railroad Terminal, and by express mail arranged with Milena an appointment in front of it. The weather at the end of June 1920 must have been pleasant, and the pair took a streetcar to the suburbs, presumably the No. 43 to Neuwaldegg at the approaches to the Vienna Woods. Kafka would never forget their strolls in the Vienna hillside. He mentioned them in several letters to Milena. "Your face above me in the forest," he wrote from Prague on August 9, 1920, "and your face below me in the forest, and my resting on your almost uncovered breast."[11]

The love relationship between Kafka and Milena, most of it epistolary, ended at his request. Two decades later she told her concentration-camp friend Margarete Buber-Neumann that for two years she had gone every day to the post office near her Vienna home in the vain hope of finding a message from Kafka. He had always written to her care of the post office, a method then widely used in Vienna by clandestine lovers. (Few people had telephones, but the mail service was reliable.) To Max Brod, Kafka's friend and an Arconaut, Milena reported in a letter that "Frank" had during their four days together shed his chronic anxiety: "I dragged him over the hills behind Vienna. . . . He was simply healthy, and his disease was to us in those days like a small cold."

Kafka returned to Vienna, where he had been happy for a brief period, for medical treatment in April 1924. He died in a sanitarium at Kierling in the Vienna Woods on June 3 in the same year, and was buried in Prague. Milena, by then a contributor from Vienna to Czech publications, wrote an obituary that the newspaper *Narodny Listy* of Prague published on June 6, 1924: "Only a few people knew [Kafka] because he was a loner, a knowing man who was terrorized by the world. . . . He was shy, anguished, gentle and good, but the books he wrote are cruel and painful. He saw the world full of invisible demons who tear defenseless man to pieces and annihilate him. He was too clear-sighted, too wise, to be able to live, too weak to fight—weak the way noble, beautiful persons are." Milena returned to Prague later, joined the anti-Nazi resistance, and was arrested by the Gestapo in 1939. She died in Ravensbrück concentration camp after a kidney operation in 1944.

In her Vienna years, Milena saw much of Franz Werfel. It was the time of the young Prague writer's deepening involvement with the widow of Gustav Mahler. Alma was then still nominally the wife of Walter Gropius, the German architect who in 1919 founded the Bauhaus art school in Weimar (it later moved to Dessau and eventually to Berlin). The romance between Alma and Werfel, eleven years her junior, had been born in the circle of the Arconauts just as Austria-Hungary was collapsing. Alma, absorbed in her personal affairs, "hardly noticed the world events" of 1918, as she would candidly admit in her memoirs. While emperors were being exiled and the map of Europe was being redrawn, the triangle comprising the famous composer's volcanic widow, her professoral, gentlemanly second husband, and the voluble author from Prague seemed made to furnish welcome diversion for coffeehouse talk.

Productive as a writer, Werfel was in company always bursting with anecdotes—funny episodes that he claimed had happened to himself or in his presence. He also had his mystical moments. When Alma was in a clinic during a difficult pregnancy, the Jewish author went to a church to pray, as he confided in his diary, "not owing to any Christian faith, but because the church is the place where people pray." He also vowed eternal faithfulness to Alma and abstinence from smoking if she only would recover, but broke the no-nicotine pledge as soon as she felt a little better. During that stressful time, he compulsively spent many hours every day at the coffeehouse. When Alma at last gave birth to a boy, Werfel inspected the baby and decided that he was "my race . . . strongly Semitic." Alma herself was not so sure who was the father. Gropius at last granted her a divorce, but Alma did not marry Werfel until 1927.

Robert Musil, today acknowledged as having been the most important of all the writers who populated Vienna between the two world wars, thought little of Werfel and made no bones about it. The litterateur from Prague represented for Musil a facile, superficial embodiment of the popular cliché of the successful author. Musil, instead, agonized over every page, was constantly rewriting, and distressed his publishers by extensive revisions of proofs. "How many pages has the gentleman red-penciled last night?," Franz Blei, Musil's friend, one day jocularly asked him at the coffeehouse. (Blei was also a friend of Werfel's and had first introduced him to Alma Mahler Gropius.)

Musil was as assiduous a coffeehouse regular as were the Arconauts, but he did not belong to their coterie. Elias Canetti, who observed him often at the Café Museum in those years, found him "standoffish," very careful in choosing the people he wanted to associate with, "and when by chance he found himself in a café or elsewhere among people he disapproved of he fell silent, and nothing could move him to open his mouth."

Standoffish Musil must have approved of young Canetti: when the future Nobel Prize–winner read sections of his then-unpublished novel *Auto-da-fé* in the auditorium of a private high school for girls in Vienna, Musil and his wife were sitting in the second row. Canetti was afraid the Musils might leave in the intermission, as James Joyce had done when the young writer had read a play of his in Zurich, but they did not move and even attended a party for Canetti in a restaurant after the reading.

The institution where the Canetti lecture took place was known as the Schwarzwald School, named after Eugenie Schwarzwald, a philanthropist and educator who in the hungry years after World War I had fed the Musils and other starving intellectuals. She was then operating a home for destitute people in a former pension at Hinterbrühl in the Vienna Woods and had invited some coffeehouse literati who, like Musil, seemed to subsist on weak coffee and strong cigarettes to join her poor guests at mealtime. Schwarzwald was an earlier admirer of Musil; when some fragments by the writer appeared in various publications, she wrote in the *Neue Prager Presse* of Prague that "Austria has a real new poet." Musil rather unkindly put her as the busybody Diotima in his *Man Without Qualities,* and Karl Kraus caricatured her and her husband, Hermann, a high civil servant, in his *Last Days of Mankind.*

In the Hinterbrühl dining room Musil, still very much the army officer, oddly found himself side by side with Egon Erwin Kisch, the cofounder of the Red Guard and member of the Arconauts, who was also glad to partake of the free meals. Musil had during the first years of the Austrian Republic been indoctrinating its military officers. When the army at last let him go with a certificate of "gratitude and recognition" in 1923, the Musils had to live mostly on fees paid by German-language newspapers in Prague for reports on art and theater in Vienna. It was good money: Czech crowns were increasingly desirable because the Austrian currency was falling into the inflationary abyss. Musil, however, was never able to manage his finances; even at the coffeehouse, he always let his wife pay the check. Martha Musil was the daughter of a Jewish merchant in Berlin, Benny Heimann; she had been married twice before and had a son and a daughter by her second husband, an Italian businessman. She had given up a painting career for Musil; in Vienna, she almost always appeared in public at his side, a laconic presence in unfashionable dark clothes on whom the dapper, reserved ex-officer appeared to rely in many things.

Musil had started *The Man Without Qualities* around 1920. This Proustian tapestry of Viennese society in the last full year of peace (1913) before the catastrophe, with Musil's ironic portrayal of its vacuousness, the cynicism of its bureaucrats, and its flashes of crime and insanity, grew only at a slow pace. The first volume appeared in print in 1930. The novel was to remain a torso, but even so, it represents a major achievement in twentieth-century literature.

THE TORCH

Although Musil was, as has been mentioned, a regular reader of Karl Kraus's journal *Die Fackel,* he found the satirist "nasty"; Kraus, on the other hand, threw Musil into his bag of despised contemporary writers, together with Bahr, Hofmannsthal, Werfel, and many others. He did concede that Schnitzler and Zweig as pacifists had shown "decency" during World War I.

Kraus himself had consistently criticized Austria-Hungary's and Germany's military policies, actions, and propaganda throughout the war, and had astonishingly gotten away with ferocious, if indirect, attacks on the warlords of the Central Powers by focusing on sycophantic journalists and writers. Kraus had started on his behemoth drama, *The Last Days of*

Mankind, in 1915, and published fragments of it in his magazine. After the war, the entire "Tragedy in Five Acts with a Prologue and an Epilogue," containing no fewer than 220 scenes, appeared complete. Kraus personally interpreted parts of it in his lectures, but ruled out that the drama could ever be performed in its entirety on a stage: this would require the time span of ten normal theatrical evenings, he wrote, since it was conceived for a "theater on Mars," and theatergoers of this world would not endure it.

Contemporary literati appear in *The Last Days of Mankind,* together with Emperor Franz Josef, Emperor Wilhelm II of Germany, real-life military leaders, and imaginary characters. One third of the text is, with devastating effect, lifted verbatim from official statements and newspaper accounts that were actually published during the war. A masterly collage, Kraus's drama is an indictment of war folly with moments of savage humor and calculated pathos. In one scene, in print as early as 1915, the voice of Pope Benedict XV imploring the leaders of the nations at war to end the bloodshed is contrasted with the voice of another personage of a similar name, Moritz Benedikt, editor in chief of the *Neue Freie Presse,* dictating an article in which he gloats over the sinking of Italian naval units by the Austrians and suggests that the fish and crustaceans of the Adriatic Sea are feasting on the bodies of the doomed crews. The tasteless article could in fact be read in the important Vienna newspaper.

The few people who approached Kraus described him as kind and considerate; the owlish polemist reserved his rages for his writings. The German language was his consuming life interest. To savor Kraus fully, however, the reader ought to be acquainted also with the Viennese dialect and Viennese phrasing. "I work longer over a word than someone else would work on a novel," Kraus said. Despite inherited wealth as well as a good income from *Die Fackel* and from his lectures, Kraus led an ascetic life. His regular visits to the coffeehouse were work, too, because he read there many newspapers that he would mordantly criticize later and soaked up information from the selected few persons he consented to meet.

From 1919 on, a standing notice in the journal warned that letters or messages to the editor of *Die Fackel* were "undesirable." Each issue sold an average of ten thousand copies in the 1920s, but the journal was almost never quoted by any other publication. The Viennese press responded to Kraus's giant spleen with the time-honored local strategy of *totschweigen* ("killing through silence").

While running his provocative magazine, Kraus found time for lecture tours to Prague and cities in Germany. In Berlin he befriended Bertolt Brecht. As a lecturer, Kraus presented material written by himself, and scenes or entire works by Shakespeare, Nestroy, and Wedekind, his favorite authors, and, most surprisingly, from the operettas of Offenbach, about whom he had copiously written. Unfortunately, no recording of a Kraus reading exists, but persons who witnessed his one-man theater —Canetti was one of them—reported that he was a born actor, masterfully able to imitate voices and mannerisms and to characterize dramatic personages. Most of his public appearances drew capacity audiences.

At times it seemed as if Kraus hated the entire city in which he lived. When a Quaker fund-raising drive for Vienna's poor did not yield as much money as the organizers had hoped to collect, Kraus suggested that Parliament vote a law "for the whipping of rich Viennese" and called for foreign air fleets to raid the city and drop excrement on its elegant streets. He poured the same venom on slow Viennese waiters and greedy cabdrivers.

The Kraus campaign that attracted the greatest attention was aimed at Imre Békessy, a Hungarian journalist who, partly with money from the financier Castiglione, became a Viennese press lord after World War I. At the height of his fortunes, in 1923, Békessy controlled the boulevard newspaper *Die Stunde* and three weeklies, received favors from the government, and was granted Austrian citizenship. *Die Fackel* kept attacking Békessy and presented evidence that he had committed blackmail. At one point, Kraus had anti-Békessy posters printed and put up at his own expense throughout Vienna, reading "The Scoundrel Must Get Out!" Békessy did get out of Austria eventually, just as an arrest warrant against him was about to be issued. (Békessy published newspapers in Hungary in the 1930s; emigrated to the United States, where he published *Barabbas: A Novel of the Time of Jesus;* and committed suicide in Germany in 1951.)

The fame of Kraus spread to countries outside the German-language area. In 1925 some professors of Paris University nominated him for the Nobel Prize in literature, but the 1926 award went to the Sardinian author Grazia Deledda; the nomination was renewed two years later, again unsuccessfully, because another woman novelist, Sigrid Undset of Norway, won the 1928 literature prize.

Only a few close friends knew of Kraus's long love affair with Baroness Sidonie Nadherny von Borutin and his periodic meetings with her at her mansion in Bohemia or elsewhere. Sidonie ("Sidie"), a descendant of old nobility, appears to have considered marrying Kraus in 1914, but friends of hers, including the poet Rainer Maria Rilke, dissuaded her, saying or hinting that Kraus's Jewish origin was a handicap. Later, to Kraus's despair, Sidonie became the wife of a Count Thun, a Bohemian aristocrat like her and a medical doctor. After the marriage broke up, there was a rapprochement between Sidonie and Kraus. He wrote her more than a thousand letters over the many years of their relationship, but apparently never discussed it with anybody else. "I don't like to meddle with my private affairs," he said in one of his many aphorisms.

CREATIVE THINKERS

One of the regular readers of *Die Fackel* seems to have been György Lukács, the Hungarian philosopher, critic, and Marxist theoretician, when he was living in Vienna in bitter poverty during the 1920s. Lukács had been a deputy commissar in charge of cultural affairs during the four-month Hungarian Communist regime of Béla Kun in 1919, and after its overthrow had fled to Austria. Lukács remained in Vienna until 1929 and then moved on to Berlin and eventually to Moscow. He and Kraus probably never met, but they had in common a preoccupation with language.

Another philosopher who owed a good deal to Kraus's obsession with words and linguistic structures was Ludwig Wittgenstein. He, too, read *Die Fackel* faithfully and was in touch with its publisher and sole writer. Today Wittgenstein is acknowledged as one of the seminal thinkers of the twentieth century; the catalog of literature about him runs to well over two thousand titles. In English-speaking academia he is remembered as a protégé and, later, critic of Bertrand Russell, as the friend of John Maynard Keynes, and as the eccentric incumbent of the philosophy chair at Trinity College, Cambridge, who gathered an elitist circle of disciples around himself. Wittgenstein's Viennese background is important for the understanding of his personality and his ideas. He belonged to the strain of intellectuals in the Austrian capital who, as if to disprove the stereotype of their city as an easygoing place, abhorred sloppy thinking, ornament, and *Schmäh*. Like Kraus, Schoenberg, and Loos in their respective fields, Wittgenstein austerely insisted on rigor, truth, and ethics.

He was born in Vienna in 1889, the youngest of the eight children of one of Austria-Hungary's wealthiest industrialists. Karl Wittgenstein, his father, who was of Jewish descent, was known as the Austrian Krupp or Carnegie, and he indeed knew, and dealt with, the German and American steel magnates. The elder Wittgenstein had run off after being expelled from high school in Vienna because of a prank. He had spent two years in the United States, and on his return home had done well in business, eventually succeeding in coordinating the iron and steel industries of Bohemia and in the Austrian Alps. When Ludwig Wittgenstein was a child, his family lived in Vienna in a palatial home with a marble staircase, and entertained Brahms and other greats of the time in their salon.

Ludwig was sent to high school in Linz, entering the institution just as Adolf Hitler, who was his age, dropped out of it. Wittgenstein later studied engineering in Berlin and Manchester, and mathematics and philosophy under Russell and George Edward Moore in Cambridge. In Derbyshire he experimented with flying machines and made various inventions, which were patented. Two older brothers had committed suicide, Hans in 1902 and Rudolf in 1904. Ludwig, too, spoke about suicide when he was trekking and camping with an English friend in Iceland and sailing in a fjord in Norway. Often oppressed by guilt feelings, Wittgenstein would consider killing himself at various times in later life too.

His father died in 1913, and he came into a vast inheritance. He decided to give away a part of it, and at Kraus's suggestion, he asked Ludwig von Ficker, the editor of the respected magazine *Der Brenner* (named after the Alpine pass in the Tyrol), to recommend needy and deserving artists. One of Ficker's nominees was the Salzburg poet Georg Trakl, a friend of Kokoschka's. Trakl was subsisting on a part-time job paying eighty crowns monthly when Wittgenstein allotted a sum of twenty thousand crowns to him; the overwhelmed poet suffered a nervous breakdown and could never be handed the money. Other recipients of donations by Wittgenstein were Kokoschka, Loos, and Rilke, who all could, and did, use the windfall.

When war broke out in 1914, Wittgenstein volunteered for military service, although he would have been exempt for health reasons. He was sent to Galicia, and for some time found himself operating the search-light on a patrol boat that sailed down the Vistula into Russian territory. Trakl meanwhile was dying of an overdose of drugs in a military hospital in Cracow; he wanted to meet his benefactor, but Wittgenstein arrived too late.

Wittgenstein won decorations for gallantry under fire, was sent to officers' school in Olomouc, and transferred to the Italian front. His regiment was encircled near Trent a few days before the armistice, and he was taken prisoner and interned in a camp below Montecassino. His brother Karl, also an officer, had just shot himself after his Hungarian soldiers had deserted. The only other surving Wittgenstein brother, Paul, lost his right arm during the war. He nevertheless stubbornly continued his career as a concert pianist; Richard Strauss, Ravel, and Prokofiev would write for him piano music that could be played with one hand.

Throughout the war, Ludwig Wittgenstein had used every spare moment for intellectual work. He read the Gospels, Dostoevski, and Tolstoi. Like Tolstoi, he was often troubled by a strong sexuality, as entries in his war diaries show. He undoubtedly had homoerotic leanings, but it is not clear whether he was ever an active homosexual. During the nine months in the Italian prisoners-of-war camp, he completed a slim, dense volume on which he had been working for years, now famous as his *Tractatus Logico-Philosophicus*. He sent the manuscript to Kraus's publisher in Vienna, Jahoda & Siegel, but it was rejected. After a sloppily edited publication in a magazine, the work eventually came out in a German-English version with a sixteen-page introduction by Russell (in London in 1922).

The little more than one hundred pages of the *Tractatus* are no recreative read. The gist of Wittgenstein's ideas is in the lapidary second sentence of the work, echoed in its last sentence: "Whatever can be said can be said clearly, and that of which one cannot speak, one must be silent about." In such a terse and seemingly cryptic style Wittgenstein investigates how human language is related to the existing world, and what can be expressed through words and sentences. "That of which one cannot speak" seems to hint at a mystical bent in Wittgenstein. The *Tractatus* and its author's posthumous philosophical writings have become fundamental texts both of the movement of logical positivism—which holds that metaphysical speculation is meaningless—and of language analysis, an important intellectual tool in the computer age.

On his release from prison camp, Wittgenstein returned to Vienna, renounced his remaining share of the family fortune in a Tolstoian gesture, attended a teachers' training school, and did summer work as a gardener in a monastery. From 1920 to 1926 he taught elementary school in, successively, three villages in the Alpine foothills fifty miles south of Vienna. His pupils and their parents later remembered him as an oddball who, among other perceived quirks, would never speak in dialect; but he was also said to have gone out of his way to impart much knowledge in all fields to his charges. He put together for classroom use a forty-two-page dictionary that won approval from the education authorities in Vienna. It was the last work by Wittgenstein published during his lifetime. He resigned from the school system in 1926 after an incident in which he had slapped one of his students in his face, and lived in Vienna for the next two years.

During that period he designed a townhouse for his favorite sister, Margarete Stonborough, who was the family rebel and a friend of Sigmund Freud's. (Ludwig Wittgenstein himself did not think much of Freud's use of language to probe the mind; psychoanalysis, he said, offered fantastic "pseudo-explanations.") The sober three-story structure that the amateur architect Wittgenstein erected for his married sister shows the influence of Adolf Loos, whom he admired: unadorned concrete walls, a flat roof, and metal doors in an interior stressing vertical lines.

Following a call from Russell and Moore, Wittgenstein returned to Cambridge in 1929 and would, with interruptions, stay there until his end. In 1930 he joined Trinity College as a fellow, and in 1939 took over Moore's chair in philosophy. Still the Tolstoian, Wittgenstein never wore a necktie, refused to participate in the high-table dinner ritual, and lived in a Spartan aerie on top of a tower of Whewell's Court. Intellectually self-assured to the point of arrogance, he totally lacked any sense of humor. He would reinforce his reputation as an eccentric, for instance, by earnestly insisting that for ethical and aesthetic reasons the only movies worth seeing were westerns. He nevertheless—or just because of his bizarreness—attracted devoted disciples; several of them were later to become influential thinkers. One of them was Alan Turing, the pioneer of the computer who during World War II broke Germany's top-secret military code.

Wittgenstein never became assimilated in England, always remaining the outsider; but after the end of Austrian independence in 1938 he applied for British citizenship, and was granted it. During Hitler's war he volunteered to serve as an orderly at Guys Hospital in London and later as a medical technician at the Royal Victoria Hospital in Newcastle. He resigned from his professorship in 1947, lived for long periods in secluded spots on the west coast of Ireland, visited the United States in 1949, and revisited Vienna. When he was found to have prostate cancer, he refused surgery; increasingly frail, he was taken in by a Cambridge physician, Dr. Edward Bevan, and his wife. Told eventually that he had just a few more days to live, Wittgenstein said only, "Good." His last words to the doctor before his death two days later, on April 29, 1951, was a message to his friends: "Tell them I had a wonderful life."

Without wanting to do so, Wittgenstein had inspired a philosophical movement at home that became known as the Vienna Circle. The founder of that group was a Berliner who taught philosophy at Vienna University, Moritz Schlick. Soon after his arrival in the Austrian capital in 1922, Schlick, a Protestant and an Anglophile, started holding informal Thursday meetings with philosophers and scientists. From the weekly gatherings it was only a step toward a scientific grouping that in 1928 called itself the Ernst Mach Society, after the Austrian physicist-philosopher.

The avowed purpose of the learned Vienna group was to search for scientific solutions to philosophical and social problems. Deeply impressed by Wittgenstein's work, Schlick selected the *Tractatus* as a basis for the discussions of the thinkers' society. Wittgenstein himself was occasionally in touch with Schlick and some of his friends, but never identified himself with the Vienna Circle. Early members of the grouping included the German philosopher Rudolf Carnap and the Austrian mathematician Hans Hahn. Other mathematicians associated with the Vienna Circle were Karl Menger and Kurt Gödel; the Vienna-born philosopher Karl Popper once expounded his ideas before members of the group.

In the 1930s several friends of Schlick's left Austria, and some reached the United States. Schlick himself was killed by a deranged student on the outer steps of Vienna University in 1936. The murderer, who professed mystical Pan-Germanic ideas, was confined in a mental institution and eventually freed by the Nazis.

The name Vienna Circle was coined by the only member of the group who took an active part in local politics, Otto Neurath. An all-round scholar, he was a supporter of Vienna's Social Democratic leaders and popularized their achievements. Neurath founded the Museum of Sociology and Economics in a space provided by the municipal government on the second floor of City Hall, and developed a pictorial language to make scientific data come to life in it. His pictorial charts—Neurath called them isotypes—were soon adopted all over the world to illustrate statistics. Neurath's City Hall museum was essentially a show window of Red Vienna.

CITY OF THE "NEW MAN"

Vienna remained the bulwark of a powerful Socialist movement after its awkward coalition with the Christian Social Party broke up in 1920. From then on, the conservative, clerical-influenced force would dominate Austria's federal government—usually with the support by German-National and other moderate or right-wing groups—until the country's annexation by Hitler in 1938. For nearly two decades Austria was thus split three ways politically and culturally. The Social Democratic Party, entrenched above all in the capital, was in permanent confrontation with a "bourgeois" lineup whose components were often bickering among themselves even when they were tactical allies. In Vienna during those years, one heard all the time about the quarrels, intrigues, patronage, and deals of the "Reds," the "Blacks," and the "Blues." Red obviously was the banner of Marxism; the nickname of the clerical party alluded to the black cassocks of the Roman Catholic priests; and the Pan-German nationalists had long chosen the blue cornflower, said to have been Bismarck's favorite, as their symbol. Another hue would soon ominously complement the political spectrum, that of the Nazis' brownshirts.

Vienna's press kept referring to the political *Lager* ("camps"). The recurring image of armed strongholds was reinforced by actual and visible military preparations. The *Lager* set up armed formations, ostensibly to protect their own leaders, rallies, and individual members. By 1925, private armies of the ideological camps were parading in Vienna or some town in the provinces Sunday after Sunday, and their uniformed militants often clashed. It was like unceasing training for civil war, and civil war did eventually break out.

The Red Guard that Kisch and other Communist intellectuals had founded in 1918 had been quickly absorbed into the republican army, the Volkswehr, but this official military body was ineffectual and unable to prevent the proliferation of the party troops. The Social Democrats organized the Republican Protection Corps, and anti-Red militants were marching in the Front Fighters detachments, which comprised war veterans and young men who could not possibly have served during World War I. The Front Fighters were later supplanted by so-called Home Defense formations *(Heimwehren)* in gray and green uniforms. Eventually the first Nazi squads in brown shirts turned up. When units of the private armies were marching on the Ringstrasse in their uniforms with buckled belts and shoulder straps, they were armed only with wooden clubs. The Viennese knew, however, that the Socialist Protection Corps and the anti-Red forces had all their caches of lethal weapons. The political mood in the city was one of cold civil war.

A constitutional reform in 1922 firmed up Social Democratic control of the capital. A special law gave Vienna the status of a *Land,* or semiautonomous region, separating it from rural Lower Austria, to which it had until then belonged. Now the Socialist rulers of the capital wielded the same legal powers as the regional governments of Lower Austria and the other seven territorial units in the federal republic. Vienna had not enjoyed such ample self-government since the Middle Ages. It was as if New York City had been severed from New York State, and its mayor had started doubling as governor of a new Big Apple State.

In the Austrian capital—where in the 1920s about two out of every three voters cast a Social Democratic ballot in every election—the Marxist party used its strength and the city's new constitutional role with skill to build a Red Vienna. It was a utopian experiment that for about a dozen years was to draw international attention to the old city while sparking fierce controversy at home.

The most effective tool in Vienna's new legal equipment was the power to tax its citizens and spend funds without much interference from the central government. Austria's Federal Chancellor could glimpse the capital's City Hall across the Ringstrasse from his office in the old Ballhaus, but he had to handle Vienna's mayor at least as gingerly as he would the chief of the Tyrolean regional government in Innsbruck, 250 miles away. The Social Democrats in the Vienna City Hall used their financial muscle to improve the living conditions of the proletariat, especially through better housing.

Ultimately, however, the avowed purpose of Vienna's municipal rulers was much more ambitious than to seek mere material well-being for the working class. In 1924 one of the leading theoreticians of what was known as Austromarxism, Max Adler (no relation to Viktor Adler), gave to one of his books the messianic title *Neue Menschen* (New Human Beings). His party was indeed endeavoring to create a "new human." The new human was to be honest, selfless, community-minded, industrious, and soberly joyful. True, Red Vienna was a political and cultural island in a country that was predominantly conservative; but the Social Democratic leadership appeared confident that the capital city would function as a laboratory for progress and that the new human beings it was to produce would eventually conquer the rest of Austria and link up with kindred movements in a Socialist Germany and other Marxist countries in Europe.

The pioneers of Red Vienna were exceptionally forceful and gifted, and their good faith and integrity rarely questioned. Many of the Social Democratic thinkers and politicians were of middle-class background; most of them could be described as intellectuals; and quite a few were Jewish.

The new-human ethos of the Social Democratic leadership was rendered attractive to the rank and file and, increasingly, to the population at large through the city's cradle-to-grave care for the working class. Julius Tandler, a prominent anatomist who was Vienna's social welfare commissioner, saw to it that young mothers received free medical attention and were given free layettes. New kindergartens, playgrounds, and wading pools were opened in the proletarian districts. When churchmen and other conservatives voiced outrage about the "immorality" of little boys and girls splashing together in the water, City Hall retorted, "Immoral, above all, is dirt."

Uncounted families were then still living in homes that not only lacked bathrooms but also running water. One out of every four deaths in the city was due to the Viennese scourge, tuberculosis. New hospitals and neighborhood outpatient clinics effectively helped fight the endemic disease, and demonstrably improved the health of the Viennese in the course of a few years.

The Social Democratic school board president, Otto Glöckel, reformed Vienna's educational system. To enliven elementary school classes, children were provided scissors, colored paper, wood, and glue and taught to use their own hands and draw upon their own observations to acquire knowledge and skills, instead of being drilled to learn by rote, as had been customary. Gifted children from poor families were enabled to receive higher education. Alfred Adler, who had once attended Freud's Wednesday meetings and was now a dissident psychoanalyst and a committed Social Democrat, held child-psychology courses for teachers and set up child-guidance clinics in the Vienna school system. Parent-teacher associations, a novelty for Vienna, sprang up, and schools experimented with student parliaments. The school board favored and promoted Social Democratic teachers. Students were no longer led to church services. Some children who went to mass or communion with the school chaplain felt they were not too popular with their Social Democratic classroom teacher.

It was over Glöckel's school reforms above all that the Roman Catholic Church in Vienna clashed with City Hall. "Red-Black" antagonism, however, spread over a much wider cultural front. The ruling party in Vienna was outspokenly anticlerical and encouraged its members to declare officially their abandonment of the church and to join instead its own freethinkers' organization. On Sundays the Social Democratic Children's Friends movement led youngsters to sports fields and on hikes, and when they were passing a church they defiantly chanted their song, "Wir sind jung, und das ist schön" (We Are Young, and That Is Beautiful).

The Social Democratic press in its cartoons pictured fat prelates arm in arm with cigar-smoking, top-hatted capitalists. Anticlericalism pervaded also the impressive adult-education program of Red Vienna. The city and the governing party opened scores of workers' libraries, a network of People's Homes and educational associations, and five suburban People's Colleges. Any Viennese was able any day to attend classes in French or English, watch slides illustrating lectures on exotic countries, or learn to appreciate music—all for a token sum or completely free of charge.

The party's Friends of Nature, sporting a badge with a red-petaled Alpine flower on their weatherproof hats, roamed the countryside around Vienna or climbed the mountains to its south and west. Worker choruses rehearsed Schubert lieder along with party chants. There were Social Democratic orchestras, stamp collectors' groups, a chess association, and a slew of gymnastics and sports clubs.

Red Vienna also supplied its citizens with bread. Good Social Democrats were supposed to buy loaves and rolls at one of the many retail

tion and at the same time benefited by it. Choice municipal apartments, City Hall jobs, and other plums were the rewards for party workers and their relatives.

In a city where the emperor's civil servants and police had for centuries exercised a paternalistic rule, the Social Democratic rank and file accepted guidance and even rigid control by the party apparatus with docility. The political adversaries of Red Vienna might scoff at the power and perks of the Social Democratic *Bonzen* ("apparatchiks"), but within the party there was little grumbling about its cadres, at least before 1927.

The presence of a number of Jews in the upper echelons of the Social Democratic hierarchy prompted political opponents to describe Red Vienna as the bulwark of the "Jewish party." It was indeed known that three quarters of the Jews in the city always backed the Social Democrats; many Jewish Viennese, it is true, voted for the party only because the other two major political forces, the Christian Social and German National parties, were anti-Semitic. Top Social Democratic leaders who had a Jewish background appear to have realized early that the party might be open to attacks by anti-Semites. Viktor Adler used to say that, because of his Jewish origin, he was a "burden" to the young Social Democratic movement, and was reported to have remarked that in its ranks "one must have Jews, but not too many." Otto Bauer, his political heir, remained—unlike Adler—a member of the Jewish community but stressed in a 1910 essay that the party of the working class was not "a Jewish protection troop."[12]

After World War I the Roman Catholic Church seemed to be the main enemy of the Viennese Social Democrats. Militant Catholics would vocally denounce the machinations of "the Jews" when Glöckel's school board permitted children to stay away from religion classes or when Tandler's social welfare department had crucifixes removed from city hospitals and priests barred from patients outside the regular visiting hours. The *Kulturkampf* atmosphere in Red Vienna fostered anti-Semitism and, in effect, played into the hands of the Nazis.

Despite the mounting wave of anti-Semitism, the Jewish leaders of Red Vienna commanded the same loyalty and even affection of the rank and file as the other top figures of the Social Democratic Party did. The power and discipline of the working-class movement was demonstrated every May 1. The Social Democratic Party formations would march hour after hour on the cobblestones of the Ringstrasse in their annual parade —the secular counterculture's answer to the church's Corpus Christi pageant. Nurses of the city hospitals, streetcar personnel, Red Falcons with scarlet crepe paper tied into the spokes of their bicycles, workers in municipal and private enterprises, athletes of the party sports clubs, and many other Social Democratic groups and their bands filed past their party leaders who were taking the salute on a grandstand in front of City Hall.

During the last years of Red Vienna, however, the city sensed that it was housing also an undefinable, volatile underclass of people who could not be controlled by the battalions of the Republican Protection Corps and the orderly ranks of the unions and the other Social Democratic organizations.

NOTES TO CHAPTER III

1. Frederic Morton, *A Nervous Splendor. Vienna 1888/89,* Boston-Toronto, 1979, p. 6.
2. From an autobiographical sketch by Stefan Zweig, 1923, quoted in *Stefan Zweig, Leben und Werk im Bild,* eds. Donald Prater & Volker Michels, Frankfurt, 1981.
3. *Der Mann ohne Eigenschaften,* Hamburg, 1978, p. 33.
4. *The Life and Work of Sigmund Freud,* New York, 1968, II, p. 171.
5. Arthur Schnitzler, *Tagebuch,* Austrian Academy of Sciences, Vienna, 1983. Entry of Nov. 22, 1916.
6. Joseph Roth, *Juden auf der Wanderschaft,* 1927, as quoted in *Versunkene Welt,* Vienna, 1984, p. 155.
7. Norbert Leser, *Genius Austriacus,* Vienna-Cologne-Graz, 1986, p. 34.
8. Erwin Ringel, *Über den Todestrieb,* in *Wien, Traum und Wirklichkeit,* Salzburg-Vienna, 1984, p. 124.
9. *Fin-de-Siècle Vienna,* New York, 1981, p. 361.
10. Alfred Polgar, *Kleine Schriften,* as quoted in Paul Michael Lutzeler, *Hermann Broch,* Frankfurt, 1985, p. 288.
11. Franz Kafka, *Briefe an Milena,* Frankfurt, 1954, passim; and Margarete Buber-Neumann, *Kafkas Freundin Milena,* Munich, 1963, passim.
12. Jack Jacobs, *Austrian Social Democracy and the Jewish Question in the First Republic,* in *The Austrian Socialist Experiment,* Anson Rabinbach, ed., Boulder and London, 1985, p. 157 ff.

4

T H E   D E M O N S

Friday, July 15, 1927, was one of those torrid days that are no rarity in the Austrian capital in summer: the city's usual leisurely pace becomes outright lethargic, its many outdoor swimming pools and the bathing beaches on the arms of the Old Danube are crowded, and business in the beer gardens and Italian ice-cream parlors soars. On that particular July day, though, Red Vienna showed a grimmer face. The Social Democratic Party apparatus unexpectedly lost control of the masses; furious mobs of workers and urban flotsam set fire to the Palace of Justice and a police station, the forces of order fired into the rioters, and by nightfall eighty-nine people were dead and hundreds of wounded filled the hospitals. That Friday started an ominous chain of events that in little more than a decade would lead to Hitler's triumph in Vienna and ultimately to the horrors and ashes of World War II.

The immediate cause of the bloodshed in July 1927 was popular anger over a court sentence in the wake of political violence in a village near the Hungarian border, Schattendorf. On January 30, members of the rightist Front Fighters had barricaded themselves in a tavern there, had fired shots into a detachment of the Republican Protection Corps that was parading in the village street, and had killed a one-eyed war invalid and an eight-year-old boy. Clashes between Socialist and anti-

Socialist militants, especially during their Sunday marches and rallies, had for years been commonplace, but few people had until then lost their lives in the creeping civil war.

After the Schattendorf shooting, three men were charged with murder and put on trial before a Vienna jury. Their defense counsel was Walter Riehl, the Nazi lawyer who had pleaded also for the assassin of Hugo Bettauer, the author of *The City Without Jews.* At the end of the eight-day trial, it took the jury only three hours and a half to acquit all three defendants by a vote of nine to three, rejecting also the prosecutor's fallback charge that the accused had "exceeded legitimate defense."

The July 15 issue of the Social Democratic Party newspaper *Arbeiter-Zeitung* published a violent editorial by its editor in chief, Friedrich Austerlitz, who branded the jurors in the Schattendorf trial as "scoundrels" and "lawbreakers without honor" and warned that their verdict would have dire consequences. The Social Democratic leadership, nevertheless, left the rank and file without any instructions as to what should be done.

Shortly after the editorial appeared, Social Democratic shop stewards in several factories called protest strikes in a seemingly spontaneous movement that took trade union headquarters by surprise. Strikers turned off the current for the streetcar system; when the trams stopped, the Viennese sensed that trouble was brewing. Workers from suburban plants trooped to the city center for what they were told would be a protest in front of the Parliament building. Groups of young radicals and apparently quite a few hoodlums showed up too. Scuffles occurred near the university as policemen tried to keep the marchers from reaching the Parliament. A vast crowd surged toward the Palace of Justice, a fifty-year-old structure in Renaissance style on a triangular square southwest of the Parliament.

Shouts against the Schattendorf sentence and against "class justice" were heard, and the first stones shattered windows. The target was inappropriate: the offices in the Palace of Justice were mainly concerned with civil cases and contained real estate records; the jury trial had been held in the gloomy criminal courts building, which was eight blocks distant and called the Gray House. The large doors of the Palace of Justice were quickly closed, but the few policemen around the building were unable to prevent young toughs from climbing through ground-floor windows and causing havoc inside.

The intruders terrorized employees, threw pieces of furniture and bundles of files out of the windows, and started fires in various offices. Soon the entire building was ablaze as thousands outside roared in delight. Government-issue desks and chairs that had been hurled into the streets were also set afire. The blaze had already reached the roof of the Palace of Justice when the fire brigade arrived, but a frenzied mob blocked the apparatus from getting close to the fire. Flames were shooting high into the sky as Mayor Karl Seitz, the popular leader of Red Vienna, appeared on top of a fire truck and tried to reason with the rioters.

Everybody recognized the mayor by his white goatee, and a few older workers cheered him, but the crowd nevertheless would not let the firemen pass. From the nearby school board headquarters its president, Otto Glöckel, came out and also attempted to calm the enraged mob, but like the mayor and other Social Democratic officials, he had to beat a retreat. Toward noon a wild horde stormed a police post opposite the south flank of City Hall and set it on fire. The rioters were by then armed with clubs, iron bars, and granite cobblestones torn from the street pavement, and a few were firing revolvers. Groups of men lifted tall cast-iron light poles from their bases and put them across the streets; others built barricades with torn-down business signs, park benches, and any other material they could get hold of.

Shortly after noon, the chief of the federal police in the capital, Johannes Schober, obtained authorization from the government to arm his detachments with rifles. The order to quell with military means what had become a revolt found the police unprepared; there was some fumbling in their barracks in the Marokkaner-Gasse behind the Music Academy before the keys to the armory were found. At last, carbines were passed out to the force present in the barracks, and the men were rushed to the Palace of Justice area. Many of them were war veterans who had some combat training or even experience at the front but had never been taught the techniques of riot control. Faced with a mob that had been running wild for hours, the police started firing into it as if they were on a battlefield.

Meanwhile, the leadership of Red Vienna was in disarray. The Social Democratic Party chief Otto Bauer was seen pacing back and forth in a caucus room in the Parliament building, "chain-smoking, not saying or doing anything. . . . The totally unexpected violence found him helpless."[1]

In the streets between the Palace of Justice and City Hall many persons, among them women and children, who had nothing to do with the rioting were caught in crossfire, and some were killed. People tried to scramble for cover in stores and doorways. From two to five o'clock, when the day's heat was at its most oppressive, police combed street after street, square after square, in a twenty-block area around the Palace of Justice, firing into any cluster of people they saw or whenever they heard a seditious shout. There were reports later that raving policemen had pursued wounded persons into Red Cross ambulances and even into first-aid wards to rough them up further. By late afternoon the entire neighborhood where fighting had gone on for many hours was eerily quiet. The death toll, it was later established, was eighty-five civilians and four policemen.

Elias Canetti, then a chemistry student at the University of Vienna, read of the Schattendorf sentence in a coffeehouse near his rented rooms in suburban Ober-St.-Veit, raced to the center on his bicycle, and was sucked into the demonstrating crowd. Reminiscing more than fifty years later, he felt that "the excitement of that day is still in my bones. . . . It was the nearest thing to a revolution that I have experienced." After the Palace of Justice fire, Canetti wrote, he could understand how the Paris populace had stormed the Bastille in 1789: "I recognized that the mass doesn't need a leader. . . . For an entire day I had before my eyes a mass that had formed without a leader."[2] Arthur Schnitzler, in contrast, was not particularly shaken as he was watching the Palace of Justice burn from the roof of his villa, nearly two miles away.

A powerful reconstruction of what happened on July 15, 1927, may be found in Heimito von Doderer's long novel *The Demons.* The son of an architect in a town near Vienna, Doderer had returned from a prisoner-of-war camp in Russia in 1920 and studied history at the University of Vienna. The Palace of Justice riot impressed him deeply. At first he felt no sympathy for the Social Democrats, became an anti-Semite, and joined the Hitler party. Later he changed his mind, and after Austria's annexation by Hitler in 1938, he omitted to renew his Nazi Party membership. In his masterpiece, Doderer viewed the events of July 1927 as the end of freedom in Austria, the historical moment when the "demons" of irrational forces were unleashed in Vienna.

On the day after the riot, the Social Democratic Party directorate and the trade union leadership issued a manifesto, calling a general strike but also urging the rank and file to avoid clashes with the government forces. The Social Democratic press charged that the demonstrators had been dealt with brutally, yet Parliament, by a majority vote, approved the conduct of the Vienna police.

The bloodshed of July 15 prompted the publisher of *Die Fackel* to launch a one-man campaign against the police chief. In September, Kraus had, at his own expense, large posters printed and put up throughout the city; they read, "Police President Dr. Schober, I demand that you resign. Karl Kraus." If Kraus thought his message would have an effect comparable to his successful crusade against the newspaper tycoon Békessy, he was mistaken; there was no reaction whatsoever from the authorities or the press. The day after Kraus's public demand for the police chief's withdrawal, a local store owner who called himself the "Gold Fountain-Pen King" and was known for his publicity gimmicks, also had posters disseminated all over Vienna, urging Schober to stay in office. The issue of how the police had handled the Palace of Justice revolt thus seemed to have become a joke. Months later, Kraus found himself in trouble with the tax office because it would not allow him to deduct the cost of the anti-Schober posters as a professional expense from his income.

Schober, a moderate Pan-German nationalist and former Federal Chancellor, emerged politically strengthened from the controversy over police methods and two years later headed an Austrian government. For the time being, however, Monsignor Seipel, the government chief who had authorized the police to take up the rifles and fire them, seemed victorious in a confrontation with Red Vienna. He told Parliament there would be "no clemency" for anyone who had incited to violence during the July riots. His left-wing adversaries henceforth called the priest-politician "the Prelate Without Mercy," and Otto Bauer, the Socialist leader, accused him in Parliament of putting politics above morality.

PRIEST AND MARXIST

During the 1920s the Roman Catholic priest Seipel and the Jewish Socialist theoretician Bauer personified the dichotomy that would eventually wreck the first Austrian Republic and pave the way for Hitler. Seipel, the son of a Vienna cabdriver, had become a professor of moral theology in Salzburg and served as minister of social welfare in the last imperial cabinet. He had urged Emperor Karl to step aside and is believed to have helped him write his ambiguous renunciation statement. As chairman of the Christian Social Party from 1921 to 1929, he harshly opposed Socialism and Red Vienna. In this strategy he could count on all-out support from the church hierarchy; before every election, the bishops urged the faithful to vote the Christian Democratic ticket.

The bald, bespectacled Seipel with the sharp profile and hooked nose was to the Socialist masses in Vienna the embodiment of clerical fanaticism. Although a son of the people, the frigid priest-statesman seemed singularly un-Viennese in his stern ways and lack of folksiness. Talking to him in private, one was struck by an alert mind and might see the flicker of an ironical smile. When a jobless worker in 1924 made an attempt on Seipel's life, gravely wounding him with revolver shots, the Social Democratic Party newspaper expressed "personal esteem" for the political adversary. And Bauer himself wrote an emphatically respectful obituary after Seipel's death in 1932, baffling the Socialist rank and file.

Seipel is known to have been similarly impressed by his political antagonist and in private conversation reportedly acknowledged Bauer's "greatness." Bauer had been born into a well-to-do family in Vienna, earned a law degree, and become a Socialist early in life. Freud is supposed to have counseled the brilliant young intellectual to stay out of politics and instead choose a scientific career. But Bauer made his name in the Social Democratic Party and served as its secretary from 1907 to 1914. He volunteered for military service when the war broke out and soon was captured by the Russians in Galicia. In 1917 the Bolsheviks released the Austrian officer at once, because they knew about his Marxist radicalism, and Bauer was able to resume party work in Vienna. After the fall of the Habsburg monarchy he belonged to the provisional republican government as secretary of state for foreign affairs, and strongly advocated Austria's union with Germany.

As the chief ideologist of his party, Bauer was the principal spokesman of "Austro-Marxism," and his relations with the Bolsheviks soured. As early as 1920, Lenin branded him as a "social traitor," observing that Bauer was at best "a learned fool who cannot be helped—the epitome of a pedant who is a petty bourgeois through and through." In the Social Democratic Party councils and in Parliament it was Bauer who above all practiced the dialectics aimed at reconciling the Marxist tenet of class struggle and democratic methods. Within his own party, Bauer's chief rival was Karl Renner, a former librarian of Parliament who had been the first government chief of the Austrian Republic. Renner, who stood for a pragmatic approach to political and social problems and often seemed amenable to compromise with the Christian Democrats, would write twenty-five years later that Bauer and Seipel obeyed "the same dogmatism." Renner was to become Austria's first head of state after World War II.

In 1927 an immediate consequence of the Palace of Justice revolt was a widening of the rift between Socialists and anti-Socialists, between Bauer and Seipel. The priest-chancellor, under the impression of the disorders in Red Vienna, started favoring the anti-Marxist private armies, the *Heimwehren*. These right-wing militias had sprung up, under various names, in the Alpine provinces of Carinthia, Styria, and the Tyrol right after the war, to repel actual or dreaded encroachments by Yugoslav, Hungarian, or Italian irregulars. The volunteer formations had presumed to defend the frontiers of the new little republic, but had soon taken on an openly anti-Socialist character and had merged with similar right-wing formations, the Front Fighters. Industrialists who were afraid of strikes and sabotage relied on the *Heimwehren* to supply goon squads, and kept subsidizing the rightist paramilitary movement as a force to oppose the left-wing labor unions. By 1927 the *Heimwehren* were strong enough in some regions to break a transport strike that the Social Democratic leadership in Vienna had called after the July events and to make the railroad trains run.

Seipel was pleased by the muscle of the *Heimwehren* and apparently decided that his party needed such a force outside the Parliament and the democratic processes to keep order in the country. He may also have been worrying about the nationalistic and anticlerical tendencies that quite a few of the anti-Socialist militias were betraying, and seems to have reasoned that the church-backed government had better take control of the rightist forces. Three months after the Palace of Justice burned, Seipel, in a statement that mixed politics with religion, declared that "if we see the enemies of Jesus Christ march in better armed and organized groups, we must do everything to correct the shortcomings in our own armament and organization." As if to make clear that he anticipated civil war, the government chief added, "True love of our people must express itself by not shunning the decisive fight within the people and for the people!"

After such language by the priestly chancellor it was not surprising that intensive military preparations took place in either of the opposing ideological camps during the next few years. Former imperial-and-royal officers and sergeants, many of them unemployed since the end of the war, now found something to do in the new permanent cadres of either the *Heimwehren* or the Republican Protection Corps. The swollen ranks of the jobless furnished any number of men who, in order to earn a few schillings, were glad to take part in semiclandestine military training during the week and get into a party-militia uniform on Sunday to march in some parade, after which there would be free beer and sausages. Soon the paramilitary forces on both sides by far exceeded the effective manpower of the thirty-thousand-man army that the World War I victors had permitted Austria in its peace treaty. The army and police, for their part, had been purged of leftists after the Social Democrats had abandoned government in 1920.

Regional and local leaders of the *Heimwehren* were in the meantime jostling for power and influence, engaging in intrigues against one another and quite often flirting with the growing Nazi movement (which was receiving support from Germany). Some local chieftains of the rightist militias indulged in Pan-German and anti-Semitic rhetoric, and all of them kept criticizing the parliamentary system. In 1931, Vienna learned one day that detachments of the *Heimwehren* had occupied government offices in a few places in the provinces in what seemed an antidemocratic putsch. The rebels were disarmed in a few hours, and the leaders of the operetta coup were charged with high treason. When a jury acquitted them, they acknowledged the verdict with the Fascist salute, grinning as they stretched out their right arms.

HOPELESSNESS

By the late 1920s the economic situation in Vienna had, after a few years of seeming recovery, suddenly turned catastrophic again. Early in October 1929 the city was stunned by the collapse of a leading bank, the Allgemeine Oesterreichische Boden-Creditanstalt. Ill-advised speculations by an inept management and overextension had caused the insolvency. It signaled the worldwide Depression; three weeks later, on October 29, the historic stock market crash hit Wall Street. The Vienna government tried to cope with the emergency by forcing another bank, the Creditanstalt für Handel und Gewerbe, to assume the liabilities of the bankrupt institution, but in 1931 the Creditanstalt also became a victim in an international chain of bank failures. Its ruin was precipitated by the recall of a large number of short-term deposits by France, following an abortive attempt by Austria and Germany at establishing a customs union. The International Court of Justice in The Hague ruled, by a vote of eight to seven, that the customs-union project violated Austria's peace treaty and the commitments the country had entered when it received a League of Nations loan in 1922.

The debacle of the Creditanstalt ushered in a period of economic hardships that hastened the end of Austrian independence. Poverty was again gripping Vienna. Between 1929 and 1933, Austrian production slumped by almost 40 percent and unemployment doubled; by 1937, the number of jobless exceeded one fifth of the entire work force. An air of hopelessness hung over Vienna. Unemployed and discontented people joined the Nazi Party, and the number of suicides, always high in the city, soared.

It seemed symbolic when Anna Sacher, the co-owner of the hotel that had been the byword of "merry Vienna," died in 1930; soon afterward the glorious old enterprise went bankrupt. (The Sacher Hotel was later rescued and restored by new owners.) Mrs. Sacher, the widowed daughter-in-law of the family business's founder, had during her long life become a famous Viennese character, loved both by the upper crust that patronized her hotel behind the opera house and by the little people she knew so well—her father had been a butcher.

Before World War I, Habsburg archdukes had dined with dancers of the opera ballet in the hotel's legendary Chambre Separée No. 7 or some other private room; Hungarian magnates with such names as Baron Major Vécsey de Vécse et Bördöllyo-Isagfá had used the Sacher as their pied-à-terre in the empire's capital; and Emperor Franz Josef, although he never set foot in the place himself, had sent Anna Sacher a napkin with his signature when Katherine Schratt, their mutual friend, asked him for it. A nephew of Franz Josef, Archduke Otto, had once crossed the lobby of the Hotel Sacher wearing nothing but his army cap and sword; the notorious libertine had died in 1906, not suspecting that his son Karl would become the last Emperor of Austria-Hungary.

Anna Sacher's cigar-smoking, her breed of dwarf bulldogs, and her earthy wit were proverbial; she spoke the Viennese dialect even to her most distinguished guests. Patrons would admiringly remark that "she knows everything and doesn't say anything" about what was going on in her house. One day soon after the fall of the Habsburgs a mob of demonstrators who had desultorily been looting the Ringstrasse hotels at last turned to the Sacher. Mrs. Sacher confronted the intruders in the lobby, cigar in her hand, and in her best butcher-shop voice roared, "Get out!" They meekly obeyed.

In the 1920s, Anna Sacher welcomed the nouveaux riches, the famous opera singers, and the film stars instead of the archdukes to her establishment. Bowing to the shimmy craze, she hired a jazz band, but would not herself listen to its music. To the end, she believed herself to be a rich woman, and she willed money to longtime hotel employees and other protégés; the bequests, however, could not be paid out because Mrs. Sacher, who had received high civic awards from both the empire and the Austrian Republic, left only debts.

She had one of those grand Viennese funerals. Thousands lined the streets, and when the cortege passed in front of the Sacher Hotel, the entire staff was lined up outside and many people cried. Among the mourners there was also the "Flower Toni," once a street figure in Vienna's center where she would wander from restaurant to restaurant to sell her roses or magnolias to patrons, now a pathetic old woman with heavily rouged cheeks. Merry Vienna had come to an end.

"JEWISH BLOOD WILL SQUIRT"

The brown tide, fed by the murky streams of old and new anti-Semitism, had been mounting for years and was soon to submerge Vienna. Telltale signs were reported from the Alpine provinces, where the term *Viennese* had become almost synonymous with *Jew*. Hitler had still been unknown outside Munich when, in the summer of 1921, posters appeared in the lake resort of Mattsee, near Salzburg, requesting all Jewish holidaymakers to leave town. Arnold Schoenberg and his wife, who were vacationing there with the composer's brother Heinrich, were asked to prove they were baptized Christians. The Schoenbergs were, but they left Mattsee at once and moved to the town of Traunkirchen on a peninsula jutting out into another one of the Salzburg region's lovely lakes. The composer liked the place and returned to it in later years. In 1922 he organized a concert in Traunkirchen to raise funds for the purchase of new bells for the Church of St. John, which dominates the town. (During World War I most church bells in Austria-Hungary had been donated as metal contributions to the armament industry.) Mattsee, at any rate, stuck to its anti-Semitic tourist policy, and no higher authority ever intervened. The 1929 Baedeker's guide to Austria noted in its entry concerning the town, "No Jewish visitors desired."

In the late 1920s some Alpine resorts had started advertising in nationalistic newspapers in Austria and Germany that they were barring Jewish guests. Eferding, in Upper Austria, stated in its publicity that "in accordance with a decision by the town council the sojourn for non-Aryans is limited to 24 hours." The small town of Schönberg am Kamp southwest of Vienna even boasted in advertisements that it had been the scene of "anti-Semitic manifestations in 1925." All this was in gross violation of the Austrian Republic's constitution.

In Vienna itself, despite diffuse anti-Semitic feeling, the Nazi Party had at first made little headway. There were, to be sure, periodic anti-Jewish outrages. At the University of Vienna they followed a long-familiar pattern: the newspapers would report that Jewish students had been beaten up at Bucharest University, the academic disorders would then spread to Budapest, and soon trouble would start in the Austrian capital. Rowdies, not all of them actual students, would block the entrances to the university's main building on the Ringstrasse and deny access to anyone they knew or assumed to be Jewish. Scuffles would break out, and if some plucky Jewish student or teacher insisted on getting into the building, a dozen attackers would maul him and kick him down the stairs that lead up to the main portal.

Police in squad cars would arrive at the scene remarkably late and seal off the approaches to the university without interfering in the violence that was going on. The policemen were supposed to be barred from "academic soil," as the university premises were called, in observance of an old privilege that was never legally spelled out. Eventually the university would close down for a few days, and the disturbances would fizzle out. In 1930 the Pan-Germanic university rector Wenzel Gleispach tried to establish a "Jewish nation" parallel to a "German nation" among the students of the institution—a proposal that was generally understood as a first step toward restricting Jewish enrollment through a racial quota system. Austria's Constitutional Court foiled that attempt at legal discrimination at the university.

In the soccer stadiums, the worst fights between opposing groups of fans occurred usually during and after games that the Hakoah, the Jewish first-division team, was playing. The Hakoah followers, however, included sturdy youths who often sent their adversaries home with more bloody noses than they themselves had suffered. Soccer was then the dominant passion of the city, giving the Viennese for a while a reason for pride. After the Austrian national eleven had beaten Scotland by five to naught and Germany also by five to naught in 1931, the sports world spoke of a Viennese Wonder Team. The miracle lasted two years. In twenty-two international games the Viennese scored seventeen victories and suffered only two defeats, three games ending in draws. After Czechoslovakia defeated the Wonder Team by two to one in 1933, the European soccer fortunes turned again.

Swastikas had first appeared in Vienna in the early 1920s when Lanz's prewar Aryan follies had long been forgotten. Dr. Riehl, the lawyer who defended Bettauer's murderer and the Schattendorf gunmen, had set up a branch of the Nazi Party. Its brown shirts and swastika armlets had slowly become familiar as one more variety of the several political uniforms that were seen in the streets. Nazi gangs started raiding Jewish coffeehouses, businesses, and clubs, and were in the forefront of the demonstrations against Křenek's *Jonny spielt auf* at the State Opera in 1928 and against the film version of Erich Maria Remarque's *All Quiet on the Western Front* in 1931.

In Parliament, shouts of "Jew pig!" and similar insults had often been heard from the Christian Social or German National sectors when Otto Bauer or some other Jewish deputy of the Social Democratic Party was speaking. The large heading of a Nazi campaign poster in spring 1932 read, "When Jewish Blood Will Squirt from the Knife." A few weeks later, fifteen representatives of the Hitler movement were elected into the city parliament. In September of that year, Joseph Goebbels, escorted by an SS commando, addressed an enthusiastic crowd filling a sports hall, the Engelmann Arena, in a Vienna working-class neighborhood. On the day Hitler came to power in Germany—January 30, 1933 —the Viennese Nazis held an outdoor victory rally in the park facing the Church of St. Charles Borromeo. Students, professional and white-collar people, and many well-dressed women cheered the Nazi orators who celebrated their Führer's triumph and predicted that Austria would soon "return to the Reich." Few persons in the crowd looked like workers.

Only a handful of Viennese Jews emigrated while they still had a chance to make an orderly move to some other country. As anti-Semitic persecution in Germany intensified, the Jewish intelligentsia in the Austrian capital, as in Prague, was even for some time reinforced by refugees from Berlin and other cities already under Nazi domination. Very few Viennese Jewish families that might have transferred funds abroad did so; almost all who were eventually to become exiles would arrive in foreign nations as beggars.

FREUD AND HIS DOUBLE

Disciples and friends of Sigmund Freud urged him again to move to some refuge in Switzerland, the Netherlands, or Britain. Over the years he had received various offers of hospitality in those countries, but had turned them all down, although he had always claimed to dislike, even to hate, the city where he had lived most of his life. After the collapse of the Habsburg Empire in 1918, he had written, "I do not want to live anywhere else. For me, emigration is out of the question."

During the 1920s, Freud had continued his busy routine, seeing patients on weekdays—up to thirteen a day during peak periods—and working on books or other writings Saturdays and Sundays. He had broadened psychoanalysis by applying it to cultural fields, although he felt, as he wrote in a 1935 postscript to his *Autobiographical Study,* that this was for him "a regressive development." His interest, he explained, "after making a long detour through the natural sciences, medicine and psychotherapy returned to the cultural problems which had fascinated me long before, when I was a youth scarcely old enough for thinking."[3] Freud kept up a lively correspondence with associates in many countries. He had known since the early 1920s that he had cancer of the palate and had at first thought that "my life would soon be brought to an end," but surgery had saved him in 1923. "I was able to continue my life and my work, though no longer in freedom of pain," he wrote. Freud endured the pain and periodic new operations with stoicism.

When Arthur Schnitzler, the famous author and nonpracticing physician, turned sixty in 1922, he received a letter from Freud in which the founder of psychoanalysis confessed he had always avoided a meeting for fear of encountering his *Doppelgänger.* The German word has spooky overtones: seeing one's double is eerie. "I have formed the impression,"

Freud went on, "that you know through intuition—or rather through detailed self-observation—everything that I have discovered by laborious work on other people." A flattered Schnitzler replied courteously and was invited to dinner at the Freud home. There must have been fascinating table talk at 19 Berggasse that June 16, 1922. Freud and Schnitzler met again fleetingly a few times later, but no close friendship developed. Schnitzler found that with the older man psychoanalytic dogma had become something of a "monomania," and declared himself more baffled than convinced by it.

As for Schnitzler's own career, he scored his last big success in 1923 with *Fräulein Else,* a novelette ending with the suicide of a young woman. In the following years, he continued turning out plays and short stories in his villa in the fashionable Cottage District. He also kept recording in his journal what he had dreamed and sometimes his interpretation of it, which music he had heard or played, and where his strolls had taken him. Increasingly hard-of-hearing, he experienced frustrations with stage and film producers and with his publishers, and had money worries. To earn more, he went on lecture tours and angled for movie contracts. In his sixties, he still managed to carry on affairs with two mistresses simultaneously, even as he foiled the attempts by his divorced wife Olga to move back in with him. Olga had during more than two decades been seeking recognition as a singer, and at one time had the conductor Bruno Walter as her teacher, but success eluded her. Now she and Schnitzler were rivals for the affection of their daughter Lili, and the author made various trips with the attractive, vivacious girl.

At age seventeen Lili fell in love with an Italian officer, Arnoldo Cappellini, in Venice. When she told her father that they wanted to get married, the author did not object, although the handsome officer was twenty years Lili's senior, a committed Fascist, and penniless. The wedding took place in Vienna's City Hall, and the young couple went to live in a small apartment in Venice they had been able to rent, thanks to an allowance by Schnitzler. The marriage was a year old when Lili shot herself with her husband's army revolver, apparently after a quarrel. She survived a few days, with her friend Anna Mahler, the composer's daughter, at her bedside. When Schnitzler and his former wife arrived in Venice, Lili was already dead. Her loss hit her father like a hammer blow. His health deteriorated, and he had dark moods. "A little yellow old man," one of his mistresses wrote in her diary. Schnitzler no longer seemed to care much about what was going on in the world; the name Hitler occurs only once in his private papers—in connection with the difficulties of producing his *Reigen.* Schnitzler died in 1931.

After Lili's death, Hofmannsthal, also in the name of his wife, Gerty, wrote to his friend Schnitzler, "We too are parents, and we are weeping with you." The following year Hofmannsthal's son Franz committed suicide. Franz seems to have been uncertain about what to do with his life, and after a sojourn in Paris he told his parents he wanted to open a travel bureau there. The elder Hofmannsthal apparently did not like the idea, and Franz shot himself in a room in the family's Rodaun house. The morning of Franz's funeral his father suffered a stroke and died. He was buried at the local cemetery, dressed in a friar's cowl. Hofmannsthal may have belonged to the Third Order of St. Francis, a religious group open to laymen, although such an affiliation was later denied by some of his closest friends. As a true Viennese, the author of *Everyman,* the play about the dying of a rich man, may have been meditating for years about his own funeral, planning it like a mystical stage production. Hofmannsthal had in his later years been suffering increasingly from depression brought on by low air pressure or by the southern wind that in Italy is called *scirocco* and in the Alps *Föhn.* Quite a few Viennese experience similar discomfort and mood alterations because of their city's special atmospherics.

Hofmannsthal had for many years maintained an elegant top-floor pied-à-terre in Vienna's central Stallburg-Gasse; there he used to confer with stage producers, literary agents, and other persons to whom he did not feel close enough to ask out to his Rodaun villa. It is typical of the small world that the city's prominent people inhabited then that other tenants in the same Stallburg-Gasse building were the famous soprano Maria Jeritza, the essayist Alfred Polgar, and a Christian Social cabinet minister who would soon become government chief, Engelbert Dollfuss.

TOWARD CIVIL WAR

Because of his unimposing height of about five feet and his political ambitions, Dollfuss was called "Millimetternich" by his enemies and soon also by his friends. He had been born an illegitimate child into a peasant family in the Lower Austrian village of Texing in 1892 and, as a

213

youth, had amazed his teachers with his intelligence. He had been enabled to attend institutes of higher learning in Vienna and Berlin, had rapidly risen in his native region's farming organization, and had eventually become minister of agriculture. Along the way, he had won a reputation as a tireless, dynamic politician who got things done.

Dollfuss was thirty-nine years old in 1932 when he became Federal Chancellor, heading a government based on a parliamentary majority of one. "Bellyache majority," the Viennese sneered, meaning that if just a couple of Dollfuss' supporters in the legislature were sick, he would be overthrown. The death of the long-ailing Monsignor Seipel in August 1932 gave the Dollfuss cabinet a new lease on life because another, healthy Christian Democrat took over the defunct priest-politician's seat and was able to cast his vote to defeat a motion of no-confidence in the government.

With all his parliamentary troubles, Dollfuss managed to secure another League of Nations loan to bolster the sagging Austrian economy. Influential non-Nazi newspapers in Germany joined the Hitlerite press on that occasion in accusing Dollfuss of having sold out to Western capitalists. At home the tiny chancellor impressed his aides by his stubbornness in seeking solutions to seemingly intractable problems, by his astuteness, and by the long hours he habitually kept. Cabinet meetings would last an entire day. Time apparently did not mean anything to the feisty government chief who was usually late for every appointment and whose many visitors had to wait endlessly to see him. Franz Josef would have been horrified by such lack of punctuality. Dollfuss liked to fly at a time when most European politicians still preferred their reserved railroad compartments and official limousines. Usually looking cheerful, the diminutive chancellor did not appear to have given much thought to long-term strategy; in a two-front fight against Social Democrats and Nazis he relied on his instincts: he was a tactician with quick reflexes. Less than five weeks after Hitler had become master of Germany, Dollfuss seized on an unforeseen development in Vienna to pull off a coup of his own.

His government's handling of a railroad strike had led to a stormy debate in Parliament, and when the clamor would not subside, the Speaker of the House declared that under the circumstances he felt unable to carry out his tasks and would resign. The officer who would no longer preside was Karl Renner, the Social Democrat who had been chancellor right after World War I. The two deputy Speakers, a Christian Democrat and a German National, taken unawares, also withdrew in quick succession. Without anybody left to declare the meeting adjourned, the legislators drifted out of the Parliament building and most of the out-of-town deputies went home for the weekend.

On Monday, March 7, 1933, Dollfuss issued a statement asserting that the national assembly had "suspended itself" and announcing that his government, in view of the parliamentary impasse, would take measures to maintain law and order. Dollfuss invoked a 1917 law that had empowered the imperial-and-royal government to direct the war economy by decree as his legal basis for governing without Parliament—a shaky prop for dictatorship.

Dollfuss was able to count on Italian support for his cold coup d'état. Mussolini had for years been subsidizing a faction of the right-wing militias, the *Heimwehren,* that was led by Prince Ernst Rüdiger von Starhemberg, a descendant of Vienna's defender of 1683, and the nobleman had become an ally of the Christian Democrats. At Easter 1933, Dollfuss went to Rome to pay his respects to Mussolini, whom Starhemberg had already met, and the little Austrian chancellor hit it off famously with the posturing dictator. Mussolini encouraged Dollfuss to proceed on his authoritarian course at home, to break the power of the Social Democrats, and to be tough on the Nazis—he, Il Duce, would back up Dollfuss against Hitler.

Curiously, it had been Hitler who had first advised Starhemberg to call on Mussolini. The seventh Prince Starhemberg, scion of a wealthy landowning family in Upper Austria, had enlisted as an underage volunteer in the Austro-Hungarian Army when he was seventeen years old and had seen action in Albania toward the end of World War I. He had then sought more adventure in the rightist movement in Bavaria and had marched behind Hitler and General Erich Ludendorff in the Munich Beer Hall Putsch in 1923. Later, back home again, Starhemberg had developed an aristocratic disdain for the Austrian Nazis, but had still been seeing Hitler occasionally.

A tall, good-looking bon vivant, Starhemberg earned himself a reputation as a womanizer, which did no harm to his political career as a leader of the paramilitary *Heimwehren.* At age thirty-one the prince found himself installed as Austria's interior minister, with the country's entire police forces at his command. Mussolini underlined his interest in Starhemberg by setting up a Vienna link between himself and the Austrian prince that was thinly disguised as the press office of the Italian legation. Mussolini's liaison man, Eugenio Morreale, was soon more influential than the official Italian envoy in Vienna. Starhemberg's *Heimwehren,* funded from Rome, were marching in the streets in new uniforms and with new battalions—the striking force of what leftists called "Austro-Fascism."

In the spring of 1933, Dollfuss, urged on by Mussolini and Starhemberg, banned the left-wing militias of the Republican Protection Corps. The Social Democratic leadership protested, but to the dismay of rank-and-file militants, it did nothing more for the time being to counter the blow. The Nazis were in the meantime stepping up their fight against the Vienna government: they released tear gas in department stores to frighten off shoppers, smeared housewalls with pro-Hitler graffiti, set off firecrackers and petards in many places to cause panic, and eventually started outright bombings. When Dollfuss had the Nazi "country inspector" for Austria, a German Reichstag deputy named Theo Habicht, arrested and expelled in June 1933, he was furiously attacked by the German press. The Dollfuss government banned all party uniforms, including the Nazi brown shirts, and Berlin retaliated by introducing a special thousand-mark tax on any German citizen traveling to or through Austria. The measure was aimed at ruining the Austrian tourist industry, which, especially in the Alpine region, depended on German guests.

A Vienna celebration marking the two hundred and fiftieth anniversary of the Siege of 1683 was in effect an anti-Nazi show of strength by the *Heimwehren.* Prince Starhemberg, whose ancestor had successfully defied the Turk, gave the keynote address at a rally in front of Schönbrunn Palace. Chancellor Dollfuss, wearing his old uniform for the first time since World War I, replied to the leader of the Austro-Fascists with a patriotic speech, stressing his determination to keep the country independent. The participants in the Schönbrunn rally then marched to the Ringstrasse amid hostile demonstrations by left-wing groups and Nazis.

A few weeks later, Nazis throwing hand grenades ambushed members of a Christian gymnastics organization near Krems, a Danubian town about forty miles upstream from Vienna. One person was killed and thirty suffered injuries. The Dollfuss government banned all activities of the Nazi Party throughout Austria and declared the SA and SS disbanded. Nazi underground networks that had been built over the years at once intensified their terrorism. Rumors swept Vienna periodically that an Austrian Legion, composed of thirty thousand Austrian Nazis who had emigrated or fled to Germany, was about to invade the country and topple its government. In October 1933 a Nazi with the Czech name Drtil fired a shot at Dollfuss, but the chancellor was only grazed by the bullet.

Dollfuss and Starhemberg agreed on creating an umbrella organization, the Patriotic Front, to comprise all political and cultural groups and all individual Austrians who were supporting their authoritarian regime and the country's independence. Soon all government workers were sporting the little ribbon in the Austrian colors (red-white-red) that was the badge of the new political structure. The Viennese called the Patriotic Front emblem the *Existenz-Bandl* ("livelihood ribbon"): one risked being fired if one failed to wear it in one's lapel or on one's shirtfront. The joke was that in any office, district, or neighborhood "half of the people are Nazis, the other half are Socialists, and all are in the Patriotic Front." The catch-all organization, which seemed to point toward a one-party state, was open to Jewish citizens, and quite a few joined and wore the red-white-red ribbon.

The Austrian chancellor felt the need for an ideological underpinning of his regime, which left-wing critics were characterizing as "clerical-Fascist." To counter the Socialist and Nazi models of a society of the future, Dollfuss invoked Pope Pius XI's encyclical *Quadragesimo Anno.* This document, issued by the Vatican two years earlier, was meant—as the first two words of its Latin text indicated—to mark the fortieth anniversary of Pope Leo XIII's encyclical *Rerum Novarum* (Of New Things) of 1891, regarding social problems. Pius XI had seized the opportunity to bring Roman Catholic social doctrine up to date and to reiterate the church's stern condemnation of socialism: "It is impossible to be at the same time a good Catholic and a real Socialist." *Quadragesimo Anno* recommended corporatism as the Christian alternative to class struggle: workers and employers in any given branch of the economy should form groupings for cooperation. The papal directives, sounding like an evocation of the medieval craft guilds, seemed to endorse the Fascist system of labor-management corporations that Mussolini had devised to smash the left-wing labor unions.

For a few years from 1933 on, the Viennese heard a lot about *Quadragesimo Anno,* but few took the trouble of reading the pontifical text with its vague, curial formulations. Dollfuss in his high-pitched voice dwelled in speech after speech on the future blessings of his "corporate state," always mentioning as an example how a peasant family with their farmhands were peacefully sitting around the dinner table. Such harmony may have existed in his birthplace, Texing, but his rural image of interclass idylls made no sense in an industrial and service economy like Vienna's. The *Heimwehren* interpreted all that talk about the "corporate state" as simply a way of saying that Austria was to adopt Mussolini's system.

Starhemberg's private army was at that time costing Italy plenty of money, and Il Duce wanted to see results. He wrote in a personal letter to Dollfuss that the time may have come for dislodging the Socialists from their "fortress Vienna." Starhemberg reinforced Mussolini's urgings with a public demand for disbandment of the Social Democratic Party and a takeover of Vienna's City Hall by the federal government. Moderate Social Democrats, mindful of the fate of their German comrades under Hitler, made secret overtures to Dollfuss, suggesting a compromise: Parliament should be reconvened, affirm Austria's determination to stay independent, and confer full powers on the government; in exchange for Social Democratic acquiescence in such a procedure, Vienna's municipal administration must remain intact. The chancellor rejected the proposed deal.

MURDER IN THE CHANCELLERY

Civil war, for years latent, broke out in earnest on February 12, 1934. Militant groups in the Social Democratic rank and file, long impatient with the cautious attitude of their party's leadership, started fighting on their own. The first shots were fired in the regional capital of Upper Austria, Linz, when police started searches for hidden weapons of the banned Republican Protection Corps. Hostilities quickly spread to Vienna. For three days, close to twenty thousand underground members of the dissolved left-wing militias battled the government forces—police, detachments of the *Heimwehren,* and eventually army units. Focal points of the fighting were the superblocks of Red Vienna. Engagements were particularly fierce around the giant Karl-Marx-Hof, whose Social Democratic defenders surrendered only after an artillery attack had caused one of the complex's central towers to collapse. Field guns and regular infantry also overcame the resistance of other superblock fortresses. Nearly a thousand persons died in the fighting in Vienna, in Upper Austria, and in the mining-industrial area of Styria. The government had proclaimed martial law at the beginning of the clashes, and fifteen captured Social Democratic leaders were hanged or shot after summary proceedings.

Otto Bauer, the theoretician of Austro-Marxism, and other prominent Social Democrats fled to Czechoslovakia and set up headquarters of their party-in-exile in Brno. Soon Viennese workers were able to read smuggled copies of the *Arbeiter-Zeitung,* then being printed in the nearby Moravian center. The power of Red Vienna, however, was broken. The Dollfuss regime named the Christian Social politician Richard Schmitz new mayor of the capital and took over former Social Democratic institutions, such as the adult-education system. Instead of taking on the illegal Nazi networks, Austro-Fascism had crushed the sole force that might have offered serious resistance to Hitler.

On May 1, 1934, the Dollfuss government promulgated a new constitution "In the Name of God Almighty, Source of all Law." Most of the charter remained on paper. Political parties, which were supposed to disappear, in fact continued to function underground or as factions within the Patriotic Front. The economic-social corporations that were to supersede the old political groupings and trade unions never came to life. The illegal Nazi Party grew stronger and more defiant by the month, recruiting members among the police, the army, and the civil service.

Twelve weeks after Dollfuss had his clerical-Fascist constitution enacted, the Nazis struck. In Vienna, high police officers and probably also one or the other member of the Dollfuss cabinet knew about the Nazi conspiracy when the putschists started their enterprise shortly after noon on a steamy day, July 25, 1934. Nearly two hundred men—members of the underground SS Regiment no. 89 and other handpicked Nazis—had gathered in a gymnastics hall in the Siebenstern-Gasse behind the former imperial stables, close to the city core. Most of them had donned stolen uniforms of the federal police and the army, and had been equipped with weapons and plenty of ammunition.

Before 1 P.M. a commando was driven in a truck to the headquarters of the government-controlled Austrian Radio, a former elementary school in the narrow Johannesgasse, near the State Opera. The insurgents penetrated into the building and forced an announcer to broadcast that Federal Chancellor Dollfuss had resigned and that the Austrian minister in Rome, Anton Rintelen, had been named his successor. Rintelen had arrived in Vienna two days earlier, but few people knew about it. A

Christian Social politician, he had for years been drifting toward the right-wing, pro-German camp and had good contacts with leading Nazis. The announcement on the radio that he had taken over as government chief was to be the signal for uprisings throughout the country, and indeed, Nazi bands in the provinces of Austria tried to occupy police stations and other government buildings, but were crushed everywhere. From Bavaria, troops of armed men belonging to the Austrian Legion invaded frontier areas in Upper Austria, but in armed confrontations with Austrian police, they were chased back into Germany. The radio headquarters in Vienna was soon retaken by steel-helmeted policemen who had appeared in the Johannesgasse with an armored car and had smoked out the raiders with tear gas. Before surrendering, the rebels threw hand grenades, killing a network employee and a policeman.

The main force of the putschists, one hundred and forty-four men, had meanwhile been driven in four trucks to government headquarters in the Ballhausplatz, where Chancellor Dollfuss was scheduled to preside at a cabinet meeting later that afternoon. The insurgents arrived just as the military guard at the main doorway was being changed, and were able to occupy the historic building and disarm the policemen in it without encountering any resistance. The invaders locked some government workers into their own offices and herded others into a courtyard. At the same time, the leaders of the conspiracy burst into the Office of the Federal Chancellor. Dollfuss tried to escape through a secret winding stair that led to a lower floor, but found the door at its end locked, and was trapped. The commander of the putschists, Otto Planetta, and an active member of the federal police who was in league with the plotters fired at the government chief at close range. Dollfuss suffered wounds on his neck and left shoulder and was put on a couch in his office, near the hall where the committee sessions of the Congress of Vienna had taken place in 1814–15. Two other members of his government who had been in the chancellery were held prisoners.

While Dollfuss was losing blood profusely, the putsch leaders insisted that he declare his resignation in favor of Rintelen and issue orders to the police and army to cease any resistance to the insurgents. Dollfuss asked for a doctor and a priest, but his assailants denied his requests. Eventually the rebels led one of their prisoners, Minister of the Interior Emil Fey, to the dying chancellor, and Dollfuss told him to ask Mussolini to take care of his family. The chancellor's wife and two children were at the time guests of the Mussolinis in their beach villa at Riccione on the Adriatic Sea, while Prince Starhemberg, then vice-chancellor, was in Venice. Three hours after the Nazi action had started, Dollfuss was dead.

The cabinet members who had not been in the Ballhausplatz building had in the meantime assembled in the Defense Ministry and ordered the police to surround the government headquarters but to abstain from any attempt at storming it, lest the putschists kill hostages. A long stalemate ensued. Press reporters who were allowed near the Ballhausplatz saw a broad no-man's-land between the chancellery building, with its main entrance closed, and the steel-helmeted, rifle-toting policemen who were ringing it.

Eventually the German minister to Austria, Kurt Rieth, arrived in the no-man's land and held a loud parley with the leaders of the rebellion, who appeared in windows of the government building. The German diplomat told the putschists that the Austrian government had promised they would be escorted to the German frontier if they evacuated the chancellery before 7:30 P.M.; after that deadline strong military forces would attack. The occupiers of the government headquarters agreed to leave, but as they came out of the building they were arrested and taken to a police barracks. The Vienna government explained that it had no longer felt bound to honor its offer of free conduct for the putschists once it had found they had assassinated Dollfuss. (The putsch leader Planetta and other insurgents were later court-martialed and executed.) On the evening of July 25, Austria's President Wilhelm Miklas appointed Kurt von Schuschnigg, who had served as minister of justice and of education under Dollfuss, as successor to the dead chancellor. In fighting in the capital and elsewhere in the country, the army and the police had lost 107 men, while 269 Nazis had been killed.

Mussolini let it be known at once that "in view of possible complications" he was ordering strong Italian army and air force units to the Austrian frontier. Il Duce, not yet an ally of Hitler, was then still cultivating close relations with Austria and Hungary—viewed as Italy's political satellites in Central Europe—and did not want to see Hitler's power reach his own nation's northern border. He was also angry that his friend Dollfuss had been murdered while the chancellor's wife and children were his own family's houseguests.

Whether Hitler knew all the details of the putsch scenario in Vienna is still not clear: he had just annihilated Ernst Roehm's SA gang in the bloody purge of June 30, 1934, and surely would have welcomed the overthrow of the Austrian regime as a means to divert attention from the slaughter in Germany.

On the other hand, Hitler appears to have then held Mussolini's military forces in higher esteem than he would later, and he surely did not at the time want a confrontation with Fascist Italy. Quickly disowning the Vienna putschists, Berlin stated officially that German authorities had had nothing to do with them and had not been involved in any negotiations; the German minister in Vienna, it was explained, had been acting on his own, and he was recalled. Hitler named his vice-chancellor, Franz von Papen, the new German envoy to Austria. Papen, whose good contacts with the Vatican and Mussolini were known, was considered a moderate, and his appointment to the Vienna post could be interpreted as a conciliatory gesture by Hitler.

Dollfuss' funeral brought hundreds of thousands into the streets of Vienna and into the Heldenplatz (where less than four years later Hitler would savor his triumph). The mourning for the little "hero-chancellor," as Dollfuss was now called by the newspapers and by official orators, seemed general and genuine. Many people were seen crying when the coffin passed on a gun carriage. The cortege was endless. World War I officers had taken their old uniforms out of mothballs to honor a former comrade. Among them was Martin Freud, the son of the founder of psychoanalysis, who had felt he should show his sympathy for a victim of the Nazis. The younger Freud had seen action during World War I and had been decorated for gallantry, as was his brother Ernst. Martin, by then a lawyer, discovered that his old lieutenant's tunic no longer fitted him, but he found a larger one at a secondhand store, pinned his decorations on it, and attended the funeral.

Martin Freud was to write much later, in exile in London, that during their last years in Vienna "the Freud family were anything but neutral . . . all our sympathies were with the chancellor Dollfuss and his successor Schuschnigg."[4] Karl Kraus did not seem his sarcastic self when he, appearing deeply moved, eulogized Dollfuss in a lecture that later was published in *Die Fackel*. Shortly before the Nazi putsch he had written, "Everybody is free to decide whether he wants to die through Hitler or allow Dollfuss to save his life."

The murder of the Austrian chancellor caused dismay in the West. The *Times* of London wrote that Dollfuss would be remembered as a leader of patriotic resistance to Nazi pressures who had put up a "fight of the utmost gallantry." Arturo Toscanini, who had long ceased to conduct in Fascist Italy but had kept making regular appearances at the Salzburg Festival, came to the Austrian capital to lead the Vienna Philharmonic in a performance of Verdi's Requiem during the official Dollfuss commemoration at the State Opera on All Souls' Day in 1934. Austria's Socialists, however, would never forget Dollfuss' acquiescence in the crushing of Red Vienna five months before his own assassination.

Rintelen, whom the Nazi plotters had chosen as successor to Dollfuss, made an unsuccessful suicide attempt, was tried and found guilty of high treason, and received a life sentence. It appeared that his assignment in the putsch had been to call a referendum—which would have been stage-managed by the Nazi Party—to make Austria's absorption by Hitler's Germany official. Rintelen was to serve two years in prison, was amnestied in 1936, and in 1938 became a member of the Nazi Reichstag, that travesty of a national assembly.

Schuschnigg, the last Austrian head of government before the country became a part of the Third Reich, always struck the Viennese as remote and somewhat alien. He was the son of an officer of the Imperial-and-Royal Army who had been transferred from garrison to garrison; he had been educated by Jesuits at their prep school Stella Matutina, an elitist institution near Feldkirch in the westernmost area of the Habsburg monarchy, and had served as an army officer on the Italian front during World War I. Schuschnigg had later earned a law degree in Innsbruck, had gone into politics, and had soon risen in the Christian Democratic Party organization in the Alpine province of the Tyrol. Elected to the Vienna Parliament, he had in 1932 become minister of justice. When German Nazis made cautious soundings for an accommodation with Vienna, Dollfuss had sent his young cabinet member on a secret mission to Munich. At the end of October 1933, Schuschnigg had met there with SS chief Heinrich Himmler and Rudolf Hess, the "Deputy of the Führer," but their confidential talks led nowhere.

THE SPELL

As Austrian chancellor, Schuschnigg soon met with Mussolini, then still regarded as the principal guarantor of the small republic's independence. Il Duce, however, liked the cool, intellectual Austrian far less than he had liked the extrovert Dollfuss. Furthermore, Mussolini was then preparing his conquest of Ethiopia and could not afford indefinitely to sustain Italy's military watch on his nation's northern frontier to protect Austria from Germany. The Fascist dictator was veering toward Hitler, and the Rome-Berlin Axis was in the making. Yet, when Italian troops invaded the territories of Emperor Haile Selassie in 1935, Viennese Nazis sported badges with the Ethiopian colors, green-yellow-red, as substitutes for the swastikas that had been banned since 1933; they did not know then that Mussolini, once Dollfuss' friend, would soon be the official ally of Hitler and that the "Steel Pact" was already being forged.

Italian recommendations to Schuschnigg to seek an accord with the Nazi government soon became pressing. New secret talks took place, and on July 11, 1936, Berlin and Vienna announced an agreement whereby Nazi Germany formally recognized Austria's "full sovereignty" and declared that the Nazi movement in Austria was an "internal matter" of that country. Vienna, for its part, pledged to pursue a policy based on "the fact that Austria professes to be a German state." An unpublished appendix to the accord obligated the Austrian government to grant an ample amnesty to Nazi detainees and to seek the collaboration of pro-German personages with the government.

An immediate consequence of the Austro-German deal was that many Viennese who had up to then been sitting on the fence jumped into the Hitler camp. At one's job and on one's block, one knew pretty well who the Nazis were; they now found themselves courted by colleagues and neighbors. The Nazi underground networks were reinforced by more members who had the Patriotic Front ribbons in their lapels. Schuschnigg, neither greatly loved nor violently hated, just did not look like a winner. Aloof, and speaking an idiom between Tyrolean and standard German that sounded stilted to Viennese ears, the prematurely gray chancellor appeared ill at ease in his embattled post. He went to church but not to the coffeehouse. He did, though, have contacts with the Viennese intelligentsia as an occasional guest in Alma Mahler-Werfel's salon.

Gustav Mahler's widow had at last become the wife of the writer from Prague when she was close to fifty and—as she noted in her diary —menopausal. The Werfels bought an apartment in Venice and a villa near the Türkenschanze, the well-to-do neighborhood on Vienna's northwestern outskirts. There, Alma had a large music room built and was holding court: Thomas Mann, H. G. Wells, Sinclair Lewis, and other international figures were her guests. After Lewis won the 1930 Nobel Prize in literature, Alma started lobbying to get her husband a Nobel too; soon his books were being burned in Germany together with those of other Jewish and "degenerate" writers. When Alma Mahler's daughter by Walter Gropius, Manon, contracted polio in Venice, Schuschnigg sent an ambulance there to take her home to Vienna. In 1937, Werfel attended a conference of the Organization of Intellectual Cooperation, a League of Nations appendage, and submitted a proposal for the creation of a "World Academy of Poets and Thinkers," a project that he had probably discussed with Schuschnigg; nothing ever came of it.

The Nazi vultures were already wheeling over Vienna, and the ranks of the city's intelligentsia were thinning. Jewish refugees from Germany who after 1933 had found a refuge in the Austrian capital moved on to Prague, Paris, London, or the western hemisphere. Hofmannsthal and Schnitzler were dead. Karl Kraus died on June 12, 1936, after having been knocked down accidentally by a cyclist earlier that year and subjected thereafter to headaches and memory lapses. During his last years, the lifelong loner had been almost completely isolated in Vienna. Kraus had seemed stunned when Hitler came to power in Germany, and it was an unusually long time before another issue of his magazine appeared. "With regard to Hitler, no thought occurs to me," Kraus wrote; he seemed to know that he was disappointing his fans by his uncharacteristically wordless attempts at grasping the significance of the Nazi tide. Bertolt Brecht justified the sudden taciturnity of "the articulate one" in a poem in which he said that silence, too, was a way of bearing witness. Kraus was at that time seeking intellectual solace in Goethe, Shakespeare, Nestroy, and linguistics. The last issue of *Die Fackel* (Nos. 917–22) contained harsh attacks on the Austrian Social Democrats, whom Kraus had for some time supported.

Robert Musil had become better known and more generally appreciated after the first volume of his *Man Without Qualities* and the fragments of a second volume had been published between 1930 and 1933. He remained nevertheless strapped financially while he kept rewriting each page of his literary production at least five times. To enable him to complete his great novel, friends and admirers, encouraged by Thomas Mann, set up a Robert Musil Fund and asked wealthy people to chip in. In 1936, Musil, always intent on staying trim and fit, suffered a stroke while swimming in the Dianabad, a Vienna indoor swimming pool.

Thereafter, he appeared to be slowing down in his work, relying on his wife in all practical matters even more than before.

Wittgenstein had long since returned to Cambridge, Popper had accepted an academic assignment in New Zealand, and Schoenberg was already in the United States (see the next chapter). In 1935 the composer received a despondent letter from his friend and former disciple Alban Berg, who complained he felt "homeless in my fatherland." Berg was in a profound depression, brought on by lack of recognition in Vienna, by money trouble, and by the death of a young friend—Manon Gropius, the beautiful, gifted daughter of Alma Mahler, who had eventually succumbed to her polio at the age of nineteen. Berg dedicated his Violin Concerto "to the Memory of an Angel" as a last tribute to Manon, and on Christmas Eve 1935 died himself, of septicemia, in a Vienna hospital.

Another Viennese who was feeling homeless in his fatherland was Stefan Zweig. The writer had been living with his wife and two daughters by her first marriage in a rambling villa on a hill overlooking Salzburg, the Kapuzinerberg. After Hitler came to power in Germany, Zweig started sleeping badly: "I always hear the rumbling of tanks in Bavaria," he said. (The Bavarian border is a few miles from Salzburg.) After the street battles in Vienna in February 1934, Zweig moved to London.

A thinker and novelist who had for years been a familiar face in the literary coffeehouses of Vienna, Hermann Broch, left the city to live in small towns in the Styrian mountains. During the hectic years after World War I, Broch, then the manager of his family's textile plant, which had several hundred workers, had cut a dashing figure in the Café Central and Café Herrenhof. Commuting from the bleak company town of Teesdorf, south of Vienna, to the capital, the elegant, handsome industrialist had mingled with the Arconauts, had had an affair with Milena Jesenska before her liaison with Kafka, and had befriended Alfred Adler, Canetti, Alma Mahler's daughter Anna, and many other members of Vienna's intellectual society. From his school days in the city Broch knew Alban Berg.

Broch's father had come to the empire's capital from Moravia at age twelve and had worked his way up from messenger boy to becoming a wholesaler in textiles and owner of the Teesdorf factory. Hermann Broch had studied the textile industry in Vienna and Alsatia, had briefly visited the United States, and had eventually taken over the Teesdorf plant. In

1909 he had converted from Judaism to the Roman Catholic faith and married the daughter of a wealthy sugar producer, Franziska von Rothermann; they had become quickly estranged, and after World War I were divorced.

Although he had never been much interested in business, Broch became involved in labor-management relations after the war and for some time acted as arbitrator in industrial conflicts. For several years he conducted a double life, as an industrial manager and as a Vienna intellectual. He contributed articles to highbrow magazines like Ficker's *Der Brenner* and in the late 1920s attended university lectures in philosophy and mathematics by Moritz Schlick and other luminaries of the Vienna Circle.

At last, in 1927, Broch made an old dream come true by selling his Teesdorf factory and establishing himself as a full-time writer. His trilogy *The Sleepwalkers* appeared 1931–32 and received good reviews, but found few buyers. The three novels deal with Germany under and after Emperor Wilhelm II and were to illustrate, as the author explained, the decay of values as shown in many individual destinies. Hannah Arendt, whom Broch was to meet in the United States much later, would call him a "poet in spite of himself." Broch's first works established his reputation as a writers' writer, which would cling to him: philosophical digressions in his novels prove his studies and meditations, but do not make for easy reading.

From 1933 on, Broch slid into near-poverty, and he disappeared from Vienna for months to hole up in the Alps. He was then working on a project that his friends called his "mountain novel"; Broch himself considered various titles, including *The Tempter* (the work was published in English in 1986 as *The Spell*). The novel is an allegory of the Nazi plague: In a secluded Alpine village a mysterious stranger turns up, wins over most of the people to his crackpot pagan cult, and eventually wields power over the entire community; the collective folly culminates in human sacrifice. The village is realistically portrayed, but the events as narrated by a middle-aged country doctor are patently symbolic of what had been happening in Germany and was going on in Austria at the time when Broch was writing.

The spellbinder Hitler could by then count on at least eighty thousand members of the illegal Nazi Party in Austria. Some of them were being held in a detention camp for suspected "antistate" activists that the Vienna government had set up in a disused industrial area at Wöllersdorf, south of Vienna; but most of the Nazis were at large and rather unrestrained. Papen, Hitler's envoy in Vienna—now with the title Ambassador—was quite openly in touch with leading Austrian Hitlerites and was also successfully wooing Austrian business executives and Roman Catholic intellectuals. Papen had his spies within Schuschnigg's cabinet, and in his secret reports advised Hitler to step up pressure on Austria by degrees.

NORTHERN LIGHTS

At the end of January 1938, Vienna saw for a few nights the luminous arches of the aurora borealis in the sky. The phenomenon, frequent in arctic regions, is unusual in Central Europe; it had last been observed, it seems, just before Napoleon's forces occupied Vienna. Many people said the northern lights were a portent of grave events to come.

On February 12, Vienna was jolted by the news that Schuschnigg was meeting with Hitler at the Nazi leader's Eagle's Nest, his vacation home six thousand feet up the Obersalzburg, a mountain near Berchtesgaden from which one can look far into Austrian territory. Papen had long suggested such an encounter, and the Austrian chancellor had eventually walked into the trap. What happened on that day in Hitler's aerie has often been told. Without any pretense to diplomatic or common courtesies, Hitler ranted at his visitor, called him a traitor to his own people, told him that no power on earth was supporting the Vienna government, and threatened a military invasion of Austria in a matter of hours unless Schuschnigg accepted all his conditions without any negotiations: "I won't change a comma!"

While Schuschnigg was exposed to Hitler's fury, Field Marshal Wilhelm Keitel, General Walter von Reichenau, and Luftwaffe General Hugo Sperrle (whose Condor Legion had destroyed defenseless Guernica the year before) were in and out of the meeting room, clicking their heels and shouting "Mein Führer!" as they were apparently reporting from time to time on the progress of supposed preparations for a military invasion of Austria. Hitler contemptuously addressed his guest as "Herr Schuschnigg," whereas the Austrian used the most deferential form of Viennese speech whenever the "Herr Reichskanzler" gave him a chance of putting in a few embarrassed words.

Schuschnigg caved in and accepted the draft "agreement" put before him. During the gloomy car trip from the Obersalzburg back to the Salzburg railroad station Papen, who had accompanied Schuschnigg, remarked airily, "Yes, that's the way the Führer can be; now you have seen for yourself. . . . Yet the Führer can also be downright charming."

The text that Hitler had presented to Schuschnigg called for inclusion of Nazis in the Austrian government; an amnesty for convicted and detained Nazis, including the surviving 1934 putschists; a blanket authorization for Nazis to carry out "legal activities" within the Patriotic Front (which had been established as an anti-Nazi organization); and close political and diplomatic coordination between Berlin and Vienna. An Austrian Nazi, Artur Seyss-Inquart, became minister of the interior and public security in the Schuschnigg government, and thus was in control of the police. The end of Austrian sovereignty came quickly.

In the Alpine provinces, especially in Styria and Carinthia, Nazis took over the schools, many government offices, and the army and police barracks. Swastika banners were seen everywhere, and jubilant crowds were parading. In Vienna, hundreds and then thousands surged into the streets, shouting "Heil Hitler!" and "One People, one Reich, one Führer!" The police no longer interfered. Schuschnigg, seeing the last shreds of power slipping from his hands, had the national assembly convened, and in an impassioned address on February 24 restated Austria's determination to remain independent. He concluded his speech with the words, "Bis in the Tod—rot-weiss-rot!" ("Until death, red-white-red!"). The deputies cheered.

At last—much too late!—Schuschnigg got in touch with Red Vienna, the underground leaders of the outlawed Social Democratic Party. They told him in a confidential meeting they had no friendly feelings toward the regime that had been shooting at workers four years earlier, but were willing to collaborate with him to defend the country from the Nazis. Schuschnigg promised he would see to it that Social Democrats could again be legally active in public life.

In the evening of Wednesday, March 9, 1938, Schuschnigg startled the world with an announcement that the country's population would be called out in three days' time, on Sunday, March 13, to vote in a plebiscite on whether they wanted a "free and German, independent and social, Christian and united Austria." Mussolini had been informed of Schuschnigg's referendum plan two days earlier and had urgently advised against it.

No ballots had been printed for the proposed plebiscite, no voting stations designated, no vote-counting commissions set up. The Patriotic Front improvised a propaganda drive with leaflets, sound trucks, and a few rallies. Despite the inadequate preparations and the lack of a campaign strategy, political experts predicted that Schuschnigg would win his referendum—if Hitler permitted it to be held. Vienna, representing almost one third of Austria's electorate, was expected to return a strong anti-Hitler vote, the Nazi street demonstrations notwithstanding. The Revolutionary Socialists, an underground organization that considered itself the heir to Red Vienna, warned the workers that the plebiscite was no occasion for "settling accounts with Austro-Fascism" but must express "our burning hatred of Hitler's Fascism." Lower Austria, the country's largest region, was also regarded as a reservoir of anti-Hitler votes. That the Alpine provinces—particularly Styria, Carinthia, and Salzburg—would overwhelmingly vote for Hitler was a foregone conclusion.

Hitler did not take any chances. Early on Friday, March 11, Germany demanded in an ultimatum that the Austrian government call off the projected referendum, and Vienna yielded. Hitler, through middlemen, ordered Schuschnigg to resign at once and to hand over the leadership of the government to the Nazi interior minister, Seyss-Inquart. The German army was poised to invade Austria within hours, Vienna was warned. Schuschnigg tried to speak to Mussolini, but Il Duce would not come to the phone. At last Rome sent word that "in the present circumstances" it could offer neither help nor advice. Paris was absorbed in another one of the recurrent cabinet crises of the Third Republic and could not just then be expected to take any initiative in international affairs. The government of Neville Chamberlain in Britain was nursing hopes for an overall understanding with Hitler's Germany and would not interfere with his annexation of Austria. Nor would the United States government contemplate any move.

After a series of confused talks with foreign diplomats and Austrian politicians and officials, Schuschnigg told Wilhelm Miklas, the head of state, that he was going to resign. The sixty-six-year-old Miklas, in office since 1928, was a Christian Social moderate, a bland, well-tailored, and at times unctuous personage who perfectly fitted the figurehead role that Austria's constitution had assigned to the President of the Republic. "Now you are all leaving me alone," Miklas said. To everybody's surprise the head of state, whom the Viennese had long considered wishy-washy, showed a measure of strength and dignity: when the German military attaché General Wolfgang Muff relayed to him Hitler's request to appoint Seyss-Inquart forthwith as Schuschnigg's successor, Miklas refused.

Hitler thought he needed some seemingly legitimate government in Vienna that would formally request the "assistance" of German forces on the pretext that it was no longer capable of maintaining law and order. All day German radio stations kept broadcasting reports about grave disturbances, and even bloodshed, in Vienna and throughout Austria. Actually there had been Nazi demonstrations as in earlier days, but no clashes or casualties.

Would the Austrian army have obeyed if an order had been given to resist Hitler? The question has been debated in Vienna ever since 1938. Austria had then sixty thousand men under arms, twice the number foreseen in its peace treaty of 1919; the World War I enemies had not objected to the introduction of compulsory military service in 1936. After the assassination of Dollfuss the police and the army had readily quelled Nazi insurgency in the provinces and had pushed the Austrian Legion back into Germany. Schuschnigg's defense chief, General Wilhelm Zehner, had assured the chancellor that the army would fight invading Germans if ordered to do so. (Zehner was to be one of the first victims of Nazi retribution in Vienna; he was shot in his apartment on March 12, 1938.) Austrian resistance to the German army would have embarrassed Hitler and stirred anti-Nazi groups even if the defenders were to succumb in an unequal fight within a few days.

Yet, Schuschnigg lost his nerve. "We are yielding to force," he told the Austrian people in a sad, fatigued voice in a broadcast from the Red Salon of the chancellor's office in the government headquarters on the evening of March 11. He spoke into the microphone a few steps from the couch on which Dollfuss had died in 1934. "Since we are not prepared—not even in this grave hour—to shed German blood," Schuschnigg went on, "we have ordered our armed forces, in case the [Nazi] invasion takes place, to withdraw without offering substantial resistance, and to await the decisions of the next hours." The chancellor closed his farewell with the words, "God protect Austria!" After he had ended, the Austrian Radio network put the same record of Schubert's *Unfinished* Symphony on the air that it had broadcast after its announcement of Dollfuss' death. The B-minor melodies would for a generation of Viennese evoke tragic memories.

Shortly after Schuschnigg's farewell address, the state broadcasting network advised that it could no longer relay any other message from him. Government headquarters filled up with tough young men wearing swastika armlets, and Seyss-Inquart started posturing like a government chief. Toward midnight, President Miklas gave up his resistance to Hitler's orders and formally signed Seyss-Inquart and his new Nazi cabinet into power, a power that was to prove short-lived. Seyss-Inquart offered to escort Schuschnigg personally to the Hungarian legation, close to the Ballhausplatz, where he might find asylum; the former chancellor refused and said he wanted to go home.

Schuschnigg had lately been living in a small building looking out on the Belvedere park, together with his father (a retired army general), his son, and a woman whom he described as his fiancée. The chancellor's wife, Herma, had died in a car accident in Upper Austria in 1935. Seyss-Inquart took his predecessor to the Belvedere apartment shortly after midnight and said goodbye to him there. Schuschnigg started waiting for the Nazis to come and get him.

Minutes after Schuschnigg's last broadcast, trucks with men in SA and SS uniforms had rumbled through the streets of Vienna's center. Bands of youths with swastika armlets had started roaming various neighborhoods, smashing the windows and tearing down the business signs of Jewish-owned stores. Large crowds had gathered in front of the government headquarters, in the central shopping streets, and in the thoroughfares of the outlying districts, and wild shouts of "Heil Hitler!" and "Juda verrecke!" ("Judah, Croak!") were heard all over the city. Suddenly, everyone was sporting the swastika. In the late evening hours enterprising street vendors had turned up with heaps of metal swastika badges, which sold briskly. Policemen put swastikas on their uniforms and were hugged and kissed by hysterical women. Swastika flags fluttered from many buildings, and householders living on lower floors put Hitler portraits into their windows.

There were also thousands of Viennese who wept on listening to Schuschnigg's farewell on the radio; they were not seen in the streets that night. They stayed at home, uneasily waiting for more news from the broadcasting network, which was already controlled by the Nazis. Long after midnight, the announcement came that all schools would remain closed on March 12 (in Austria classes were then held on Saturdays too), and the population was urged to put out swastika flags to mark "the historic day." There seemed to be no lack of Nazi flags.

The shouting in the streets went on through most of the night. People who had remained indoors called friends by telephone to exchange news and impressions. There were nasty surprises: people whom one had trusted were now boasting they had been Nazi sympathizers or even party members all along. A few Viennese who had most to fear and had the quickest reflexes made dashes to one of the city's rail terminals to catch the first train and get out of the country before the Germans arrived. There were rumors—which later proved to be true—that packs of young Nazis armed with handguns were raiding the apartments of well-known business and professional people, and were harassing them.

Guido Zernatto, a writer and poet from Carinthia who had been minister in charge of the Patriotic Front in the Schuschnigg government, grabbed a car and, with his wife, drove to safety across the nearby Czechoslovak border. Erwin Schrödinger, who in 1933 had shared the Nobel Prize in physics with Paul A. M. Dirac of Britain, found himself with his wife, Annemarie, in the Nazi delirium of Graz. They drove to the Italian border and walked across it. Later the Schrödingers had trouble getting across the Italian-Swiss border because the Swiss policemen were baffled by their lack of any luggage. In Switzerland at last, Schrödinger put through a telephone call to Ireland's Prime Minister Eamon de Valera, who was also a mathematician. De Valera at once appointed Schrödinger dean of a new Institute of Advanced Studies in Dublin. For refugees from the Nazis who were not Nobel laureates the reception abroad would be much cooler.

At dawn on Saturday, March 12, a sinister pair arrived at Vienna's Aspern Airport: SS chief Heinrich Himmler and his deputy, Reinhard Heydrich. They went to work at once. During the next few days the Viennese whispered to one another the news of sudden deaths. Among the first victims was Major Emil Fey, a leader of the *Heimwehren* who during World War I had won Austria-Hungary's highest decoration for gallantry (the Maria Theresa Order); in February 1934 he had, as vice-chancellor, played a decisive role in defeating the Social Democratic rebels, and during the Nazi putsch in July of that year he had for a few hours been a prisoner of Dollfuss' assassins. Ever since then, there had been rumors that he had known of the Nazi conspiracy in advance. After the *Anschluss,* Fey, his wife and son, their maid, and even their dog were found shot dead in their home. The official version was suicide-murder, but many Viennese were convinced that the Feys had been massacred. Another alleged suicide was Odo Neustädter-Stürmer, a member of the right-wing militias who, as a minister in the Dollfuss cabinet, had negotiated with the Nazi putschists in July 1934.

It was still dark in the early hours of March 12 when the Viennese heard the droning of low-flying Luftwaffe aircraft; the planes kept circling over the city for hours to intimidate the population. On land, the military invasion began in the west of Austria in the first light of the morning. Not everything went as smoothly as Hitler's generals had planned: scores of tanks and troop carriers broke down or ran out of fuel and had to limp to Austrian service stations. No armed resistance was encountered, however, and the population welcomed the occupiers jubilantly, to the visible surprise of many German soldiers.

Hitler had waited to give his forces marching orders until he was sure Mussolini would acquiesce. Late in the evening of March 11, Prince Philipp of Hesse, a Nazi who was a son-in-law of the Italian king and served as a go-between from one dictator to the other, had reported to Hitler by telephone from Rome that he had called on Mussolini at his office in the Palazzo Venezia and had received the assurance Italy would not move a finger. Hitler then sent his famous message: "Duce! I shall never forget this."

FINIS AUSTRIAE

The Italian press attaché in Vienna, Cristano Ridomi, came to his office near the State Opera while the propellers of the Nazi aircraft were churning overhead and with a smirk, wrote on the day's leaf of his desk calendar "Finis Austriae" (The End of Austria). Ridomi was the man of Count Galeazzo Ciano, Mussolini's son-in-law and foreign minister. When he had been named to the Vienna post as successor to Eugenio Morreale, Prince Starhemberg's friend, the international community in Vienna sensed that Mussolini was writing Austria off. Now, Ridomi's high spirits contrasted with the dejection of other Italians in the city. That morning, foreign diplomats, on the phone with one another and with their home governments, were speculating on how long they would be allowed to stay in the Austrian capital.

Sigmund Freud heard newsvendors shout "Extra! Extra!" in the usually quiet Bergasse. "Quick, Paula, get me the *Abend!*" he told the maid. Paula was never very quick, but Freud eventually got to read the latest news about the Nazi takeover, and he, too, wrote "Finis Austriae" on the calendar-diary that was always on his desk. He had "often expressed warm admiration for the brave Schuschnigg," Martin Freud reported later in his reminiscences about his father.

Schuschnigg and those with him were isolated in their Belvedere park residence, subjected to petty harassment by young Nazi guards. The former Austrian chancellor underwent the first of many questionings only two weeks after the invasion. Four Gestapo officers wanted to know from him what property he owned (Schuschnigg said he had none); whether he was a Freemason (no); what his relationship with Baron Rothschild had been (none); and what dealings he had had with the Habsburgs (evasive reply). The questioners told the prisoner also that Cardinal Innitzer, the Archbishop of Vienna, had spoken unfavorably of him. It figured.

The former chancellor was eventually transferred to the Vienna Gestapo headquarters and held there in a bare top-floor room for seventeen months. He recalled later that some of the Nazis who were guarding him around the clock were more sadistic than others. After a time, he was allowed to marry his fiancée, Vera Czernin, by proxy. In 1940, Schuschnigg was moved to the Gestapo prison in Munich, and in December 1941, to Sachsenhausen concentration camp. His wife was authorized to join him, and a daughter, Maria Dolores Elisabeth, was born to them in a prison clinic. During the last stages of World War II the Schuschniggs were moved, successively, to the Flossenburg and Dachau concentration camps, and eventually to the South Tyrol, where they and other prominent prisoners were liberated by United States forces.

The first German army units reached Vienna in the evening of March 12, 1938. The chunky infantry soldiers in their gray-green uniforms under steel helmets grinned from their trucks as crowds of Viennese were cheering them. During the following days quite a few members of the invasion force confided to their new Viennese friends that they had feared being shot at when they had crossed the Austrian border and that the flowers showered on them and the general enthusiasm were a big surprise. The Viennese, on the other hand, were astonished to observe how the newcomers were marveling at all the butter, sausages, cakes, and whipped cream they could buy with their marks. Many German soldiers fashioned food parcels and sent them home: in Germany, guns had long been higher than butter on Hitler's list of priorities.

Task forces of the Gestapo and the SS had turned up in Vienna even before the regular German army arrived. Local SS and SA men in their uniforms and with handguns were strutting in the streets, deferentially saluted by the Vienna policemen. Gangs of civilians, many teenagers among them, with swastika armlets and a variety of weapons, kept ransacking apartments and stores of Jews and of known supporters of the Schuschnigg regime. Nazis with grudges were carrying out private vendettas. Jewish and anti-Nazi schoolteachers and office workers were ordered to stay away from their jobs or found it advisable to do so without being told.

Members of SS Regiment no. 89, the unit that had staged the putsch in which Dollfuss was murdered, occupied Vienna's main synagogue. Nearby, on the Morzinplatz off the Danube Canal, the Gestapo installed itself in the two-hundred-and-fifty-room Hotel Metropole and adapted entire floors as detention pens. Within days, the name Hotel Metropole became the synonym for terror and torture. In Vienna's streets anyone who was not wearing a swastika risked being mauled by roving gangs of young hoodlums. The city's coffeehouses had overnight become eerie, nearly empty places while the beer halls and taverns were thronged with celebrating Nazis and, after a few days, with off-duty German soldiers. The *Anschluss* kept the brewery trucks busy.

On Sunday, March 13, Vienna learned that it was no longer a capital city. Hitler had on his triumphant progress into conquered territory paused in Linz—where he had grown up and dropped out of school—and issued there a law "On the Reunion of Austria with the German Reich." In Vienna, Seyss-Inquart and his Nazi ministers hurriedly voted ratification of the law, but President Miklas, still holding out, refused to put his signature under the text. The Nazis thereupon told the Austrian head of state that he was through; Miklas did sign a resignation statement.

Excitement in Vienna peaked when Hitler at last arrived and savored victory in the city where he had once lived as an outcast. To the deafening cheers of the vastest crowd that the capital had ever seen, he declared in an address in the Heldenplatz, "As Führer and Chancellor of the German nation I report now, before History, the entry of my native land into the German Reich." The World War I corporal who had taken orders from sergeants now was reporting to History.

News photos and newsreels convinced the world at large that the Viennese enthusiastically wanted to join Hitler's Third Reich. The images and press reports seemed to justify the inertia of the governments that Schuschnigg had in vain begged for help. Only the Soviet Union, Republican Spain, Mexico, Chile, and China lodged official protests against the annexation of Austria. The United States, Britain, France, and most other countries soon downgraded their legations in Vienna to consulates.

During the following weeks, the Gestapo arrested tens of thousands of Viennese; an estimated seventy thousand people were sent to prisons or concentration camps. Christian Social and Social Democratic politicians, who had for many years been feuding, were caught in a VIP dragnet, together with labor leaders and anti-Nazi officials. They were all herded into a special railroad train and shipped to Dachau; during the nightmarish journey, young SS men—most of them Austrians—took turns beating up the prisoners.

The Nazi rage did not spare the dead either. As Jewish cemeteries were being desecrated, raiders caused havoc in the apartment where Karl Kraus had lived and worked, destroying books and memorabilia kept there. Kraus's publisher-friend Richard Lanyi was beaten to death in a concentration camp. Kraus's brother and favorite niece also were to die in a camp.

Hitler still wanted a semblance of legitimacy and called a plebiscite in which Austrians were to state whether they wished their country to be a part of the Great German Reich. Cataracts of Nazi propaganda poured down on Vienna and the Austrian provinces during three weeks; pressures and blandishments were used to induce influential personages and groups to recommend a yes vote.

It was easy to get Vienna's archbishop, Cardinal Innitzer, to endorse the Nazi takeover. Had not he obsequiously called on Hitler on his first day in the city, and given the Nazi salute? Now, the cardinal convened the other Austrian bishops and with them issued a pastoral manifesto urging the faithful to do their "national duty" by voting for the *Anschluss*. Innitzer did even more: he had his signature under the church document preceded by a handwritten "Heil Hitler!" Reproductions of the cardinal's obeisance to the Nazi dictator were disseminated in posters and leaflets without number.

The muted masses of Red Vienna in the factories and in the municipal superblocks were disconcerted when Karl Renner, the first chancellor of the Austrian Republic, declared in a newspaper interview that "as a Social Democrat" he would vote yes in Hitler's plebiscite. He recalled that he had come out in 1918 for union between Austria and Germany. "Although it has not been brought about by the methods I profess," the Social Democratic leader went on, "the *Anschluss* has nevertheless been achieved and is a historic fact. . . . The aimless twenty-year journey of the Austrian people has now ended." Renner would make a political comeback after World War II as chancellor and eventually as president of a resurrected Austria. A biographer suggested after his death that Renner's pro-*Anschluss* statement in 1938, "which was also in keeping with his German-national conviction," was to some extent prompted by the circumstance that his son-in-law was Jewish. The Gestapo had arrested Hans Deutsch, a former director of the city-controlled Hammer bakery who was the husband of Renner's daughter Leopoldine; Deutsch was later released and allowed to emigrate to England. Renner's 1938 declaration may thus have been "a personal arrangement with the people in power at the time."[5] In any case, it convinced many Social Democrats that it was useless to resist the Nazis.

With a prince of the church and an elder statesman of Red Vienna calling for a yes vote in Hitler's plebiscite, the Nazis easily obtained a slew of similar *Anschluss* endorsements from writers, scholars, artists, actors, and other well-known personages. Among them was Josef Weinheber, the author of formally perfect poetry in Viennese dialect; he would commit suicide in 1945. Another public supporter of Austria's annexation was the conductor Karl Böhm, who was to reap honors at home and abroad after World War II.

On the eve of the plebiscite, Hitler revisited Vienna and rhetorically told its new Nazi mayor, Hermann Neubacher, "This city, in my eyes, is a gem! I shall mount it in a setting worthy of it, and entrust it to the care of the entire German Reich!" And in an address to a frenzied crowd filling the disused Northwest Railroad Terminal, Hitler boasted, "My name will endure as that of a great son of this country. I believe it was God's will that a boy was sent from here into the German Reich, to let him achieve greatness, to make him the leader of the nation and enable him to take his native land into the Reich."

Before 7 A.M. on Sunday, April 10, 1938, thousands of Viennese were already lining up at the polling stations; by noon the majority of enfranchised voters—no Jews, of course—had already cast their ballots. Foreign news correspondents who had toured voting places reported that the plebiscite was being conducted in an orderly way and that they had seen no sign of coercion. Swastika emblems and Nazi uniforms were everywhere, it is true, and many voters did not bother to enter the polling booths but demonstratively crossed the yes circle on the ballot right in front of the precinct commission. Anti-Nazi Viennese confided to trusted friends they, too, had voted yes because they were convinced the Nazis had ways of finding out who had cast a no ballot and would take reprisals.

After the steamroller Nazi propaganda in the weeks before the plebiscite—when no opposition voice was to be heard—and in the climate of Hitlerite hysteria and implicit or open intimidation on voting day, no one was surprised at the official outcome: 99.73 percent for the end of Austria.

"I am so happy," Hitler broadcast from Berlin to a huge Nazi victory rally in Vienna.

NOTES TO CHAPTER IV

1. Hans Ziesel, *The Austromarxists in "Red" Vienna: Reflections and Recollections,* in *The Austrian Socialist Experiment,* Anson Rabinbach, ed., Boulder and London, 1985, p. 126.
2. Elias Canetti, *Das Gewissen der Worte,* Frankfurt, 1981, pp. 243ff.
3. *Works,* Standard Edition, London, 1959, XX, p. 72.
4. *Sigmund Freud, Man and Father,* New York, 1958, p. 196.
5. Norbert Leser, *Genius Austriacus,* Vienna, 1986, p. 194.

5

UP AND DOWN SOMEBODY
ELSE'S STAIRS

Two days after Vienna had all but deified Hitler, one of the wittiest and most provocative residents of the city, Egon Friedell, heard an SS squad come up the stairs. As the Nazis were already outside his apartment door, he called down from his window to warn passersby to clear the sidewalk, and jumped.

Friedell, close to sixty when he chose death, had been a brilliant embodiment of the Viennese coffeehouse civilization. An essayist and sometime actor, he had hung out at the Café Central, had been a friend of Peter Altenberg and other literati, had kept criticizing Freud in print, and had temporarily managed the avant-garde cabaret Fledermaus. He had surprised all those who thought they knew him when he published in 1927–32 the three-volume *Cultural History of the Modern Age,* which spans the period from the black plague to World War I. Crammed as it is with anecdotes, catchy chapter headings, and sweeping conclusions, the work became fashionable reading in the early 1930s, as Oswald Spengler's *Decline of the West* and Hermann, Count Keyserling's *Travel Diary of a Philosopher* had been a few years earlier. Seemingly frivolous, Friedell had not let on that when he was not seen at the coffeehouse, he was doing serious research—another Viennese closet toiler. Academic scholars might dismiss many of Friedell's judgments as superficial, but nobody could deny the impressive range of his interests and the sustained sweep of his writing.

Franz Theodor Csokor, an author who had decided to leave Nazi-ruled Austria although he was not Jewish, called on his friend Friedell and urged him to flee too. Friedell gestured toward his files and card indexes, saying, "I can't possibly leave all this behind." A few hours later he was dead.

Friedell's suicide was one of many hundreds in Vienna in the weeks and months after the Nazi takeover. According to City Hall statistics, 1,358 people killed themselves in Vienna in 1938; the 1937 figure had been 973 (which, at around 60 suicides per 100,000 inhabitants had already been an international record). In 1939 the official number of suicides was 1,075. However, the *Jewish Morning Journal* of New York reported in 1940 that during the first year of Nazi rule, 3,741 Austrian Jews had taken their own lives; "Austrian" in that context was almost synonymous with "Viennese."

Not all of those counted as suicides in Vienna in that period were Jewish. One non-Jewish Viennese who died by his own hand was Karl Sindelar, a star of the soccer Wonder Team whom his many thousands of fans had idolized as *der Papierene* ("the Paper-Thin One"). Suicide, at any rate, as a way out of hopeless situations had always been considered an honorable option in the city. To be sure, some Jews and Gentiles who had allegedly taken their own lives in March 1938 and in the following months had actually been victims of Nazi criminals.

A census held in 1934 established the number of Vienna residents professing what was officially called the "Mosaic faith" as 176,034; at the beginning of 1938 the figure was 168,652. During the seventy years preceding the *Anschluss,* 38,318 Viennese had formally left the Jewish community. The survivors among these nonreligious Jews and converts to Christian confessions, and their descendants, were estimated in 1938 to number at least 30,000; under the Nazi racial laws they all were "non-Aryans."

Goering asserted in an address in the Northwest Railroad Terminal two weeks after the *Anschluss* that 300,000 Jews were parasitically living in Vienna, and promised his listeners amid wild cheers that their city would within four years be *judenrein* ("purged of Jews"). The Nazis were to more than fulfill Goering's commitment: by the end of 1938 the Jewish population of the city had dropped to 64,000, and a little more than six years later, when the Red Army entered the Austrian capital, the number of Jews who had somehow managed to survive there was variously given as between 136 and 220.

From the first days after the *Anschluss* the Nazi policy was to take over Jewish businesses and apartments, deprive Jews of their livelihood and property, and force them to emigrate with at most ten German marks in their pockets, an amount that would barely cover their living expenses for one day abroad—if they ever succeeded in reaching a foreign country. To speed the exodus, the Nazis subjected Jews to continual harassment. Even before Hitler made his first visit to Vienna as its conqueror, Nazi gangs forced Jews to scrub billboards and sidewalks to remove all traces of Patriotic Front propaganda. Several victims of such humiliation had to seek hospital treatment for burns from the sharp lye given to them when they had been ordered to do the cleaning work with their bare hands.

The anti-Semitic laws and practices that had been gradually introduced in Germany over the preceding five years were enforced in Vienna in one stroke. All Jews had to adopt Israel or Sara as their new middle names, and any document issued to them spelled out their identity as "non-Aryans." Yellow stars made their appearance. Jews were not allowed to sit on park benches and had to request special permits for using public transport. When the foreign press reported the violence and robberies that the Viennese Jews were suffering, the city's new Nazi chief, Joseph Bürckel, a German, blamed such acts on "certain people" who did not belong to the party. Many Jewish stores and homes were in fact looted by long-envious neighbors, riffraff, or habitual criminals wearing swastika armlets. Most of the German soldiers who were occupying Vienna abstained from tormenting the city's Jews; this was essentially the work of homegrown Nazis and of rabble who felt encouraged to let themselves go. Eventually the new authorities banned the display of the swastika symbol by persons who were not members of the Nazi party.

Gangs of young people who did belong to Nazi units, wearing uniforms and swastika insignia, continued rounding up Jews at random in the streets. A young Jewish Viennese might go out on an errand and never come home again. Days later someone might tell the desperate parents their son or daughter had been seen on a truck with other white-faced prisoners, guarded by grinning youths in brown shirts. Many such vanished persons were never heard of again; only a few of the arrested or kidnapped Jews were released later and could tell of their brutal experiences. The clear intention was to terrorize all of Vienna's Jews into emigrating at once, leaving all their possessions in Nazi hands.

EICHMANN AT WORK

In the course of a few weeks thousands of large and small commercial enterprises reported publicly, and announced in show windows and on business signs, that they had been "Aryanized." The term meant that Jewish owners and partners had been ousted without any compensation, Jewish employees had been fired without severance pay or any other benefits, and Jewish suppliers had been cut off without any payment to settle outstanding bills.

During their underground period the Viennese Nazis had identified their prospective victims and mapped the expected loot. Individual greed and resentment against specific persons or groups might explain why many Viennese had a personal interest in anti-Jewish measures. Yet, no one who was a witness can evade the memory of the overwhelming majority of the Viennese denying any help to, or active compassion for, their Jewish fellow citizens.

Jews whose families had been living for generations in the city, who had thought of themselves as thoroughly assimilated, and who maybe had lit the candles on a Christmas tree twelve weeks earlier now suddenly found they had not one Gentile friend in all of Vienna. Maids walked out on Jewish families who had always treated them well; the building superintendent who had been given the customary money gift at the beginning of the year no longer greeted Jewish tenants; the neighbors scowled or looked away; and the corner grocer would serve a timid Jewish householder who had for years been a good customer only after the other people in the store had left, or not at all. Civil servants to whom a Jew might have to turn, maybe for a passport or some tax matter, would be sarcastic or outright rude. Thrown out of their jobs, their businesses, and their professional organizations, shunned by people whom they had regarded as friends, ostracized in their neighborhoods, Vienna's Jews felt that the fabric of everyday life had been torn to shreds overnight and that they were being deprived of home and identity. A Gentile Viennese who called on a Jewish friend to pay back a loan that was not yet due because he thought the money might now be needed saw the creditor break down in sobs: "It's the first decent thing anyone has done to me since the *Anschluss.*"

Jewish Viennese who, often after long family discussions, eventually decided they had to leave found that all exit doors seemed closed. All foreign consulates—the former legations—in the ex-capital were beleaguered by visa seekers day after day, but were generally unhelpful. Many of the foreign diplomats who had remained in Vienna as consular officers appeared unsympathetic, and their small staffs were often gruff. If a visa application was accepted at all, instructions from the home government had to be awaited. Weeks and months would pass, during which the would-be emigrants wrote letter after imploring letter to remote cousins, friends, international humanitarian organizations, former business or professional associates, or any other contact abroad they could think of. The mail, fortunately, kept functioning; the Gestapo did open letters, but mainly to search for money that might have been stuffed into envelopes.

The British consulate near the State Opera posted a terse sign at its entrance stating that no visas would be issued. The French consulate in its elegant building near the Belvedere would not accept any visa applications either. The United States consulate near St. Stephen's Cathedral did, but it requested an affidavit from someone living in America who would guarantee the upkeep of the penniless visitor; there was no hope of getting an immigrant's visa soon, because the Austrian quota had long been filled and there was an endless waiting list.

Many Jewish Viennese nevertheless applied for admittance to the United States and somehow obtained the necessary affidavits. Among them was Anton Kuh, one of the coffeehouse literati, who even in desperate straits had kept his sardonic sense of humor. "Schnorrer kann man überall brauchen" ("Schnorrers are welcome anywhere") was his explanation for the decision to emigrate to America, although he spoke little English and had no clear idea of how to survive there. His maxim became proverbial among Viennese refugees. Kuh did eventually reach New York and died there in 1941, aged fifty-one.

Switzerland allowed German citizens to enter its territory without a visa, but had suggested to the authorities in Berlin that Jews should be identified by a *J* stamped into their passports so that its frontier guards would be alerted and could bar them. When a Viennese Jew managed to obtain a German passport—all Austrian passports had been invalidated when the Germans arrived—the red *J* was already on its first page, and the chances of wangling a visa from any country were dim. According to a grim joke that made the rounds of Vienna in those days, there were only two kinds of countries in the world—"those where Jews can't live and those that don't admit Jews."

An Austrian ambassador to Switzerland in the 1970s who some thirty years earlier had been among the Viennese who were wandering from consulate to consulate in search of a visa wrote, "When I see today the attentions with which refugees from the Communist area are being received in Western Europe, I am glad for them; at the same time, I am haunted by feelings of oppression and shame when I think of the truly inhuman treatment that we death candidates were accorded by presumedly civilized countries."[1] Switzerland, for years terrified at the prospect of being swamped by refugees from Hitler, did eventually grant asylum to about four thousand Jewish and other Viennese.

Initially it was still possible to be admitted to some Caribbean or Latin American country like Cuba, the Dominican Republic, or Bolivia, at least for a limited time. Until the beginning of World War II it was also fairly easy to immigrate to Shanghai if one had the money for the long journey; however, making a living in the Chinese metropolis was another matter. The Taussigs of Vienna spent their life savings in 1938 to book the last available passage on a boat that was to sail for China. "You are lucky," they were told by the travel agent. "You got the space because the couple who had originally reserved it have just committed suicide." In Shanghai, Franziska Taussig worked as a cleaning woman and as a baker of sweets for other emigrés, for Chinese customers, and eventually for Japanese occupation officers. At times she was on her feet from 4 A.M. to midnight. Her husband, a Hungarian-born Vienna lawyer, never found any job in China and, after a few years, died of an infection.

Another Viennese, the film director Arthur Gottlein, set himself up as a puppeteer when he found himself stuck in Shanghai, and operated marionette shows. He had success with the local Chinese and earned plenty of money, at least until the Japanese interned him. Gottlein had come to Shanghai from Manila, where he had produced various movies. He recalled later that at first he did not understand why his Filipino crew bristled whenever he gave directions, prefacing about every other sentence, as many Viennese will, with the German word *also* ("well, now . . ."). At last he was informed that in the local patois *also* means "dog."

In 1939, when Shanghai was about the only place on earth where a

Jewish immigrant did not need a visa, more than twenty thousand Jews had found a refuge there. They included at least three thousand Russian and Baghdadi Jews who had been living in Shanghai before 1938, and some seventeen thousand people from Germany, Poland, and Vienna. Most of the hundreds of exiles from the Austrian capital had reached Shanghai via the sea route, out of Trieste; a few others had managed to travel across Poland and the Soviet Union. Almost all of the Viennese had arrived penniless and had no experience of East Asia, and many spoke only poor English. Some had to live in refugee camps, and most of the others in the drabbest districts of the city of four million. Under increasing Japanese pressure, the Shanghai authorities curbed immigration in 1939, and in February 1943 they established a "restricted area" that was in effect a Jewish ghetto in the International Settlement. There, the Jewish refugees were living in forty blocks of squalid housing, mostly on narrow side lanes, off the main streets. Japan's defeat in 1945 opened the Shanghai ghetto, and virtually all of its inhabitants soon sought a haven elsewhere.[2]

The only countries that would admit Viennese Jews "were those they would not have picked, had they had a choice," as Bruno Bettelheim wrote much later.[3] The Vienna-born psychoanalyst and child psychologist, who made it to the United States in 1939 after spending a harrowing year in Nazi camps, reported that within months of the annexation of Austria the prisoner population of the Dachau complex jumped from six thousand to nine thousand and that during 1938 some sixty thousand prisoners were added to the total number of inmates in all Nazi concentration camps. During Bettelheim's transfer from Vienna to Dachau, several prisoners died of exhaustion or torture, and he himself received a bayonet wound and a heavy blow on his head, the "initiation" that the SS guards—many of them Austrians—routinely administered to the people in their power to undermine their self-esteem and will to resist.

The Viennese Jews who wanted to go abroad found "assistance" of a sort at a new Nazi agency that had ensconced itself in the graceful palace that a Parisian architect had built for Baron Albert von Rothschild in 1884. The new administrative unit at 22 Prinz-Eugen-Strasse was called the Central Office for Jewish Emigration; it could be reached by telephone at the numbers U 45-4-40 and U 45-4-45. Its chief was a thirty-two-year-old SS bureaucrat, a native of the cutlery city of Solingen in the Prussian Rhine Province who had grown up in Austria—Adolf Eichmann.

Nearly seven hundred prospective Jewish emigrants were processed in Eichmann's office every business day during its peak period. The assembly-line procedure was aimed at ferreting out and seizing any property or assets the applicant possessed. At the end, a German passport, duly stamped with a red *J* was issued with the warning that its holder must leave the Great German Reich within two weeks, on pain of being sent to a concentration camp.

Eichmann was seven years old when his family moved from Solingen to Linz in Upper Austria, where his father had landed a job with the local Electric Power & Tramway Company. The younger Eichmann got most of his education in the Danubian city but, like another Adolf before him, did not finish high school. He tried for some time to make a living as a salesman for a motor oil firm and crisscrossed the region on a motorbike; eventually he was recruited into the SS by a young Linz lawyer, Ernst Kaltenbrunner. In 1933, Eichmann joined the Nazi Austrian Legion in Germany, a protégé of Kaltenbrunner who himself was quickly rising in the SS hierarchy. Placed in charge of the new Vienna agency for the despoliation of Jews by the SS, Eichmann showed organizational skills and the complete absence of any humane feeling that within a few years would help him to become the chief administrator of the Final Solution. It must be recalled here that Austrian Nazis played a conspicuous role in all phases of the Holocaust; most of these myrmidons of genocide were natives of the Alpine provinces rather than of Vienna.

FREUD'S VISITORS

Despite the increasing harassment, the humiliations, the iciness of neighbors and former presumed friends, the deepening insecurity, the looting and the roundups, many Jews, particularly elderly ones, were still hesitant to leave Vienna. One of them was Sigmund Freud. His English disciple, friend, and future biographer, Ernest Jones, worriedly rushed to Vienna in March 1938. He found Freud, the day after Hitler's arrival in Vienna, still adamant in his decision to stay on: "This is my post, and I can never leave it."[4]

A few days later, a bunch of Nazis with swastika armlets and rifles raided the Freud apartment at 19 Berggasse. Freud's wife, Martha, kept her North German composure and politely asked the unbidden visitors to leave their weapons in the hall. Their commander, a former Austrian army officer, observed the civilities and addressed the master of the house as "Herr Professor." (It seems that this show of respect cost the leader of the intruders his job.) The Nazis searched the apartment and took off with 6,000 schillings, an amount then the equivalent of $840. When Freud was told by his wife how much money had been seized, he remarked, "Dear me, I have never taken so much for a single visit." Anna, Freud's favorite child, was detained by the Gestapo ten days after the *Anschluss* and questioned for several hours before she was allowed to return home. Even then, Freud did not want to leave Vienna. Martin Freud would much later recall that his father believed, as many educated Europeans at the time did, "that the Nazi eruption was out of step with the march of civilization . . . that a normal rhythm would soon be restored."

An old pupil and friend, Princess George of Greece and Denmark, was more clear-sighted and at last succeeded in persuading Freud to seek a refuge abroad. The princess, then fifty-five years old, was known in psychoanalytical quarters by her maiden name Marie Bonaparte; she had far-reaching international connections. Alerted by Ernest Jones, the princess enlisted the help of William C. Bullitt, who had once worked with Freud on a study project regarding President Woodrow Wilson and was then United States ambassador to France. Bullitt appealed to President Franklin Roosevelt, and Washington intervened on Freud's behalf in Berlin. Eventually the Nazi authorities in Vienna granted the Freuds the *Unbedenklichkeitserklärung* that was required for leaving. The long word of German bureaucratese means a declaration that someone is unobjectionable; the term may be rendered as "statement of harmlessness."

Marie Bonaparte and her husband, a cousin of King George of Greece, visited Vienna, where they stayed at the former Greek legation. Spending most of the day at the Freud home in the Berggasse (then marked by a large swastika sign over the doorway), the princess helped in the preparations for the move. The Nazis had permitted the Freuds to take some furniture, a part of their library, and the professor's famous collection of antiquities with them, but hundreds of books had to remain behind. Marie Bonaparte also paid the $4,824 ransom for the Freud family that the Nazis exacted; there was another lengthy—and grimly comical—bureaucratic term for such ultimate blackmail: *Reichsfluchtsteuer,* or "tax on fleeing from the Reich." Freud repaid the money to the princess later.

Marie Bonaparte is credited with having saved the lives of some two hundred Jews during the Hitler years. She was a granddaughter of François Blanc, the founder of the Monte Carlo gambling casino; her wealthy mother, Marie-Félix, had married Prince Roland Bonaparte, a grandson of Napoleon's brother Lucien. During her sojourn in Vienna in the spring of 1938, Marie Bonaparte also recovered documents she had earlier deposited in a safe at the Rothschild Bank in the Renngasse, including 284 letters by Freud to his onetime friend and confidant Wilhelm Fliess in Berlin, which the princess had bought from the latter's widow. Nazi police officers were present when the princess was allowed to retrieve the contents of the bank safe, but they appeared interested only in whether there were any valuables or money, not in letters written long before World War I.

Before Freud received his declaration of harmlessness, a party of SS officers called at his home and requested a formal statement by him to the effect that he had no complaints. Under dictation, a poker-faced Freud wrote, "I, Professor Freud, herewith declare that after the reunion of Austria with the German Reich I have been treated by the German authorities, and especially by the Gestapo, with the esteem and regard due to my scientific reputation; that I have been able to pursue my activities freely; and that I do not have the least reason for complaint." Freud is supposed to have volunteered to add the sentence, "I can very much recommend the Gestapo to anyone," but his visitors, who may have sensed his irony or just did not think that the wording was right, said the statement was sufficient as it was. Freud, his wife, and their daughter Anna, with Freud's beloved chow chow, Jofi, left Vienna by train on June 4, 1938. Marie Bonaparte and Ambassador Bullitt were at the Gare de l'Est in Paris next day to meet them. The other Freuds left Vienna separately.

The British authorities were far more welcoming to the Freud family than they were to other refugees of the period. Freud proceeded from Paris to London and lived for a short time in rented quarters at 39 Elsworthy Road. On September 27, 1938, he moved into a spacious house at 20 Maresfield Gardens, Hampstead, that he had bought for sixty-five hundred pounds. Paula Fichtel, the Freuds' faithful maid in Vienna for decades, rejoined the family in London. Although increasingly racked by cancer pain, Freud started a new book, *An Outline of Psychoanalysis* (which he was not to complete), and received patients and followers until he died on September 23, 1939, at the age of eighty-three. Anna Freud lived in the Hampstead house until her death in 1982. With her friend Dorothy Tiffany Burlingham, she established there her Hampstead Clinic, developing and practicing her methods of child analysis. In the 1970s, Anna Freud revisited Vienna on various occasions and attended the unveiling of a plaque in the arcaded courtyard of the University of Vienna commemorating the academic activity of her father, who had never attained a full professorship in the institution.

Alfred Adler, the early associate and later rival of Freud, had started visiting Britain and the United States in the 1920s and had been lecturing there, although his English was halting. When the Austrian Social Democratic Party, with which he identified, was outlawed by the Dollfuss regime in 1934, Adler moved to the United States. During a lecture tour in 1937 he died of a stroke in Aberdeen, Scotland. Adler's daughter Alexandra and son Kurt continued his work in the field of individual psychology in New York.

THE SONG OF BERNADETTE

The Viennese writer Hermann Broch, who had undergone analysis by a disciple of Freud and was a friend of Adler's, reached the United States by way of Britain, but his road to freedom was arduous. Broch had for some years been living in mountain villages, which were less expensive than Vienna. He had eventually been allowed the free use of a vacation house in Alt-Aussee that belonged to Viennese friends. The day after the *Anschluss* local Nazis arrested Broch and took him to the prison at nearby Bad Aussee. The writer must have been blacklisted after the local mailman had reported to his Nazi underground network that the Jew from Vienna was regularly receiving a German-language magazine, *Das Wort,* from Moscow. Broch had never been a Communist but had subscribed to that emigré publication. In Bad Aussee he was held for three weeks in a cell, together with the former chief of the local Patriotic Front organization, until a decent Austrian official declared him in writing "politically harmless."

On his return to Vienna, Broch, like uncounted other people, lined up outside consulate after consulate in vain quest of a visa. At last, a woman friend of his in Paris asked James Joyce to help the Viennese writer. Joyce had never met Broch, but remembered a lecture the Austrian had given in Vienna on the occasion of his fiftieth birthday in 1932; its text had later been published. The Irish novelist asked French authorities and, through a friend, the British government to admit Broch; after complications and delays, a visa was issued. During the interminable weeks when Broch was waiting for a break, he often rode Vienna tramcars for hours, for fear some Nazi squad might arrest him in the streets and tear up the Bad Aussee certificate of political harmlessness that he was carrying in his pocket. Broch's widowed mother would neither then nor later hear of emigration. The writer put her up with a former mistress of his, Ea Von Allesch, who in the period of the Arconauts had been called "the Queen of the Café Central." Mrs. Broch, like many other elderly Jewish Viennese, was eventually picked up by the Nazis and sent to the concentration camp of Theresienstadt (Terezin) in Bohemia, where she soon died "of old age."

Thomas Mann and Albert Einstein, who were both living in America, had signed affidavits for Broch, but it would take some time before the Viennese writer was able to sail for New York. He spent a few months in London and in St. Andrews, Scotland, as guest of his English translators, Edwin and Willa Muir. In London, Broch met such Viennese fellow emigrés as Stefan Zweig, who had been in England since 1934, and the irrepressible Alma Mahler Werfel, who had her base then in Paris.

The Werfels had been in Italy at the time of the *Anschluss.* Alma left her Jewish husband behind and returned to Vienna to look after their villa and other assets, and discovered that her stepfather had been a Nazi all along and was exercising a strong pro-Nazi influence on her mother. Alma and her daughter Anna Mahler managed to reach Prague hours before the frontier between Austria and Czechoslovakia was closed, and from there traveled to Milan by way of Budapest, Zagreb, and Trieste, to be reunited with Werfel. Alma and her husband moved on to Paris, where they found a colony of Viennese refugees that over the next few months was to grow considerably. Bertha Zuckerkandl—who in Vienna had been a friend and, as a party giver, a rival of Alma—was already in Paris; as a sister-in-law of the late premier Georges Clemenceau, she had entrée to the highest circles there. For a few months both Alma and Bertha tried to organize something like a Viennese intellectual salon—or coffeehouse—in the French capital.

Werfel, together with the emigré writers Alfred Polgar and Joseph Roth, founded in Paris the Ligue de l'Autriche Vivante (League of Living Austria) as a forum for anti-Nazi intellectuals. Polgar and Werfel were also on the board of the short-lived Central Association of Austrian Emigrants, together with Sigmund Freud and other noted refugees from Vienna. Polgar, whom we have met as an early critic of the Ringstrasse architecture, had been one of the Viennese who rushed to the Vienna West Railroad terminal and caught the train to Switzerland as German troops were approaching the city; he arrived in Zurich all right but soon found he was not universally welcome. Swiss newspaper and magazine editors were ready to publish his polished essays, but his local colleagues were miffed; eventually the Swiss Writers' Association petitioned the authorities to deny Polgar a work permit, and he left to try his luck in Paris.

Joseph Roth was by then a tragic figure. The novelist from Galicia had for years lived in Germany but had moved to Paris when the Nazis came to power. After the *Anschluss* he started publishing *Oesterreichische Post* (Austrian Mail), a periodical that advocated a Habsburg restoration after Hitler. Roth, however, was drinking himself into stupefaction. Friends suggested that Archduke Otto might be able to save him, if anyone could. Otto, the oldest son of Austria-Hungary's last emperor, was then living in Paris too. The archduke, twenty-six years old at the time, called on Roth, and the writer and former army officer sprang to attention. Otto told him to stop drinking. "I shall obey, Your Majesty!," Roth gasped. But it was too late.

Three days before Roth died of alcoholism in a poor people's hospital in Paris on May 27, 1939, Stefan Zweig wrote to him, "You have only one duty—to write decent books and to drink as little as possible to conserve yourself for us and for yourself." At a memorial ceremony for the dead writer and patriot in London, Zweig said in his eulogy that Roth had chosen "slow self-annihilation."

The outbreak of World War II led to instant internment of most Austrian refugees in Paris. They were first kept at a bicycle-race stadium at Colombes, on the northwestern outskirts of the capital. Presumed German Nazis could be seen camping on the rafters there side by side with such Jewish Viennese as Karl Farkas, the former cabaret star. (Farkas would eventually reach New York and score a Broadway hit with his musical *Marinka.*) After the fall of France in June 1940, many of the emigrés fell into Nazi hands; others succeeded in the general confusion to squeeze onto boats sailing for England; and quite a few ended up in the south of France, which was soon to find itself under the Vichy puppet government. The Werfels and Polgar were fortunate enough to get out of Paris in time, heading south.

One of several places where the Werfels stayed during the following months was Lourdes. The Jewish author had long shown mystical leanings, and in the Roman Catholic shrine he became enthralled by the figure of St. Bernadette Subirous and by her visions of the Virgin Mary in a local grotto in 1858. "One day in my great distress I made a vow," Werfel wrote later. "I vowed that if I escaped from this desperate situation and reached the saving shores of America, I would put off all other tasks and sing, as best as I could, the song of Bernadette."[5] His book on the girl saint and the film based on it, with Jennifer Jones as Bernadette, were to make Werfel's name better known throughout the world than all his earlier works had.

Werfel, the compulsive raconteur, would later in California dine out on funny accounts of how Alma and he had been on the run: how they had always been just a step ahead of the Nazis in southern France; how they had crossed the Pyrenees on foot, together with Thomas Mann's brother Heinrich, Heinrich's wife, Nelly, and Thomas Mann's son Golo; and how they had been defrauded by a friend of an Austrian friend in Lisbon before sailing to New York on the Greek liner *Nea Hellas* in October 1940. Polgar was a fellow passenger during that voyage. Like other Viennese refugees, Werfel in retrospect was able to see farcical aspects of his flight from Hitler's Europe; at the time, however, he suffered from severe depressions and had crying spells, as Alma recorded in her memoirs.

"SO MANY JEWS AMONG THE NAZIS"

The Viennese author who had never liked Werfel, Robert Musil, might have stayed put, despite his Jewish-born wife, but he would not. Soon after the *Anschluss,* the Hamburg publisher Eugen Claasen visited Musil in Vienna with a proposal to work for him, hinting that Goebbels' propaganda ministry in Berlin was in favor of such a collaboration. Musil declined. "I cannot breathe in this air," he told a coffeehouse friend, the writer Oskar Maurus Fontana. Musil and his wife left for Italy in the summer of 1938 and from there proceeded to Switzerland. During the less than four years he had still to live, Musil would always be oppressed by money worries.

One of the few people close to the Musils in their Swiss exile was the Viennese sculptor Fritz Wotruba. Living in Switzerland since the end of 1938, Wotruba was comparatively well off, thanks to lucrative commissions; he had been able to enlist the help of the Swiss president, Philipp Etter, to obtain a visa for his Jewish wife. After the war the successful sculptor would be called back to Vienna to join the faculty of the Art Academy.

With all their international prestige and connections, with the President of the United States, Nobel laureates, and other prominent personages interceding for them, Freud and the other illustrious Viennese who wanted to escape the Nazis still found their journey to freedom rough going. It was immeasurably more so for tens of thousands of other, obscure refugees from Vienna. When they had at last decided to leave— usually after agonizing family discussions—they all had to make the rounds of unsympathetic consulates; write pleading letters to everybody in other countries they knew or had heard of; dodge Gestapo dragnets; make arrangements for elderly relatives who refused to budge; and, if they were Jewish, run the gauntlet of Eichmann's office to be methodically robbed of all their belongings.

Some older Jewish men who during World War I had served in the emperor's army, maybe as officers, and possibly had even won decorations for gallantry in the field were convinced that the Nazis would respect their military record. Others persuaded themselves and wavering relatives and friends that things could not get any worse and that one should sit out the storm and wait for the inevitable return to some sort of normalcy. One had, after all, a long experience with anti-Semitism in Vienna! Virtually all those Jews who stayed on in Vienna were rounded up and deported by the Nazis, at the latest during the first years of World War II. At least fifteen thousand Jewish Viennese who had found a refuge in France or some other European country fell into the hands of the Nazis when Hitler's army later marched in.

Those Viennese who did get away were scattered all over the globe in a myriad of individual destinies and adventures. They all took their personal share of bitterness with them, and after the collapse of the Third Reich, only a small percentage of the emigrés cared to return to what had been home.

Of the twenty-three graduates of a typical Vienna high school class, all of the ten Jewish students and one Gentile emigrated after the Nazi takeover.[6] Five of those who stayed behind died in combat as members of the German armed forces or owing to other war-related causes; six Gentiles lived in Vienna after the war; and one, who had been the class Nazi (he had a Czech name), could not be traced and was supposed to have gone to live somewhere in northern Germany. Of the emigrés, three reached the United States (two by way of Italy and one by way of Belgium and Bolivia); three found new homes in Australia (one after some years in what was then still Palestine); two moved to France and one each to Brazil and England; and one enlisted in the French foreign legion, never to be heard of again. One of the two who survived the war in France had joined the Maquis and, on surfacing from the underground, had a French name, apartments in Paris and Nice, and the red ribbon of the Légion d'Honneur in his buttonhole; a shadowy French agency sent him on a mission to Vienna, and the day after his arrival he was found shot dead in his hotel in the French occupation zone—a sinister twist worthy of a Graham Greene novel.

Except for the foreign legionnaire and the Maquisard, the emigrants from that Vienna high school class achieved professional success in their host countries: three taught at universities, one headed a research institute, and the rest held executive positions or made good in other ways. A few of the group would later revisit Vienna occasionally, but four said they would never go back again, even for a few days.

Hindsight prompts us to wonder today why so few Jewish and anti-Nazi Viennese in 1937 and 1938 correctly read the signs of impending doom and went abroad while they still could have made orderly arrangements. Widespread hopes in Vienna that the Western powers would never allow Austria to fall prey to Hitler was one reason, but the almost general reluctance to abandon Vienna must be ascribed to the simple fact that the human mind resists change even in the most dire conditions.

People who had lived in the Austrian capital through the grim years of World War I and the immediate postwar period might—wrongly—feel that with the vaunted Viennese adaptability they would be able to survive somehow Nazism too. Anyone who has not ever had to take a decision on which life or death might depend ought to be cautious in assigning blame or guilt.

The luckiest anti-Nazi Viennese were those who, by chance or design, happened to be traveling abroad at the time of the *Anschluss;* Werfel was one of them. Another—one who would have been arrested at once by the Nazis if he had been at home—was Prince Starhemberg. The wealthy former vice-chancellor was spending what he described as a "prolonged winter vacation" in Switzerland with his wife, the Burgtheater actress Nora Gregor, and their son in March 1938. The prince, who had been an early admirer of Hitler, then a friend of Mussolini's, and eventually a leader of rightist militias that fought the Social Democrats and the Nazis, moved later to Paris. While his wife was doing film work with the French director Jean Renoir, Starhemberg enlisted in the French air force as *lieutenant à titre étranger* (foreign volunteer lieutenant), asking never to be sent on a combat mission over Austria. After the fall of France, Starhemberg flew his French fighter plane to England and joined de Gaulle's Free French forces. He served in French Equatorial Africa, fell sick with malaria, and in 1942 moved to Argentina, where he had friends and where his wife and son were already living. The prince took care of a rich Spaniard's hunting reserve in the Argentinian pampas while his wife accepted film engagements in Chile; she died there in 1949. Starhemberg returned to Austria in 1955 and, in the following year, succumbed to a heart condition.

Former leaders of Red Vienna were also abroad at the time of the *Anschluss,* exiles since the civil war of 1934. Among them was Otto Bauer, who had been the chief of the Social Democratic Party's headquarters-in-exile in the Moravian city of Brno for a few years before moving to Paris, where he died in 1938. (Such a formidable antisocialist theoretician as Ludwig von Mises later described Bauer as the sole outstanding Marxist thinker he had ever encountered.) The former social-welfare chief of Red Vienna, Julius Tandler, died in Moscow in 1936. Otto Neurath, the protean mathematician and economist of the Vienna Circle who had founded the museum of Red Vienna's social achievements, had emigrated to the Netherlands in 1934; when the German army overran the country in 1940 he and his fiancée fled in a rowboat and were picked up by a British destroyer.

International humanitarian groups, including the Quakers, in tenacious negotiations with the Nazi authorities, succeeded in evacuating more than twenty-eight hundred Jewish children from Vienna to France, Belgium, the Netherlands, Britain, Sweden, and the United States. Some of the young passengers on the special trains to the host countries and seaports were infants, and all of the children left without their parents, whom few of them would ever see again.

During the first year after the *Anschluss* close to one hundred thousand Viennese emigrated. The Nazis stopped issuing exit permits to Jewish men between the ages of eighteen and forty-five in August 1939, and soon afterward all Jewish emigration from Vienna came to a halt. The last Jewish refugee group from Vienna, headed for Portugal, left at the end of October 1941.

Several passengers of the children's trains from Vienna were interned as "enemy aliens" in Britain, together with about twenty-five thousand other Austrians, Germans, and Italians, in and after 1940, when a Nazi invasion seemed imminent. The enemy aliens who were detained in British camps for varying periods included Sigmund Freud's son Martin; the composer Egon Wellesz, who had become an honorary fellow of Lincoln College in Oxford; the newcomer Otto Neurath; the musicologist Otto Erich Deutsch, who was then working on his fundamental catalog of Franz Schubert's works; and many other Jewish scholars, scientists, and intellectuals from Vienna. Max F. Perutz, a Viennese graduate student who had come to Cambridge in 1936 for research work on the structure of proteins, was another such internee. More than forty years later, when he had long been a Nobel laureate, he reminisced about the commander of his camp at Huyton, near Liverpool, a white-mustachioed World War I veteran: "Watching a group of internees with skullcaps and curly sidewhiskers arrive at his camp, he mused, 'I had no idea there were so many Jews among the Nazis.' He pronounced it 'Nasis.' "[7]

EXILE IS A DISEASE

Internment in England brought three young Viennese musicians together, the violinists Norbert Brainin and Siegmund Nissel and the violist Peter Schidlof. After their release in 1942 the three refugees banded together with the British cellist Martin Lovett to found the Amadeus Quartet. The name chosen by the new group signified its repertoire: it would concentrate on Wolfgang Amadeus Mozart and other Viennese composers. The quartet made its debut in London's Wigmore Hall in 1948 and was to become one of the great chamber ensembles of the twentieth century, offering four thousand concerts all over the world and selling millions of records during its nearly forty years before the public. When Schidlof died in England in 1987, the three survivors said they would not try to replace him.

More than seven thousand of the internees, including Perutz, were removed from Britain to Canada and Australia. The deportees included avowed or suspected Nazis; Italian waiters; the Italian banquet manager of the Savoy Hotel, who had been working in London since 1906; and many Jewish Viennese. At least 650 of the deportees drowned in July 1940 when a German submarine sank the former luxury liner *Arandora Star,* which had sailed from Liverpool and was bound for Canada. Another transport, the *Dunera,* narrowly escaped two German torpedoes during its voyage to Australia. The ship was packed with 2,500 refugees, several survivors of the *Arandora* sinking among them. Germans and Austrians who had been on board the *Dunera* complained later to Australian authorities that they had been treated harshly and had been robbed of valuables by their British guards. An investigation led to court-martial of three Britons; the commander of the military escort aboard the *Dunera* received a severe reprimand, and a sergeant major was sentenced to a year's imprisonment.

In Australia the "enemy aliens" were first taken to inhospitable sites. The intellectuals among them nevertheless soon managed to organize cultural activities. In the bleak camps scholars and scientists lectured on Shakespeare, astronomy, physics, and chemistry; musicians who had built their own violins and fashioned their flutes from cactus and eucalyptus wood gave concerts. Erwin Frenkel, the son of the cantor in a synagogue in Vienna's Leopoldstadt district, opened a Viennese coffeehouse in the Tatura Camp.[8]

From 1941 on, internees in Australia were permitted to return to England, and some of them who did so volunteered for the British military forces. Several Viennese chose to remain in Australia and applied for naturalization when the government decided in 1944 that former internees might become "desirable citizens." Viennese Jews who had been deported from Britain to Canada found that when they were eventually released from the camps there, the United States would not even admit those who had held immigration visas before their internment. Some stayed on in Canada, while others went to Cuba and various other countries in the western hemisphere or returned to Britain.

Quite a few emigrés from Vienna found new homes in the one country in the entire world that had officially declared Jews to be welcome: the Dominican Republic. The government of Rafael Leonidas Trujillo Molina, dictator of the Caribbean island state since 1930, had offered to issue immigration visas to one hundred thousand Jews when the problem of the refugees from Central Europe was discussed at an international conference at Évian four months after the *Anschluss.* President Roosevelt had taken the initiative for the meeting in the French spa on Lake Geneva and had named Myron C. Taylor, a former chairman of the United States Steel Corporation, as his representative there. Of all the thirty-two countries that sent delegations, only the Dominican Republic came up with a seemingly viable proposal. Trujillo, the tyrant who was ruling the small republic as if it were his private property, took up an idea that had first been aired in Santo Domingo in the nineteenth century—to promote the settlement of Russian and other European Jews to spur economic development. Early in 1940 the Dominican rubber-stamp parliament passed a law granting Jewish immigrants full civil rights. The Dominican Republic Settlement Association was founded, and it assigned land at Sosua on the country's north coast to Jewish applicants.

Candidates for settlement in the Dominican Republic discovered, however, that Trujillo's bureaucrats had a farming colony in mind and wanted only immigrants with an aptitude for agricultural work—not intellectuals. Instead of one hundred thousand Central European Jews, only about seven hundred actually went to live in the Dominican Republic, most of them lower-middle-class people. The newcomers to Sosua were first assigned dilapidated houses that the United Fruit Company had vacated, but they soon built their own neat homes, a synagogue, and eventually a small power plant, an aqueduct, a school, and a clinic.

One of the first settlers was a baker from Vienna. Jewish butchers from Germany and Vienna bred cattle and developed meat and dairy industries that won great renown all over the Dominican Republic. The Jewish colony also grew and exported tomatoes. It had its own fortnightly newspaper, *La Voz de Sosua,* and received some reinforcement when former Shanghai refugees arrived in 1947. When I visited Sosua during the Dominican civil war in 1965, trucks from the Jewish model farms at Sosua were traversing the island regularly to supply the capital, Santo Domingo, with butter and steaks. I found a few elderly Viennese in Sosua, but their children had moved on to the United States, first to get a college education and then to enter the American mainstream. In Sosua one could still hear old stories about supposed dalliances between male Viennese immigrants and the wives of fellow settlers from Germany, and there was also gossip about the amorous Viennese having allegedly fathered a crop of illegitimate children born to Dominican women. Many Sosua settlers, it seemed, had never learned to speak correct Spanish; their community had remained something of an alien enclave in the Caribbean nation. The immigrants' feeling of cultural superiority appears to have been the reason.

Many Jews who escaped from Hitler had to cope with their own superiority complexes even in more-advanced host countries. Hilde Spiel, a Viennese who had studied philosophy under Moritz Schlick and had emigrated first to Paris and then to London in 1936, found that the Jewish newcomers in France often indulged in disparaging remarks about that nation. An anecdote had it that two of them were critically watching a detachment of somewhat ragged French soldiers march by; one emigré said to the other, "Our SS march more smartly." The Parisians by then called their faultfinding guests the *chez nous* because their frequent unfavorable comparisons between French conditions and pre-Hitler life in the cities where they had come from were invariably prefaced by the two French words, meaning "at home."

In London, Spiel found many emigrés, and later the Viennese Jews, too, complaining about insipid food, the lack of double windows, drafty rooms, and the standoffish attitude of the British. Viennese who were used to lingering at the table after a meal were appalled that they were not supposed to do so in English eating places. Refugees who had accepted humble jobs just to make a living, maybe working as a butler or a maid, tended to bore everybody with tales of how important they had been at home. They were known as the "St. Bernard dogs," who actually had only been dachshunds in the old country. Spiel's conclusion: "Exile is a disease."[9] Werfel said it in almost the same words in France in 1939: "Being an emigrant is a disease."

Arnold Schoenberg wrote to friends in Europe from California that he had become "homeless and speechless." His English was then still halting, although he worked hard to improve it. Schoenberg was conducting master classes at the Berlin Academy of Arts when Hitler came to power in 1933. With his second wife, Gertrud, he left Germany at once, arriving in Paris only with hand luggage. Soon afterward, Schoenberg asked a rabbi in the French capital to receive him back into the Jewish community; Marc Chagall, the Russian-born painter, signed the composer's statement as a witness. Schoenberg accepted an offer to teach at a new private conservatory in Boston and arrived in New York with a visitor's visa in his Czechoslovak passport. (Czechoslovakia had issued the passport to him on the strength of the circumstance that Schoenberg's father had been born near Bratislava.) The composer found life in Boston and New York hard to take, and moved to Pasadena in the hope that the West Coast air would ease his chronic asthma. At age sixty, he felt uncomfortable in California too.

Another Viennese who ended up in California was Alfred Polgar. The sixty-seven-year-old essayist who spoke only broken English was lucky enough to get hired as a writer by Metro-Goldwyn-Mayer. He had, however, great difficulties in adapting to Hollywood and was homesick for Europe. "My life is 99 percent memories," he confided to a friend. "I'm not very interested in the hundredth part." His dejection brought forth a bitter short story, *His Last Mistake:* An American editor is telling an emigré writer that what is done and said in his fiction is not done and said in the United States; the writer's characters live, love, laugh, and cry in ways that are not American ways; the emigré jumps out of the window of the thirty-second-floor office, and the editor, now really angry, shouts after him, "In America one doesn't jump out of the window!" Polgar became a United States citizen, moved back to Europe in 1949, sensed a "secret hostility toward returnees" in Vienna, and went to live in Zurich —where he had not been allowed to work in 1938—and found a congenial coffeehouse there. He died in 1955.

Many refugees were shocked to encounter racism in the West. When Broch was awaiting his departure for the United States in Scotland, quite a few local people who thought he was a visiting German made anti-Semitic remarks to him. The Werfels were a little later outraged by the pro-Hitler attitudes that officials of the Vichy government in southern France were striking. And when Herbert Feigl, the favorite disciple of Moritz Schlick and one of the members of the Vienna Circle, applied for an academic position in the United States, some inquired, "Is he a Jew?"[10] Feigl did eventually teach at Iowa State University and won the chair of philosophy at the University of Minnesota.

From the Bible and Thucydides to this day, world literature offers any number of witnesses to the miseries, nostalgia, depressions, resentments, alienation, and schizophrenia of exile or emigration. Dante wrote of the salty taste of other people's bread and of how hard it is to have to walk up and down other people's stairs. Joseph Roth, maybe with those verses from the *Divine Comedy* in mind, chose "The Bitter Bread" as the title of an essay, written for an emigré newspaper a few months before his death. In it, he described how refugees from Nazism were vegetating in Paris, trying to pick up a few francs hawking pencils or ladies' stockings, always worrying about their sojourn permit and the rent for their dingy rooms.

Roth himself was then living in the last of the many cheap hotels he had inhabited between Marseilles and Warsaw, the Hôtel Café de la Poste near Paris' Luxembourg Palace, and at his death would leave nothing but one threadbare suit, a thin overcoat, and a bundle of manuscripts. German emigrés who had been in Paris for years were advising newcomers from Vienna to shun hotels and look for a modest rented room in some private home, never to enter a restaurant but to cook their own meals, and to order a small beer rather than the more expensive café crème in the cafés where most of them were spending many hours every day. The refugees who had just arrived from Vienna did not always find the veteran emigrés from Germany welcoming and friendly; there was a "the boat is full" mood, as there always is in host countries during emigration waves. Karl Marx, himself an expatriate, had spoken in London nearly a century earlier of "emigré pigs."

ALRIGHTNIKS AND COMPLAINERS

There are, on the other hand, countless examples of immigrants in all ages who made good in their host countries, adjusted quickly and successfully, and in a few years felt completely at home in what had been a strange ambience at first. The Viennese who emigrated to the United States because of Hitler soon saw themselves divided into two categories: alrightniks and complainers. The newcomers of the first, larger group did not seek—or may even have shunned—the company of other recent immigrants, with their quarrels and intrigues; tried to learn English and the American idiom quickly; tackled any job offered to them; and adopted their new environment's way of life with enthusiasm.

Anecdotal evidence suggests that the great majority of the Viennese who arrived in the United States in the 1930s and early 1940s assimilated speedily and thoroughly. By 1950 the number of American residents who had been born in the territory that had remained Austrian after World

War I was estimated at around two hundred thousand. (Close to four hundred thousand residents of the United States were listed as Austrian-born, but they included natives of Bohemia, Moravia, Galicia, and other areas once ruled by the Habsburgs.) Most of the immigrants from the Austrian heartlands had come from Vienna, often by adventurous detours. Not surprisingly, those big-city people usually settled in New York, Los Angeles, or some other metropolitan area.

"They often adjusted emotionally to the new country with remarkable rapidity," wrote E. Wilder Spaulding, an American cultural attaché in Vienna from 1949 to 1955 who has investigated the Austrian immigration to America.[11] "They applied immediately for citizenship, made a tremendous effort to find friends outside the emigré circle, worked hard to improve their English, and sometimes even changed their names and their religion. Most Jews went over to Reform Judaism or to liberal Protestant churches like the Unitarian."

Spaulding went through *Who's Who in America* and found that the 1952–53 edition listed 127 distinguished Americans who were born in Austria, and the 1962–63 edition, 225: "Only Canada, Great Britain, Russia and Germany provided more entries of distinguished Americans than Austria." Of four Austrian or Austrian-born Nobel Prize–winners in physics, three—Victor F. Hess (1936), Isidor Isaac Rabi (1944), and Wolfgang Pauli (1945)—lived and worked in the United States, and the fourth, Erwin Schrödinger (1933), spent some time in America before going back to Vienna. Those who focus on such success stories "will too often ignore all the frustrations, disappointments and failures" that the Viennese immigrants to the United States experienced, Spaulding warned.

One general complaint by the newcomers from Vienna was that the social security system in the United States, even after the New Deal legislation, compared poorly with Austria's. Viktor Adler, the Social Democratic leader, had conceded as far back as 1891 that Austria-Hungary's social laws were among the best in the world, surpassed only by Britain's and Switzerland's; yet, Adler's party kept pressing for further improvements. After World War I new laws on mandatory workers' vacations, labor representation, and collective bargaining were enacted by the Austrian Republic.

The ease whereby American employers could fire someone whom they had just hired and the skimpiness of pensions—if there were any pensions at all—startled the immigrants from Vienna. On the other hand, the many emigré intellectuals soon found out that generous grants for research projects or creative work could be obtained from foundations or other private groups and that lecture fees were easy to come by. Schoenberg, however, was appalled when Princeton University offered him only a hundred dollars for a lecture on his twelve-tone system and would not refund his travel expenses. George Gershwin and Leopold Stokowski, with others, contributed to a small fund set up to enable young Americans to study with Schoenberg in Boston and New York; his move to the West Coast was prompted not only by his asthma but also by expectations that he could make more money there.

Eventually the composer did land a job at the University of California at Los Angeles. His last salary for holding music classes there was $5,400 a year. When Schoenberg had to retire at the age of seventy in 1944, he had qualified for a university pension of just $28.50 a month, increased to $40.38 in 1945. Until his death in 1951, Schoenberg was forced to give lessons and to take on small composition work to support himself and his family, which had again grown when, at age sixty-six, he had another son by his second wife. Big money seemed to beckon only once during the American years of modern music's pioneer: soon after his arrival in California, Schoenberg received an offer from Hollywood to compose the score for a film version of Pearl S. Buck's *The Good Earth,* which was to star a Viennese, Luise Rainer. He asked for $50,000, but Metro-Goldwyn-Mayer found the requested fee too high, and the world of music was deprived of a Schoenberg exercise in Chinese sounds and instrumentation.

Like millions of immigrants before and since, Schoenberg and many other Viennese newcomers had to realize that living in rich America did not mean they themselves would become rich too. There were also other adjustment problems. Shortly after arriving in New York from Britain, Broch wrote to a friend he did not like "the noisy roughness" he had found. (Yet, New York must have been even less sophisticated when Broch first visited the city before World War I on a study trip to acquaint himself with textile manufacturing in the United States.) Kokoschka in a letter from New York complained to Schoenberg about the "lack of culture in this amusement world." Schoenberg himself kept wondering in conversation and correspondence about the poor preparation of the music students he was obliged to instruct. He did not like the way Americans overheated hotel rooms either. At the Ansonia Hotel on

Broadway at Seventy-third Street in Manhattan, he would keep the windows open during music lessons in winter, which must have troubled his pupils; Schoenberg also detested American railroad trains, finding them torrid, "like a crematorium."

As for human relations, the flinty composer had his reservations too. In a letter to his sister-in-law Mitzi Seligmann, who had just arrived in the United States, he struck a note of caution: "All Americans look honest and are likable and helpful, but they immediately spot a greenhorn and will take advantage of one." Assimilated immigrants were the worst, Schoenberg remarked on another occasion, adding that he preferred to have to deal with native Americans.

The extrovert Werfels took to America with greater ease than did their sometime friend Schoenberg. The film version of *The Song of Bernadette* made its author famous and helped sell his other books. (Thomas Mann observed in a letter to his friend Agnes E. Mayer that *Bernadette* was a "mystification novel"; it was, he said, "humiliating" that it had sold 350,000 copies and film rights had been bought by Hollywood for $100,000.)

Alma Mahler Werfel became the frequent hostess of a German-Austrian coterie in California that included Thomas Mann and his family, Bruno Walter, Max Reinhardt, and occasionally the Schoenbergs. At her gatherings, one also saw Igor Stravinsky, Benjamin Britten, and other resident or visiting notables. Katia Mann, the Nobel laureate's wife, to be sure, did not like Alma, finding Mahler's widow overfond of sweet liqueur and a fearful gossip. There was indeed a lot of piquant talk, for instance, about Schoenberg's late fatherhood or about his quarrel with Thomas Mann over the novelist's association of the twelve-tone system with the demonic composer Leverkühn in his novel *Dr. Faustus* (1948). Mann eventually agreed to have the book appear with an author's note acknowedging that the tone-row technique was "in truth the intellectual property of a contemporary composer and theoretician, Arnold Schoenberg," and not the invention of the fictional musician.

Werfel died in Beverly Hills in 1951, and Bruno Walter played the organ at his secular funeral. Alma moved to New York the year afterward and lived in a two-room apartment at 120 East Seventy-third Street until her death in 1964. In New York she tried to run something like a Viennese salon with the assistance of a butler and steady escort, August Hess, whom a biographer has described as a "caricature of an imperial-

The Karl Marx Hof, erected from 1927 to 29, is the largest working-class housing project built during the Socialist decade of Red Vienna. Prominent architects such as Josef Hoffmann designed some of the new residential buildings.
(Courtesy of the Austrian Press and Information Service)

Joseph Maria Olbrich's Secession building, a masterpiece of Jugendstil (youth style), housed the exhibitions of the Secessionist artists who broke with the traditional Association of Visual Artists in 1897. *(Courtesy of the Austrian Press and Information Service)*

Egon Schiele, in a self-portrait of 1913. He survived Klimt by half a year. *(Bildarchiv d. Österreichisches Nationalbibliothek, Courtesy of the Austrian Institute)*

Hermann Bahr, coffeehouse chameleon, was a leader of the literati clique known as Young Vienna. He championed the avant-garde artists associated with the Secession. *(Bildarchiv d. Österreichisches Nationalbibliothek, Courtesy of the Austrian Institute)*

Modernist Oskar Kokoschka signed his paintings "OK." This was not the opinion of his detractors; visitors to his 1908 artistic debut were shocked by the eroticism in his work. *(Courtesy of the Austrian Institute)*

Photograph of satirist Karl Kraus in 1908. Kraus carried on a lifelong campaign against Hermann Bahr and Young Vienna in his magazine *Die Fackel (The Torch)*. *(Bildarchiv d. Österreichisches Nationalbibliothek, Courtesy of the Austrian Institute)*

Critics have compared the novels of Robert Musil to works by Joyce and Proust. *(Bildarchiv d. Österreichisches Nationalbibliothek, Courtesy of the Austrian Institute)*

Arthur Schnitzler was a member of Young Vienna. His plays and novels portray the lives of the Jewish intelligentsia of the period. *(Bildarchiv d. Österreichisches Nationalbibliothek, Courtesy of the Austrian Institute)*

Vienna physician Alfred Adler founded the School of Individual Psychology. He had been an early member of Dr. Sigmund Freud's famous Wednesday Society. *(The Bettman Archive, Inc.)*

TOP: Josef Breuer was one of the physicians associated with Freud's early psychoanalytic movement in Vienna. *(Courtesy of the National Library of Medicine)* BOTTOM: Theodor Herzl, the founder of modern Zionism, was a convinced assimilationist during his student days in Vienna. *(Bildarchiv d. Österreichisches Nationalbibliothek, Courtesy of the Austrian Institute)*

Friends had to convince Dr. Freud to leave Vienna after the Nazi annexation. "This is my post," he said. He is photographed arriving in Paris with his friend Princess George of Greece (*left*) and William C. Bullitt, U.S. Ambassador to France, on May 13, 1938. (*UPI/Bettmann Newsphotos*)

This shop window sports the swastika and graffiti scrawled *Jude* (Jew). Jewish Viennese were immediately deprived of their businesses and apartments in the days following the *Anschluss*. (*UPI/Bettmann Newsphotos*)

Elderly Jews were forced to scrub the streets of Vienna in the first flush of the Nazi takeover. Of the three hundred thousand Jewish Viennese of 1938, only about two hundred managed to survive in the city for the liberation of 1945. (*UPI/Bettmann Newsphotos*)

Adolf Hitler strides into Vienna in the company of his military staff on March 13, 1938. His entry formalized the annexation of Austria to the German Reich. Hitler had twice been rejected as an art student at the Academy of Fine Arts in Vienna. *(UPI/Bettmann Newsphotos)*

Many Viennese welcomed Hitler. Nazi flags sprouted from the windows and sales were brisk in swastika armbands and badges. *(UPI/Bettmann Newsphotos)*

The Vienna Court Opera House,
photographed in the autumn of 1938.
(The Bettman Archive, Inc.)

The Court Opera House was heavily damaged in the bombing
that liberated Vienna from the Third Reich. *(Courtesy of the
Austrian Institute)*

St. Stephen's Cathedral burns during the battle of Vienna, April 1945. *(Courtesy of the Austrian Institute)*

The 1952–53 edition of Who's Who in America listed 127 distinguished Americans who were born in Austria. Viennese exile Billy Wilder directs Marilyn Monroe in *The Seven Year Itch*. *(UPI/ Bettmann Newsphotos)*

Director Otto Preminger looks out over Hollywood in a 1977 photo. Few Jewish artists or intellectuals returned to live in Vienna after the war. *(UPI/Bettmann Newsphotos)*

Austria's President Kurt Waldheim shares a Nazi past with many Viennese. This poster of June 9, 1986, has an added legend for the supporters of the victor in the June runoff elections: "Thank you for your trust." *(UPI/ Bettmann Newsphotos)*

royal Rittmeister [cavalry captain]."[12] Alma revisited Vienna, but had no desire to move back to her native city; there were enough Viennese in the United States for her strenuous social life.

HOLLYWOOD'S LITTLE VIENNA

The artists and entertainers from Vienna who had drifted to America long before the Hitler era had formed little cliques, especially in New York and Los Angeles. One of them was Erich von Stroheim, who for moviegoers around the world was the very embodiment of the arrogant, monocled German officer—"the Man You Love to Hate," as studio publicity portrayed him. In his native Vienna he had been plain Herr Erich Oswald Stroheim, without the particle of nobility that was later to become his trademark (like his monocle) and give rise to his nickname, "the *von.*" His career in the army of Austria-Hungary had not taken him higher than the modest rank of a corporal. After his military service Stroheim had immigrated to the United States in 1906 at the age of twenty-one and had for years led an obscure existence. The outbreak of World War I had found him in Hollywood, where he played bit parts in the silent pictures of the nascent movie industry. By 1917 he had perfected what was to remain his screen persona for the remaining forty years of his life—that of the haughty Prussian officer.

Stroheim repeatedly visited France, worked in French films, and in *La Grande Illusion* (1937) delivered the most admired interpretation of his basic role. He appeared on Broadway and on tour (in *Arsenic and Old Lace*) in the early 1940s and married the French actress Denise Vernac, opposite whom he had appeared in the film *The Mask of Dijon* (1946). Stroheim directed various motion pictures, usually driving their producers to distraction by his love of detail, a common Viennese trait. Irving Thalberg, making fun of Stroheim's insistence on having long sequences shot to capture ambience and mood, called him a "footage fetishist." By then, many people who had to deal professionally with Stroheim complained that the arrogance that characterized his film roles had rubbed off on him in real life. Stroheim offered a caricature of himself in the part of Gloria Swanson's butler, ex-director, and ex-husband in Billy Wilder's *Sunset Boulevard* (1950).

Wilder, born in Vienna in 1906, started out as a local-beat journalist and court reporter with a good ear for how people talked. He did a lot of interviewing, but may have a bit overdrawn his early life as a journalist when he said in a television appearance much later that back in Vienna he had, in the space of a couple of days, had to interview personages like Richard Strauss and Sigmund Freud. Neither was easily accessible to news reporters. He moved to Berlin and made a good living there as a writer of scripts for film romances and other light fare. He reached the United States by way of France, worked at Paramount as a script writer for Ernst Lubitsch, the German expatriate, and eventually came into his own as a director. Wilder brought to Hollywood a substantial dose of Viennese cynicism and a litterateur's knack for sparkling dialogue and the telling line. Disenchantment, failure, and human weakness became his favorite themes, as in *The Lost Weekend* (1945), on alcoholism, and *Sunset Boulevard,* which portrays Hollywood pretensions and delusions. In such comedies as *Some Like It Hot* (1959) and *Irma la Douce* (1963), he offered a virtuoso display of his Viennese gifts for brilliance and manipulation.

The other successful Vienna-born Hollywood director in the decades after World War II was Otto Preminger, almost of the same age as Wilder. The son of a magistrate and himself a graduate of Vienna University's law school, Preminger had, after an early acting stint, tried to bring legitimate drama to what is now Vienna's Volksoper. The experiment did not last long. Later Reinhardt had called Preminger to his Theater in der Josefstadt as a stage director and producer. After a few years' film work in Berlin, Preminger had moved to New York in 1934 but after one Broadway season had gone on to Hollywood. There he directed numerous films, notably the classic mystery *Laura* (1944); *The Moon Is Blue* (1953); *Saint Joan* (1957), with his young discovery Jean Seberg in the title role; and *Exodus* (1960). He also acted, often playing Stroheim-like Nazis.

Another Viennese fugitive from Hitler who had been successful in the German film industry, the actor and director Fritz Kortner (originally Fritz Nathan Kohn), always felt like an outsider in California. He disliked Hollywood parties, and whenever he decided to attend one to meet influential movie people, he was ill at ease. He particularly recalled an evening in the home of the scriptwriter Ben Hecht when he did about everything wrong. After dinner the host and his guests sat down to a friendly poker game, and Kortner had to confess he did not know how to play; he sensed he was "completely washed up." After World War II he returned to Germany and successfully resumed his career.

Vienna's quintessential man of the theater, Max Reinhardt, had visited the United States with his German company in 1924. After Hitler's rise to power, Reinhardt left Europe, arriving in New York with his first wife, Else Heim; his second wife, Helene Thimig; and his lover, Eleonore von Mendelssohn. Reinhardt's son Gottfried, an actor and producer, had moved to the United States earlier. Now an immigrant, the older Reinhardt filmed his version of *A Midsummer Night's Dream* (1935, with William Dieterle as codirector) in Hollywood and opened an actors workshop in the film capital. On Broadway he directed various plays, including Thornton Wilder's *Merchant of Yonkers,* an adaptation of Nestroy's classic *Einen Jux will er sich Machen.* Reinhardt shuttled between New York and California in the epoch's crack railroad trains the way he had incessantly kept traveling between Vienna, Berlin, and Salzburg. His best work, however, had undoubtedly been done in Europe.

Reinhardt's second wife, Helene Thimig, who belonged to a famous Viennese theatrical family, landed parts in some of the period's many anti-Nazi films, such as *The Hitler Gang* (1944). German and Austrian refugee actors, whom Hollywood had earlier spurned because of their accents, suddenly found themselves in demand exactly for that reason after the United States entered the war in December 1941: there were suddenly plenty of roles for emigrés who could credibly impersonate Nazis or their victims.

As for Reinhardt himself, he never forgot his stagestruck early years in Vienna when for forty kreuzers, a trifling sum, he could enjoy any Burgtheater production, and did so almost every night. "I was born in the fourth gallery," he reminisced. "From there I saw for the first time the stage lights; there I was nourished . . . with the rich artistic fare of the imperial-royal institution." Reinhardt's last production, a *Fledermaus* adapted to American tastes as *Rosalinda,* was presented by his son Gottfried in 1942, shortly before the great director's death. In 1986, when a memorial to him was to be rededicated in Salzburg, Gottfried Reinhardt did not want Kurt Waldheim, just elected President of Austria, to attend the ceremony: "At the very time my father died in exile, victim of a pernicious regime, you were loyally and, I presume, effectively serving it. I urge you not to desecrate the Reinhardt testimonial with your presence." Waldheim did stay away.

Reinhardt, Wilder, and Preminger, three successful Viennese who fled to Broadway and Hollywood because of Hitler, were alike in that they never shed their accents in their spoken English and they often manifested lingering traces of nostalgia in the perfectionism and brilliance of their work. Yet, during their long years in Hollywood the two younger men thoroughly absorbed the idiosyncracies and moods of their new country and became universally regarded as pillars of the American motion picture industry—sought after, admired, and often criticized as such.

Several former Reinhardt associates and protégées also reached the United States. Among them was the actress Elisabeth Bergner, whose outstanding American stage success was her portrayal of a wife whose husband tries to poison her in *The Two Mrs. Carrolls* (1943). The play by Martin Vale (Marguerite Vale Veiller) had a Broadway run of 585 performances. The waiflike Luise Rainer, also a Reinhardt alumna, was a Viennese who won best-actress Academy Awards in two successive years, in 1936 for *The Great Ziegfeld* and in 1937 for *The Good Earth*.

The Viennese actor and playwright Hans Jaray, together with a few other Austrian and German emigrés, and Lilli Darvas, the wife of the Hungarian dramatist and novelist Ferenc Molnár, founded a drama troupe, The Players from Abroad. They performed in German in New York (at the Barbizon Plaza Theater) and other American cities. In California, Jaray was one day a dinner guest in the house of the German writer Carl Zuckmayer, at the time one of the emigrés who were (like Polgar) populating the "writers' buildings" of the major Hollywood film studios. Zuckmayer had lived near Salzburg in Austria from 1926 to 1938, and his second wife, Alice, was Viennese. When she put an authentic *Tafelspitz* (Vienna-style boiled beef) with cabbage on the table, Jaray "was moved to tears," Zuckmayer recalled in his memoirs. The exiles' nostalgia was sharpened also by a yearning for the food they had been used to in the old country. Brecht, Zuckmayer's old friend, used to say in California that among the things he missed most was German bread. "There is no bread in America."

Mention should also be made of Hedy Lamarr, who arrived in the United States in 1937, preceded by lurid publicity. The glamorous Viennese, whose real name was Hedwig (Hedy) Kiesler, had appeared in a brief nude sequence—then judged outrageously daring—in the Czechoslovak film *Ecstasy* in 1933. In the Vienna of Chancellor Dollfuss' clerical-rightist regime, *Ecstasy* had caused sensation and scandal; furthermore, its young star had nurtured coffeehouse gossip by her reputed entanglement with influential personages.

The Viennese colony on the West Coast included, in addition to several Hollywood scriptwriters, the composer Erich Wolfgang Korngold. The former child prodigy of the Court Opera immigrated to the United States in 1934. Reinhardt induced him to move to California, and the versatile Korngold started writing musical scores for films and ultimately won two Academy Awards. Schoenberg, who had demanded— but not gotten—fifty thousand dollars for the musical commentary for *The Good Earth,* said he despised Korngold's sellout to the movie industry, but the younger composer appears to have been quite content with his Hollywood career. He died in 1957.

In San Francisco, Kurt Herbert Adler of Vienna embodied operatic culture for nearly three decades. An alumnus of his native city's Music Academy and university, Adler had made his debut as a conductor in Max Reinhardt productions at the age of twenty. He worked later in opera houses in Germany, Italy, and Czechoslovakia, and in 1936 served as an assistant to Toscanini at the Salzburg Festival. Adler immigrated to the United States in 1938, was engaged by the Chicago Opera, and in 1943 joined the staff of the San Francisco Opera. As chorus master and subsequently as artistic director and eventually as general director of the institution he expanded the repertory, brought many European and young American singers to San Francisco, and built there one of the world's leading opera ensembles.

The Viennese conductor Erich Kleiber, who had all but dominated Berlin's musical life before Hitler, immigrated to Argentina. His son, Carlos Kleiber, was also to win great acclaim as an orchestra conductor and eventually accepted Austrian citizenship. Another Vienna-born conductor, Erich Leinsdorf, went to New York after the *Anschluss* and at the age of twenty-six was engaged by the Metropolitan Opera—the beginning of a distinguished American musical career. His successor as music director of the New York City Opera in 1957 was another, younger Viennese conductor, Julius Rudel. Sir Rudolf Bing, born in Vienna in 1902, reached New York by way of Berlin, the Edinburgh Festival, and the Glyndebourne Opera in England, and served as general manager of the Metropolitan Opera from 1950 to 1972. Maria Jeritza, who had sung in the 1921 Vienna premiere of Korngold's *Die tote Stadt,* moved permanently to the United States and often appeared at New York's Met. She also remarried; her new American husband was Irving P. Seery.

271

After World War II, as musical bonds between Vienna and New York became increasingly close, Schoenberg on the West Coast was thinking about revisiting his native city. When Vienna—against strong opposition by conservatives in the municipal administration—conferred honorary citizenship on Schoenberg to mark his seventy-fifth birthday in 1949, he wrote back that he hoped to see again the city he had "always loved." The aging composer, who had earlier seemed so unsentimental, now had his nostalgic moods. In 1950 he wrote a summing-up of his life and political credo. He had been proud to be called up to military service during World War I, he reminisced, and had carried out all his army duties with enthusiasm as a loyal supporter of the House of Habsburg. He still considered himself a monarchist, Schoenberg added, but as a naturalized American citizen, thought he had no right to take part in the politics of his adopted nation; he stressed that "I never was a Communist." Death prevented him from seeing Vienna again.

HOMELESS WANDERING

Broch, too, was one of the Viennese emigrés who were planning to go back to the old city, for a visit or maybe even for good. He wrote to a friend that "the United States is not the right place for dying. Being laid out, makeup on one's face, in a funeral parlor is a spooky thought; death is being negated here." As for living in America, Broch discovered that one could subsist for years on foundation grants and support from friends. He stayed for six weeks at the Yaddo artists' colony at Saratoga Springs, New York, was a houseguest successively of Albert Einstein and Erich Kahler in Princeton, and later lived in a series of rented apartments and rooms in New Jersey, New York, and Connecticut. Working up to eighteen hours a day with his radio always tuned to a classical-music station, he wrote and rewrote his great novel *The Death of Virgil,* which he had started in prison in Bad Aussee, and tackled his voluminous correspondence. He wrote seven or eight letters on an average day, each usually four or more pages long and always containing complaints about his heavy mail. He was "committing a constant, slow suicide," Broch wrote in 1943 in the familiar Viennese vein of self-pity and fascination with death.

He suffered bad falls that required surgery, often had bouts of flu, and was also beset by money troubles. Whenever he visited New York, he crisscrossed the city by subway and bus to see as many of his old and new friends as he could fit into his day. When Broch learned that Franz Blei, the onetime magazine publisher and Café Central habitué, was sick in a hospital in Westbury, Long Island, he visited his fellow Viennese, who was dying a lonely death far from home. Blei was one of thousands of elderly refugees who had not been able to build a new existence for themselves in America and had to rely on handouts.

Those who met Broch during World War II and in the first postwar years reported that, in his sixties, he was still handsome—a tall, slightly stooped pipe smoker who could be very witty. Despite all his dark good looks and considerable charm, people nevertheless wondered what really attracted women to him. Broch was as notorious for his erotic entanglements in New York, Princeton, and New Haven as he had been in Vienna when he was young and rich. One of his several American affairs led eventually to marriage. Broch's second wife was Anne Marie Meier-Graefe, an immigrant from France who had introduced him to Hannah Arendt, the German-born thinker and writer who became his friend. Arendt's husband, Heinrich Blucher, was a witness at Broch's wedding in New York's Municipal Building in 1942. The second Mrs. Broch went soon back to France.

When Broch's *Death of Virgil* appeared in translation in 1945, the long, philosophical novel received good reviews, including one on the front page of the New York *Times Book Review;* financially, however, it was not a success. The book recreates the Roman poet's last day in Brundisium, his feverish night, reminiscences of his childhood, and dialogues with friends and with Emperor Augustus. Hardly the stuff for airport paperback racks. Although the novel remained almost unknown in Europe for years after its appearance, the Vienna chapter of PEN nominated Broch for the 1950 Nobel Prize in literature, but the award went to Bertrand Russell.

During the last months of his life, Broch lived drably at a rooming house in New Haven, Connecticut. He had become a lecturer on modern German literature at Yale University, but the position paid no salary. Expecting to rejoin his wife in the south of France soon, Broch drove himself hard as usual and suffered a fatal heart attack in May 1951. "Poet and Philosopher" reads the headstone of his grave in Union District Cemetery at Killingsworth, Connecticut.

One of several Viennese exiles for whom Broch had tried to obtain a

U.S. visa was Musil. In the old days the two had known each other from their regular coffeehouse visits, but had not always gotten along well. In the United States, Broch used to remark that the prickly Musil really had a rotten character and would deserve to experience some hardship, but it was a shame that such a talented writer should be just vegetating in Switzerland. Musil, informed of efforts to get him to America, wrote to Broch that he was worrying about how he could live over there: "I am unable to write anything but *The Man Without Qualities.*"

Musil was still working on the book in the morning of April 15, 1942, a few hours before he died of a stroke while going through his daily calisthenics in the bathroom of his Geneva home. During their nearly three years in Switzerland, Musil and his wife had been chronically short of money and had difficulties with renewing their residence permit. The Swiss bureaucracy had never heard of the Viennese writer and requested testimonials. Hermann Hesse and Thomas Mann, whom the Swiss officials did know, had supplied statements that the author of *The Man Without Qualities* was indeed worthy of being granted asylum. No more than eight mourners were present when Musil's remains were cremated. The Zurich pastor Robert Lejeune, who had done much to help the writer during his Swiss years, gave the eulogy. Musil's ashes were scattered in a forest near Geneva.

The end of the Viennese emigré writer Stefan Zweig was even sadder. He had moved to Brazil, and from there wrote to Broch, with whom he had always liked to discuss literature, "I am sorry you don't stay here with me." Zweig, the biographer of Marie Antoinette, Mary Stuart, Fouché, and other historical figures was then well known in the English-speaking world; his books were selling well, and he had enough money. When he first chose Petropolis as his residence, the resort in the hills north of Rio de Janeiro seemed to him "a miniature Ischl." He was thinking of the Alpine spa near Salzburg where Emperor Franz Josef and many Viennese aristocrats, socialites, and intellectuals had used to spend summers in the old days. But the Brazilian Ischl only deepened Zweig's nostalgia, leading to a lasting depression.

Zweig, an outspoken pacifist during World War I, had regarded himself as a citizen of the world. Now "he found that his homeland, after all, meant more to him than he thought."[13] When Zweig had arrived in New York from London at the beginning of World War II he was bitter that the British authorities had stamped "Enemy Alien" into his passport and searched his luggage as if he were a suspected criminal or spy. In New York he had found he could not cope with all the refugees who, overrating his influence, were seeking his help. "I am not blessed with the wise economy of [Thomas] Mann, who can get rid of people after an hour—with me they all stay three," he complained.

In New York City and upstate Ossining, Zweig lived for a few months in a triangular relationship with his first wife, Frederike, and her successor, Charlotte Elisabeth ("Lotte"), whom Frederike had originally hired as the writer's secretary. Eventually the young woman, the granddaughter of a German rabbi, had become the second Mrs. Zweig.

In the United States and Brazil, Zweig had written *The World of Yesterday,* his evocation of the Europe that was no more. His mood at the time was even better expressed by the alternate titles he considered for the book: "We, a Hard-Proved Generation," "These Days Are Gone," or "A Life for Europe." The Zweigs made new friends in Petropolis; one of them was Gabriela Mistral, the Chilean lyrical poet who was then living in the Brazilian resort and would win the 1945 Nobel Prize in literature. She and other Petropolis intellectuals noted the Viennese writer's despondency. His creed of secular humanism and pacifism offered no consolation to him. When a Brazilian rabbi invited him to give a Yom Kippur lecture, Zweig wrote back that "like most Austrians I was brought up in the laxest fashion in matters of faith and would not be able to overcome a feeling of uncertainty in an assembly of real believers."

In February 1942, disheartened by the bad news from the war fronts, especially the fall of Singapore to the Japanese, Zweig and his wife canceled plans to visit Rio de Janeiro during carnival, and took lethal doses of Veronal. In a written statement left on his tidy desk, the writer thanked the Brazilian authorities for their hospitality and explained that "after one's sixtieth year unusual powers are needed in order to make another, wholly new, beginning; those that I had have been exhausted by the long years of homeless wandering." There was a stack of farewell letters, including one to Zweig's first wife in the United States, the envelopes complete with the necessary mail stamps. Books that Zweig had borrowed were neatly marked for return to their owners. The pencils on the writer's desk had been freshly sharpened: he had concluded his life in the orderly way a Viennese court counselor might go into retirement.

HABSBURG AND ROTHSCHILD

The dismal war situation that contributed to the Zweigs' suicide prompted other Viennese emigrés in the United States and elsewhere to think about actively joining in the Allied military effort. Archduke Otto, the oldest son of the last Emperor of Austria-Hungary, tried for some time to organize an Austrian battalion to fight against Hitler side by side with American forces in Europe. The archduke established headquarters at Essex House on Central Park South in New York, conducting himself like the official pretender to the hypothetical thrones of Vienna and Budapest. Otto had access to the White House and the State Department, and did not object whenever some former Austrian in the United States addressed him as "Your Majesty," the way Joseph Roth had done in Paris. A few Austrian refugees in New York rallied around him, including Guido Zernatto, the writer who had been a member of the Schuschnigg government and was then teaching at Fordham University. The U.S. Defense Department favored the archduke's military plans for some time until it realized that most of the Austrians in America and in other parts of the world were not interested in a Habsburg restoration; the department concluded that if they were to take up arms against Hitler, they should do so as volunteers or draftees in the regular military forces of the United States or its allies.

Archduke Otto, one of eight children of Emperor Karl and Empress Zita, was six years old when the imperial family was expelled from Austria in 1919. He grew up in Switzerland, on the Portuguese island of Madeira, in Spain, and in Belgium, and graduated with a degree in political and social sciences from the Roman Catholic University of Louvain, Belgium. During his Belgian years he resided in a small castle at Steenokerzeel, near Brussels, that the Belgian royal family had placed at the Habsburgs' disposal. Visitors from Vienna around the middle of the 1930s found the young, Italian-looking archduke well informed on the minutiae of politics in the Austrian capital. Early in 1938, when Hitler was about to order the invasion of Austria, Otto urged Schuschnigg in a secret letter to win the backing of the Social Democratic workers "who cannot be poisoned by National Socialism." If Schuschnigg were to feel unable to resist Nazi pressures, the letter went on, he, Otto, was ready to take over as chancellor, being determined "to go to extremes for the protection of the people and the state." In other words, Otto offered to take responsibility for armed resistance to Hitler.

Schuschnigg was at heart a monarchist. He replied to the archduke in writing that if Austria were to yield to Nazi force, it should happen "without involvement of the dynasty"; annexation of Austria by Germany would probably lead to a new war that would result in a completely new Europe and permit some hope for "resurgence." The chancellor gravely added, "To lead [our] country into a fight that from the beginning would be hopeless cannot in my opinion be responsibly countenanced under any circumstances. I know what war is like, and have also experienced civil wars." Schuschnigg, however, did not know what the Nazi tyranny would be like. After the *Anschluss,* Otto moved to Paris and, during World War II, to the United States. His mother and other Habsburgs went to live in Athol, Massachusetts, but were also frequently seen in New York. The Habsburg family returned to Europe after the war and eventually were readmitted to Austria.

The richest Viennese during the 1930s, Baron Louis Nathaniel Rothschild, too, had found a refuge in the United States and had bought a large farm in East Barnard, Vermont. Back home, people used to say that the baron, with his slim figure, his neatly trimmed mustache, his sparse gray hair, and his unflappable manner, looked more the English lord than what he actually was—the shrewd owner of the largest fortune in Central Europe. He was the Rothschild clan's "silkiest, most stoic and untouchably finished grand seigneur."[14] He was also an amateur scholar, an avid polo player, and a notorious ladies' man. In December 1936, Baron Rothschild had played host to ex-King Edward VIII, who had just abdicated. While the future Duchess of Windsor, Wallis Warfield Simpson, was whiling away the time in Cannes, Edward was staying at a Rothschild castle at Enzesfeld, near Vienna, until they could get married.

Baron Louis Rothschild's brother Eugene had moved to Paris, but the bachelor chief of the family's Vienna branch refused to budge. Only the day after the Nazi takeover did the baron attempt to leave. He appeared at the Aspern airport, accompanied by a valet, ostensibly to fly to Italy for a polo match. SS officers seized their passports and sent them back to town. The next morning, a Gestapo detail called at the baron's sumptuous residence to arrest him. He sent word he would be ready to surrender to them "after lunch," and impassively did so.

Adolf Eichmann installed himself in the Rothschild palace, and the fifty-six-year-old baron was held for more than a year on a floor below the cell of former chancellor Schuschnigg in the infamous Metropole Hotel. Nazi investigators insistently questioned both men, but always separately, about their alleged collusion to sell out Austria to "international Freemasonry" and "Jewish capitalism." Both Schuschnigg and Rothschild indignantly denied any plotting.

Later Goering started negotiations with the Rothschild family by way of Switzerland and other intermediaries, with a view to ransoming the imprisoned baron. Himmler apparently wanted a piece of the action, too, and at one point paid Rothschild a visit in his cell at the Metropole. The baron agreed to the transfer of all his properties in Austria to the German government and to the sale of another important asset, the iron-and-steel works in the Vitkovice district of Moravská Ostrava, Czechoslovakia, to Germany by the nominal owners, a Rothschild-controlled British group. There were probably also hefty cash payments to Nazi bigwigs before Baron Rothschild was freed in May 1939 and allowed to leave the Great German Reich. After World War II he married an Austrian countess, Hildegard ("Hilda") Auersperg, and revisited Vienna, but he did not move back to the city. The baron drowned while bathing in Montego Bay, Jamaica, in 1955.

OUTSIDERS IN ACADEMIA

Language being a major hurdle in the assimilation process, young immigrants had a better chance than older ones because of the ease with which they usually picked up American accents and idioms. Rudolf Flesch, who arrived in the United States in 1938 at the age of twenty-seven with a practically useless Austrian law degree, became an authority on the English language. As a writer, lecturer, and editorial consultant, he tirelessly castigated woolly prose and the gobbledygook of bureaucrats. His many books, among them *The Art of Plain Talk* (1946) and *Why Johnny Can't Read* (1955), advocated clear writing and better reading education. The Viennese emigré thus wanted to teach Americans how to read and write English, and was heeded.

Henry Anatole Grunwald was eighteen years old when he arrived in New York; he would later say he learned English above all from the movies. He early joined *Time* magazine and rose to the position of editor in chief. On Grunwald's retirement in 1987, President Ronald Reagan appointed him United States ambassador to his native Vienna. Another Viennese, Felix Rohatyn, reached New York via Paris, Lisbon, and Rio de Janeiro. He studied physics at Middlebury College in Vermont and became an outstanding investment banker and a New York civic leader. As state-appointed chairman of the Municipal Assistance Corporation, he was credited with rescuing New York City from its dire financial troubles in the late 1970s.

Many Viennese scholars and scientists who had already been established at home met with difficulties when they tried to continue their careers in the United States. The biochemist Erwin Chargaff, no alrightnik, wrote in his memoirs, after a forty-year association with Columbia University, that it would be a mistake to think that academic refugees had been received with open arms in America. The younger ones, he recalled, had simply had to swallow their pride, but the more eminent a scholar had been at home, the cooler had been the welcome in the United States. Chargaff always felt himself to be a "misfit" and an outsider, despite his naturalization and his work at Columbia University. Chargaff professed nostalgia for the Europe that no longer was, but not for Vienna. The famous Viennese *Gemütlichkeit,* he remarked, often concealed "a really bestial incivility."[15]

The Viennese mathematician Kurt Gödel, a colleague of Einstein at the Institute for Advanced Study at Princeton, had circled the globe to reach the United States. A member of the Thursday meetings of the Vienna Circle, Gödel (born in Brno in 1906) was lecturing at the University of Vienna when the Nazis took over. He was called up to military service in 1939, was released after basic training, and was surprised when he was not drafted at the beginning of World War II. Gödel applied for a passport and, to his astonishment, obtained one. He left for Lithuania, then still an independent country, made it from there to the Pacific coast by way of the Soviet Union and Manchuria, and sailed for San Francisco. By 1940 he was installed in Princeton and eight years later became a U.S. citizen. Colleagues recall the slightly built Viennese, who was a giant in mathematics, as a loner who would lock himself up in the basement to be safe from unwelcome visitors. Gödel died in Princeton in 1978.

Other former members of the Vienna Circle also managed to get to the West and find academic positions in the United States—Rudolf Carnap at the University of Chicago; Herbert Feigl at the University of Minnesota; and Karl Menger at the universities of Notre Dame and Chicago. The logical positivism of the emigré scientists from Vienna, with their rejection of metaphysics, for some time reinforced technocratic trends in American thought.

The Viennese philosopher Karl Popper, who had had early contacts with the Vienna Circle, moved from New Zealand to London after World War II. In 1946 he met for the first time his fellow Viennese Wittgenstein, but their encounter at an academic gathering in Cambridge was not relaxed. Popper made what he thought was a jocular remark, and Wittgenstein, apparently crabbier than usual, walked out of the seminar room and slammed the door. The rebuff did not harm Popper's career in England; in 1964 he became Sir Karl.

In the field of the social sciences, two Viennese, Ludwig von Mises and his onetime associate Friedrich August von Hayek, were leading advocates of liberalism in the West. Mises, a chamber of commerce official in Vienna from 1909 to 1938, started teaching as *Privatdozent* (unsalaried lecturer) at the city's university in 1913 and became an associate professor in 1918; he remained an academic outsider because he was not backed by any political party. "A Jewish intellectual who justified capitalism seemed a monstrosity" to most Viennese social scientists, Hayek wrote later about his master. Mises served as an artillery officer during World War I, and in 1917 he was called into the government's war economy department. During the 1920s he held informal seminars on socioeconomic problems every two weeks that inevitably ended in late-night discussions in some coffeehouse. Mises was instrumental in the stabilization of the Austrian currency in 1924, met and disagreed with about every Marxist theoretician in Western and Central Europe, and founded the Austrian Institute for Business Cycle Research, which won international esteem.

In 1934, Mises accepted a teaching job at Geneva University while keeping his Vienna posts. The annexation of Austria by Hitler found him in Switzerland. Mises moved in 1940 from Geneva to the United States, where nobody seemed to have ever heard of him. For some time he lived in small New York hotels, in vain seeking some academic employment. At last, in 1945, he became an unsalaried visiting professor at the graduate school of business administration of New York University; he had also received small foundation grants, enabling him to continue his scientific work. His book *Socialism: An Economic and Social Analysis* appeared in 1949 and suddenly made his name known in academia and among politicians all over the world. He had more than two decades of productive life in the United States still before him.

After Mises' death in 1973, at the age of ninety-two, a slim volume of his *Recollections* came out. In it, he recalled the "unbridgeable chasm between a minuscule group of Vienna intellectuals and the mass of the so-called educated people" in Austria during his younger years. His observation provides a key to understanding the baffling contrast between the Vienna that was a cultural crucible in the first few decades of the century and the Vienna that seemed delirious in its 1938 welcome for Hitler.

Tart though Mises was in appraising the intellectual ambience in Vienna before Nazism, he also sounded an emotional note—unusual for him—when he wrote about the events that led to the *Anschluss.* He blamed Britain, France, and Czechoslovakia for their failure to come to the aid of the last pre-Hitler government in Vienna, and went on, "One people on the European continent only carried out serious resistance to Hitler—the Austrians. Only after successfully resisting for five years little Austria, abandoned by all, capitulated. The entire world heaved a sigh of relief. Now Hitler was at last saturated, now he would peacefully deal with the other nations."[16]

Hayek had joined Mises' Institute for Business Cycle Research in Vienna as a young university graduate and later was named its director. He was called to Britain in 1931 to teach at the London School of Economics and became a friend, but also an implacable theoretical critic, of John Maynard Keynes. He helped bring Popper from New Zealand to London. Hayek's indictment of socialism, *The Road to Serfdom,* established his international fame. He accepted a teaching post at the University of Chicago in 1950, and in 1974 shared the Nobel Prize in economics with Gunnar Myrdal of Sweden. Later Hayek returned to his native country, taught for some time at Salzburg University, and then moved on to the University of Freiburg in West Germany.

Of the hundreds of noted Viennese scholars and scientists who were forced into exile by the Nazis, only one out of every five returned to the old city after World War II. Many, to be sure, were content with their new lives and felt at home in their host countries, and even more among them could not forget the horror of their last days in Vienna and the fate their relatives and friends had met. It is equally true that post-Nazi Vienna had made no special efforts to induce onetime citizens who had been successful abroad to come back. As the Viennese psychologist Friedrich Hacker put it, "The perpetrators cannot forgive their victims for what they did to them."[17]

NOTES TO CHAPTER V

1. Hans J. Thalberg, *Von der Kunst Oesterreicher zu Sein,* Vienna-Cologne-Graz, 1984, p. 66.
2. David H. Kranzler, *The History of the Jewish Refugee Community of Shanghai, 1938–1945,* Ph.D. Thesis, Yeshiva University, 1971.
3. *Surviving, and Other Essays,* New York, 1980, p. 41.
4. *The Life and Work of Sigmund Freud,* New York, 1968, I, p. 293.
5. *The Song of Bernadette,* New York, 1943, p. VIII.
6. Class of 1930, Bundes-Realgymnasium Vienna VIII.
7. M. F. Perutz, *That Was the War. Enemy Alien.* The New Yorker, August 12, 1985, p. 35.
8. Peter and Leni Gillman, *Collar the Lot,* London-Melbourne-New York, 1980. This well-researched book provided much of the information used in the section regarding the Viennese internees in Britain.
9. *Kleine Schritte,* Munich, 1976, pp. 35ff.
10. Donald Fleming and Bernard Bailyn (eds.), *The Intellectual Migration,* Cambridge, Massachusetts, s.a., p. 327.
11. *The Quiet Invaders,* Vienna 1968, passim.
12. Berndt W. Wessling, *Alma, Gefährtin von Gustav Mahler, Oskar Kokoschka, Walter Gropius, Franz Werfel,* Düsseldorf, 1983, p. 13.
13. D. A. Prater, *European of Yesterday,* Oxford, 1972, p. 307.
14. Frederic Morton, *The Rothschilds,* New York, 1962, p. 249.
15. *Das Feuer des Heraklit,* New York, 1979, passim.
16. *Erinnerungen,* Stuttgart-New York, 1978, p. 91.
17. As quoted by Wolfgang Müller-Funk, *Geschichte, mit Tränen geschrieben,* Die Presse, Vienna, October 24–26, 1987.

6

WALDHEIM'S VIENNA

The Nazis had been masters of Vienna for almost two years when a forbidden word, declaimed on a local stage, touched off a storm of applause in the darkened theater: *Austria.* During a repeat performance the handclapping and cheering reached the intensity of a demonstration. The Security Service of the SS reported the incidents to Berlin, expressing the suspicion that the ovations had been organized. The production disappeared from the repertoire.

The play was *König Ottokars Glück und Ende* (King Ottokar's Fortune and End), by Franz Grillparzer, the poet and dramatist who wrote the eulogy delivered at Beethoven's graveside. He used the figure of Ottokar II, the ambitious and able thirteenth-century king of Bohemia, in an apotheosis of his conqueror Rudolf of Habsburg and the dynasty that was to rule Austria for 640 years. The drama had been produced to mark the fiftieth anniversary of the Deutsches Volkstheater (German People's Theater), which is visible from the Ringstrasse near the former imperial castle and is now officially called simply Volkstheater.

The house had seen many avant-garde productions during the 1920s when its director, Rudolf Beer, was a local rival of Max Reinhardt. Beer committed suicide after the Nazi takeover. The word *Austria* had not been heard in public since March 1938, nor did the newspapers ever print it. At first, the official Nazi term for Hitler's homeland was Ostmark (Eastern March), a word that went back to the early Middle Ages, long before Ottokar's and Rudolf of Habsburg's time. Soon, even Ostmark sounded dangerous to the Nazis because it seemed to suggest some geographical and historical unity; the designation Alpine and Danubian Regions was eventually used whenever the territory of the former Austrian Republic had to be mentioned.

Vienna had become a provincial city of the Third Reich, but few of its inhabitants could get used to its downgrading. The diplomatic missions had been closed or become consulates, and most of the foreign press correspondents had moved elsewhere. German Nazis were filling the best jobs in Vienna's City Hall and in the departments of the former Austrian government, now mere regional offices that were taking orders from Berlin. Austrian Nazis might win influential positions in the *Altreich* ("Old Reich," meaning Germany before the annexation of Austria) and later in the German-occupied territories, but they were being systematically squeezed out of power in their party and in local government at home. The Nazi archives captured at the end of World War II contain plenty of reports by worried informants who described the mood in Vienna as "depressed" as early as 1939. The enthusiasm of the days immediately following the *Anschluss* had soon fizzled out.

"PIEFKE, GO HOME!"

Union with Germany was not such a good thing as had been claimed, the Viennese quickly found out. They had been given one German mark for an Austrian schilling and a half when the Reich's currency was introduced, but the exchange rate was unfair, and the result was a sudden increase in the cost of living. At the moment of the Nazi takeover, the schilling had been covered by gold and hard currencies to the extent of 38.4 percent, whereas the backing of the German mark amounted to a measly 1.4 percent. The ninety-one tons of gold and the large foreign-currency sums that the invaders had found in the safes of the Austrian National Bank were at once transferred to Berlin.

The Nazis also removed the regalia of the Holy Roman Empire from the treasury of the Hofburg and moved them to Aachen, the city where Charlemagne is buried and where the German emperors were crowned.

The golden crown, the imperial mantle, and the other historical paraphernalia were returned to Vienna by the Americans after the end of World War II.

What upset the Viennese much more than the whereabouts of the imperial relics was the scarcity of butter and other fats, of meats and vegetables, and of whipped cream and chocolate long before the wartime rationing of food was to start. If somebody dared to complain to the grocer or to a restaurant waiter, some German would cut in, remarking in an unfamiliar accent, "You Viennese still live far too well; people at home, where I come from, work harder than you do and aren't so spoiled." Such tactlessness and arrogance, encountered also in many other situations and on many levels, soon helped make the Germans unpopular in the Austrian capital.

One reaction was that many local people who up to then had spoken the kind of refined Viennese German that one might hear in government offices and in coffeehouses started switching in public to broad suburban dialect. Instinctively or intentionally they were signaling, "I have my roots here, I'm not a Prussian." Quite a few Viennese Nazis who had been bossing their neighborhoods or their colleagues at work sensed the change in the city's state of mind and became noticeably subdued. Many others who had personally profited from the Nazi conquest—perhaps by having moved into an apartment once inhabited by a Jewish family or by having become manager of a formerly Jewish-owned business—professed their trust in Hitler almost to the end. There had been, sure enough, jobs and homes suddenly for anyone who was not Jewish or on the Gestapo's list of suspects. Most of the Viennese had grabbed what advantages they saw, while muttering their discontent in private or with close friends at the coffeehouse.

Occasionally there were public outbreaks of anti-Nazi and anti-German feeling. Whenever a German soccer club played against a local club, the guests were greeted with a barrage of boos, and anyone in the bleachers who dared to root for them risked being roughed up. Young working-class fans yelled anti-German slogans in Viennese dialect, such as—to quote the tamest—"Piefke, go home!" Piefke, supposedly a frequent Prussian name, is a Viennese nickname for North Germans, implying dour pettiness and pedantry. Some soccer games ended in near riots.

In St. Stephen's Square, after Sunday mass in the cathedral, churchgoers broke into cheers for Pope Pius XI who had snubbed Hitler; the cheers were meant, and understood, as an anti-Nazi demonstration. The old pontiff had summoned Cardinal Innitzer, the Vienna archbishop, to Rome to reprimand him for his Pan-German gestures and had pointedly moved from the Vatican to his summer residence at Castel Gandolfo before Hitler visited Rome in the spring of 1938. Reprisals for the shouts in St. Stephen's Square came quickly when young toughs raided the archiepiscopal palace and nearby church-owned buildings. The Reverend Johannes Krawarik, who was thrown out of a window during the disorders, suffered severe injuries, but survived.

The first organized anti-Nazi resistance groups in Vienna after the *Anschluss* were set up by Communists who had a long experience in underground work. Some former Social Democrats joined them. According to the Gestapo records, found after the war, sixty-three hundred alleged Communists were arrested in Vienna during the Nazi occupation, and some three hundred of them were executed. The Communist resistance cells above all disseminated leaflets against the Nazi domination and, after Hitler's attack on the Soviet Union in 1941, against the war.

Non-Communist Viennese characteristically gathered often in coffeehouses. Regulars who had long known one another commented on news in the press and exchanged information much in the way the restless students and other intellectuals had done in the coffeehouses of Metternich's Vienna about a century earlier.

An Augustinian monk, the Reverend Roman Karl Scholz, founded the secret Austrian Freedom Movement and, from Klosterneuburg Abbey, near Vienna, coordinated the meetings and propaganda of anti-Nazi networks. He was betrayed, arrested, and after long imprisonment hanged on a butcher's hook in Vienna's Gray House (the court building near the university) in May 1944, at the age of thirty-two.

The outbreak of World War II scarcely a year and a half after the *Anschluss* stiffened Vienna's passive resistance to the Nazi regime. While many officers and soldiers from Austria's Alpine regions were fighting valiantly, at times heroically, on all war fronts, Nazi commanders regarded Viennese members of the Wehrmacht as slack and unreliable. In the course of the war, hundreds of Viennese who had been drafted into the German armed forces were court-martialed and executed for insubordination, desertion, or "cowardice in the field." Many more Viennese were sent to the dreaded Penal Division no. 999 whose front-line units were employed for the clearing of minefields and other desperate assignments.

One young Viennese who was illegally wearing the uniform of a master sergeant of the German army was in reality a member of an Austrian resistance group who had linked up in Switzerland with the U.S. Office of Strategic Services (OSS), the forerunner of the Central Intelligence Agency. He was Fritz Molden, a son of the former editor in chief of the Vienna newspaper *Neue Freie Presse* and of Paula von Preradović, the poet who had written the words for Austria's new national anthem. Molden had been wounded on the Russian front, done underground work in Paris and Berlin, joined an anti-Nazi partisan group in Italy, and, using an alias and a German military uniform, slipped from Switzerland into Austria to contact resistance cells. After the war, following a brief stint in government service, he became a Vienna book publisher.

Anti-Nazi groups made up of Communists, Social Democrats, Roman Catholics, and liberals in Vienna eventually established contacts with one another and started carrying out concerted leaflet, graffiti, and sabotage actions. Three years after the *Anschluss,* in the spring of 1941, an estimated one thousand Viennese were not just grumbling, like a large part of the population, but were actively defying the Nazis in the resistance movement. The Gestapo knew of this underground and spared no effort to infiltrate it with informers. One of the Nazi spies was a popular, good-looking actor of the Burgtheater, Otto Hartmann. He enabled the Nazi investigators to track a clandestine network and round up many of its members in July 1941. Hartmann was arrested after the collapse of the Hitler regime, found guilty of having acted as an informer and agent provocateur for the Gestapo, and sentenced to life imprisonment.

In 1942 the Gestapo arrested a forty-eight-year-old Franciscan nursing nun, Sister Maria Restituta (the former Helene Kafka), who had distributed anti-Nazi and antiwar literature. She refused to tell how she had gotten it, was sentenced to death for "preparation of high treason," and guillotined in March 1943.

According to a memorandum that the Austrian government presented to representatives of the United States, the Soviet Union, Britain, and France in London in 1947, some six thousand political death sentences were carried out in Vienna under Nazi rule. The Nazi judicial bureaucracy never forgot to bill the relatives of persons who had been put to death for the cost of their detention and trial, including a flat fee of

120 marks for the executioner. In other words, the families of the victims had to pay for the hangman.

Vienna's busy Nazi-dominated courts had to deal also with what the natives called *Mundfunk,* a play on words denoting seditious rumors and jokes. (The neologism rhymed with *Rundfunk,* "broadcast," and might be rendered as "mouthcast.") Many a Viennese received a prison term or was sent to a concentration camp for whispering an anti-Hitler joke to the wrong person in some coffeehouse. One defendant was sentenced to two years in jail because he had sung a parody of an old tune with substitute lyrics that prophesied a Vienna "without Nazis" soon because they would all "hang from the lampposts."

In July 1941, Hitler appointed his former youth leader Baldur von Schirach as *Gauleiter,* or regional Nazi party chief, of Vienna. By then, Hitler may have realized that the mood in the city of his squalid early years had soured; Schirach at any rate soon sensed widespread hostility to the regime. In a rare admission of mistakes he told a meeting of medium-level Nazi functionaries in Vienna in October 1942 that "some" Germans had been acting in the city in a high-handed manner and that "negative reactions" were therefore understandable. Vienna's disillusion with Hitler deepened further as food rations were gradually reduced and as Allied air raids on the city became frequent.

At first, Allied bombers started from North Africa to attack targets in Austria, but after the invasion of Italy in 1943 their bases were much closer. The Viennese began sitting down to their meager lunches at 11 A.M. because they knew that American and British squadrons that had taken off from the runways at Foggia, in southern Italy, in the morning would be overhead by noon and would unload their bombs on the city.

Between 1943 and 1945, Vienna suffered fifty-two bombing attacks, which took, according to official figures, 8,769 lives and totally destroyed 37,000 homes. When Schirach in 1944 requested more antiaircraft batteries for the city, Hitler turned him down with the cold remark that the Viennese should not be spared the experience of air raids that other Germans were having.

In the autumn of 1943 the Viennese who were listening to enemy broadcasts—and by then, many did—learned that the Allied powers had formally promised to restore Austria as a free and independent country. This Moscow Declaration of November 1, 1943, described Austria as the first victim of Hitler and stressed that its postwar treatment would depend on how much the Austrians themselves were going to contribute to their own liberation. This Allied document would later make it easier for the Austrians to shake off any responsibility for the rise and the crimes of the Hitler regime.

The plot by high German military officers and well-placed civilians to assassinate Hitler and overthrow the Nazi regime in July 1944 had dramatic repercussions in Vienna. The local contact man of the conspirators was a Captain Karl Szokoll. He had armed forces units that had placed themselves under his command occupy telephone exchanges, the radio station, railroad terminals, and other vital installations, and had high Nazi party and Gestapo officials rounded up and held in the building of the former imperial-and-royal war ministry on the Stubenring, then the seat of military staffs. For several hours on July 20, Szokoll wielded total control of Vienna. During the night of July 21, SS troops retook the city, freed the detained Nazi bigwigs, and arrested many military men and civilians. Among the victims of the Nazi reprisals was Jakob Franz Kastelic, a Vienna lawyer who had organized one of the earliest resistance groups from his regular coffeehouse in the Hietzing district; he was executed in Berlin.

The remaining few months of Vienna's domination by the Nazis became increasingly grim. When the State Opera at the end of June 1944 ended what was to be its last season under the Hitler regime, it performed, with unintended symbolism, Wagner's *Götterdämmerung* (The Twilight of the Gods), conducted by Hans Knappertsbusch. (Curiously, Knappertsbusch had also been on the podium on the night of March 12, 1938, as the first German troops were entering Vienna. That time he had conducted Wagner's *Tristan und Isolde,* with Rosette Anday, who was Jewish, singing the part of Brangäne.) At the end of August 1944 the last few theaters in Vienna that had kept operettas and light comedy on their programs closed down.

Early in October 1944 a group of Austrian industrialists and some senior military officers called on Schirach to request that Vienna be declared an open city and that the Allied powers be notified that no defense in the case of an enemy advance on it was contemplated. The regional Nazi boss promised to take up the matter with Hitler. Ten days later a cowed Schirach was back from Hitler's headquarters with orders that Vienna must be defended "to the last stone" and that anyone opposing his decision was to die.

During the harsh winter of 1944–45 the Viennese spent many hours, day and night, in the air raid shelters. Early in 1945, graffiti reading "O5" had appeared all over the city, including on the walls of St. Stephen's Cathedral: it was the code of a new umbrella organization of all resistance groups, meaning the letter *O* and the fifth letter of the alphabet, *E,* together forming the beginning of the name Oesterreich (Austria). One of the underground federation's members was Captain Szokoll; he had managed to convince his superiors that during the abortive anti-Hitler putsch in July 1944 he had just been "following orders" and had not been a plotter. On March 16, 1945, Hans Blaschke, an SS officer who was their last Nazi mayor, told the Viennese, "The worse our cities are destroyed, the more we become invincible. . . . Hunger, ruins and ashes are guarantees of our greatness." It was the language of madness at a time when the Soviet forces were already advancing in Hungary.

BATTLE OF VIENNA

On March 12, 1945, exactly seven years after the *Anschluss,* Vienna suffered its most devastating British-American air attack. The State Opera, hit by several bombs, burned out; St. Stephen's, too, was heavily damaged. Less than three weeks later Red Army units crossed the frontier between Hungary and Austria, and the Nazi authorities prohibited anyone from leaving Vienna in a truck, car, or horse-drawn vehicle. As fuel had become scarce, horses had lately returned to the city streets in sizable numbers. Many residents fled into the countryside on foot in the hope of being taken in by some relative or friend. Streetcar service in Vienna ground to a complete halt.

The Battle of Vienna started on April 5, 1945, and lasted more than a week, during which the civilian population, shaking with cold and fear, was huddling in air raid shelters and basements. Hitler had sent one of his few remaining first-line army units, the Panzer Division "Der Führer" to defend the city. The other forces supposed to assist the crack troops included ragged Volkssturm (People's Storm) battalions, last-ditch formations into which fifteen-year-old boys and sixty-year-old men had been pressed; they quickly melted away as the Red Army was approaching Vienna from the south and the east. When the Russians were already in Baden, the spa that is almost a suburb of the capital, Brahms's

German Requiem was performed in the concert hall of Vienna's Musikverein.

The bulk of the German troops was then concentrating on the northeast bank of the Danube; Nazi demolition squads blew up all bridges across the river but one. SS forces were still holding the area between the Danube River and the Danube Canal, including the Leopoldstadt district, which had for generations been home to many thousands of Jewish Viennese, and since World War I also to Jews from Eastern Europe. As Soviet troops were battling their way to the city center, heavy fighting took place in the vast Prater area. The Prater's old amusement park with its merry-go-rounds, funhouses, roller coasters, and other rides and attractions became a bizarre battlefield. Artillery shells bent and twisted the Giant Ferris Wheel, the Riesenrad, which had been erected in 1896 and had long acquired landmark status; all its gondolas burned and dropped to the ground.

On April 8 someone managed to climb halfway up the tower of St. Stephen's Cathedral, which had already suffered extensive damage, and hoisted a red-white-red flag, Austria's historic colors. By then, Soviet artillery was firing into the city center. St. Stephen's was hit repeatedly and gutted by fire.

At various sections of the battle front, Austrians serving in the German armed forces tried to establish contact with the Russians to negotiate an orderly withdrawal or surrender of their units to save Vienna further destruction. Beyond the Danube, on April 8, the SS hanged three of these army officers—Major Karl Biedermann, Captain Alfred Huth, and First Lieutenant Rudolf Raschke—in the main square of the Floridsdorf district, a working-class neighborhood. Their officers' shoulder straps had been ripped off their army tunics, and the three corpses dangling from utility poles carried signs reading, "I tried to strike a deal with the Bolsheviks."

Two days later the Red Army reached the Ringstrasse. SS troops blew up the bridges across the Danube Canal, and from their positions between that waterway and the Danube River shelled the city center. Soviet guns returned fire, and the result of the artillery duel was a broad belt of ruins and debris on either side of the Danube Canal. Fires were raging all over the inner city and remained unchecked. Tanks churned the flower beds and wartime vegetable patches in the Augarten, the park that Emperor Josef II had opened for the enjoyment of "all the people." Amid that inferno, special murder commandos of the SS still found the time to seek out and kill Jews who had somehow survived in the Leopoldstadt district; SS men shot the patients of a Jewish hospital in their beds. Meanwhile, Red Army commandos in a surprise action captured the only intact bridge still spanning the Danube River, the Reichsbrücke, and established a foothold on the northeast bank.

The Battle of Vienna was over by 2 P.M., April 13, 1945. All German forces either had withdrawn to the left bank of the Danube, where they were being hard pressed by the Soviet troops, or had been captured. Moscow Radio, in a victory broadcast, praised the Viennese for having supported the Red Army and thereby "saved the honor of the Austrian nation." Frightened civilians at last stumbled out of the basements and found the streets littered with corpses and carcasses of horses between wrecked vehicles and mountains of rubble. The historical center, the lower-middle-class and workers' districts in the city's east and south and, as already noted, the Prater and the strip along the Danube Canal had suffered the worst damage.

One of the first things the Russian conquerors of Vienna did was to look for the storehouses where the Nazis had kept stocks of food—canned milk and meat, dried vegetables and flour—and open them to the civilian population. Starved Viennese swarmed into these places and helped themselves to the supplies; anyone who did not would later be sorry because for weeks afterward no food rations were to be given out. There was some fraternization between Soviet soldiers and the Viennese; many people in the city knew at least a little Czech, a language related to Russian, and thus were able somehow to communicate with the new occupiers.

Within a few days, however, the Soviet soldiery had made themselves thoroughly unpopular, feared, and eventually hated. Wine played a role in this quick change of mood. The conquerors found plenty of it in Vienna's cellars; the grape harvests of the last few years had been copious. In some instances, the new masters of the Austrian capital did not bother with drawing off the vintages in the proper way but fired their guns into the casks and filled their steel helmets with what poured out of the holes. In many basements soldiers stood ankle-deep in spilled wine. According to a story that soon made the rounds of Vienna, a drunken Soviet infantryman had fallen into a giant vat of Klosterneuburg Abbey's renowned winery and had drowned in it: "What a way to die for the Russian fatherland!"

Discipline in the Red Army in Vienna broke down almost immediately after the Nazis had been ousted. Thousands of Viennese women were raped; on every city block the cries of victims were heard, and horror stories abounded. Nuns who had become pregnant after being assaulted by the Soviet soldiery later received tacit permission from the church authorities to request "therapeutic" abortions. Vienna's women eventually found out, many too late, that they were relatively safe on the upper floors of buildings: for some reason the Russian soldiers would not climb stairs if they could help it.

Much later, Moscow requested and obtained a choice plot of city land —a park in front of the former palace of Prince Schwarzenberg facing the Ringstrasse near the Belvedere—for a huge Red Army memorial. The Russian inscription on the semicircular colonnade around a statue of a Soviet soldier in heroic Stalinist style proclaims "eternal glory" for the conquerors of German fascism. A solemn treaty makes the local authorities responsible for the upkeep of the site, which the Viennese call the "Monument to the Unknown Rapist."

Unforgotten in the city is also the Soviet soldiers' passion for wristwatches. During the first few months after the end of the Nazi domination, numberless Viennese were stopped in the streets by some Russians in uniform who demanded, "Oorah, oorah!," their pronunciation of the German word *Uhr* ("watch"). Some members of the Red Army were seen with three or four wristwatches on their forearms. Shootings between drunk or marauding Soviet soldiers were no rarity.

The official figure of suicides in Vienna during all of 1945 was 1,979, or about 130 per 100,000 population. Many of those who killed themselves, it is true, were Nazis who feared punishment. Among the Viennese who died by their own hand was Josef Weinheber, a lyrical poet who had been crafting formally perfect verses in the local dialect for many years while reluctantly working as an employee in a Vienna post office. He was a Nazi, and at age fifty-two took his own life in a village near the capital as the Soviet forces were approaching.

There were, sure enough, also episodes of individual kindness by Russians. They were generally friendly and often affectionate toward children. Yet, the gang rapes and the robberies remained foremost in the memory of a metropolis that the Soviet troops were supposed—as Moscow kept repeating—to have liberated from the Nazi yoke. The record of the Red Army as an occupying force is a major reason why the Communist Party remained weak in Vienna after World War II, as it had after World War I.

In Moscow there were apparently hopes that Vienna's working class could still be won for Communism and that a pro-Soviet regime could be set up at once. Stalin, who had sojourned in Vienna for a few weeks thirty-two years earlier, personally picked the man for the purpose—Karl Renner. The former leader of Vienna's moderate wing of Social Democrats and first Austrian government chief after World War I was then seventy-four years old. He was living in retirement in the town of Gloggnitz, forty-eight miles south of Vienna, had kept fit with cold showers and calisthenics every morning, and was working on a long didactic poem praising astronomy and modern science as avenues toward truth. The Battle of Vienna was still raging when the commander of the Third Ukrainian Front, Colonel General Aleksei S. Zheltov, sent for Renner and received the goateed old Social Democrat at his headquarters in the Alpine foothills south of the capital to tell him what the Kremlin wanted him to do.

Renner responded with characteristic Viennese flexibility. He wrote a personal letter to "His Excellency Marshal Stalin," addressing him as "Very Esteemed Comrade," to assure him that the Austrian working class had "limitless trust" in the Soviet Union and that the reorganized Social Democratic Party would "fraternally" cooperate with the Communists. Somewhat naively, Renner added that he personally had offered hospitality in his Vienna home to many refugees from czarism and had "continually frequented" Trotsky during the Russian's years in the Austrian capital. Stalin apparently did not mind this reference to his mortal enemy, nor were Renner's Pan-German declarations only seven years earlier a handicap in Soviet eyes. Stalin must have known that the aged Social Democratic leader was still popular in Vienna and reckoned he would do as head of a provisional government until it could be replaced by an all-out Communist regime.

Viennese Communists who had found asylum in Moscow during the war were flown home as soon as the Red Army had conquered the city. The Soviet commander in chief in Vienna, Marshal Fyodor I. Tolbukhin, met with former local politicians, among them the Social Democrat Adolf Schärf and a Christian Social leader who during the Battle of Vienna had escaped from his death cell in the Gray House, Leopold Figl. After sixty-two months of detention in Nazi concentration camps, Figl had been released, but had been rearrested in 1944 when the Gestapo received information that he was trying to revive the Lower Austrian Farmers' Association, which he had once headed. Marshal Tobulkhin ordered Figl to organize food supplies for the capital's hungry civilian population.

Ten days after the rout of the Nazis from Vienna, a new Austrian government was formed under Soviet sponsorship. It was headed by Renner, who had arrived in the capital two days earlier, and comprised Social Democrats, Christian Socials, and Communists. In the last democratic elections in Austria in 1930, the Communists had polled only 0.6 percent of all votes cast, against 41.1 percent for the Social Democrats and 35.7 percent for the Christian Social Party. Now the Communists were given equal standing with the two traditional political forces, which changed their names to Socialist Party of Austria and Austrian People's Party.

A Communist intellectual, Ernst Fischer, became secretary of state for popular enlightenment, instruction and education, and cultural affairs. The son of an Austrian general, he had escaped to Moscow in 1934. Fischer's name appeared also as editor in chief in the masthead of the first daily to come out in Vienna after the Nazi defeat, *Neues Oesterreich* (New Austria).

Two weeks after the Battle of Vienna had ended, tramcars were again clanking on some routes. The Burgtheater, whose sumptuous palace on the Ringstrasse had been damaged, presented Grillparzer's *Sappho* in a former cabaret, the Ronacher. The State Opera started a brief makeshift season with Mozart's *Nozze di Figaro.* Since the opera house on the Ringstrasse had been nearly destroyed, the performances took place in the Volksoper, a theater on the northwestern belt boulevard, the Gürtel, that an anti-Semitic group had built in 1897 as a "Christian-German" stage. It had gone bankrupt only six years later and since then had had a checkered history. The theater saw drama, opera, and operetta, and in the early 1930s was for some time directed by Otto Preminger. Quite a few coffeehouses, too, were soon in business again, but what they served tasted like dishwater.

FOUR MEN IN A JEEP

Most of the well-known Nazis had disappeared from Vienna. Some had left when the Red Army was still advancing in Hungary, others had fled with the SS, and some who had stayed on until the end had managed to reach the western regions of Austria, which had been occupied by American and French forces, or British-occupied Carinthia in the south. The Soviet authorities in Vienna picked up a number of Nazis who had not gotten away in time; most of them came back from the east years later. The occupation of the Austrian capital by the Red Army lasted four months and a half. During that period, the Allies were negotiating about how to administer Austria, while the provisional Renner government made efforts to be recognized in the western part of the country, where many regarded it as a mere Soviet puppet show.

Beginning on September 1, 1945, Vienna was carved up into American, British, French, and Soviet occupation zones around an inter-Allied core, the central district within the Ringstrasse. This area, the heart of Vienna, was policed by patrols comprising members of the four occupation powers—"four men in a jeep."

Some of the American servicemen in the city and a few members of the other Allied contingents were former Viennese who had emigrated years earlier and had enlisted in, or been drafted into, the armed forces of their host countries. They had odd and depressing experiences. Unknown people were living in the apartments they had once inhabited, sometimes among furniture that had belonged to relatives of whom nobody seemed to have heard. The coffeehouses that the returnees had once patronized were peopled with ambiguous characters. The city with its ruins, rubble, and shot-up trees and business signs, was disheartening; the parks were unkempt and dangerous. The only constructions that had withstood all the Allied air raids and the Soviet artillery were the six flak towers, monstrous concrete emplacements for antiaircraft batteries that the Nazis had erected in various parts of the city and that overlooked all buildings around them. The flak towers mar Vienna's skyline to this day because blasting them away would require so much explosive that the surrounding neighborhoods might be endangered, and dismantling them with jackhammers would need armies of laborers.

In the first few months of the four-power occupation, the Viennese fawned on anyone wearing an Allied uniform, but they soon found out that the Americans could be played off against the British, and both against the French, and all three against the Russians, or the other way around. Such manipulation was useful for wangling permits, safe-conducts, and other favors. It sometimes worked also for slipping through the meshes of the denazification proceedings on which the Allied authorities had insisted. As soon as local people discovered that a member of the occupation forces spoke German or even the Viennese dialect, they would resort to any blandishment and begin whining about their city's sad plight.

Former Viennese were given to understand that the catastrophe that had befallen the city was the Soviet occupation, not Hitler's conquest. In the intervening seven years many of the Viennese who had survived in the capital had profited from the expulsion of the Jews. Most of the other residents, while grumbling about the Nazis and the "Prussians," had somehow, in the tradition of their city, muddled through. The Allied air attacks, it is true, had hit the city hard and had strained Viennese nerves, but they had caused more anger and hostility against the Americans and the British than against Hitler. With most of their men in Wehrmacht uniforms somewhere on the war fronts, many Viennese had to the end identified with the armed forces of the Third Reich.

Most galling to former Viennese in Allied uniform was to be told, "Ah, you were smart to leave in time. You saved yourself so much trouble, all those horrible things we here had to see!" Self-pity has always been a conspicuous trait among the Viennese, most of whom had been callous when fellow citizens were being robbed of their belongings, their dignity, and even their individual identities in 1938.

The first postwar winter, 1945–46, was a trying time for the Austrian capital, but no more so than it was for London and many cities on the Continent. The Viennese shivered with cold and went hungry. In the municipal slaughterhouse of St. Marx eight head of cattle a day had to suffice for the entire city of 1.6 million. The official food rations provided 760–1,000 calories a day for the "normal consumer," but to get them one had to queue up for hours. As they had done after World War I, philanthropic groups in the United States, Sweden, and other countries sent supplies for another generation of Viennese children.

Even to secure fodder for the Lipizzaner horses required much logistical skill. General George S. Patton, who commanded the U.S. forces in Austria and was a keen horseman, is credited with having rescued the famous performers of the Spanish Riding School from being scattered and ending up in front of farmers' carts or from meeting an even worse fate. The once-pampered white horses had been evacuated by the Nazis from Vienna and from their stud at Piber, Styria, and taken first to Bohemia and then to Upper Austria. There, General Patton found them eventually. In November 1945 the seventy Lipizzaner stallions and two hundred and fifty mares were returned to Vienna or to their stud. (A fictionalized version of their adventures became the Walt Disney film *The Miracle of the White Stallions.*)

In a broadcast on December 24, 1945, the new Austrian government chief, Figl, told his countrymen, "I can't give you anything for Christmas; I can't give you any candles for your Christmas tree, provided you have one at all. No piece of bread, no coal for heating, no glass for replacing shattered window panes. We don't have anything. I only can beg you, keep faith in our Austria!"

What the powerless Vienna government and local tradespeople could not supply, and the occupying powers would not, the black market did, at least to some extent. Military and civilian personnel of the Allied forces were partners in the illegal traffic. Its center was an open-air bazaar in front of the Vienna Polytechnic, in Ressel Park, named after Josef Ressel, the Austrian engineer who in 1829 invented the screw propeller and thereby revolutionized navigation. The association with the sea was fitting enough: many of the things that could be bought in the seedy park around the Ressel monument had indeed been shipped from far away, usually from America—cigarettes, canned food, clothing, liquor, and medicines. Payment was to be made in dollars or military scrip, if the buyer somehow (most often, illegally) possessed them, or in gold, jewelry, works of art, rugs, or other valuables.

Black-market deals were also pulled off in many other places in Vienna, particularly in the coffeehouses. "There is here an entire stratum of society," the young daily *Neues Oesterreich* editorialized, "that one may describe as a greatly enlarged Ressel Park." It was the Vienna of the *Third Man,* Graham Greene's story of the gangster who sold spurious penicillin—then a new wonder drug almost impossible to obtain legally in the occupied city—and thereby caused the death of children. "The smashed dreary city of Vienna" was how Greene remembered the city— in the Prater, part of the Soviet sector, the rusting iron of crippled tanks that nobody had cleared away; ruins and rubble everywhere; the once fashionable Kärntnerstrasse existing only at eye level because the ground floors of damaged buildings alone had been repaired; prostitutes hanging out at a U.S. information office; the Sacher Hotel, a transit billet for British officers; men in overcoats sipping ersatz coffee behind coffeehouse windows.

Greene also recalled the kidnappings that continually occurred not only in the Soviet sector but also in the zones of the three other occupying powers—"a Ukrainian girl without a passport, an old man beyond the age of usefulness, sometimes, of course, the technician or the traitor." In a few rare instances members of the Western forces or even local civilians who witnessed such abductions managed to wrest the victim from the Russians, but it was at any rate the prudent thing to shun the Soviet zone altogether, if one could, and never to go out anywhere after dark. The local newspapers had by then started using sarcastic quotation marks whenever they referred to the soldiers of the four occupying powers as Vienna's "liberators." The implication was that it was not so bad under the Nazis after all.

The Austrians' feelings about the Russians were revealed by the first postwar election, in November 1945, when only four Communists were elected to the country's new Parliament, against eighty-five representatives of the Austrian People's Party and seventy-six Socialists. Known members of the Nazi Party had been barred from voting. Following the election, the conservatives and the Socialists decided to govern jointly as a "grand coalition." Renner became President of the Austrian Republic and Figl, as has been mentioned, Federal Chancellor.

The collaboration between the two main forces in Austrian politics, which had bitterly fought each other between the two world wars, was to last more than two decades and would be resumed in 1987. This grand coalition stemmed from the experiences of Austrian conservatives and Socialists in the Nazi concentration camps, where they had endured the same brutal treatment, got to know one another personally, recognized the mistakes and follies of the past, and pledged to work together in public life if they and their country were ever free again.

The small Communist Party stayed on in the Vienna government as a junior partner for a while, but eventually withdrew from it; Communists were never again to play more than a marginal role in Vienna politics. Their party remained a sect of Marxist-Leninist doctrinaires who usually followed the Moscow line. But not always: in 1956 the Austrian Communist leader Fischer publicly condemned the Soviet military action to crush the Hungarian uprising as *Panzer-Kommunismus* ("tank Communism").

Between 1948 and 1953, Vienna and Austria benefited from Marshall Plan aid to the tune of nearly one billion dollars (calculated in United States dollars of that time). The quantity of American goods shipped to Austria—mostly by way of Trieste—under the European Recovery Program amounted to almost a ton for every single man, woman, and child in that country. American aid permitted a gradual increase in the food rations for the Viennese. The heaps of rubble in the city's streets disappeared, and the war-damaged buildings were repaired or demolished to make way for new construction.

One of the vanished ruins had been the Metropole Hotel, off the Danube Canal. A plaque at the site now reads, "Here stood the House of the Gestapo. It was inferno for those who believed in Austria. It was the forecourt of death for many of them. It crashed to pieces like the Thousand-Year Reich. But Austria has resurged, and with it our dead, the immortal victims."

Vienna's rehabilitation and economic comeback were achieved in a remarkably short time, but the occupying powers were still in control of their respective sectors and jointly patrolled the city center. In a New Year's broadcast in 1950, President Renner compared the occupiers to "four elephants in a rowboat" and pleaded with their governments, "Leave us alone!" Renner was to die a year after that address and would be replaced by another Socialist, Vienna's former mayor Theodor Körner.

In the cold-war climate in world affairs, the two superpowers were tortuously negotiating a concerted withdrawal of the occupying forces from Vienna and the rest of Austria. The last difficulties were overcome exactly ten years after the Red Army's conquest of Vienna when an Austrian government delegation visited Moscow. The Viennese politicians, conservatives and Socialists, hit it off with their Soviet hosts, and full agreement was reached in only three days. The Viennese told one another afterward that Federal Chancellor Julius Raab and Foreign Minister Figl, both conservatives, had made a better impression on Soviet leader Nikita S. Khrushchev and his aides than did the Socialists in the Austrian delegation because of the two men's capacity for drinking innumerable vodka toasts. One of the Socialists in the group that conducted the decisive Moscow talks was Bruno Kreisky, an undersecretary in the

Austrian Foreign Ministry who was later to head the Austrian government for nearly thirteen years.

TEARS AT THE BELVEDERE

The Soviet government undertook to withdraw its forces from Austria, as did the three other occupying powers. Moscow's condition was that Austria was to commit itself to remain perpetually neutral, not to join the North Atlantic Treaty Organization or any other military alliance, and never to grant any military bases on its territory to another power. The East-West accord on Austria in 1955 would for decades remain the sole instance of the Soviet Union voluntarily giving up an area its armed forces had occupied.

Secretary of State John Foster Dulles and the foreign ministers of the Soviet Union, Britain, and France—Vyacheslav M. Molotov, Harold Macmillan, and Antoine Pinay—went to Vienna to sign the Austrian State Treaty, enshrining the country's full independence and sovereignty. The ceremony on May 15, 1955, a Sunday, was held in a hall in the Upper Belvedere Palace, where Prince Eugene of Savoy had once given receptions and Archduke Franz Ferdinand had lived for years before he was assassinated at Sarajevo. Figl, the former government chief who was now foreign minister, put his name to the document after the representatives of the occupying powers had signed. Molotov, Macmillan, Dulles, and Pinay gave addresses, and at the end Figl declared that "with our thanks to the Almighty we have signed the treaty, and we joyfully announce today: Austria is free!" Then the five government representatives stepped out on the balcony to greet a cheering crowd of several thousand Viennese who had gathered in the Belvedere Park. Figl, tears in his eyes, held up the treaty document. Many among the people below also wept. During the next few months all foreign troops left Vienna and the rest of the country.

The powers that allowed Vienna to govern again a sovereign state seventeen years after its takeover by Hitler did not press very hard for a thorough purge of Nazis. There was, it is true, a denazification drive during the first few years after World War II, but it was bland. Former Nazis soon reemerged in the Viennese bureaucracy, in the education system, in the professions, and in the information media. Vienna's Socialist mayor, Körner, while declaring that "Nazis don't belong in high-level positions," characteristically held out the possibility that exceptions from this principle might be made whenever it was "absolutely necessary for professional-technical *[fachlich]* reasons." Ex-Nazis found a political refuge in a new group, the Freedom Party, but the two big vote-getting machines, the People's Party and the Socialist Party, also welcomed new members who once had enthusiastically applauded the *Anschluss.* The two major parties had begun wooing unreconstructed Nazis as early as 1949, during the campaign preceding the parliamentary elections.

Officially, Vienna was Red again and did not like to be reminded of its infatuation with Hitler in 1938. Viennese self-glorification reached a peak a few weeks after the departure of the last foreign troops when the rebuilt State Opera was inaugurated. The shattered opera house had been repaired and thoroughly modernized at a cost of fifteen million dollars (in 1955 dollars). The British press, still vividly remembering the pageantry surrounding the start of Queen Elizabeth II's reign in 1952, wrote about an "Austrian Coronation." Beethoven's *Fidelio,* with its prisoners' hymn to freedom, was chosen for the solemn reopening of the old house.

A glittering international audience filled the State Opera on November 5, 1955, and a worldwide broadcasting hookup relayed *Fidelio* to listeners around the globe. Karl Böhm was the conductor; he had publicly welcomed Hitler's conquest of Austria in 1938, as had many other prominent Viennese, but all this seemed now forgotten. Bruno Walter, who had been artistic director of the State Opera when the Nazis were besieging Austria and who later had been driven into exile, was among the invited guests.

The authorities had also asked Gustav Mahler's widow and Maria Jeritza to attend the gala in a box together with another State Opera veteran, Lotte Lehmann. Alma Mahler Werfel, however, was miffed that she had not been offered a box for herself alone, while Jeritza would not meet with her old rival Lehmann and was offended that her new American husband had not been invited too. In the end, only Lehmann showed up. Hundreds of Viennese stood outside the State Opera long before the performance was to start, gawked at the arriving ticket holders, and then listened to the music that poured out of a public address system improvised for the occasion.

NEW SMUGNESS

The old Spanish Riding School was also back in business in 1955, presenting its horse ballets to foreign tourists, who were visiting Vienna in increasing numbers. The Vienna Boys' Choir, to which the young Haydn and the young Schubert had once belonged, sang again in the former Court Chapel every Sunday morning and went periodically on world tours. The Giant Ferris Wheel in the Prater was turning again, as in the good old days, though only with half the original number of its gondolas. Picture postcards of old Emperor Franz Josef were displayed in show windows along the streets. One might have thought the Hitler period had never happened. The Viennese seemed to congratulate one another on how, through hard work, they had made the World War II ruins and rubble disappear in a few years and how, with plenty of good old *Schmäh*, they had swept the Nazi past into the Danube.

In the climate of the 1950s, marked by renascent smugness and a new prosperity, there were nevertheless a few Viennese who, to general embarrassment, kept reminding their fellow citizens of what really had happened. One of them was a cabaret performer, Helmut Qualtinger. He had been fifteen years old when the Nazis shanghaied him and his schoolmates into a Volkssturm antiaircraft company, and he had seen other boys in his outfit die under enemy bombing and strafing. Later, as an actor, he created the character "Herr Karl," the archetypal Viennese opportunist and characterless heel. In a long monologue, repeatedly switching from dialect into the kind of stilted standard German in which lower-middle-class Viennese address someone in authority or, at times, their own children, Herr Karl reminisced how he had always gotten by, how he had taken advantage of the persecution of the Jews without actually being a Nazi Party member (just an air raid warden), how he had stolen a few liters of wine here and made a squalid pass at some woman there, how he had weathered the war and postwar periods, cheating and scrounging—all the time surviving, surviving.

Qualtinger's Herr Karl act was soon available also on records, and they sold well. To anyone who has seen real-life models for Herr Karl in action, Qualtinger's performance, long after it was recorded, has a demonic ring, with its well-remembered sounds of insensitivity, latent cruelty, and shabbily complacent selfishness. Small wonder that Qualtinger collected many enemies. He started drinking, had marriage and money troubles, suffered from depression, and painfully died of kidney failure in 1986. City Hall assigned an "honor grave" at the Central Cemetery to the remains of the actor who had made himself Vienna's conscience.

Emigré Viennese who revisited their native city found it unfamiliar in many respects. For one, the way many people dressed seemed odd. Even in 1946, when Hilde Spiel returned to the capital of restored Austria as a correspondent for the *New Statesman,* she was "struck by the Tyrolean hats that every resident of the once so elegant city now wears."[1] That was only the beginning.

Today foreigners who arrive in Vienna for the first time will at once note that many of the local people sport Alpine attire. Women in dirndls with diamond rings on their fingers and makeup on their faces wear mountaineers' hats with a wild-grouse feather or a tuft from a chamois' coat, and munch torte and gossip in the local *Konditorei* ("confectioner's shop"); civil servants carrying briefcases walk to their offices disguised as Styrian gamekeepers; and on trolley cars half of the passengers wear loden. The tourist, too, may dutifully pick up a loden hat or coat as a useful and durable souvenir.

Viennese have for generations loved to dress up like Alpine hunters, but only during their vacations in the mountains. During his Alpine holidays Freud would don a Tyrolean costume—leather shorts with the braces visible and a green hat with a chamois brush—and roam the forests to look for mushrooms; whenever he found one, he would briefly put his hat over it. The literati who migrated every summer to the resort town of Alt Aussee, near Salzburg, strolled on its promenades in Alpine garb whenever it was not raining, as it frequently does in those mountains; when it did rain, they had to stay in their villas and face their writer's block. Even Emperor Franz Josef, an avid huntsman, had fancied loden outfits, instead of his customary army uniform, during his Ischl vacations.

In their own city, however, the Viennese used to wear urban clothes, leaving the regional costumes to the picturesque visitors from all over the empire—the Hungarian magnates with their embroidered tunics, the Galician Jews in their black kaftans, the Bosniak soldiers with their white fezzes, and the Tyroleans with their chamois tufts. Loden had made inroads in Vienna between the world wars, when Austria had become essentially an Alpine republic. Since 1945 the city has looked like a permanent folklore festival.

This greening of Vienna through a prevalence of loden, which visitors may find quaint or even appealing, is an outward sign of the provincialization of a once cosmopolitan metropolis. It goes hand in hand with demographics. Until 1918, Czechs, Slovaks, Hungarians, Poles, Ruthenians, Croats, Italians, and people from other parts of Austria-Hungary were continually immigrating to the imperial capital. After World War I, newcomers, when there were any, arrived mainly from the Alpine provinces. After World War II, waves of political refugees from Hungary, Czechoslovakia, Poland, and the Soviet Union swept into Vienna, but most of them soon moved on to other countries. Turkish, Yugoslav, and Greek guest workers have brought new ethnic elements into the Austrian capital, but its rural-Alpine character has remained considerably stronger than it was before 1918.

The idiom, too, has changed, as it always does everywhere. Returning Viennese who have long lived abroad discover that the dialect they spoke in their early years is not always understood. The sounds and the intonation are the same, but the vocabulary is different. Migrants all over the world have similar experiences when they return home after an absence of half a lifetime or so. In Vienna, many words and phrases from North Germany have infiltrated the spoken language, dislodging old dialect expressions.

Seven years of Nazi rule in the city and the circumstance that hundreds of thousands of Viennese served for long periods in the German armed forces are reasons for the linguistic shifts. German tourism, now a mainstay of Vienna's service industries, influenced the local idiom too. To please patrons from Hamburg or Frankfurt, waiters would say *Sahne* instead of *Schlagobers* or *Schlag* for "whipped cream," and the term slipped into the city's everyday language. *Metzger* ("butcher") began to supplant *Fleischhauer* or *Fleischhacker;* and *Bescheid sagen* ("to send word") seems to the Viennese more efficient now than their own old *ausrichten* because they hear it from "efficient" North Germans. Similar new usages could be quoted by the score. Television shows imported from Germany are speeding the homogenization of language, resulting in an idiom that earlier generations of Viennese would have rejected as "Prussian" and outlandish.

Subtler and harder to grasp were the changes in Vienna's intellectual atmosphere after World War II, but they were unmistakable too. Sure enough, the city remained still among the world's music capitals. The Vienna Philharmonic Orchestra, playing under Herbert von Karajan or Karl Böhm, earned new praise at home and abroad. The State Opera was again in the same class as La Scala in Milan and the New York Metropolitan Opera. At the Vienna Music Academy the Schoenberg disciple Hans Swarowsky was training such young conductors as Claudio Abbado and Zubin Mehta in his master classes. American musicals were vying with revived Viennese operetta. Concerts and recitals were held virtually every day in the year, and glutted the schedule of the new Vienna Festival each spring. Legitimate theater was kept alive, thanks to government subsidies. The Viennese were again reading all the newspapers they could lay their hands on in their coffeehouses.

Vienna's *Fasching* ("carnival"), renowned through the centuries, was soon nearly as frenzied a season again as when the Strausses were conducting their waltzes; in fact, waltzes were still being played and danced. On the Thursday before Ash Wednesday the State Opera skipped a performance to transform itself for the glittering *Opernball:* debutantes in long white gowns danced with handsome young men in white tie and tails on the huge floor formed by the stage and the raised pit and auditorium floor, while their elders beamed down from their boxes, some maybe figuring up in their heads what it all was costing. The President of the Republic, members of the government, and foreign diplomats were present, and perhaps the prime minister of neighboring Bavaria too. And after all the champagne, the opera buffets at dawn served the traditional goulash soup, which is supposed to be an antidote for hangover. Year after year, from New Year's Eve to the beginning of Lent, some three hundred thousand Viennese would revel at the ball of the Philharmonic Orchestra and at the shindigs of soccer clubs, student fraternities, and the chimney sweepers' guild, and up to five hundred other affairs.

It was almost like the good old times. Yet, something seemed to be missing: creativity and originality. The bookstores displayed a multitude of works dripping with nostalgia for the Habsburg Empire and the era of Franz Josef. The press was filled with maudlin and narcissistic reminiscences of Vienna's past. The authorities and the cultural establishment did not seem to care that few of the Viennese emigré scholars, scientists, and artists returned to what had been their home.

At the same time, new talent in the Austrian provinces appeared to feel little love for the country's capital and no urge to live and work in it.

The writers and dramatists Peter Handke and Thomas Bernhard did not need Vienna to win international renown. Bernhard, in a short story on a Viennese inventor who committed suicide because his city would not recognize his work, described Vienna as "the largest cemetery of fantasies and ideas," a city where "a thousand times more geniuses decayed, shriveled up and were annihilated than actually emerged."[2] Ingeborg Bachmann, a native of Carinthia like Handke and the most important Austrian woman writer of her generation, lived for a time in Vienna, then traveled extensively, and eventually settled in Rome, where she died in 1973 in circumstances suggesting suicide.

Vienna's Jewish community remained small in the decades after World War II—between 5,000 and 10,000 people in a population that had shrunk to 1.5 million. No exact number of Jews in the city was available because quite a few of them never bothered to register with their community's religious-cultural center. Two rabbis were sufficient to care for the spiritual needs of their coreligionists. There was plenty of subterranean anti-Semitism; anyone who understood the local language and had an ear for its overtones could sense it. With around one half of a percent of the city's inhabitants being Jewish, Vienna's post-Hitler anti-Semitism was like Poland's, an anti-Semitism almost without Jews. It was also an anti-Semitism without declared and militant anti-Semites; there were probably more swastika daubings on Long Island than in Vienna.

Rather, the suppressed, hidden, or even subliminal anti-Jewish feeling betrayed itself through attitudes and casual remarks. A medium-level civil servant observed to a visitor whom he knew only slightly, "Vienna is today a city of banks, and they are all linked internationally. And you know who controls the banks—the Jews. My grandfather and my father both used to say, 'The disaster of Vienna is the money Jews,' and it still is." In fact, since the end of World War II the historic Vienna branch of the House of Rothschild has never reopened, and all the big Austrian credit institutions have been controlled by the government, which has had a Jewish personnel that is negligible.

Many Viennese seemed never to omit mentioning in conversation that somebody's father had been a "baptized Jew," that this or that fellow resident had a Jewish wife, or that some visitor was an "American Jew." When the New York *Times* opened a bureau in Vienna in the 1970s, its new chief correspondent soon received a luncheon invitation from a government official; years later the host owned up that he had been instructed by his superiors to find out whether the newly accredited

American journalist was Jewish. Clearly, the xenophobia of many Viennese survived the war.

In the autumn of 1956 the Viennese were jolted by the anti-Soviet insurrection in neighboring Hungary and the brutal way in which the Red Army crushed it. Hardly a year had passed since the last Soviet troops had left Austria, and the Viennese felt that, but for the grace of God, they too might have had to confront a fate like that of their old sister city Budapest. During the next few months, more than a hundred thousand Hungarian refugees poured into Vienna, and for once the city showed itself compassionate and helpful to foreigners in need. Almost all of the Hungarians who sought asylum eventually moved to other countries—most of them to the western hemisphere and to Australia—although some returned home.

For a few days in 1961, Vienna had the heady illusion of being again a world capital when President John F. Kennedy, who had been elected a few months earlier, and Premier Khrushchev of the Soviet Union held their inconclusive summit meeting in the city. Austria's foreign minister was then Bruno Kreisky; he was soon to become chairman of the Socialist Party and, later, his country's government chief.

EMPEROR BRUNO

A period of nearly thirteen years in Vienna's recent history has become known as the Kreisky era (1970–83). Under the Socialist leader as Federal Chancellor, the country prospered and gained in international prestige, and many of its citizens appeared increasingly self-satisfied. At the height of Kreisky's popularity, the Viennese called him *Kaiser Bruno* (Emperor Bruno). There was a mockery in the sobriquet, for the government chief who usually spoke in the local dialect expertly manipulated the information media with a view to enhancing his public image as a father of the fatherland; but there was also the affectionate suggestion that he had indeed become a patriarchal figure like Emperor Franz Josef.

Despite all the nostalgia for the dead Habsburgs, the living members of that historic family had not caused much of a splash when they had reappeared on Viennese soil. The last Habsburg pretender to the imaginary throne of Vienna, Archduke Otto, had formally renounced any dynastic claims in 1961 and declared himself a "loyal citizen of the

Republic." He had thereupon been authorized to return to Austria. Otto of Habsburg had married a German princess, Regine von Sachsen-Meiningen, had established his residence in Bavaria, and eventually would also acquire citizenship in the Federal Republic of Germany and be elected to the European Parliament in Strasbourg as a West German representative. He occasionally revisited Vienna during the years when Emperor Bruno was governing Austria and later.

Kreisky's appeal to the Viennese was the more remarkable in that he was Jewish. He was a descendant of an upper-middle-class family in the textile business that, like so many other ones, had moved from Moravia to Vienna. While he was a student, Kreisky had joined the Social Democratic Party. He had been active in its underground organization after the 1934 civil war, had been arrested and sentenced to a short prison term, and had eventually found a refuge in Sweden during World War II.

When Kreisky was in power, I once asked him about anti-Semitism in his city and country. "Yes, there is latent anti-Semitism in Austria," he said, "the same way as there is elsewhere in the West, including the United States. But anti-Semitism here isn't worse than it is in other Western countries. It isn't a threat to Jewish existence." Kreisky pointed to the many Viennese and other Austrians who had voted for him in election after election. "And yet, they all know I'm a Jew," he added, using the short form *Jud* instead of the standard German *Jude*. In the Viennese idiom *Jud* is slightly disparaging, but it is also employed in a self-mocking vein by local Jews. Kreisky did not usually dwell in public on his Jewish ancestry; whenever his background was brought up, his stock explanation was that he was an Austrian, a Socialist, and a religious agnostic. An unrepentant Viennese Nazi with whom I discussed Kreisky's acceptance by many local people remarked, "Yes, he is a Jew, but an exceptionally intelligent one."

Former Nazis and neo-Nazis had reason to be grateful to Kreisky, for he stressed that, so many years after World War II, the time for purges and accusations should come to an end, except in cases of clear and hitherto unknown war crimes. Such pragmatism won Kreisky the support of the Freedom Party, the right-wing group that included many Pan-German nationalists, ex-Nazis, and even former members of the SS, enabling him to govern without the conservative People's Party. The social climate, at any rate, remained remarkably peaceful.

During the Kreisky era, as before, labor-management conflicts were quietly settled by negotiation and compromise. While millions of workers in neighboring Italy went on frequent and bitter strikes, just a few hundred Austrian wage earners at most might stage short work stoppages in any given year. The per capita share of production time lost annually by walkouts in Austria was measured in seconds (for instance, 5.7 seconds in 1984), whereas the yearly statistical average of the Italian strike waves came to many hours off the job for every worker.

The much-envied Viennese mechanism for strike avoidance was known as "social partnership." It is based on a Viennese invention that is characteristic of the city's propensity for finessing a problem rather than fighting over it, the Paritätische Kommission (Committee of Equals). The body, unique in Europe, comprises representatives of organized labor, of employers' associations, and of government departments. The committee's activities are not regulated by any law; it meets voluntarily and has no legal powers to enforce its decisions. Yet, this bargaining apparatus, established in 1945, has kept functioning in Vienna under all governments, has solved almost all disputes over wages, working hours, and productivity, has guaranteed and increased the real income (measured by purchasing power) of laborers and employes, and has contained inflation.

Another Viennese sociopolitical procedure also survived all government changes and flourished in the Kreisky era—*Proporz,* which may be translated as "proportional spoils system." Though unofficial, *Proporz,* a quasi-institutional perpetuation of the old *Protektion,* is ever present in Vienna. All desirable jobs in the bureaucratic hierarchy, in the state broadcasting network, in the cultural establishment, and in many other fields are allotted, according to intricate calculations, to protégés of one of the three major political parties—Socialists, conservatives, and national-liberal rightists. You may be a genius and a candidate for the Nobel Prize, but you will not get that university chair or position as chief of a clinic unless you are sponsored by one of the three political machines. Ambassadors, chief executive officers of state-controlled industrial concerns or banks, and managers of the federal railroads are all chosen in accordance with the *Proporz* system.

It is not surprising that such universal logrolling and patronage in Vienna soon engendered corruption. The city's bureaucracy, which had enjoyed a reputation for scrupulous rectitude under the Habsburgs, was embarrassed by scandals even while the four occupying powers were still supervising the government. Funds were squandered, and banks mismanaged; government money was diverted into private pockets, and public work projects resulted in outrageous cost overruns. The Kreisky era, too, had its share of unsavory affairs, although the chancellor personally was untainted by scandal, one of the reasons for his enduring popularity among the cynical Viennese.

In foreign affairs Kreisky acted as if he were the chief of a major power. He invited the leader of the Palestine Liberation Organization, Yasir Arafat, and on another occasion the Libyan dictator Colonel Muammar Qaddafi to Vienna and hugged them in front of the television cameras. Israel reacted with anger.

In 1973, Arab terrorists commandeered an Austrian railroad train near Vienna, seizing three Jews who had been allowed to leave the Soviet Union and an Austrian customs official as hostages to press their demand that Austria close down a transit camp for Jewish emigrants, Schönau Castle, south of the capital. Kreisky personally directed the negotiations with the terrorists, who released their hostages and were flown to Libya after receiving a promise from the chancellor that Schönau Castle's use as a refugee center would indeed cease. Golda Meir, then Prime Minister of Israel, flew to Vienna and tried to persuade Kreisky, her comrade in the Socialist International, to reverse his decision. The two had a tense confrontation, during which Kreisky remained adamant. Schönau Castle was closed, and a majority of Viennese appeared to support the chancellor in this issue. Soon afterward, alternative transit facilities for Jewish refugees were set up.

More than two hundred thousand Jews from the Soviet Union passed through Vienna during the 1970s and 1980s. When Moscow, yielding to American insistence, eased the restrictions on the emigration of Jews somewhat, it requested that all those who had been permitted to leave the Soviet Union, ostensibly bound for Israel, be routed via Vienna. As during World War I, Jewish refugees from the east became again a familiar sight in the Austrian capital. The emigrés who had chosen to proceed to Israel were usually flown to Ben Gurion Airport, near Tel Aviv, within forty-eight hours. Those who wanted to settle in the United States, Canada, or some other country except Israel—the majority—were put up in boardinghouses in Vienna by Jewish relief organizations, pending completion of visa and immigration procedures.

A few hundred of the many thousands of Russian Jews who had passed through Vienna on their way to Israel returned to the Austrian capital after months or years, having found for some reason that they could not adjust to Israeli society. They drifted back to Vienna because no other country would take them, for by first immigrating to Israel they had technically lost their refugee status. Some of the returnees petitioned the Soviet Embassy in Vienna to allow them to go back to Russia, others found jobs and obtained work permits in Vienna, and still others had to live on charity.

In 1988 the Vienna government announced it would grant Austrian citizenship to about 5,000 Soviet Jews who had been allowed to emigrate but had eventually decided against settling in Israel and were not being accepted back into the Soviet Union. Austrian citizenship, it was explained, would make them eligible for social welfare benefits.

For many years the state of American-Soviet relations at any given time could be gauged from the volume of Jewish emigration flowing through Vienna. During periods of East-West tension just a handful of Russian Jews would arrive at Vienna's South/East Railroad Terminal, but whenever Moscow wanted to please Washington, trains would bring scores of emigrés. They all had a long journey behind them. After years of waiting for permission to leave the Soviet Union they usually had to depart by rail from the Ukraine. At the Soviet-Czechoslovak border station of Tchop they were thoroughly searched and routinely despoiled of any valuables they were trying to take with them to the West; after slowly traversing Slovakia they boarded another train in Bratislava and shortly afterward left the Soviet orbit.

After the Arab attack on a refugee transport in 1973, the daily morning train from Bratislava to Vienna was boarded by a special security detail of the Austrian police as soon as it crossed the Czechoslovak border. Before reaching Vienna, all Jewish emigrés on the train were asked by Austrian officials whether they wanted to proceed to Israel—they all had exit visas for Israel—or to some other country. At the South/East Terminal policemen, their submachine guns at the ready, awaited the train and provided a grim reception for the emigrés. The travelers from the Soviet Union split into two groups: one to be taken into waiting buses by Israeli officials, and the other to be met by representatives of America-based Jewish organizations. This procedure went on almost every day for many years. Things seemed to look up for Russian Jews who wanted to leave when another East-West summit took place in Vienna in 1979; President Carter met with Premier Leonid I. Brezhnev, with

Kreisky playing the genial host. Later the number of Jewish emigrés passing through Vienna went down and up again like a yo-yo.

During his nearly thirteen years as government chief, Kreisky pushed hard for Austrian involvement in global affairs, and he strove to make this outwardly and permanently visible in Vienna. An imposing complex of new buildings for international bodies and conferences was to serve the purpose.

The Organization of Petroleum Exporting Countries, OPEC, established its permanent secretariat in the Austrian capital in 1957 (although it held many of its periodic meetings in Geneva or elsewhere). In the same year, the revived Austrian Republic obtained, through strenuous lobbying, the selection of Vienna as the seat of the International Atomic Energy Agency, a specialized body of the United Nations. Washington, Rome, and Geneva had also offered to host the fledgling nuclear organization, but the Soviet Union had favored the Austrian capital. Later a few smaller units of the world organization also established headquarters in Vienna, and in 1979 the city proclaimed itself the "third United Nations center," next to New York and Geneva. An Austrian, Kurt Waldheim, was then secretary-general of the world body, and with an eye toward his own future career, he favored Vienna's new international ambitions.

Kreisky often explained why Vienna should try to attract as many United Nations offices and other international groups as possible. When Hitler was about to invade Austria, Kreisky recalled again and again, the Schuschnigg government's pleas for help from other nations were in vain because the world did not care about the little country. The presence of global organizations in Vienna would create a new identity and image for the city; this might guarantee that it would not be forgotten, written off, or bartered away in times of crisis. Furthermore, the Socialist chancellor used to point out, the influx of international civil servants, of top experts from all over the world, and of foreign diplomats and government representatives would keep Vienna from sinking into provincial torpor.

The reputation for stolidness that Vienna had acquired since the end of World War II was in fact a reason why United Nations personnel in New York were unenthusiastic about relocating to Vienna. The international staff in Geneva, too, opposed moving to the Austrian capital; although the Swiss lake city is much smaller than Vienna and is not exactly "swinging," its location permits one to spend pleasurable weekends in

Paris. Kreisky, at any rate, went ahead with plans for a vast new United Nations center on the Danube that a previous conservative government had originated. The Socialist chancellor contended that the money for the mammoth project was much better spent than was that appropriated for the modest Austrian armed forces.

A location for UNO City, as the proposed Vienna International Center is commonly called, was found near the northeast bank of the Danube amid factories and truck farms, a site that to the Viennese was about as glamorous as the New Jersey meadowlands are to Manhattanites. More than half a billion dollars were spent on a cluster of three Y-shaped office towers of different heights, a circular conference hall, and ancillary buildings.

Later an international convention center was added, but delegates to the East-West talks on arms reduction who started using its facilities denounced the structure as a "bunker in a desert"—too much concrete, too many security precautions, and no decent restaurant or cozy bar anywhere in the vicinity. Representatives of the North Atlantic Treaty Organization and the Warsaw Pact bloc had been holding negotiating sessions in the Hofburg to discuss cuts in the strengths of their troops and in their conventional weapons since the early 1970s; they had enjoyed the mellow comforts of the city center until, much to their displeasure, the host government had told them to move beyond the Danube to UNO City.

To make Vienna more attractive to diplomats and other foreigners, the authorities opened an international school. Near the United Nations cluster, also on the left bank of the Danube, a white mosque with a minaret and a Moslem center rose. A few years after the international complex was officially inaugurated in Waldheim's presence in 1979, it was linked with Vienna's nascent subway network and thus could be quickly reached from the heart of the city. Viennese officials suggested privately that one day, perhaps, the United Nations might move from its glass palace on New York's East River to the Danube or at least might decide to hold one of its General Assembly sessions in Vienna. Such hopes, however, have remained unfulfilled.

Subway construction, incidentally, underlined the renewal of the infrastructure of a city that was afraid of drifting into provincialism. Vienna's first subway project was discussed in 1910, when Austria-Hungary's capital ranked among the world's largest urban centers, almost in the same league as Paris, London, and New York, all of which already had efficient underground transit systems. The Vienna subway blueprints then slumbered in office drawers for fifty years, during which the city experienced two world wars and was overtaken in population by neighboring Budapest and left far behind by such expanding urban areas as Sao Paulo, Mexico City, Cairo, and Shanghai.

By the early 1960s, Vienna was choked with automobiles and trolley cars, and prosperous enough to think about a billion-dollar subway project. Digging started in 1969 near the State Opera. A new sound-absorbing track structure, with plastic sleepers coated with rubber, was developed to curb subterranean noises and vibration around the opera house and the nearby concert halls. Elaborate engineering shielded the Cathedral of St. Stephen's while a multilevel subway station was being built near it for almost a decade.

As the subway network expanded, City Hall soothingly reassured the population that its beloved red trolley cars would remain in service on the streets "for a long time to come." On the Ringstrasse and on the radial avenues leading to the suburbs, the tramway (locally pronounced TRAN-vie) cars kept leisurely rolling, their bells jangling, as they did in the days of Emperor Franz Josef.

Once the World War II damages had been repaired, Vienna took on new, merrier colors. For generations the predominant gray of the house facades in a broad belt between the Ringstrasse and the outer suburbs— Districts II through XI and District XX—had had a depressing effect. From the late 1960s on, many buildings in the residential areas surrounding the Ringstrasse started blossoming in bold yellows, ochre, pastel blue, and strawberry; the mood of entire neighborhoods seemed friendlier.

In the mid-1980s a painter who hated rationalism and fancied bright colors and wavy lines, Friedensreich Hundertwasser, obtained City Hall approval for a fifty-unit housing project that, when it was finished, admirers found dreamy but critics dismissed it as nutty. Bulbous golden cupolas, fairy-tale chimneys, trees, grass, and statuary top the gaudy building's irregular roofs and terraces. Apartments on different levels have exteriors painted in aquamarine, peach, pistachio, or white, with curved dividers of silver and gold tiles. Multilevel apartments contain "adventure rooms" with floor slides for children. The bizarre four-million-dollar structure in the formerly humdrum Kegelgasse in eastern Vienna became an instant sight-seeing attraction, and thousands of families applied for its apartments.

At the same time, Jugendstil, the Viennese version of Art Nouveau, was being relentlessly resurrected throughout the city in hotel design, café and restaurant decor, furniture, storefronts, and posters. One emblematic episode in the neo-Jugendstil manner was the restoration of a public toilet on the Graben; the old underground facility in the fashionable shopping street was lovingly redone in marble and burnished wood, with copper fittings, in lines that might have been drawn by Gustav Klimt or Otto Wagner.

Claudio Abbado, the conductor, told me in 1986, "When I studied at the Vienna Music Academy from 1956 to 1958, the city was gray, and there seemed to be only old people around then. But Vienna has spruced itself up; now it's full of vivid colors, it's lively and cosmopolitan. There are plenty of young people, and many of them are interested in the arts." Abbado, a Milanese, had just taken over as music director of the State Opera; since the Baroque era, Italians have played an important part in Vienna's musical life.

Abbado had succeeded Lorin Maazel, who as State Opera director from 1981 until 1984, had been the first American ever to head the institution. Maazel had become internationally renowned as a guest conductor and as music director of the Cleveland Orchestra; in Vienna he had tried to cope with both the artistic challenges and the administrative chores of the State Opera, while also accepting engagements abroad. From the beginning, he tangled with the Viennese bureaucracy and soon found himself embroiled in intrigues not unlike those that had exasperated Gustav Mahler and Herbert von Karajan before him. Critics conceded that Maazel was a good enough conductor but found him an indifferent administrator, one who all too often tried to run the august opera house as an absentee manager. The circumstance that he was Jewish seems to have contributed to the growing enmity toward him, although nobody would say so. (Leonard Bernstein, another Jewish American, has for more than two decades enjoyed great popularity in Vienna and is the object of adulation whenever he makes an appearance in the city.) Maazel resigned two years before his State Opera contract was to run out, and the authorities hired a new general manager, Helmut Drese from the Zurich Opera, to share responsibilities with the new music director, Abbado.

SMILES AND SCOWLS

"There must be spectacles." Empress Maria Theresa's observation is more valid than ever in present-day Vienna. The government funding of the State Opera, the Volksoper, the Burgtheater, and their affiliates, as well as the Spanish Riding School, is no longer as lavish as it used to be, but it is generous enough to keep all these institutions going. Even Viennese who never buy tickets to them and are content with watching television at home and reading about the opera gossip in their newspapers will readily agree that their city needs plenty of music and shows to attract visitors from abroad.

Local intellectuals, not too happy about the tourist industry, say that only a vibrant cultural life will prevent Vienna from sliding into obscurity. The trouble is that almost all of the official *Kultur* is ruminative and looks backward, while creative artists are usually busy elsewhere. As the Vienna Philharmonic Orchestra lovingly and masterfully records yet another set of Beethoven symphonies and Mozart concertos and the city organizes yet another blockbuster exhibition to celebrate its own past with a wealth of detail, new ideas and trends seem to come only from outside.

With all its cultural conservatism and parochialism, present-day Vienna has retained, and even augmented, a cosmopolitan veneer. This is a result above all of its flourishing tourist business. Foreigners flock to the Austrian capital by the hundreds of thousands every year and write nearly fifty million postcards during the travel season. To accommodate all those visitors, new hotels have sprouted in the center, doubling the number of guest beds in the city to nearly forty thousand in the decade between 1975 and 1985. All cabs seem to be new, all waiters seem to understand English, and store signs in Japanese and Arabic are multiplying. Fancy restaurants and nightclubs cater almost exclusively to foreign diplomats and the expense-account crowd.

Until shortly before Pope John Paul II's trip to Vienna in 1983, the tabloids and some weeklies used to run column after column of advertisements for massage parlors, sex clubs, and call girls. In view of the pontifical visit, the major newspapers tuned down the publicity for prostitution, but the sex ads soon crept back into the press. While bordellos are officially outlawed throughout the city (but not in the surrounding region of Lower Austria) and streetwalkers remain banned from the center of the capital, thousands of prostitutes are known to be practicing and finding native and foreign clients galore in present-day Vienna.

The Austrian capital is also said to be crawling with spies. Every now and then an espionage affair in some faraway nation reveals that agents had met with their control officers, or had established other clandestine contacts, in safe houses or at such unobtrusive locations as suburban tram stops in Vienna.

From time to time, the city is frightened by terrorists, but they are never natives—Arabs who cause a massacre at the main synagogue or shoot up Schwechat Airport; Armenians gunning down Turkish diplomats; or left-wing extremists from Germany on the run. Vienna's green-uniformed policemen have less trouble with street crime than do their colleagues in many other European cities; they must instead pound sidewalks around the clock on guard duty outside foreign embassies, Jewish establishments, and United Nations offices.

What the tourists see in Vienna they seem to like. The streets are clean; there are fewer graffiti than in Zurich. Fashionable women from Milan or Turin who at home are afraid of going out in their mink or sable coats fearlessly parade them in Vienna at night and wear their jewelry without dreading chain snatchers. If there are muggings, foreign robbers are usually blamed. There are almost no panhandlers either, but the Kärntnerstrasse, long ago converted into a pedestrian mall, becomes in the early evening hours an open-air stage where British rock artists, Spanish guitarists, music students, Latin American dancers, and maybe a Macedonian flute player with a fez perform to pick up a few schillings.

The tourist industry and general prosperity have swelled the new Viennese underclass: there are the Turkish and Greek maids in the hotels, the Yugoslav busboys in the restaurants, the young Arabs and Indians in pink windbreakers who peddle newspapers in the evening hours, the Poles and Czechs who sneak out of the refugee camps in search of a chance to wash windows, unload a truck, or do other occasional work for a pittance. Employers may or may not show friendliness toward their own Croatian or Anatolian laborers, but in the streets and trolley cars the swarthy foreigners with their many children encounter hard stares and maybe hear mutterings. Foreign manual labor is needed but resented.

Other foreigners who live in Vienna do not find the local people much more pleasant either. The natives seem to reserve their smiles and politeness for the tourists who stay in hotels, spend money, and soon leave. An American student at the Vienna Music Academy reported, "In more than a year here I have been unable to come to know any Viennese outside school. Socially I meet only with other foreigners."

Nor has anything apparently changed in the old Viennese harshness toward children. To them "the city today still shows a senile, icy, hostile face," the Viennese writer Friedrich Heer found.[3] The relatively large number of elderly persons among the local population may explain why a prevalent Viennese mood is *grantig,* local patois for "bad-tempered" or "peevish."

Anyone who understands the dialect and overhears the everyday conversations in waiting rooms, taverns, and streetcars will be struck by how *grantig* many Viennese seem to be in their well-functioning, moderately affluent city. Listen to their litany of gripes about colleagues at work and neighbors, their complaints about the ingratitude of their own children and the outrageous behavior of young people in general, and their endless tales of diseases, hospitals, and complicated surgery. Death and cemeteries are still favorite topics. Vienna's municipal mortuary service is said to be the largest enterprise of its kind in the world, with some five hundred employees arranging thirty thousand burials and cremations every year; they provide costumed wreath-carriers, elaborate hearses, and all the paraphernalia for four classes of obsequies, from plain to gala. More than half of all funerals are in the gala bracket, costing from five thousand dollars upward.[4]

There are nevertheless enough alert young people in the ancient city to let whiffs of fresh air into the prevailing mustiness. Cultural innovation and intellectual curiosity in Vienna seem indeed confined to youth groups, jazz clubs, small experimental stages, and marginal art galleries. The chasm between a small intelligentsia and the mass of the "educated middle class" about which Ludwig von Mises wrote may have widened. Despite television and tourism, few Viennese appear attuned to what is going on in the world at large. The local press is insular and chauvinistic.

Like many old people who seem to have total recall of events that happened in their early years but have forgotten what they were told last week, Vienna dwells with loving *Schmäh* on the centuries of Habsburg rule but seems struck with amnesia regarding its recent past. "Austria has been instrumental in causing two world wars, but in Vienna this is forgotten," a Netherlander wrote to the *International Herald Tribune* in Paris in 1987. "Not long ago I took a sight-seeing tour to Schönbrunn

Palace. The young Austrian guide gave us a ten-minute history of his country over the microphone. After a detailed discussion of Prince Eugene and Empress Maria Theresa only two sentences were left for the twentieth century: 'In 1918 the Kaiser abdicated and Austria became a republic. In 1938 Austria was occupied by the Germans and in 1945 liberated.' "

THE ART OF AMNESIA

A memory gap, typical for many Viennese of his generation, bedeviled Kurt Waldheim when he sought the presidency of the Austrian Republic in 1986 and after he won it. The disclosure of "Waldheim's disease," as scoffers called it, hit the Viennese like the announcement that a shameful plague had long been raging among them, denied by some and hushed up by others, an illness that had now come into the open.

Like so many other Viennese, Waldheim was not a native of the city but a genuine product of it. He was born in 1918 in St. Andrä-Wördern, a village west of the capital, and brought up in the nearby town of Tulln on the Danube. His father, Walter Waldheim, was a teacher and eventually a school superintendent; he had had his original name, Watzlawik, legally Germanized into a sylvan compound word that translates as "forest home." This was not unusual. Many Viennese with Teutonic-sounding names had once had Slavic ones like Watzlawik; other Viennese, mostly Jews whose ancestors had been forced to adopt German names in the eighteenth century, would have them anglicized after their emigration to the West. The older Waldheim, who had not liked his Czech name, was no Nazi; he was in fact known as a supporter of Schuschnigg's Christian Social Party and, for that reason, lost his job and was briefly imprisoned after the *Anschluss.*

His son Kurt also appears to have had some political trouble; he is said to have passed out Patriotic Front leaflets in Tulln just before the Nazi takeover and to have been beaten up by Nazis. Young Waldheim nevertheless adjusted quickly to the new situation: a few weeks after the *Anschluss* he joined the Nazi Student Union. This, the ambitious eighteen-year-old son of an anti-Nazi father may have thought, was the thing to do if one wanted to continue his law studies and attend classes at the Consular Academy, a school that trained future diplomats. Half a year later Waldheim joined the cavalry branch of the Nazi SA, or Storm Troopers, which did not mean full membership in the Nazi Party but would make him appear a Nazi sympathizer. Waldheim later described the SA unit as a "riding club," as if to say a young student who liked horses just had to become a Storm Trooper.

Waldheim became engaged to Elisabeth Ritschel, a member of the female arm of the Hitler Youth Organization; she transferred to the Nazi Party rolls at age eighteen in 1940 but quit the party and reentered the Roman Catholic Church (which she had earlier abandoned) before getting married to Waldheim in 1944. After the outbreak of World War II, Waldheim who had already done military service in the Austrian army, was drafted into the Wehrmacht and assigned to the cavalry. He participated in the campaign in France, was then sent as a lieutenant to the eastern front, and suffered a slight foot injury. He repeatedly stated later —as in his autobiography, published before his presidential campaign— that he had been granted a medical discharge from the Wehrmacht, which had enabled him to spend the rest of the war finishing his studies and winning a law degree from the University of Vienna in 1944.

Waldheim did mention that during the last three years of World War II he had served with the German army in the Balkans when he filled in a so-called denazification questionnaire at the end of 1945. He was then applying for a job with the foreign service of the new Austrian government, and Foreign Minister Karl Gruber, a leader of the wartime anti-Nazi resistance movement, thought that the tall, twenty-seven-year-old ex-officer who spoke English, French, and Italian would make a good diplomat. When the minister learned of rumors that Waldheim had a Nazi past, he asked an aide to investigate. The aide was Fritz Molden, who had been an associate of Gruber in the Austrian underground movement and now was in government service (briefly, as it was to turn out). Waldheim seems to have been able to convince the foreign minister and his staff that he had not been more deeply implicated in the Nazi system than innumerable other Austrians had been.

From then on, Waldheim's rise in the world was quick. He served in the Austrian Embassy in Paris from 1948 to 1951, as an ambassador to Canada from 1958 to 1960, and as political director of the Foreign Ministry in Vienna, the department's third-highest post, when it was headed by Kreisky. Waldheim was by then well versed in the intrigues that are legendary in the Ballhaus, the historic palace in which the government chief and the foreign minister cohabit, while their respective personnel continually maneuver against each other for higher budget appropriations and plummier assignments, as well as for more desirable office space, with a better view from the windows and fancier desks and rugs.

A cool and diligent careerist, Waldheim did not strike his colleagues as an intellectual or as a person with above-average intelligence. He was a linguist, to be sure, but never managed to shed his thick Viennese accent in the tongues he spoke. Always ready to do favors for people who might later be useful to him but arrogant toward underlings, Waldheim was soon a byword for undisguised ambition and manipulative skills. He became Austria's permanent representative at the United Nations—a coveted post—and eventually foreign minister. In 1971 he ran unsuccessfully for the Austrian presidency as candidate of the conservative People's Party.

After a Social Democrat, the Vienna mayor Franz Jonas, was elected president, Kreisky, by then government chief, nominated Waldheim for the post as United Nations secretary-general—a consolation prize in the spirit of *Proporz*. Waldheim lobbied insistently for himself at United Nations headquarters in New York; his campaign vita did not mention his wartime role in the Balkans.

The United States and the Soviet Union backed his candidacy, and he was elected successor to U Thant of Burma, defeating Max Jakobson of Finland. His success, an official publication in Vienna asserted, was "not only an appreciation of Dr. Waldheim's personality but also evidence of the trust that neutral Austria is enjoying throughout the world."

Waldheim never attained the prestige that an earlier United Nations secretary-general, Dag Hammarskjold of Sweden, had earned, but neither had U Thant. The Viennese put in long hours at headquarters, and with his wife, "Sissy," graced diplomatic cocktail parties, luncheons, and dinners—sometimes three or four such affairs a day. He traveled often, visiting trouble spots around the globe and conferring with world leaders. Those who dealt with him usually found he was no Metternich, but rather a plodding bureaucrat. Since the weight of the United Nations in world affairs was already dwindling, even a diplomatic genius probably would not have achieved much more than the Viennese did. He was generally perceived as one who would not oppose the powerful. "He invites pressure," a Swedish diplomat observed.

Waldheim was reelected to another five-year term in the United Nations job, but when he was seeking a third term in 1981, China objected, and Javier Perez de Cuellar of Peru became his successor. Back in Vienna, collecting handsome pensions from the United Nations and the Austrian government, Waldheim went about preparing a second candidacy for the post as head of state. The People's Party again nominated him as its candidate, and large posters with his gaunt likeness went up all over the country, proclaiming him: "The Man the World Trusts."

Waldheim started addressing electoral rallies, but audiences seemed chilly toward him, and an aide confided privately that he was a "bad campaigner." His opponent was a Socialist physician and former minister of health and environment, Kurt Steyrer, who had gray-haired good looks but was little known and was no captivating orator either. Then the presidential campaign suddenly became inflammatory and world attention focused on it.

From the beginning there had been mutterings within the Socialist Party that Waldheim had a Nazi past that ought to be brought to public knowledge. Fred Sinowatz, the Socialist who had succeeded Kreisky as government chief, was said to have mentioned Waldheim's "brown past" in a closed meeting of a local party unit, alluding to the brown shirts that Nazi Storm Troopers had worn. (Sinowatz denied having ever made such a remark, but a Vienna court later upheld a witness who affirmed she had heard it.)

The Vienna newsweekly *Profil,* which for years had been attempting to shake Austrians out of their complacency, started investigating Waldheim's background, and so did other researchers. The World Jewish Congress, an organization based in New York and dedicated to protecting and fostering Jewish life everywhere, received information about the initial findings and commissioned a thorough search in archives for material regarding Waldheim. The New York *Times* learned of the discovery of hitherto little-known details of Waldheim's wartime activities and confronted the presidential candidate with them.

The correspondent of the New York daily who interviewed Waldheim during his campaign had the same experience as the Austrian researchers who had earlier seen him: the presidential candidate first denied anything that might reflect unfavorably on his conduct between 1938 and 1945, but when shown a piece of evidence, he would reluctantly admit that, well, yes, there might be something to it, but he just could not remember very clearly, and those had been hectic times, hadn't they? When Waldheim was confronted with more material, he uncomfortably admitted fact after fact, offering bland explanations—he had been just a tiny cog in an awesome military machine, a desk-bound subaltern army bureaucrat without any decisional power.

Documentary evidence that became available piecemeal during the months after the early disclosures proved that First Lieutenant Waldheim had been attached to high staffs of the German armed forces in Yugoslavia and Greece between the spring of 1942 and the end of World War II. He acted as an interpreter between German and Italian generals, and served for long periods in quartermaster and intelligence sections of German Army Group E at a time when Nazi forces were carrying out brutal reprisals for attacks by Yugoslav and Albanian partisans, were rounding up civilians for slave labor in Germany, and were deporting thousands of Jews from Greece. Yugoslavia hanged the former commander of Army Group E, General Alexander Löhr, an Austrian, as a war criminal in 1947. (Early in 1985 a group of Austrian air force officers put up a plaque commemorating Löhr as a pioneer of their country's military aviation, but the plaque was later removed.)

The Croatian government of Ante Pavelić, a Nazi and Fascist vassal, awarded Waldheim its King Zvonimir Medal for "brave conduct" in the antipartisan operations. Later the Tito government listed Waldheim as a war criminal, charging him with a part in the execution of hostages. His file, with thousands of others, was handed over to the United Nations War Crimes Commission, a body that was later dissolved, and the material remained buried in the world organization's archives.

While there was no definite proof that First Lieutenant Waldheim had personally been involved in any atrocities, many questions remained unanswered. Why had not Yugoslavia or Greece brought up Waldheim's wartime record when he was first nominated for the United Nations post and when he was elected and reelected? Had the United States, Soviet, and Israeli secret services known his background? Had some power, or more than one, been blackmailing Waldheim during his decade as secretary-general to extract information or other favors from him? Or had Waldheim simply assumed the Yugoslavs, the Soviets, or somebody else knew about his past, and had he accordingly been acting with great circumspection, thereby rendering the United Nations even more ineffectual than it already was?

In Vienna, Waldheim maintained at first that during the war he had just "done my duty" as a soldier. This assertion angered not only former members of the small anti-Nazi underground movement who had been risking their lives but also many young people: they had suspected all the time that many older Viennese, perhaps their own parents, had been Nazi collaborators. Peter Handke branded the presidential candidate a "master of excuses" and a "controverter of facts" who would become the head of a "split people, a non-nation." More than a thousand intellectuals came out publicly against Waldheim, yet hundreds of thousands applauded him.

As more and more facts about his past became public, Waldheim reacted the way many Viennese do whenever a police officer or judge, their boss or their own spouse, catches them in a *Schmäh:* they first deny everything, then fall back on a rearward line of defense, and, when that position becomes untenable, withdraw further, but never tell the whole story. To those who questioned or interviewed him, Waldheim appeared as his own worst enemy: what did his vagueness and reticence hide?

The charges leveled at the presidential candidate from abroad touched off a chauvinistic backlash in Vienna. The big newspapers sprang to his defense. What did foreigners know about the agonies and hardships we have gone through? they asked. Editorialists wrote that people in other countries had no right to meddle in Austrian affairs. There were clear anti-Semitic sounds too. That the World Jewish Congress should have spearheaded the anti-Waldheim campaign was deeply resented. Was it not a Zionist vendetta for his evenhandedness regarding Middle Eastern problems when he was Secretary-General of the United Nations? The very name of the Jewish organization was taken as a sign that a conspiracy by "World Jewry" was afoot to humiliate and punish not only Waldheim but all of Austria. Vienna's press denounced an international plot to whip up "Austrophobia." Natives who suggested that their compatriots should at last begin to cope with their equivocal recent past were pilloried as "soilers of their own nest."

Such a groundswell of paranoid self-pity—"The whole world is against us!"—was nothing new in Vienna. The roots of such collective neuroses may go as deep as the unforgotten fears of Turkish conquest; they are surely grounded in the "reduction complex" caused by the much more recent dismemberment of the Habsburg Empire. In 1972, when the Austrian skiing champion Karl Schranz was disqualified at the Winter Olympic Games at Saporo, Japan, Vienna erupted in an astonishingly incongruous mass reaction: a crowd of more than a hundred thousand protested in the Heldenplatz against the alleged injustice, and Chancellor

Kreisky, always attuned to the city's moods, added his official outrage in an irate harangue.

Some leaders of the Jewish community in Vienna and Simon Wiesenthal, the nemesis of Nazi war criminals, publicly deplored what they described as an interference in Austria's domestic politics by the World Jewish Congress. They also voiced concern that its anti-Waldheim drive might inflame Austrian anti-Semitism again. Wiesenthal, who had once helped track Adolf Eichmann in Argentina, said that Waldheim must have known about the Nazi atrocities committed by the military units in which he had served but there was no proof of his personally being guilty of any crime. Quite a few Jewish Viennese said later they had voted for Waldheim.

The Socialist Party advised its candidate Steyrer not to mention the war crimes issue in his campaign. The most biting remark about Waldheim from any Socialist leader came from Chancellor Sinowatz. Alluding to the conservative candidate's explanation that by joining the Storm Troopers' riding unit he had not become a Nazi Party member, Sinowatz quipped, "Waldheim wasn't a Nazi; only his horse was." Anti-Waldheim demonstrators henceforth would carry a dummy horse with them.

Waldheim was elected President of Austria in a runoff on June 8, 1986, by 53.8 percent of the vote—but only one third of all enfranchised Viennese cast ballots in his favor. When he was sworn in at a session of the Federal Assembly, some Socialist members stayed away while a few others attended with black neckties as a sign of mourning. The United States and the Soviet Union were represented by their chargés d'affaires instead of their mission chiefs, whereas Britain and France sent their ambassadors to the inauguration. No Israeli diplomat was present. In his address, Waldheim called for reconciliation and cooperation, denounced anti-Semitism and recalled "the horrors of the Holocaust."

At the same time, a dozen anti-Waldheim protesters, among them an American rabbi and a Roman Catholic nun, were parading in the striped uniforms of Nazi concentration camp inmates in front of a gate to the Volksgarten, near government headquarters and the presidential office. A police cordon separated the demonstrators from a jeering crowd. One Waldheim fan shouted in Viennese dialect, "Why don't you go back to Mauthausen? That's where you belong!" Mauthausen, a town on the

Danube eighty miles west of Vienna, was the site of the largest Nazi concentration camp in Austria; nearly 200,000 prisoners died there.

During the first few weeks after Waldheim's election to a largely ceremonial office, his entourage predicted that the attacks on him would soon die down. But they did not. In a parliamentary election in November 1986 the Socialists remained the country's strongest political force, while the right-wing Freedom Party, in which neo-Nazis appeared to be gaining ground, polled 9.72 percent of the vote, against 4.98 percent three years earlier. Vienna was still red: the Socialists won nearly 53 percent of all votes cast, and in a municipal election in 1987 polled 55.3 percent.

In April 1987 the U.S. government declared President Waldheim an undesirable alien and placed his name on the Justice Department's "watch list" of nearly fifty thousand persons to be barred from American territory. He was the first head of state thus stigmatized. "Voluminous evidence" that Waldheim was implicated in Nazi atrocities during World War II was cited in Washington as the reason for the unusual measure. Outraged supporters of Waldheim asked in Vienna, Why isn't Pol Pot, the chief of the genocidal Cambodian regime, on the watch list? Why not Idi Amin of Uganda? *Die Presse,* Vienna's most serious newspaper, printed readers' letters recalling the attacks by the U.S. Air Force on the Austrian capital during World War II as examples of "American war crimes."

Vienna's diplomatic service was at that time attempting frantically— almost to the exclusion of any other task—to line up foreign support for Waldheim. The effort scored an important success, thanks in part to intervention by highly placed churchmen, when Pope John Paul II consented to receive the Austrian president in a solemn state visit. On June 25, 1987, Waldheim called on the pontiff in the Vatican and beamed when the head of the church in an address praised the visitor's activities in international life, "always devoted to securing peace among people." The pope did not mention Waldheim's World War II record. Israel and Jews around the world responded with bitterness to the honors accorded to Waldheim in the Vatican.

An international commission of experts on military history, appointed by the Austrian government at Waldheim's suggestion, was meanwhile investigating the president's past. The panel was headed by Hans Rudolf Kurz of Switzerland, and included General James Lawton Collins, Jr., president of the United States Commission on Military History, as well as specialists from Belgium, Britain, Greece, Israel, and West Germany.

In a 202-page report published in Vienna at the end of its activities in February 1988, the historians' group declared it had found no proof that Waldheim had been directly involved in any war crime; yet the document portrayed him as a liar. He had, it stated, "tried to let his military past slip into oblivion and, as soon as that was no longer possible, to make it seem harmless." Waldheim, the commission found, had in the Balkans been much more than just a second-rank desk officer, and had been "especially well informed" on what was going on in the area. The historians' panel conceded that Waldheim as a junior staff member had had "only extremely modest possibilities for resisting injustice," but it pointed out that a few other German officers had courageously opposed or thwarted military orders without being punished. "A certain guilt could arise just from knowing about the violations of human rights in the place where a person was stationed if the person concerned—out of lack of strength or courage—violated his human duty to take steps against injustice," the report contended.

Waldheim in a nationwide broadcast told Austrians the commission report had cleared him of charges of "personal guilt and implication in war crimes." He admitted that he had made a mistake two years earlier when he had said he had done his "duty" as a German soldier, and added that he respected "the heroes and martyrs of that time." As always in history there had been few of them, the president remarked; "we others in my generation were submerged in the machinery of war, in fear and in the effort to survive." Waldheim said he had a clear conscience and would not resign because a head of state must not yield to "outside pressure."

A few weeks later a subdued Vienna marked the fiftieth anniversary of the Nazi takeover. Waldheim attended an official commemoration of the date, March 11, but as a silent member of the audience; Socialists and other members of Parliament had threatened to walk out if the president were to be among the orators. In a characteristic compromise Waldheim had been permitted to deliver a television address to the nation in the evening of March 10. In his broadcast he apologized to the world for Austrian participation in Nazi crimes.

As a belated winter storm was tormenting the city, a few thousand Viennese took part in anti-Waldheim demonstrations, and Austrian intellectuals issued another manifesto urging the head of state to resign. Waldheim, however, reaffirmed his determination to serve his full six-year term.

LOATHING AND LOVE

Austria's sixth head of state since the end of World War II can be considered typical of a certain kind of Viennese—there are different ones too! The disputes churning around him again drew the world's attention to the old city. In other countries a presidential candidate finding himself in Waldheim's predicament might have withdrawn from the race, or at least have resigned immediately upon election. Waldheim's refusal to step aside had one important, though unintended, result: it kept his case alive and caused some young Viennese to wonder and to ask questions of their elders.

A disconcerting number of Waldheim's fellow citizens, to be sure, seemed to approve of his conduct and his eellike defenses. But there were others who said they had for the first time realized how many older people who may not have been Hitlerites before the *Anschluss* had quickly adapted to it afterward, and to what extent the Viennese, although they may have grumbled, had collaborated with the Nazis. A group of Waldheim opponents kept candles burning in front of St. Stephen's Cathedral every day for weeks in 1987, and again in 1988 to honor the victims of the anti-Nazi resistance movement; angry discussions with rightist hecklers ensued regularly.

The international response to Waldheim's election brought home to the Viennese that their image abroad contrasted starkly with their smug self-perception. It dawned on them that they were far less popular in the world than they had always believed. This painful discovery released much xenophobia.

The city was culturally and morally split. While a large part of the population appeared unrepentant, a few Viennese continued to denounce past guilt and warn that the capital of Austria would drift into sullen isolation unless a catharsis occurred at last. Such a collective repudiation of the mistakes and misdeeds of the 1930s and 1940s cannot be expected without radical changes in education, political leadership, and the information media. The chances for such large-scale transformations do not seem bright.

A few Viennese at home and many more in the diaspora are again experiencing the familiar ambivalence: loathing and love for that ancient metropolis on the great river, its suburbs nestling in the ultimate spur of the Alps—the city that has nurtured so much genius, created so much art, stifled so many talents, seen so much tragedy. A native, Franz Grillparzer, just before the end of the deceptively placid Metternich era, summed up the well-known feeling in the first sentence of his poem *Farewell to Vienna:* "Beautiful thou art, yet dangerous too."

NOTES TO CHAPTER VI

1. *Rückkehr nach Wien,* Munich, 1968, p. 35.
2. Thomas Bernhard, *Der Stimmenimitator,* Frankfurt, 1978, pp. 173ff.
3. Friedrich Heer, *Dunkle Mutter Wien, Mein Wien,* Vienna-Freiburg-Basel, 1978, p. 60.
4. Hilde Schmölzer, *A Schöne Leich,* Vienna, 1980, passim.

INDEX